William Edward Hearn

The Theory of Legal Duties and Rights

an introduction to analytical jurisprudence

William Edward Hearn

The Theory of Legal Duties and Rights
an introduction to analytical jurisprudence

ISBN/EAN: 9783337313258

Printed in Europe, USA, Canada, Australia, Japan

Cover: Foto ©Suzi / pixelio.de

More available books at **www.hansebooks.com**

THE THEORY

OF

LEGAL DUTIES AND RIGHTS:

AN INTRODUCTION TO

ANALYTICAL JURISPRUDENCE.

BY

THE HONOURABLE
WILLIAM EDWARD HEARN, LL.D., M.L.C.

MELBOURNE:
BY AUTHORITY: JOHN FERRES, GOVERNMENT PRINTER.

LONDON:
TRÜBNER AND CO., 57 AND 59 LUDGATE HILL.

M DCCC LXXXIII.

TABLE OF CONTENTS.

CHAPTER I.

THE THEORY OF COMMAND.

CHAPTER II.

THE THEORY OF SOVEREIGNTY.

CHAPTER III.

THE EVIDENCES OF LAW.

CHAPTER IV.

THE THEORY OF LEGAL DUTY.

CHAPTER X.

RIGHTS *IN REM* RELATING TO OWNERSHIP.

CHAPTER XI.

THE ACQUISITION AND EXTINCTION OF RIGHTS *IN REM.*

CHAPTER XII.

RIGHTS *IN PERSONAM.*

CHAPTER XIII.

THE COMBINATIONS OF RIGHTS.

CHAPTER XIV.

THE TRANSFER OF RIGHTS.

CHAPTER XV.

THE SUCCESSION TO RIGHTS.

CHAPTER XVI.

THE RECOGNITION OF FOREIGN RIGHTS.

CHAPTER XVII.

THE CODIFICATION OF THE LAW.

CHAPTER I.

THE THEORY OF COMMAND.

§ 1. From many motives men seek to influence
the conduct of other men. Sometimes they look
exclusively to their own personal interest; sometimes they
desire the advantage, or what they think to be the advantage,
of those whom they wish to control; sometimes they believe
that they are doing God service; sometimes they are eager to
diffuse what they consider to be some great truth; sometimes
the motive is the mere love of power; sometimes it is a strong
self-will that can brook no contradiction. Although the
motives are thus varied—and I neither need nor profess to
furnish an exhaustive enumeration of them—the methods by
which the desired projects are carried into effect present much
less diversity. There are indeed but three expedients by which
human conduct is effectively controlled. These expedients
are the application of pleasures or of pains or of purposes.
Some persuasive influence, some present good, or some expectation of future good, may be brought to bear upon the
actor. Or, again, some evil may be threatened to him as
likely to befall him in case of his refusal, or as likely to be
averted in case of his compliance. Or, lastly, his mind may
be so trained, his habits may be so formed, that use becomes
a second nature, and spontaneous action takes the place of
obedience.

These motives and these means operate sometimes separately, sometimes in concurrence. They must all be taken
into account by the student of society. In a more rough and
ready way, regard must be had to them by all those persons

(marginal note: Command as a Social Force.)

who have to deal with human character, and especially with
the spontaneous conduct of masses of men.   This intermixture both of causes and of means is one of the principal
difficulties in any scientific investigation of human character.
But, even where the phenomena are the most complex, it is
possible, under favorable conditions, to isolate a particular
class of causes, and to examine its effect apart from other
influences.   The result of such an inquiry is necessarily as
imperfect as its premises are limited.   Sometimes, however,
although perhaps not frequently, the cause is so distinct,
and the effects are so practically important and so free from
the action of other influences, that the attempt may be made
with a reasonable prospect of success.   It is by this expedient alone that, at least in our present state of knowledge,
any advance appears possible in the unwieldy perplexities
of social science.   How many cases may be found that
are susceptible of separate treatment, I do not attempt to
inquire ; but there are at least two which are now sufficiently
well known.   The universal desire to obtain the maximum
of result with the minimum of effort furnishes a basis for
the purely scientific part of Political Economy.   In like
manner, the universal desire to influence in certain circumstances by certain means the conduct of other men furnishes
a basis for the purely scientific part of Jurisprudence.

One great cause of such a desire, whether we regard the
motive or the opportunity for giving effect to the wish, is
the inequality of conditions.   This inequality is a universal
phenomenon.   Diversity of power, whether of body or of
mind or of wealth, arises out of the conditions of human
nature, and is consequently essential to human society.
Within certain limits, such diversity may perhaps be artificially restricted ; its presence can never be wholly banished.
There always must be the difference between infancy and
manhood, between manhood and old age, between male and
female, between strength and weakness, between wisdom
and folly, between energy and apathy, between experience

and inexperience, between virtue and vice, between wealth
and poverty, between co-operation and isolation. Further,
where inequality exists, the mode of influence always takes
one characteristic form. Men do not need to persuade where
they can command. Where there are on the one side relative
power and on the other side relative weakness, and where
the conduct of the one party is likely to affect the well-being
of the other party, command invariably appears. But a
command—that is, a direction from a stronger to a weaker
as to his conduct—necessarily implies a threat. The motive
to obey a command, in the true sense of the term, is never the
hope of pleasure, but is always the fear of pain. Pleasure
is indeed a powerful inducement to human action, but it is
not that inducement which operates in the circumstances
that we are now considering. Commands are not enforced
by sweetmeats; they must be made of sterner stuff. In
other words, commands, properly so called, do not include
every possible means of securing in human beings a certain
course of action. They relate only to one such method;
and the method which they adopt is exclusively the fear
of pain.

Thus, out of all the circumstances in which human beings
seek to influence the conduct of other human beings, and
out of all the means which for this purpose they adopt, it is
possible to deal with one set of circumstances and with one
class of methods. The circumstances are those in which
there exists between two parties an inequality of power. The
method is the dread which the weaker party entertains that in
the event of his disobedience he will sustain some evil at the
hands of the stronger. Even when thus limited, the position
needs further restriction. Jurisprudence does not profess to
deal with all cases of unequal power, but with that particular
case of inequality which exists between a political community and its several members. Nor even in this case
does it go beyond the existence of certain commands and
the consequences which these commands, when rightly

understood, may be reasonably supposed to include. It does not discuss either the wisdom of the command or the circumstances which have led to its issue. The form and not the substance of law is the subject-matter of Jurisprudence. Consequently I am not now concerned either with the merits of the law or with its history. I have not to inquire whether any particular statute does or does not effect the object for which it was framed, or to trace the steps by which any particular department of the law attained its present shape. I accept the present state of the law as for my immediate purpose an ultimate fact, and I shall attempt to describe its structure and its correlations. I propose, in short, to deal with the anatomy and physiology of law, and not with its natural history. To attain this object the first step is to analyze the great generic notion of command. .

The Analysis of Command.　§ 2. A command implies two parties at least. The term party does not necessarily mean a person. It may be either a person, or a group of persons who are in the same circumstances and occupy the same relation to the other person or group of persons. One of these parties gives the command ; the other party, whom I venture to call the commandee, receives it. The command so given and received is an intimation of the will of the commander as to the conduct of the commandee. The former signifies his desire that the latter should do some act or observe some forbearance. The latter accepts this intimation as a guide or a warning for his future conduct. The term, however, has a further connotation. Every command implies a menace. The commander either expressly or by implication intimates that in the event of his command being disregarded he will cause some painful consequence to come upon the offender. The particular character of that consequence is not now material. It is enough that some ulterior proceeding is indicated, and that that proceeding will be an evil. But it is essential that the commander should have, or at least should appear to the commandee to have, ability to give to his menace practical effect. If he have not the power to inflict, in case of disobedience, the threatened evil, the idle threat will not influence the commandee's conduct. If he have that power, the commandee will, in proportion to his belief as to the extent of that evil and to the certainty of its infliction, govern himself accordingly.

There are thus six elements in a command. There are first the two parties. There is secondly the desire of one of these parties as to the conduct of the other. There is thirdly the act or the forbearance which forms the object of the desire. Fourthly, there is the notification of that desire to the party who is affected by it, and his consequent duty to comply therewith. Fifthly, there is the menace—more or less definite and always implied if it be not always expressed —which indicates the evil attendant upon disobedience. Finally, there is the assumption that of these two parties the one has in some way the power of giving effect to his threat and of bringing upon the other, in case of his disobedience, serious evil.

§ 3. Of the various species of commands, law is **Difference of a Legal Command from other Commands.** one. That law fulfils all the conditions essential to a command is readily seen. There are the two parties of unequal power, the sovereign and the subject; there is the direction to act or to forbear which the one gives to the other; there is the evil which awaits disobedience, and the belief that that evil can and will be inflicted. So much we may assume. That which has now to be determined is the essential difference of law. We have to search for those marks by which this particular species of command is distinguished from all other such species. Law is a command of the State. I will not now discuss the precise meaning of the term State. It expresses what is called in popular language the Government of the country. We know in a general way what the Government is, and that it is different from an individual, or from the Church, or from a trading company; just as we know, even though we have not the assistance of experts in biology, what is meant by a man, and that he differs from other animals. Assuming then the separate existence of the State, we may allege that law is a command of the State. In other words, law is the intimation of the will of the State to its subjects concerning their conduct, an intimation usually expressed through certain appropriate organs, and enforced by other organs. This is what is meant by law as administered by Courts of Justice, and as enacted by Parliament or accepted by tradition. Law is a command of the State by which, so far as it extends, the subjects of the State regulate their conduct, and which its officers duly authorized in that behalf enforce.

This definition at once removes a multitude of obscurities and ambiguities. The command of the State is different from any other form of command. It is not the command of a house father. It is not the command of a bishop. It is not the command of any voluntary association of men. It has of necessity much in common with all these commands, just as they have much in common between themselves, and for the same reason—namely, that they are all species of the same genus. A master gives an order to his servant, and intimates that neglect will be followed by dismission. A schoolmaster desires a pupil to learn a certain lesson, and tells the boy that if he fail to learn it he will be punished. A trades union orders its members not to work beyond a certain time or for less than a certain wage, and threatens various penalties if they disobey. A land league forbids tenants to pay their rents, and men are shot if they fulfil their legal obligations. All these cases contain the essential elements of command, of duty, and of sanction; but they are not law, and some of them are contrary to law. They are commands indeed, but they are not commands of the State.

In like manner we are thus disembarrassed of a number of so-called laws which have in their time impeded jural thought.

The cases I have mentioned were, according to their several varieties, true commands ; but those to which I now refer are Customs are not commands at all. Their resemblance to law not Commands consists in the effect, not in the cause ; in the uniformity of conduct in which they result, and not in the means by which that result is obtained. Such is the law of honour, or the law of fashion, or the law of nations. These so-called laws are not commands but customs. In each of these cases men, for some reason, habitually act in a similar way. The force of habit produces a uniformity of conduct as exact as that which is due to law. There is more than this. Public opinion operates with all the weight of a heavy sanction, and in a similar manner. The disapprobation of those among whom a man lives is often a more formidable penalty than fine or imprisonment. Such a case may reasonably appear to fulfil all the conditions of a true law. Yet it fails even more completely than those domestic or private commands of which I have spoken. Not only is it not a command of the State, but it is not a command of any kind, in the proper sense of the term. It is not a command of the State, even though it be universally accepted by all the people of the State, because the State implies a political organization, and its commands must be expressed through its accredited organs. But these customs are the outcome of an unorganized public will, mere uniformities of action, and not the deliberate intimation of a settled purpose. Further, they are not commands, whether of the State or of any other authority, because they have not the essential characteristic of a command, a true sanction. No definite penalty is attached to the breaches of these customs, but only the vague sentiment of general disapprobation. If a person offend against the law, he meets with a specific punishment, and there are proper officers to ascertain his guilt and to inflict the penalty. But the consequences of a breach of custom is that indefinite persons think in various and indefinite degrees less well of the offender than otherwise they might have done. There is another distinction also, and one that is hardly less important. Custom uses for the attainment of its object approbation as well as disapprobation. In other words, it seeks to secure uniformity of conduct by rewards as well as by punishments. But a legal sanction is something very different. It has nothing to do with rewards ; and relies on punishment alone. Thus the idea of custom is distinct from that of law. A custom may, and often does, become law, but never by its own inherent force. Such a result* is attained when, and only when, to the vague and indefinite sense of popular approbation or disapprobation, there is added, by competent authority, the distinct and specific penalty with which the law visits the breaches of its commands.

Law an Equivocal Term. Closely connected with this subject is the unfortunate ambiguity that has grown up around the word law. This confusion has been so often explained, and when it has been once understood is so apparent, that it seems scarcely to deserve further notice. But error is always difficult to kill ; and a verbal error, so powerful is the influence of words upon thought, seems to bear a charmed life. At the risk, therefore, of seeming to write mere truisms, I must add a word of warning. Law produces uniformity of conduct : uniformity is observable in the course of nature : and so we have got the expression "laws of nature." This unlucky equivoque has found such favour with the public, the final arbiters as we know of language, that there is an appreciable risk that the word law will ultimately be exclusively appropriated to the uses of physical science. But between the laws of nature and the laws of the Queen there is no resemblance and no means of comparison. Commands apply to rational beings and not to things or events. A rule of conduct is one thing, and an invariable unconditioned sequence is another thing. A precept and the allegation of a sequence are disparate, and any possible relation between them can only be metaphorical. The application of the word law to two such unlike objects merely amounts to a similar combination of letters, or at most to different applications of a common root. The ideas which this alphabetical coincidence happens in our language to express are related in the same manner and to the same extent as in Latin *jus* meaning law is related to *jus* meaning sauce.

Difference of Law from other Commands of the State. § 4. Law is thus distinguished from all other classes of commands—it is a command of the State. But a further limitation is still required. Law and the command of the State are not equivalent terms ; the latter expression is the wider. It includes indeed all law, but it also includes much that no person supposes to be law. Every law is a command of the State, but it is not every command of the State that is law. The order of a judge in any given case, the order of a general to his soldiers or of an admiral to his fleet, the order of the head of a department to his subordinate officials, the order of the Queen to any officer in whatever service, are all commands of the State. These several functionaries are the proper officers to give effect, in their respective spheres of action, to the intimation of the public will. Yet none of these commands is what we call law. To obtain accuracy there must be added to our definition the words " with intent to establish a rule of conduct." That is to say, the acts and the forbearances to which the command relates are not specific but general. The difference does not consist in the number of persons to whom the command applies. A law which regulates a particular occupation, or exclusively concerns the conduct of even a single individual, is not less a law than one whose application is universal ; but a proceeding which determines merely a particular act or forbearance, or even the existence of a particular right, is not a law, even though it be taken by the proper legislative organ, and assume the legal style and title : it is merely an executive or a judicial act, which is performed by a body whose usual duty is not administration but legislation. Thus a private Act of Parliament is never regarded as equivalent to a public Act. It is deemed to be a superior form of contract, and is construed according to the rules which govern the interpretation of contracts, and not according to the rules which govern the interpretation of statutes. So, too, when divorces * were granted by Act of Parliament, the procedure in Parliament is held to have been part of our judicial system, and not true legislation. The object, then, of a law is to furnish a standard of conduct ; it prescribes a rule of action in the matter to which it relates. The rule so prescribed may extend to all persons, or to some persons in exclusion of others. When this general rule is applied to a particular set of facts new relations arise. The case is no longer one of legislation but of executive duty. In all advanced communities separate organs are provided for these respective functions. Cases may indeed occur which are, as it were, on the border line, and in which it may be difficult to say whether the marks of the one class or the marks of the other class are the more conspicuous. But the difference between legislation and the consequences of legislation is in itself distinct, and in practice the line which divides them can usually be drawn with reasonable precision.

Objections to the Theory that Law is a Species of Command.

§ 5. Some misgivings seem to have lately arisen as to this famous analysis, and recent writers looking at the actual course of events are disposed to doubt whether it covers the whole field of modern legislation. It has been alleged † that, "laws purely permissive, laws declaratory, rules of procedure, rules for public convenience, rules conferring faculties, and rules conferring privileges, cannot, without undue violence to language, be brought under any strict partition of all law into rights and obligations." It may be that this passage is intended as a protest, not against the theory of legal command, but against Austin's adoption of right as the basis of

---

* See Shaw v. Gould, L. R. 3 E. & I. Ap. 80.
† By Mr. Frederic Harrison, Fort. Rev., N.S., xxiv., 607.

his system. If this be its meaning, I have nothing to say against it. But other writers* succeeding Mr. Harrison regard his remarks as a conclusive argument against the proposition that every law consists of a command, a duty, and a sanction. In this respect I think that the cases mentioned admit of explanation. I adhere indeed to the maxim, " *Rectum et sui index et obliqui,*" and I believe that the establishment of the truth is the best refutation of error. But in the present case the discussion of the opposing arguments will serve both to illustrate what I have said and to remove, as I hope, reasonable difficulties.

There are laws which on the face of them create no duty and express no sanction. They merely repeal or amend other laws or declare or otherwise interpret the meaning of such prior laws. Austin speaks of these laws as laws improperly so called ; and advantage has been taken of this admission to found an argument against his entire scheme. But the explanation is simple. These laws are in reality, what in form they usually profess to be, parts of the Principal Acts. They are to be incorporated and read together with these Acts. A repealing Act merely withdraws a previous command. An amending Act modifies a previous command, either by way of addition or of diminution or of change. A declaratory Act explains a previous command which was otherwise doubtful or obscure. In all these cases the command of the State with the usual duty and sanction had already been issued, and that command subsequently receives certain changes by the authority from which it originally emanated. The old law and the new taken together amount merely to a new and revised edition of the original command.

With respect to Acts conferring a franchise or a faculty, it must be observed that, as I shall presently have occasion more fully to show, a right cannot be created otherwise than by imposing a duty. Consequently the creation of a franchise or a privilege, or a monopoly, or any other

* See Mr. Wise, Outlines of Jurisprudence, 9.

exclusive right, presupposes a duty of forbearance in all other persons. In the instance cited by Mr. Harrison, the right to serve on a jury, the duty is apparent. It is in substance to the following effect :—" Subject to certain specified disqualifications and exemptions, every man shall when required so to do serve on a jury. If he offend herein, he shall be liable to fine or imprisonment." The case is one not of a right but of a positive absolute duty, a kind of duty which not unfrequently occurs when the State for its own purposes desires the active assistance of its subjects. Thus, a member of Parliament, a sheriff, an alderman, are bound to serve in their respective offices. A more striking example is the case of the electoral franchise. Certain persons are empowered to elect members of Parliament. All other persons are prohibited from doing so. To the latter injunction a penalty is attached ; but the law does not think it necessary, although it obviously has the power, to compel electors to record their votes. Yet in its origin the franchise was certainly a duty ; and doubtless ought still so to be regarded, although it has now become a duty of imperfect obligation. In all these cases the apparent difficulty arises from the circumstance that the duty, which in its origin was burthensome, has subsequently become advantageous. It simulates a right ; but its true nature is not thereby changed.

The case of enabling or permissive Acts is the complement of those which confer franchises or other positive rights. They exempt the party concerned from the operation of an existing restriction. In each case the grantee may do what others may not do. But under the enabling Act he is relieved from a duty of forbearance ; under the grant of a franchise or privilege the duty of forbearance from which he is excepted is cast upon others. The difference is expressed in our law by the terms privileges and immunities. The person who enjoys a privilege may do what others are forbidden to do. The person who has an immunity may forbear in cases where others are bound to act. The person who enjoys both a privilege and an immunity is in fact *solutus legibus*, exempt from the operation of the statutes in such case made and provided ; and he may do any specified act or observe any specified forbearance, anything in any law to the contrary notwithstanding. An Act which contains such provisions is substantially an amendment of a previous law. It corrects that law and limits its operation. In place of the proposition that no person shall do such an act or observe such a forbearance, it substitutes the proposition that no person except the person or the class described shall so act or forbear. Sometimes the same result appears in the form of a justification. In this case the exception is not personal, but some special circumstances are limited in which the law does not apply. Thus, no person may, as a general rule, restrain another person of his liberty ; but when a felony has been committed, any person may, notwithstanding the general rule, arrest the offender, and the law will support and protect him in doing so.

There is another class of laws which at first sight may not seem to come within this analysis. I mean those which regulate dealings with rights. These laws, however, are merely extensions of the command by which the right is created, and are intended to furnish means or facilities for ascertaining the person in whom the right resides. The law requires all persons to forbear from interfering with the property of John Doe, his heirs executors administrators and assigns. All that great body of law which relates to the devolution and the transfer of that property and to the dealings with it for the purpose of rendering it a financial security, and which for the better accomplishment of these objects provides various forms of pre-appointed evidence, is ancillary to the original command, and furnishes means or facilities for its execution. Thus, when Mr. Harrison asks in effect where is the obligation or the sanction in the familiar rule that every Will must be in writing, the answer is, first, that the rule is a subsidiary provision which presupposes a right, and consequently a duty and a sanction ; and secondly, that this particular rule actually contains within itself both a duty and a sanction. It casts upon the intending testator the duty of making his Will in a specified way, and it enforces compliance with this command by the sharp penalty of nullity.

Rules of judicial procedure, and rules for the control either of the other servants of the State or of such occupations as the State thinks fit to regulate, are laws in the sense in which I have used the term. They consist of commands given either to the public officers or to the persons who have to deal with those officers. In the former case, the sanction, if it be not otherwise expressed, is the dismission of the officers. In the latter case, it is the refusal of the assistance which the persons concerned ask the officers to render. When private occupations are regulated, duties are imposed upon the persons engaged in these occupations, and a breach of their duties is usually punished by the ordinary methods. In all these cases there is a sanction, although it may often happen that the sanction is not of a proper kind. In the case of procedure, for example, the Legislature often gives very minute directions, and omits to state what it intended to be the consequence of a breach of these directions. This excessive detail, and this want of specific sanction, are indeed infallible indications of bad drafting ; but bad drafting is unfortunately not unknown. In such circumstances one of two consequences usually happens. Either the courts hold that the Act is merely directory, which is a polite form for declaring that it is in fact not a law: or the sanction of nullity is applied, and the whole proceeding is set aside as void. No more fertile source of irritation to judges and of vexation and expense to suitors is known, nor one which causes such frequent miscarriages of justice. But these disasters arise from the badness of the law, not from the absence of it. Thus the general conclusions, at which in the earlier part of this chapter we arrived, remain unshaken. Law is a command of the State. It implies always a duty under sanction, and sometimes, as we presently shall more fully see, a right. It differs from other commands of the State, because it regulates men's conduct generally, and is not limited to mere individual acts. These characteristics are always present in every true law, even though their presence may not always be readily discernible.

CHAPTER II.

THE THEORY OF SOVEREIGNTY.

The State. § 1. Of the elements which collectively constitute a command, three may be included in the relation of sovereign and subject. These terms respectively connote the two parties, their unequal powers, and the desire of the one to regulate the conduct of the other. I have already said that I postulate the State. Human anatomy and physiology are studied without any settled opinions upon the origin of man. In like manner, one portion of the anatomy and physiology of the social organism may be studied without regard to the origin of society or to the stages through which, at different periods of its development, that portion of the organism may have passed. It suffices then, without any discussion as to the commencement or the history of the relation, to describe as it now exists the character of sovereignty. Austin's treatment of this subject suggests two observations. The first relates to his arrangement. He thought fit, probably for temporary and polemical purposes, to leave the arrangement of his predecessors, and to discuss the meaning of law of duty and of sanction before he considered the nature of sovereignty. That is, he studied the function before he studied the organ. By this course he has given to the earlier part of his work the unfounded appearance of dogmatism. The logical consequences of admitted premises are thus presented as though they were the mere opinions of the writer. But although the effect of Austin's book is by this means considerably marred, the error is one which subsequent writers can easily avoid. The second observation relates to a more formidable difficulty. The words sovereign and subject have associations that are dangerously misleading. They have been borrowed from a particular stage of political development, and they retain the memories of their origin. They imply, or seem to imply, that the sovereign is external to the community, and that his power is different in origin and in kind from that of the people over whom he rules. I am not concerned with the theories of Divine right and of the Original Contract. These theories have long since served their purpose. They were invented to explain certain temporary phenomena. They mark perhaps what Comte would have called the supernatural and the metaphysical stages of Jurisprudence. The proposition that I now desire to maintain is that the power of every Government is simply the power of the people itself, and that the State means nothing more than the organized community.

Every society is, or at least closely resembles, an organic body. In super-organisms, as they have been called, not less than in organisms, the higher forms, as compared with the lower, have a more elaborate structure and a more full development. The forms of the political organs vary, but the functions which they perform are alike. These functions are, among other things, to make and enforce general rules for the conduct of members of the community. Thus, where there is a political community, whatever may be the circumstances in which that community was organized, whether it arose spontaneously or was the result of the deliberate consent of its members, the political organs furnish the machinery by which in any given direction, either within or without the body politic, the whole national force can be applied. That body may, if it think fit, with more or less of disturbance and of inconvenience, change the form of its organ; but while the organ, whatever be its form, continues, it and it alone expresses the national will, and it and it alone directs the national power.

The Jurisdiction of the State. § 2. Law is thus a species of command of the State or politically organized community. I do not now propose to discuss the various forms of political organs which exist or which have existed in different communities, or to estimate their comparative merits or defects. It is enough that every political community possesses some such organ, and that the place of each community in the political scale may be measured by that organ's development. I proceed then briefly to inquire to what persons the commands of the State are given, or, in other words, who are the subjects of the State, or, to again change the expression—who are the members of the community and their dependents. This question, like so many others, cannot be fully answered without the aid of history, and I have elsewhere* expressed in some detail my views upon its historical aspect. I shall therefore merely state, as accurately as I can, the general rules of modern law upon the subject. These rules are taken from English authorities, but they are, I think, substantially true in other European countries.

Personal and Territorial Jurisdiction. There are two grounds on which a State claims jurisdiction—one is personal, the other is territorial. The first arises from birth, the second from residence. Both these causes are generally combined, since natural-born subjects of a State usually live within that State's territorial limits. But this is not always the case. Natural-born subjects may reside abroad. Strangers may come to live within the Queen's dominions. The jurisdiction of the State thus presents itself under a double aspect. It may claim to follow its own subjects, even though they be in another jurisdiction. It may, indeed from the nature of the case it must, as a general rule, exercise authority over all persons who are found within its territory, whatever other claims upon their allegiance may exist. The extent to which different States press their claims, or rather their claim, over their natural-born subjects, varies considerably. In France,† which seems to mark the extreme limit of the personal theory, it has been recently enacted that an offence by a Frenchman against French law, in whatever country it be committed, is punishable by the French courts. The English practice has been to decline, with but few exceptions, all concern for the conduct of any subject of Her Majesty outside her dominions. In

* See "The Aryan Household," cc. xv. and xvi.
† See Prof. Holland's Jurisprudence, 310 (2nd ed.).

some few cases, such as slave-dealing, bigamy, and homicide, our law has made punishable certain offences by any of Her Majesty's subjects in whatever part of the world they are committed. In all other cases, if an Englishman be charged with any serious offence against the laws of another country, he is, on certain conditions, surrendered to take his trial according to the laws of that country. On the other hand, we enforce against all offenders every breach in our own country of our laws. In all circumstances it is a fundamental rule that no State can enforce its laws even against its own subjects within the territory of another State. The sea, which is the common highway of nations, has its own customs. For our present purpose it suffices to say that the rules as to territorial jurisdiction apply to the ships of each nation on the high seas. Such ships are sometimes described as floating islands. But this somewhat poetical expression merely means that persons and property on board ships at sea are subject to the jurisdiction of the country to which the ship belongs.

On the whole, then, the following rules seem to be generally accepted. In the first place, every State may legislate for its own subjects in all places, whether in its own territories or on the high seas or in the territory of any other State, but may not execute any such law in any territory or upon any ship that is not its own. In the second place, every State may legislate for all strangers within its boundaries, or on board its ships on the high seas, or on board a foreign mercantile ship within its harbours or territorial waters, but not further or otherwise. Thirdly, subject to the exceptions I am about to enumerate, every State has exclusive jurisdiction over all persons and property within its territories.

Exceptions to Territorial Jurisdiction. The exceptions to the rule of territorial jurisdiction are in the first place sovereign princes, ambassadors, and the retinue of such princes or ambassadors. In the case of such retinues the privilege is not that of the

servant but of the master; and it consequently extends so far
as the personal convenience of that master is concerned, and
not further. The exceptions also include a foreign army in
licensed transit through the territory of the State, ships
bearing the commission of another State, and vessels of
pleasure in the personal use of a foreign sovereign prince.
In accordance with the Custom of Nations, no proceedings
may in any circumstances or for any breach of law be taken
in the courts of any country not their own against any of
these persons. If they commit any offence, they may be
required to leave the country ; and redress may be sought by
diplomatic methods, but not by any judicial remedy. But
any such person may, if he think fit, waive his privilege, and
invite the aid of the court or submit to its authority. In such
cases the once privileged plaintiff or defendant is treated in
all respects in the same manner as an ordinary suitor.

Law not
Universal.
Law in the strict sense of the term is not a
universal phenomenon. Rules of conduct indeed of
some kind exist wherever human beings live together; but
rules of conduct are not necessarily laws. Law, as I have
said, is a command of the State, that is, it is the deliberate
command of the community, through its definite organs
established for that purpose, and enforced by these organs,
with the intent of producing a general course of conduct in or
among its members or its dependents. But the State itself
is of recent growth, and the function which it exercises cannot in the nature of things have preceded it. The State is
only one out of several forms of society, and is not the oldest
of those forms. The larger part of mankind still live under
their ancestral customs, and without any approach to what
we call political organization. Except in those countries
which are descended from the Roman Empire, or to which
the influence of the Roman law has reached, the true State
seems to be unknown. There have indeed been elsewhere
mechanical aggregations of persons, such as the tax-taking
empires of the East ; but out of Europe and the countries

peopled from Europe no politically organized and law-making empire is found. Thus in Asia the depths of the great ocean of human life remain undisturbed in their changeless repose, regardless of the fierce and desolating tempests by which its surface is continually tossed. Its units live their humble life under their old ancestral traditions. They obey the orders of their master so long as he is their master; but whether they have a master, or whether they have none, their standard of conduct is the custom of their forefathers. Such a condition is very different from the legislative activity of English-speaking peoples. Yet we seldom reflect how very recent is this activity. The conquerors of Crecy looked with undisguised alarm at any new project of law, and the fact that a reform necessitated a new statute* was an admitted and often a fatal obstacle to its success. All the volumes of our statutes, from their beginning under Henry III. to the close of the reign of George II., do not equal the quantity of legislative work done in a decade of any subsequent reign.

The Services of the State. § 3. Some misconception has existed as to the services which the State has rendered to society. Various important social institutions are usually described as though they were the creatures of law. Thus Bentham † remarks that "Property and law are born, and must die together. Before the laws, there was no property. Take away the laws, all property ceases." The statement also that the end of Government is to maintain tranquillity at home and peace abroad is ordinarily accepted as an axiom. Yet it may confidently be alleged that none of these statements is historically true. Property existed long before the State, and consequently before the laws which proceeded from the State. It now exists in many parts of the world without the State. It would probably, although in this case we can but conjecture, survive, at least in some degree, the State. The same observations apply to other objects of enjoyment, such as the domestic rights. Even expectations belong to

* Hallam's Middle Ages, III. 49.   † I. 509.

the same class. Regard for the plighted word has charac-
terized and still characterizes, at least as between themselves,
many societies of men who know nothing of laws or of legal
sanction. The *nexum* and the *sponsio* existed before the
Twelve Tables ; that is, they were part of the customs of the
Latin clans long before the Prætor held his court. The
Teuton who lost not his property only but his freedom
at the gambling table, quietly held out his hands for the
fetters of the slave. So too men settled their disputes
before there was either judge or jury to decide between them.
The Bedaween Arabs do so at this day. Nor was an Act of
Parliament, or any other command of the State, necessary to
induce men to unite in repelling an invader or in themselves
invading any foreign territory which they happened to desire.
All this is merely to say that men once lived, and in some
cases are still living, in a condition of society different from
that in which we live and which we call political. Yet it
cannot be denied that under political society an immense
advance has been made in all that we vaguely describe as
civilization. It is in these societies, and none other, that the
progress of the human race is most conspicuous. The
question therefore arises in what way and to what extent
does the State tend to produce such great results? It will
not be expected that, in a single section of a chapter of a work
in which the subject only incidentally presents itself, a complete answer can be given to questions of such magnitude.
Yet it may be possible to indicate to some extent the direction which such an answer when it arrives is likely to take.

Although it is true that in an archaic society the
great objects with which law is practically concerned are
already formed, their development is very incomplete. They
must be exercised *certis verbis*, in a fixed and often complex
form and without the least deviation or mistake. They are
even in this form available only as between members of the
same community or the few strangers to whom the special
privilege of the " commercium " was sparingly granted. Even

in the case of its own members, the house fathers only of the
community could act; and it is probable that at least in any
important transaction custom further required the consents of
various persons interested. Further, custom controlled every
phase of human activity, and thus little room was left for any
improvement. The blood feud too rendered life insecure to
an extent which we happily can but dimly realize. I think
then that we cannot be far wrong if, among the most important domestic consequences of the growth of a moderately
strong and orderly Government, we enumerate the following
advantages :—First, such a Government substituted the
Formless for the Formal method of transacting all kinds of
ordinary business; that is, it substituted the intention of the
parties as expressed in any reasonable way for the onerous
ceremonies of the older time. Secondly, it substituted citizens
for clansmen, and thus rendered possible the existence of
larger communities; that is, it increased the number of
persons between whom co-operation and exchange could take
place; and it strengthened for all purposes, both internal and
external, the whole community. Thirdly, it substituted contracts and wills for the fixed customary rules of dealing with
property both during life and after death; and thus individual energy was enabled to make in a great measure its own
laws in relation to its own affairs. Fourthly, it took into its
own hands not merely the terrible custom of vengeance but
all offences against person and property. It thus secured not
only internal peace and good order, but also the fulfilment
of promises between persons who had otherwise no mutual
special relations. But none of these changes were immediate
in their operation. The State was of slow growth, and was
at most but one of various competing social forces. Its
influence varied in different cases, and in the same case at
different times according to the degree of its own power.
When it was successful, it gave to the community in which
it was placed such an impulse towards both wealth and well-
being as in no other circumstances the world has ever seen.

§ 4. It is not material to my present purpose to inquire into the motives by which men are induced to adopt or to acquiesce in any particular form of government. Their conduct rarely proceeds from any carefully balanced considerations of expediency. They are influenced sometimes by what we should call the superstitious desire to be ruled by a member of some particular family. Sometimes the dominant influence is mere custom : sometimes it is an intelligent reluctance to exchange evils which they know for evils which they can only dimly foresee, and a well-grounded belief that destruction is easy but that construction is almost impossible. Sometimes the motive is simply fear and an inability to offer any successful resistance, as where a conquered country is held under the yoke of a harmost or a pro-consul, of a pasha or a major-general. It is not necessary to inquire into cases of constitutional disturbance, of the irregular supremacy of an adventurer, of a discontented minority or of the inadequate expression of the will of a majority. All such questions belong to a different department of study. The super-organism not less than the organism has its pathology as well as its anatomy and its physiology. But before we can understand the conditions of disease, we must ascertain the standard of health. Accordingly, I assume, as the type or normal form of a society in which law prevails, an autonomous community with definite political organs. Such a community deliberately makes laws for its own guidance through its proper organs, whatever those organs may be. In such circumstances, as I have said, the community possesses machinery by which its entire force can be directed without hindrance to any particular object. As regards, therefore, any single member of the community, the law is irresistible. He cannot struggle against the whole force, physical and moral, of the society in which he lives. It is this inability of any private person to resist in any circumstances the public power that is meant by the expression the omnipotence of the law.

In practice this bold metaphor must be received with much reserve. Law is impotent to change, even in the most insignificant respect, the ordinary course of nature. No Act of Parliament can add a cubit to our stature. The master of thirty legions confessed his inability to alter the usage of one poor word. But these considerations relate to the substance, not the form, of legislation. They show that foolish laws may be made, but they do not disprove the proposition that the law may expend the last man and the last shilling of the community in enterprises which are manifestly absurd. There is, however, an important limitation which affects the form of law. It is that of time. An existing Legislature may do what it likes so long as its power continues, but no independent Legislature can by any contrivance, or by any words, tie the hands of its successor. That is, no independent Legislature is bound to regard any limitation upon its powers or its discretion that its predecessors may have attempted to impose ; and no court of justice will interfere to require the recognition of any such limitation, or will refuse to accept the later enactment. " And albeit, says Lord Coke,* it appeareth by these examples and many other that might be brought what transcendent power and authority this Court of Parliament hath, yet, though divers Parliaments have attempted to bar, restrain, suspend, qualify, explain, or make void subsequent Parliaments, yet could they never effect it, for the latter Parliament hath ever power to abrogate, suspend, qualify, explain, or make void the former in the whole or in any part thereof, notwithstanding any words of restraint, prohibition, or penalty in the former : for it is a maxim in the law of Parliament *quod leges posteriores priores contrarias abrogant.*" This doctrine has received some remarkable illustrations in recent times. The Acts of Union of England and Scotland and of Great Britain and Ireland provided in effect that the existing established Churches and Ecclesiastical arrangements of Scotland and of Ireland respectively should remain

. * See 4 Inst. 43.

unchanged for ever.   Yet within four years after the Union
with Scotland an Act relating to lay patronage was passed
in direct contravention of the Treaty of Union, and the
House of Lords in the present reign judicially decided that
the later Act must prevail.   In Ireland, within the life-time
of persons who were living when the Act of Union had
declared the Established Church was to last for ever, that
same Church was disendowed and disestablished.

The Practical   § 5. It does not follow because the State has
Limits of
Legislation.   absolute control over the persons and property of its
subjects that such power is exercised without restraint.   In
every well-governed State provision is made for protection
not only by the Government but against the Government.
Such provision, which is one of the leading subjects of constitutional law, applies to the Executive Government only;
and the fact still remains that the legislature is always beyond
any legal control.   Law, which supplies the machinery for
directing at its will the national force, supplies no machinery
by which the lawful exercise of that force can be limited or
controlled.   But not the less is the power actually controlled,
although the influences to which it is subject do not belong
to law.   Men rarely do all that they have the power of doing.
There is the great force of public opinion, itself the result
partly of the history of the people, partly of their traditions
and customs, partly of the existing state of knowledge,
partly of the existing standard of morality.   All these and
other influences determine the discretion of the nation, and
insure more or less completely that in general the legislative
power shall be exercised in a measure consistent with the
prevailing public sentiment.   Nor is this all.   It is not
merely that the legislators are checked by the dread of the
disapprobation of others or are encouraged by their approval.
They are themselves members of the community, and their
habits and purposes are formed under the like influences as
those of their fellow-citizens.   They spontaneously, therefore,

use their derived powers in the way in which they use their original powers. In countries with representative institutions the members of the legislative bodies are usually, from various causes, keenly sensitive to the prevailing tone of public sentiment. But these are matters which do not belong to the theory of jurisprudence, nor should that theory be blamed because it omits subjects of which it never pro fessed to treat. Jurisprudence deals merely with the form . of law, and from that stand-point declares that every independent community has, through its legislative organs, the power to frame whatever laws it pleases, whether these laws be wise or foolish, beneficent or cruel, conducive to virtue or conducive to vice. It does not profess to treat of the art of legislation, and it therefore intentionally omits the consideration of those numerous and complex and powerful forces which collectively form the total of national character and national life. It neither denies the existence of such forces nor under-estimates their importance. It only asserts the obvious fact that these forces are not law, and do not therefore come within the sphere of jurisprudence. It has never been imputed as a fault in Comyn's Digest that the very learned author simply states that the king has the sole authority to declare war or peace, and that he does not enumerate even the most obvious influences by which the Royal discretion in the exercise of that momentous power is controlled. That famous work was written upon law, and not upon the principles of constitutional government. In like manner we must be content to ascertain the precise character of sovereignty before we investigate the counteracting influences which limit its practical operation.

ThePrinciple of Political Liberty. § 6. It is indeed the primary function of the State to protect its members against foreign enemies or domestic evil-doers. But this is not the only protection of which these members stand in need. They require protection against the State itself. Means must be found of guarding against the very guards. " The only insecurity," says J. S. Mill,* " which is altogether paralyzing to the active energies of producers is that arising from the Government or from persons invested with its authority. Against all other depredators there is a hope of defending oneself." It becomes necessary then to provide, first, that while the power of the State is sufficient to effect its objects, it shall not be more than sufficient for that purpose ; and second, that that power shall not be applied to any other objects. These limitations upon the powers of the State, both as regards their extent and their direction, constitute that which is termed political liberty. It is idle to suppose that liberty consists in the total absence of all restraint. Such a state of things is anarchy, and anarchy is not liberty. Political liberty implies such a well-ordered arrangement of the political organs that both the combined action which is sought shall be secured, and that the reasonable limits of that action shall not be exceeded. These expressions are indeed vague, and admit of many varieties of degrees. Nevertheless, in practice and under favorable conditions, a gradual advance has been made in several countries, but most of all in England, to unite the desired conditions. Even in England the attainment of the ideal standard is still far remote. But in no other country has so much been practically done to insure that the State shall have all the powers of sovereignty, and that it shall exercise these powers with wisdom and with justice.

The Functions of the State. The most difficult, and at the same time the most important, of all social problems is to determine the precise limits of the functions of the State. It cannot be said that this problem has yet received complete solution. It is indeed beyond the scope of jurisprudence, but jurisprudence may nevertheless furnish some help in the inquiry. We shall presently see that a distinction must be made between those matters which directly and immediately concern the State and those matters in which the State is asked to assist or to restrict the action of individuals. To

* Political Economy, I. 139 (4th ed.).

the former class belong those duties which are known as absolute. To the latter class belong all the duties and rights which relate to particular persons. Between these two classes stands the mixed class of general duties, in which both the State and individuals claim an interest. For the present purpose these duties may be classed with the absolute duties. As to those duties, then, in which the State issues its commands without reference to the wants or the claims of individual persons, the State should not seek to extend its commands beyond those matters which in good faith directly and immediately concern itself and its own proceedings. As to particular duties, the State should abstain from all interference with *bond fide* contracts and wills, except where these arrangements interfere with some provision fairly contained within the former class of duties. Where legislation is needed in the absence of any private disposition, the State should so far as possible follow the prevailing custom. The practical danger is twofold. One danger is that matters which are merely of private right should be included under public duties. The other danger is that absolute duties should be multiplied beyond the point which the reasonable requirements of the State demand. The action of the State is indeed a great force ; but the greater the force, the greater is the care that is needed in its application. It by no means follows that because some object is desirable it should on that account only be the subject of legislation : much less does it follow that everything which appears to us to be desirable should be carried into effect by legal pains and penalties. I know of but one test in such cases ; and in that test I think that both reason and the early history of law concur. That test is the question whether any proposed absolute or general duty does or does not directly concern the well-being of the State, or whether the power which the Executive seeks is or is not in the circumstances of the case reasonably required for the proper exercise of State functions. Burke* observes that every nation has some particular subject

* III. 253.

which forms, as it were, its point of honour, and expresses
in a concrete form its abstract idea of liberty.   Among the
Romans this ideal standard was the right of electing magis-
trates.   Among our forefathers it was the right of self-
taxation.   The choice of such subjects is not arbitrary.   It
arises from purely historical causes, and the tradition
survives the actual occasion.   But these sentiments and
the ceaseless discussions on the best form of government,
although the practical statesman can never afford to lose
sight of them, are of little use to the student of society.
What he needs is some general principle which explains the
effect of legislation on the advanced societies, and which,
when it is sufficiently understood, may furnish the basis of
a rule for their practical guidance.   I think that I have
above indicated the outline at least of such a principle.
The classification of law, the principles of Political Economy,
and the hints of archaic history, all seem to point in the
same direction.   But the full development of such a principle must be sought elsewhere than in a treatise on
Analytical Jurisprudence.

CHAPTER III.

THE EVIDENCES OF LAW.

The Source of Law.

§ 1. In his history of the Decemvirate, Livy describes the Twelve Tables as "*Fons omnis publici privatique juris.*" It was perhaps this passage that gave rise to the well-known expression, "*fontes juris.*" Like most metaphors, this phrase is ambiguous. It means either the source of the authority of law, that is the legislator ; or the source of our knowledge of law, that is its evidences. Were it not for this ambiguity, the subject would present no special difficulty. So far as regards the first and proper sense of the expression, there is no room for doubt that the express command of the community duly notified through its proper organs is a source of law. But whether such a command is the sole source of law is a question that is less readily answered. I have already shown that the limitation of the term law to the commands of the State excludes other standards of conduct. Revelation, morality, expediency, may separately or concurrently govern men's conduct ; but none of them is law. The same reasoning which leads us to distinguish these standards from law applies with even greater force to custom. Law is essentially a command, but custom, "*mores consensu utentium comprobati,*" depends simply on the free will of those who observe it. The relation of custom to law is so close, and is, as I think, so generally misunderstood, and the weight of the authority in favour of the proposition which I dispute is so great, that I propose to offer a few remarks upon the subject.

Justinian* in his "Institutes," declares, although it is noteworthy that Gaius is silent on the subject, that customs approved by the consent of those who observe them imitate

* L 2, 9.

law. That resemblances exist between custom and law is
certain. The former denotes a uniformity of conduct; the
latter connotes that uniformity as the object which it desires
to attain. So far, therefore, we may accept the doctrine of
the "Institutes," although we may have misgivings as to its
practical value. But a passage in the Digest* carries that
doctrine much further. It in effect alleges, not that custom
imitates law, but that it is law. It observes that law derives
its force solely from the will of the people, and that it is
immaterial whether that will be expressed by their formal
vote or by their conduct. Accordingly, it was held under the
Roman system that laws were repealed not only by express
enactment but by simple desuetude. I need not repeat the
arguments by which Austin† refuted this fallacy. I will only
say that in every country customs are generally observed
which are not laws; that customs which in their original state
were only partially observed have become laws; that when a
custom becomes law it binds all persons, and not those only
who had assented to it by their observance; and that no
custom, however generally adopted, can be deemed to be law
against the express provision of an Act of Parliament. It is
true that the conversion of custom into law is of frequent
occurrence; but such a conversion takes place‡ when and only
when the custom is adopted by the Legislature and is enforced
by its authority. There is no greater difficulty in adopting
by way of reference and in terms of general description a
body of customs than there is in adopting in like manner a
body of laws. Parliament has given legal effect to the then
existing canons of the Church; it has directed the Indian
judges to have regard to the usages of India; it has introduced into New South Wales the then existing laws of
England; and it has confirmed in Lower Canada the then
existing laws of France. But although these canons and
these customs and these laws of England and of France were
in existence long before the enactment of any of the statutes
to which I have referred, they never could of themselves

---

* I. 3, 32.   † I. 555 *et seq.*   ‡ See "The Aryan Household," 395 *et seq.*

and without such express enactment have ripened into law. They lacked the one essential element of law—they were not in the circumstances the command of the State. Nor is this all. Law cannot exist without the command of the State; and the command of the State which generates law can only be given through the appropriate organs. The order or resolution of either House of Parliament, or of both Houses, or Her Majesty's proclamation, is not sufficient to produce law. The original constitution of every State, however it may have been formed, provides certain organs by which, and by which alone, the will of the people is expressed. While these organs continue in existence, they and none others are legislative. To the question, therefore, of Julianus, in the passage from the Digest which I have cited above—what is the difference between the consent of the people expressed by their suffrage and the consent of the people expressed by their conduct?—the answer is that there is all the difference that exists between the conduct of a mere aggregate of human beings and the conduct of a duly organized community.

This view of the relations of Custom and of Law does not offer, and is not intended to offer, any explanation of the origin or the continuance of society. The nature of custom and the nature of law and their mutual relations are in themselves important subjects of inquiry, even though the result of that inquiry does not explain why men entered into society or why they remain in it. This treatise does not touch a subject of still greater practical interest, the tendency, namely, of obedience to the law to become a habit, and so at some future day to dispense in a greater or less degree with the need of sanctions. I assume, as I have said, the existence of a State; that is, I assume that a community exists which is organized in a particular manner, and has organs of a particular kind; and I inquire into certain functions of these organs. In this inquiry I contend that, for the reasons I have assigned, the ideas of custom and of law are in fact

C

distinct. I do not allege that law is the exclusive element
of social cohesion, or that it is more than one out of many
influences by which in the existing condition of society
human conduct is determined and social life is maintained.
But law admits of separate examination to an extent that
is very unusual in social phenomena. It does not tend to
facilitate that examination if we insist either that all custom
is law, as the Digest argues, or that, as a recent writer*
contends, all law is custom. Jurisprudence is not sociology,
but it is one branch of it, and a branch which in existing
circumstances admits of more successful study than almost
any other such branch. Its success, however, as a contributory study depends upon an exact understanding both
of what it undertakes and of what it declines to consider.

The Sources of the Knowledge of Law.
§ 2. Although there is but one source of legislative authority, our knowledge of the commands
which that authority issues is derived from various sources.
The command may be notified directly and in express terms.
In this case there is no difficulty except such as arises in
its interpretation. Or there may be customs, or the laws
of another country, which the Legislature has adopted as a
whole and without any specific enumeration, and which must
therefore be ascertained and compared with other existing
legislation. This process involves a long course of judicial
decisions or other authoritative exposition ; and from the
materials thus accumulated generalizations are made and rules
of law are extracted. Thus both statutes as interpreted· by
the courts, and customs as ascertained and established by the
same authority, furnish new and improved data by which in
subsequent cases the judgments of these courts are directed.
Further, the law provides that under certain conditions and
with certain exceptions the laws of foreign countries may for
certain purposes be accepted as having the force of law in
our country. This courtesy both towards the foreign Legislature and the foreign courts in no way implies any political

* Mr. Leslie Stephen, Science of Ethics, 146.

dependence upon that country. It is simply a mark of goodwill to neighbours of like habits and institutions to our own, and a means of doing complete justice both in the case of our own citizens who have entered into engagements abroad and in the case of foreigners who are resident in our own country.

In like manner, and under certain conditions, and subject to certain restrictions, the law permits that the agreements between parties shall, so far as these parties are concerned, have the force of law. Under this power each man in his dealings with other men is permitted to no inconsiderable extent to be his own lawgiver. But it is necessary to ascertain in the first place whether any particular agreement has complied with the conditions upon which alone the law will recognise and enforce it, and in the second place what the true intention of the parties actually was. On this subject also the assistance of the courts is required, and a great body of decisions has been accumulated. Another direction in which law may be sought is in the delegated legislation of public bodies. The Legislature often authorizes various associations of men to make rules for their own government, and gives to these rules as against the members of the association the force of law. Thus colonies have their local Acts of Parliament. Municipal councils have their by-laws. Academic bodies have their statutes. Trading companies have their articles of association, and other societies their rules or regulations. These cases of subordinate legislation differ in their names, but they agree in their substance. They imply that powers more or less extensive of legislation have been conferred upon the particular body by the authority of the State. Such legislation is the act of the State itself through its agents authorized for that purpose ; and, consequently, so long as the agents keep within the limits of their authority, their acts are equivalent to an Imperial Statute. I propose now to consider in detail each of these classes of evidences, namely, statutes, customs, foreign laws, judicial decisions, agreements, and delegated legislation.

c 2

Statute Law. § 3. The simplest and fullest evidence of the law is the direct declaration of the Legislature, or, as we term it indifferently, a Statute or Act of Parliament. When such an Act is passed, nothing remains but to ascertain its true meaning. This task, however, is not always easy. Partly from ordinary literary defects, partly from the necessity— a necessity which legislators do not always recognise—of reading together the various Acts upon the same subject so as to give their full effect to each, above all from the like necessity in regard to the common law, serious difficulties sometimes arise in the work of interpretation. The rules of interpretation form a special branch of law, and are not within the scope of my present undertaking. It is enough to say that an Act of Parliament, when it is duly passed, is according to its true intent conclusive evidence of the law. Such is the effect of a statute if it be duly passed. It is necessary therefore to consider the circumstances in which a statute is not duly passed and the consequences of any defect in its enactment. In other words, the questions arise, can a statute be *ultra vires*, and can the courts go behind a statute?

The answer to the first of these questions requires a little explanation. In the case of a sovereign State, that is of a political community not subject to any external authority, its legislation can never be *ultra vires*. There are no degrees in sovereignty; and when the will of the community has been expressed by its proper organ, no court can disregard it, and no force can lawfully impede its operation. Consequently in England the authority of an Act of Parliament is never disputed, and its provisions are never measured by any external standard. In the United States, on the other hand, although the principle is the same, its application is different. It is not easy to decide what in that country is the organ of sovereignty. It is unnecessary now to pursue the inquiry. But this much is certain, that the Congress is not that organ. The standard of legality is the written constitution, and every statute inconsistent with that constitution may be set aside by the Supreme Court. There are of course methods by which the constitution can be amended ; nor can any one doubt that, if it were desired, an entirely new organ of sovereignty could be created. The will of the community is as uncontrolled as it is in England; but the organ for the expression of that will is somewhat complicated and somewhat obscure.

Upon the question whether the courts will entertain an objection that a document which professes to be an Act of Parliament is not really such the English Reports do not furnish any definite authority. The nearest approach to an authority is a case* that occurred in the time of Charles II. An objection to an Act passed by the Convention Parliament was taken on the ground that that body had not been summoned by the Royal writ, and was not therefore a Parliament. The objection does not appear formidable, because, as the king had accepted the Convention as his Parliament, the omission of the writ was only an irregularity which the Royal ratification might be fairly held to cure. The court refused even to entertain the objection, and seems to have thought that it was bound by any instrument in which His Majesty professed to declare his will in Parliament. But although there is no conclusive legal precedent on the subject, grave questions have sometimes arisen in practice, and the rules concerning them may now be regarded as definitely settled. When any breach of the rules of Parliamentary procedure with regard to Bills takes place, no advantage can be taken of such breach after the Bill has left the House in which it has occurred, although in that House it forms a good ground of objection up to the moment at which the Bill is passed. Each House has the exclusive control of its own procedure, and no other authority is competent to inquire into the steps by which it arrived at its final conclusion. It is with its results, not with its processes, that the other branches of the Legislature are concerned.

* See Hallam, Const. Hist. II. 316 *Note.*

But when a Bill has inadvertently received the Royal assent, either in mistake or without having been assented to in its final form by either of the two Houses, the case is much more serious. Such an error is in fact incurable. The practice,* when any such untoward event has occurred, is to pass in due form at the earliest possible moment a validating Act, and so the question has never come to the courts.

A recent case further illustrates the supreme authority of a Statute. There is no maxim of the law more clear or more frequently observed in practice than that of "*Fraus vitiat omnia.*" Yet, as this case shows, even an allegation of fraud will not induce a court of justice to go behind an Act of the Imperial Parliament. A firm of solicitors† brought certain proceedings for their costs against shareholders in an unsuccessful railway company. The main defence was that there was not and never had been any such company or any shares or shareholders therein. In support of this position, it was contended that Parliament had been induced by fraudulent recitals to pass the Act under which the company was formed. On this contention Mr. Justice Willes observed— "These Acts of Parliament are the law of this land, and we do not sit here as a court of appeal from Parliament. It was once said, I think in Hobart, that if an Act of Parliament were to create a man judge in his own case, the court might disregard it. That dictum, however, stands as a warning rather than an authority to be followed. We sit here as servants of the Queen and the Legislature. Are we to act as regents over what is done by Parliament with the consent of the Queen Lords and Commons? I deny that any such authority exists. If an Act of Parliament has been obtained improperly, it is for the Legislature to correct it by repealing it ; but so long as it exists as law, the courts are bound to obey it. The proceedings here are judicial not autocratic,

---

* Sco Sir T. E. May's Practice of Parliament (6th ed.), 500.

† Leo r. Bude and Torrington Junction Railway Co., L. R. 6 C. P. 576.

which they would be if we could make laws instead of administering them. The Act of Parliament makes these persons shareholders or it does not. If it does, there is an end to the question. If it does not, that is a matter which may be raised by a plea to the *scire facias.* Having neglected to take the proper steps at the proper time to prevent the Act from passing into a law, it is too late now to raise any objections to it."

Customary Law.   § 4. Where a State adopts certain customs as a whole, such an adoption is subject to the ordinary rules of interpretation. These rules provide that customs shall not be unreasonable and shall not be inconsistent with existing legislation. That is, the common law supplies in such a case the needful restriction which in similar cases statutes express by the words "so far as the same can be applied therein," or by equivalent terms. Such restrictions, needful though they be, give a wide latitude to those who administer the law. "What is reasonable, says Lord Coke,* is not to be understood of every unlearned man's reason, but of artificial and legal reason warranted by authority of law." In these circumstances it is the duty of the judges to ascertain what particular customs come within the true meaning and intent of the legislative adoption. They must decide whether a given usage be one of the good customs of England, or whether it be reasonable, or whether, having regard to the circumstances of the community and to the other legislation in force therein, the legislature can fairly be supposed to have meant that it should be adopted. When a general usage has thus been judicially ascertained and established, it becomes† part of the law, which courts of justice are bound to know and to recognise. English law contains abundant instances of this transmutation of custom into law. The common law consists of

* Co. Litt. 62 *a.*
† See *per* Lord Campbell, Brandao *v.* Barnett, 12 Cl. & F. at p. 805; and *per* Cockburn C. J., Goodwin *v.* Roberts, L. R. 10 Exch. at p. 346.

general customs judicially ascertained and recognised. These
customs have dropped their original description, and are now
called emphatically law. The word custom is now restricted
in legal language to special customs which prevail in particular localities, and is contrasted with those general customs
from which they derogate. The Law Maritime means the
general maritime law, that is the customs observed in navigation, as administered in England; and is in truth, as it has
been judicially declared,* "nothing more than English law,
though dealt out in somewhat different measures in the
Common Law and Chancery Courts, and in the peculiar
jurisdiction of the Admiralty." The Law Merchant is
hardly even a custom, but is rather, as we shall presently see,
the application to the construction of mercantile contracts of
an ordinary rule of interpretation. Thus all these customs,
whether of the land, or of the sea, or of the market, are
enforced by the officers of the State in pursuance of the
command of the State ; and these several branches of the law
as they now exist are the result of the manner in which
successive generations of judges have performed their duties.

Foreign
Law.   § 5. Another class of the evidences of law is
Foreign Law. I have said that law applies only to
an independent community, that is a community which is not
subject to the command of any external authority. It follows,
therefore, that foreign law cannot of itself be either a source
or an evidence of law in any other community. As between
separate communities, various customs exist which are
observed with more or less exactitude. In the intercourse
between European nations, or nations of European descent,
these customs are known as International Law. This use of
the term law is metaphorical and often misleading. Law
cannot be predicated of mere customs which are not even
true commands, much less the commands of any competent
State. Some of these customs, especially those which relate
to the sea, have been accepted by most nations, and form

* *Per* Willes J., Lloyd *v.* Guibert, L. R. 1 Q. B. at p. 123.

part of their respective laws. They start from the same point, and retain a distinct family resemblance, "*quales decet esse sorores.*" But the maritime law of the present day as administered in England is by no means the same as the maritime law administered elsewhere. That this law is essentially the law of each country appears from the fact that a judge in Admiralty is bound by Her Majesty's Orders in Council, even though such Orders are repugnant to the known customs of nations. He is Her Majesty's servant, and must obey her lawful commands. If any other nation be aggrieved by his decision, the remedy is not by way of appeal to any other tribunal, but by diplomatic methods. The dispute in such circumstances is a matter not of right but of expedience.

Private International Law occupies a different position. The expressions public and private international law are not altogether happy. The former system is international, but is not law. The latter system is law, but is not international. Private international law, as it is called, is merely the recognition *ad eundem,* if I may so speak, by the courts of one country of rights of action that have accrued in another country. Such a right will, subject to some exceptions and limitations, be generally recognised elsewhere, and will be enforced in the recognising country in the same manner that it would have been enforced if it had originated in the latter country. · This recognition is said to result from the "comity of nations," but it is not necessarily reciprocal. Whatever be the motive for the practice, the authority is always, and necessarily, that of the recognising State. In like manner there exists, or did exist, a *comitas academica* between the learned bodies of Europe. At the present day colonial universities accept and recognise the degrees of the older universities, although no such comity is extended to them. They do so, not because they are under any obligation in the matter, nor from any wish to flatter by unappreciated attentions a somewhat ungracious sisterhood; but because, in the circumstances of colonial society, such a policy is expedient to themselves. When, therefore, foreign laws are administered in any court, they are so administered, not because they are foreign, but because, although originally foreign, they have by some means become national. Thus French law is administered in Quebec or in the Mauritius, not because it is French law, but because, when these countries came under British rule, they obtained a grant of their own laws and customs. Again, in contracts, the parties may expressly stipulate that their agreements shall be construed with reference to certain specific laws or usages. That which they may expressly stipulate they may by their conduct tacitly imply. In such cases the foreign law is imported merely as a term of the contract, and must be interpreted in the same way as any other such term is interpreted. But by whatever method the foreign law is introduced, the court of the country into which it is brought administers it according to its own procedure, and enforces it by its own remedies.

§ 6. When one system of rules of conduct is superinduced upon another pre-existing system, there is obvious need for interpretation. The two systems must be made to fit. That is, in determining the intention of the Legislature, regard must be had not simply to the actual provision of the new law but to its relation to the old law. It is not material whether the customary law or the express law, the *consuetudo* or the *lex lata*, be the earlier. Judges must construe the new custom by the old law, and the new law by the old custom. Law, therefore, greatly needs authoritative exposition. This need is especially felt when the two kinds of evidence co-exist, and most of all where one of them is, from the nature of the case, not easily ascertained. Thus the importance of the judicial function is apparent both in ascertaining, as I have said, the common law, and in construing with reference

Authorized Exposition of Law.

to the law so ascertained the provisions of the statutes. The cause which has practically given to the decision of the judges their almost legislative weight is the rule that every decision until it be overruled by superior authority is binding upon the judge who pronounces it and upon all other judges of equal or inferior degree ; even the ultimate court of appeal, the House of Lords itself,* is bound by its own decision. The policy of this rule is the urgent need of certainty in law. " It is generally more important, said Lord Cottenham,† that the rule of law should be settled than that it should be theoretically correct." And Lord Westbury,‡ speaking of the rules which govern the transmission of property, observes that " their justice or injustice in the abstract is of less importance to the community than that the rules themselves shall be constant and invariable." In other words, uncertainty is the gravest defect to which a law can be exposed, and must at whatever cost be avoided. Accordingly, a previous decision§ binds a judge as much as the words of an Act of Parliament. Even in a new combination of circumstances, when he has no decision and even no opinion of his predecessors to guide him, a judge is not at liberty to decide merely upon his own notions of expediency and of justice. " Our common law system, said a distinguished judge,‖ consists in the applying to new combinations of circumstances those rules of law which we derive from legal principles and judicial precedents ; and, for the sake of attaining uniformity, consistency, and certainty, we must apply those rules, when they are not plainly unreasonable

---

* " It is your Lordship's duty to maintain as far as you possibly can the authority of all former decisions of this House ; and although later decisions may have interpreted and limited the application of earlier, they ought not (without some unavoidable necessity) to be treated as conflicting. The reasons which learned lords who concurred in a particular decision may have assigned for their opinion have not the same degree of authority with the decisions themselves. A judgment which is right and consistent with sound principles upon the facts and circumstances of the case which the House have to decide need not bo construed as laying down a rule for a substantially different state of facts and circumstances, though some propositions wider than the case itself required may appear to have received countenance from those who then advised the House."—Caledonian Railway Co. r. Walker's Trustees, 7 App. Cas. at p. 275, *per* Lord Selborne.

† Luzon r. Pryse, 4 Myl. & Cr. 617.

‡ Ralston r. Hamilton ; 4 Macq. Sc. App. Cas. 405.

§ See, for a remarkable instance of this rule, Chapman r. Monmouthshire R. & C. Co., 27 L. J. Exch. 97.

‖ Sir James Parke, Mirehouse r. Rennell, 1 Cl. & F. at p. 546.

and inconvenient, to all cases which arise; and we are not at liberty to reject them and to abandon all analogy to them in those to which they have not been judicially applied because we think that the rules are not as convenient and reasonable as we ourselves could have devised."

There are other forms of authorized exposition. One of them is text books, of which some few are received as evidence of the state of the law at the time when the author wrote. In general, however, text writers have no special authority. Their opinions are merely those of experts, and depend for their value in each case upon the reputation of the author. Another such form may be found in the *Responsa Prudentum* of the Roman law, an institution which to us is so strange, but which seems peculiar to or at most a survival of archaic society. In modern law, however, the authorized exposition rests exclusively upon decided cases. From this stand-point some observations suggest themselves. The first is that the standard is the official opinion of the judges, or I should rather say their conduct in the exercise of their office. It is not what the judges say* but what the judges do. Thus an opinion,† though it be erroneous, if it conclude to the judgment of a court, is a judicial opinion, and binds other judges. But an opinion given out of court, or given in court if it be not necessary to the judgment, is extra judicial, and has no legal efficacy. It is simply the opinion of a lawyer of repute, and its weight depends not on the position of the speaker but upon its own merits. The second observation is that the business of the judges is not to promote jural science, or to make rules, but to decide cases. They are above all things practical men. Their office does not relate to any speculative question, much less to any matter of legislation. They are appointed to hear and determine disputes. "The Courts, it has been said,‡ do not deal in definitions." Neither, it may be added, do the judges make laws. A judge supplies materials for generalization, but he does not necessarily

---

generalize. His materials arc, from the very fact that he supplies them, trustworthy, but his generalizations are subject to criticism. In the third place, we can thus appreciate the force of the Roman maxim "*non ex regula jus sumatur, sed ex jure quod est regula fiat.*" The rule is the evidence, not the cause, of the law. Like the mariners' compass, to use Lord Bacon's illustration,* it points out the law but does not make it. The authority precedes the decision, and the rule is a generalization from many decisions. If the process of generalization have been skilfully performed, the rule is sound. If that process be inexact or incomplete, the rule is not sound. But unless and until it receives recognition either from the legislature or from the court of ultimate appeal it remains a mere statement of uniformities, a summary of decided cases, and is liable to be set aside or modified by a single contradictory decision. Thus, although it was a common opinion† that the doctrine that a share in the profits of a trade created a partnership therein, "had become so inveterately part of the law of England that it would require legislation to reverse it," and although legislation actually did take place on the assumption that this statement of the law was correct, the House of Lords decided a case on principles inconsistent with the rule. The result of that decision is that the former rule is not now accepted as a correct statement of the law, and a different rule has taken its place.

Agreements. § 7. Another evidence of law is the agreements of parties. Such agreements do not indeed make the law, but they prove it. No agreement has any legal effect without or against the law. Some agreements do not give rise to any legal objection ; none can be effectual when any Act of Parliament or rule of law is repugnant to them. But, subject to certain conditions and restrictions, the State commands that the agreements of parties shall as between themselves be carried into effect, and undertakes the duty of

---

* De Aug. Sci. viii. c. 3, Aph. 85.   † *Per* Blackburn J., L. R. 1 C. P. at pp. 109, 112.

enforcing them. "*Pacta conventa qua neque contra leges neque dolo malo inita sunt omnimodo observanda sunt.*" When au agreement is such that the law will recognise and enforce it, it is called a contract. The legal duties to which a contract gives rise are included under the term obligations. For the purpose of distinguishing them from obligations which arise not from consent but from the direct command of the law, they may perhaps be called consensual obligations. Thus, not by virtue of the mere agreement but by virtue of the legal power to make under certain conditions such an agreement, the parties to a contract may, as between themselves and those who claim through or under them respectively but not as regards any other person, determine their mutual duties. So far as they are concerned, their agreement is law, even though in the absence of such agreement the law would have made different provisions. To such au extent is the principle carried, that the parties may choose their own judges; and the award of these arbitrators, as they are called, will be enforced in the same manner as a judgment of the court.

A remarkable application of this principle and one which has been attended by important practical consequences is found in the case of associated but unincorporated bodies. Where a number of men act together for a common object, they may make rules for the furtherance of that object; and these rules are regarded as contracts, and may be enforced accordingly. But the courts do not pretend to consider the merits of such rules any more than they consider the merits of the bargains of our daily life; and they deal with them only so far as they relate to the disposition of property or other collateral objects. This principle occurs at a very early period of the history of law. In the Twelve Tables* it is written "*ut sodalibus legem sibi ferre liceat*" — the gildsmen may make their own rules; and a like rule† is said to have existed in the early law of Athens. The same principle which applied to the

---

* Tab. IV. fr. 27.   † Dig. XLVII. 22, 4.

"Sodales" of a Roman association now governs the relations[*] of the various branches of the Christian Church. Except in the case of an established Church, and then only so far as that church is concerned, the State does not interfere with ecclesiastical affairs. If men choose to co-operate for such affairs, they may make their arrangements in the same manner and to the same extent as they arrange their secular business. These agreements are binding, as between the parties to them, exactly as the by-laws of a company are binding; and they are enforced through the same tribunals and by the same remedies as ordinary contracts are enforced. It is noteworthy how satisfactorily even in delicate matters a system works in which the State is content to limit its action to its proper sphere.

Custom and Contract. There is a curious relation between Custom and Contract. They mark contrasted periods in the history of society. In each of these periods they severally perform a similar function. Custom is characteristic of archaic society, contract of modern society. In archaic society, composed, as it was, of small independent quasi corporate bodies, there was no room for individual freedom of action. Each such corporation was almost if not altogether self-sufficing, and the intercourse of these bodies was carried on rather by a kind of treaty than by the spontaneous exchange system of modern life. When the State became developed, the old household and the clan gradually gave way before it. Custom in its new form of law grew definite and fixed. It could no longer adapt itself to the wants of the society, for all change in it was effected not from within but from without, not by the tacit consent of those who used it but by the express enactment of the State. As the old order gradually passed away, provision for the new order became necessary. When the individual emerged from the "Familia," his personal relations were multiplied and were often new. But it never was the object of the State to

---

[*] Eden r. Forbes, L. R. 1 Sc. App., *per* Lord Cranworth, at p. 581.

interfere with men's mutual relations so long as these relations
did not interfere with public interests. It was not for the
regulation of private relations that the State was organized;
and whenever it has undertaken any such duty, it has invariably been unsuccessful. In the absence, therefore, either
of corporate control or of political control, men settled their
relations by mutual agreement. Accordingly, as the State
grew, contracts also grew. They were not indeed unknown
in archaic times, but their condition was so rudimentary that
they may practically be regarded as creatures of the law.
The movement of the progressive societies has, in a phrase
that has become almost popular, been described* as "a movement from status to contract." With the substance of this
proposition I concur, but its form seems to me inexact. It
compares in two sets of sequences the antecedent of the one
with the consequent of the other. The statement would, I
think, be free from objection if it were alleged that the course
of jural evolution is from custom to contract.

Where a political organization is established, custom
often passes into law. Its former character is thereby
changed, and no alteration in it is possible except that which
the Legislature may from time to time intentionally make.
But a change in the form of society or in its organs does not
change the nature of man. So potent a social influence as
custom, although its direction may be changed, must always
continue to exercise some effect. In matters of public law,
custom now operates by affecting legislation. In matters of
private law its effect is different. Both customs and contracts
when they are adopted by law are not adopted unconditionally,
and consequently both of them require judicial interpretation.
But in the attempt to ascertain the true nature of any agreement one of the most important elements in the transaction
is the ordinary course of the business to which the transaction relates. To this course the parties may fairly be
presumed to have referred, and by this course their language
must therefore be limited. This course of business is only

* Sir H. S. Maine's Ancient Law, 170.

custom under another name, and thus the influence of custom
is maintained not indeed as a direct command but by way of
interpretation. To this effect it has been said* that the Law
Merchant "is neither more nor less than the usage of
merchants and traders in the different departments of trade,
ratified by the decisions of courts of law, which, upon such
usage being proved before them, have adopted them as settled
law, with a view to the interests of trade and the public
convenience—the court proceeding herein on the well-known
principle of law that, with reference to transactions in the
different departments of trade, courts of law, in giving effect
to the contracts and dealings of the parties, will assume that
the latter have dealt with one another on the footing of
any custom or usage prevailing generally in the particular
department. By this process, what before was usage only
unsanctioned by legal decision has become engrafted upon or
incorporated into the common law, and may thus be said to
form part of it."

Delegated
Legislation.
§ 8. There is little difficulty as to the theory of
delegated legislation. Where any act is done under
a power, it is taken to be the act of the grantor of that
power. Delegated legislation is, therefore, simply the legislation of the superior Legislature through its authorized
agent. I have already observed that this principle underlies
the theory of contract. But the expression is generally used
to denote the rules which the law authorizes public bodies
that have been incorporated by competent authority to make
for the regulation of their own affairs. The authority depends
in each case upon the terms of the grant; and the matter,
although it forms an important branch of practical law, does
not belong to this inquiry. On one part of it, however, I
may offer some observations. The Imperial Parliament has
granted to the greater colonies large powers of legislation.
I propose to inquire how far, in their case, those answers
must be modified which in a previous paragraph I have, in

* *Per* Cockburn C. J., Goodwin *v.* Roberts, L. R. 10 Exch. at p. 346.

D

relation to sovereign States, attempted to give to the questions whether an Act of the Legislature can be *ultra vires*, and whether a court of law can inquire into the validity of a document professing to be such an Act.

It has always been held that Englishmen, when they emigrate from England to some other part of Her Majesty's dominions for the purpose of forming there a new community, take with them their liberties and free customs, which are their birthright. This birthright includes, among other things, those powers which collectively are called the power of self-government. But the necessities of the case limit some of these liberties and modify the exercise of others. Hence arises a very peculiar organization—peculiar, I mean, in its results, for it is a mere extension of a simple and familiar principle. As every town in England makes its own by-laws, while it is subject to the general laws of the land, so in the extended aggregate which we call the Empire each colony makes its own laws for its own wants, while in all other respects it remains subject to the Imperial Government. Thus, in every self-governing colony, there are two distinct legislative organs. The one is the Imperial Parliament; the other is the Colonial Parliament, which exercises the power that the Imperial Parliament has in its Constitution Act given it. In practice, and according to the rules of constitutional exercise of power, the Imperial Parliament rarely interferes in the internal affairs of a colony that has a Parliament of its own. Its legal competence to do so cannot be disputed. No Imperial Act applies to the colonies unless they are expressly or by necessary intendment included in it. But hardly a session passes without some colonial legislation; such, to take but a few recent examples, are the Acts relating to naturalization, to extradition, to merchant shipping, to kidnapping, to jurisdiction in territorial waters. On the other hand, their Constitution Acts usually give to the colonies within their respective boundaries almost plenary powers of legislation. Her Majesty, with the advice and consent of the Colonial

Parliament, may, with some inconsiderable exceptions, make laws in and for the colony in all cases whatsoever. The effect of such a grant has been explained* by the Judicial Committee of the Privy Council. Lord Selborne, delivering judgment on behalf of that Committee, says—" The Indian Legislature has powers expressly limited by the Act of the Imperial Parliament which created it, and it can, of course, do nothing beyond the limits which circumscribe those powers. But when acting within those limits, it is not, in any sense, an agent or delegate of the Imperial Parliament, but has and was intended to have plenary powers of legislation as large and of the same nature as Parliament itself. The established courts of justice, when a question arises whether the prescribed limits have been exceeded, must of necessity determine that question ; and the only way in which they can properly do so is by looking to the terms of the instrument by which affirmatively the legislative powers were created, and by which negatively they are restricted. If what has been done is legislation within the general scope of the affirmative words which give the power, and if it violates no express condition or restriction by which that power is limited (in which category would, of course, be included any Act of the Imperial Parliament at variance with it), it is not for any court of justice to inquire further or to enlarge constructively these conditions and restrictions."

The method by which these two powers of legislation are harmonized is simple. When a Colonial Act is repugnant to an Imperial Act which binds the colony, the Colonial Act† is, to the extent of the repugnancy, void. This rule is a part of the law in force in the colony as much as that colony's Constitution Act, and it is enforced in the same way that all law is enforced. The judges administer the law in force in the colony ; and the Imperial Acts affecting the colonies are a part of that law with the administration of which the judges are charged. If there be a collision, or a seeming collision, between any parts of that law, there are

* Reg. r. Burah, 3 App. Cas. at p. 904.   † See 28 & 29 Vict. c. 63, s. 2.

D 2

rules which guide the judicial decision. The statute law may conflict with the common law ; two statutes may conflict with each other ; the schedule may conflict with the body of its Act. For all these cases rules of construction are provided. So, too, when the Colonial law conflicts with the Imperial law, the judges have to administer both Acts, and their judgment is determined by a definite rule of construction. Thus, from the nature of the case, Colonial judges may, and if need be must, inquire into the validity of Colonial statutes, because the Colonial Parliament exercises merely delegated powers of legislation, and the supreme law of the Empire is the command of the Queen in the Imperial Parliament.

CHAPTER IV.

THE THEORY OF LEGAL DUTY.

§ 1. When a command has been issued, certain new relations follow from it. The person who gives the command expects that obedience will be paid to it. The person who receives the command has the alternative either of obedience or of suffering. Further, the nature and the extent of that suffering and the mode of its infliction become to both parties matters of immediate interest. Thus a person subject to a command is under a duty to obey. When he breaks that duty, he is under a liability. The character of that liability, the mode of its enforcement, and the party at whose suit it is enforced, vary according to circumstances. The general fact, however, remains. Command implies duty. Breach of duty implies liability. Liability, when enforced, implies sanction.

It follows that the terms command and duty are co-extensive. The same observation applies to each of them and to sanctions. Each of these three terms implies the other two. Every command implies a duty, and unless it were enforced by a sanction it would not be a command. A duty becomes such because it has been commanded, and because the command is enforcible. A sanction anticipates a breach of duty, and, consequently, the disobedience to a command. In the words of Austin,* "Each of these three terms signifies the same notion, but each denotes a different part of that notion and connotes the residue."

It is material to observe that the duty is prior to its breach, and that it is distinct from the consequences to which that breach gives rise. The primary or original duty is to obey the command ; the secondary duty, where any such arises, is to submit to the sanction. This so-called secondary

* L 94.

duty is really not a duty but a liability. It raises no ques
tion of obedience or of disobedience ; it merely implies
suffering. There are, indeed, cases in which a second
or subsidiary command is given ; these are the cases
where an intermediate sanction is employed. Where a person
is sentenced to pay a fine, it is his duty to pay it, lest he
be imprisoned. Where a person is sentenced to imprisonment, it is his duty to submit to the regulations of the
gaol, and not to escape or attempt to escape, lest a worse
thing happen to him. In such cases the ultimate sanction
is postponed, although it is never absent. But where a man
is sentenced to death, or to mutilation, or to flogging, no
further duty is imposed upon him. He merely suffers. Thus
the breach of duty brings with it liabilities, sometimes immediate sometimes mediate, and nothing more. When a
duty is broken, a sanction sooner or later takes its place.

Another aspect of this matter requires notice. Liability
expresses the immediate consequences attendant upon a
breach of duty. It is a state accessory to the command and
conditional upon its breach. But it also becomes specific
even where that command is general. A man may be subject
to a duty whether absolute or general ; that is, he, as well
as all other persons, may be commanded to do a certain act
or to observe a certain forbearance. When he has broken
that duty, he is no longer included, at least as to that transaction, in his original class. He, and he only, must bear the
consequences. Thus, a breach of duty, whether the duty be
general or be particular, always results in a specific liability.
If a new duty be apparently substituted for the former duty,
that new duty is always particular. If, on the other hand,
there arise merely what Austin calls an obnoxiousness to a
sanction, that state of things attaches to the offender and to
no one else. Thus a breach of even a general duty results
in a particular relation. The legal syllogism of which the
major premiss expresses the sanction is not in *Barbara*, but
in *Darii*.

These observations are true of all duties, whatever may be their origin. Every command creates a duty; and as there may be different and inconsistent commands concerning the same object, so there may be a conflict of duties. With such questions I am not now concerned. I deal with legal duties, and with legal duties only. I assume that in case of a breach of legal duties, whatever may be the motive which induces such disobedience, the legal sanction will come into operation. Whether the motive be such as would from another aspect warrant the resolution to brave the terrors of the law, whether the legal sanction be in any particular case sufficient or insufficient, whether in such a conflict the legal duty is to prevail or is to give way, whether the law should crush its opponent or be itself set aside by reason of the opposition—these are questions which the jurist must leave to the moralist or to the legislator. He merely accepts the law as from time to time he finds it, and concerns himself with its form alone. He leaves to others the task of bringing it into harmony with other standards of conduct or of adjusting it to the present exigencies of society. *" Ita scriptum est "* has always been the lawyer's motto. He may admire or he may condemn the opponents of the law; but whatever may be his personal feelings he declares that, whether they be saints or whether they be sinners, whether they be traitors or whether they be patriots, these opponents have broken a legal duty, and that they are consequently liable to a legal sanction.

Division of Legal Duties. § 2. In the case then with which alone we are concerned, that is to say in the case of legal duties, the State is the commander. But who is the commandee? If we admit that he must be a person over whom the legislating State has or claims to have jurisdiction, the question still remains whether the command of the State extends to all its subjects or to particular classes of them

or to some specific individual. The first case is that of
general law, that is of duties imposed upon all, or, at all
events, upon most persons indefinitely. The second case is
that of exceptional or special legislation, that is legislation
which imposes duties upon certain kinds or classes of
persons, and not upon any persons outside the limits of
such class. This division comprises the law of Conditions,
or, as it has been sometimes though less happily called,
the law of Status. Thus the law relating to merchant
seamen or to licensed victuallers is important to seamen
or to licensed victuallers respectively ; but no person who
is not a seafaring man or a licensed victualler or a person
having dealings with such men cares to become acquainted
with it. In the third case this specialization is carried to
its extreme length. The command applies to a particular
person, and it may be to his legal representative, but to
no one else. Thus, if a man by a properly executed deed
undertake to pay another person a certain sum of money,
the law imposes upon him and his executors or administrators the duty of fulfilling his engagement. To no other
person, however, is any legal command given in the matter.
If the engagement be bilateral and not unilateral, like
consequences will follow. The two parties will be respectively liable to the extent of their several promises ; but no
other person is directly affected by the transaction. Thus
legal duties attach either to all people or to some people,
and these particular duties concern either certain classes of
persons or merely the parties.

There is another principle upon which duties may be
divided. Commands, whether they be universal or particular,
may be given with relation to some third party or without
such relation. In the latter case the duties are called
Absolute; in the former case they are called Relative. Thus
an absolute duty is one in which the operation of the
command ceases with the person to whom it was given.
A relative duty relates to some third party who has an

interest in the performance of the duty. Thus this double
division gives four classes of duties. One of these classes,
that of absolute particular duties, is special in its character,
and deals exclusively with certain classes of the community.
It thus forms the law of Conditions, and is distinct from
and subsequent to the general law. Consequently, duties
considered as part of the general law form three divisions.
They are absolute general duties, relative general duties,
and relative particular duties; or, as we may briefly term
them, they are Absolute, General, and Particular. Absolute
duties are those which do not concern any person but the
commandee. General duties are those which relate to
indefinite persons. Particular duties, or, as they are otherwise called, obligations, are those which relate to definite
persons.

Absolute
Duties.   § 3. Absolute duties have hitherto received from
jurists but little attention. Austin[*] dismisses the
subject in half a page, which unfortunately does not exhibit
at their best the powers of that great thinker. His successors have contented themselves with merely repeating his
observations. The only duties which he specially mentions
as absolute are those which prohibit suicide and cruelty to
the lower animals. He adds two other classes, where the
duty is to be observed either towards indefinite persons or
towards the sovereign. The latter case merely serves to give
rise to a vigorous though purely verbal dispute as to the
meaning of the word sovereign. The former case seems, and
I say it with all reverence, to confound the distinction
between absolute and general duties. This opinion derives
some support from the fact that, in a footnote in which a
few examples of absolute duties are enumerated, Austin[†]
includes among absolute duties libel, although this offence
plainly correlates a third party. But absolute duties occupy
a much more important place in our legal system than these
scanty notices of them would lead us to suppose. They

[*] I. 413.   [†] Ib. 415.

constitute in fact more than half * of our whole criminal law. Their importance has been obscured by two circumstances. In the first place, Austin's system was based upon the consideration of rights, and he was consequently embarrassed by a class of duties which did not correlate rights, and for which he could therefore find no fitting place. In the second place, in the minds of the administrators of the criminal law, the breach of the duty has practically smothered the duty itself. But whatever the cause may be, it is certain that absolute duties have never been examined in detail, and that, consequently, their true importance has not been appreciated.

Self-regarding Duties.   The first division of absolute duties includes those duties which Bentham calls self-regarding, or duties which affect the person of the individual upon whom the duty is imposed. This division is but small, and contains only prohibitions against suicide, drunkenness, and other acts of immorality. Most of these prohibitions are affected by considerations of time, place, and circumstance, and thus are for practical purposes placed in other divisions of the law. Thus drunkenness, although it is so far unlawful that a contract to procure it will not be enforced, and that it forms in certain circumstances an excuse for not performing a contract, is not now punishable. But drunkenness in a public place, or while in charge of any dangerous thing, or when attended with certain circumstances of aggravation, is an offence against public order, and is punished accordingly.

Household Duties.   The next division is household duties, that is duties which a man is required to perform in the management of his family, apart from any right on their part to the enforcement of such duties. Thus a man may not have about his house disorderly persons, or may not during the continuance of a valid marriage marry a second woman, or may not marry a girl under age without the consent of her parents or guardians. He must register the birth of

* If all the duties, both absolute and general, which now compose the criminal law of Victoria, were reduced into one code, the absolute duties would contain about 474 sections. The general relative duties would contain about 354 sections.

his child, and must cause the child to be properly vaccinated. Further, he must provide for the maintenance of his wife and children, and for the education of the latter. These family duties are, for two reasons, especially difficult to classify. In the first place, they include both absolute duties and general duties, and also those special and peculiar duties which, taken collectively, form a status or special condition. In the second place, the secondary object of the duty is a person; that is, the act or forbearance which the duty enjoins has to be done or observed towards a person who may be different from the person for whose advantage the duty is imposed. It is sometimes also difficult to determine whether a person be merely the secondary object of the duty or whether he has a right to its performance. Thus it may be doubted whether the duty of maintenance should be described as absolute or as relative. Such a difficulty, however, is only a question of fact, not of principle. The doubt is *whether the particular case has more marks of one class than of another class. But the classes are, at least in thought, distinct; and the merits of the division are consequently not affected.

Concerning Occupations. A larger division than either of the two preceding relates to occupations. The law requires men not to follow at certain times their ordinary callings, or not to pursue certain kinds of business without leave given and received, or it in some way regulates their industrial operations. The first of these classes comprises the laws relating to the observance of Sunday. The second includes a miscellaneous host of licensed occupations. The third deals with certain matters concerning the medical profession, printing and publishing, factories and mines. There is no connexion between these cases separately. They only agree in this— that duties concerning the exercise of these occupations are imposed upon all people.

Concerning Imports and Exports. Further, the law makes provision for the persons and the things that may not enter the country, or that may enter subject to certain conditions. Many of these

* See Mill's Unsettled Questions in Political Economy, 79.

regulations concern the general public, and are not matters of mere Custom-house or harbour routine. Such provisions form part of the general law, and should be kept distinct from matters of administrative regulation. The duties towards the Aborigines form in this country another branch of absolute duties. These duties are commands given for purposes of public policy to all persons, requiring them to observe certain forbearances in respect to these natives. That is, the Aborigines are the objects to which the prescribed forbearances apply, but they are not the third parties for whose benefit the forbearance is intended. They are thus in the same position as those lower animals in whose behalf the law in certain circumstances thinks fit to interpose. Duties are cast upon the owners of cattle concerning the treatment of these animals, the mode of slaughtering them, and their management when suffering from certain diseases. Provision is also made for the preservation and the capture of game and of fish. It would be absurd to say that these animals, whether tame or wild, had rights. They are simply the secondary objects of absolute duties.

Towards Aborigines, and towards Lower Animals.

The duties I have mentioned may be regarded as private. But the absolute duties which are of a public nature are so important and so numerous that they require separate consideration. The main divisions of this branch of absolute duties are duties relating to allegiance, that is, the negative side of the Royal Prerogative ; duties concerning public servants, that is, not the duties which such servants are required to perform, but the duties which the public are required to observe towards them ; duties concerning elections, concerning the administration of justice, concerning the public peace, decency, good order, safety, and convenience ; concerning coins, weights, and measures ; and concerning the public revenue and its protection. In all these cases the State simply issues its commands and enforces obedience to them. No question arises as to the

Absolute Public Duties.

presence or the position of a third party. There is nothing
but the duty and obedience to it.

General Duties. § 4. Relative duties are either general or particular;
that is, they relate either to indeterminate persons or
to determinate persons. Of general duties some relate to the
persons or to the feelings of our neighbours ; some to their
families, or to their homes, or to their property ; some to the
exercise of their lawful enjoyments, or to the fulfilment of
their expectations ; while some require towards our neighbours and for their benefit the observance of veracity and of
circumspection. I shall endeavour to state in general terms,
and subject to the rules of exculpation, the operation of these
duties. No person may, by way of violence insult or annoyance, touch even with his finger any other person. There is
no question of degree in such matters ; the slightest touch,
or even an attempt to touch, is prohibited. No person may,
by word or sign or writing, expose any other person to
public aversion, contempt, or ridicule, or cause him any loss
by attacks upon his reputation. In these cases the qualifications and the exceptions to the rule are unusually
numerous and important. But, subject thereto, the rule
is peremptory. It extends too beyond defamation, and
applies to insults and to threats. A like prohibition applies
to blasphemy with intent to offend; not, indeed, in contravention of the maxim *"Dis injuriæ dis curæ,"* but because
words of this description naturally shock and pain the
persons to whom they are addressed. No person may in
any way interfere with the wife or the children or the servants of any other person, or may directly or indirectly
prevent, or try to prevent, his enjoyment of their society or
of their services. Nor may any person enter without permission the dwelling of any other person when it is closed,
and especially after dark. In this case, too, the prohibition
is of the widest. Without the house master's consent, not a
finger may be inserted in any part of the building, not a

latch of any unlocked door may be lifted, for "a man's house is his castle and his surest refuge." In like manner, no man may interfere even in the least degree with his neighbour's property. He must not destroy, he must not injure, he must not take, he must not touch "anything that is his." No person may interrupt any enjoyment other than those I have already mentioned to which any other person is lawfully entitled, or disappoint any other person in his lawful expectations. Nor may any person by any act or any representation mislead any other person to his loss. Nor may he use his own property, or manage his own business, or govern his own conduct in such a manner as to cause other persons any unlawful harm or loss. Finally, he must take such order with every person and every thing under his control as in their case also to insure for his neighbours a like security.

How Abso-
lute Duties
differ from
General.
Certain differences may be noted between these general duties and the duties which in the next preceding section were under our consideration. In the first place, absolute duties may be either positive or negative. The command may be either to do an act or to observe a forbearance. The latter class is the more numerous, but there are many absolute public duties of a positive kind. Such, for example, are the registration of domestic events, the vaccination of a child, service as a juror, assistance to the police in the arrest of criminals, the giving true evidence as a witness in courts of justice. But except as regards those who are specially dependent upon the commandee, and who are unable to protect themselves, general duties are always negative. The command in their case is to forbear from interfering with the person or the feelings or with the enjoyments or it may be with the expectations of the third party. The law does not require any man to give any property or to render any service to another to whom he owes no special duty. It merely provides that men shall leave their neighbours alone. Thus a man may not strike

another, much less cause him grievous bodily harm, least of all kill him. Except, however, where some special relation exists, such as that of a shipmaster and one of his passengers or of his crew, a man is not legally bound to rescue another from danger; nor does any such duty arise even though such rescue would not be attended with risk or inconvenience to himself, and even though he may have known that upon his refusal to help death must follow, and though he may have desired that result.

Thus in " Daniel Deronda " Mr. Grandcourt and his wife Gwendolen have been living unhappily. They go out together on the sea in a pleasure-boat without any attendants. Grandcourt accidently falls overboard. He could have been saved if Gwendolen had only thrown him a rope. She might easily have done so, but did not, and deliberately let him drown. Morally, indeed, she was responsible for this man's death, but no court could have found her guilty of murder. It was not her legal duty to save his life, but only to abstain from doing him positive harm. He, like every other person, must take care of himself. Her conscience, however, did not so readily absolve her, nor did the opinion of the only person to whom the facts were known. But where, as I have already intimated, one person, whether from contract or from some direct command of the law, is under a legal duty to provide for another, and where such other person is otherwise helpless and unable to provide for himself, if the person under the duty fail therein, and if death or serious injury thence ensue, that person will be criminally liable for the consequences of his neglect. Thus, if a father starve his child, or a master his apprentice, or a gaoler his prisoner, or the keeper of a lunatic asylum the patients under his charge, the offender comes within the range of the criminal law. So, too, when at sea a passenger or seaman falls overboard, the master of the ship is by express legislation required to make reasonable efforts for his safety. Bentham,[*] indeed, has urged that this duty of assistance

* I. 149.

should be made universal. But the law has never gone so far, and leaves to the spontaneous impulse of humanity that help which it would be both difficult and dangerous to enforce as a legal duty.

Sanction in Absolute and in General Duties. For the breach of absolute duties the sanction is always by way of punishment. The State and the State alone has cause of complaint, and no other person is directly concerned in the matter. Where the sanction in such cases consists in a pecuniary penalty, the whole or a part of that penalty is sometimes, for the better detection of offenders, given to the informer, and he is allowed to sue in his own name for the amount. Thus, if a disqualified person be elected to Parliament and sit and vote therein, he is liable for each such act to a heavy penalty, which any person who chooses to do so may recover in his own name and for his own use. But these arrangements do not alter the nature of the case. The offence is the breach of an absolute public duty. The sanction for the offence is a fine. That fine is not regarded as the property of the informer, but may like any other penalty be remitted by the Crown. Its proceeds are specially appropriated, and the procedure for its recovery is, as a matter of convenience, assimilated to that in a civil action. In substance the case does not differ from that of a reward offered and paid for information in the case of a felony. The sanction is, as I have said, by way of punishment. But in the case of general duties, in addition to the State and to the party upon whom the duty lies, a third party is interested. Consequently, the sanction must have a double aspect. A breach of duty involves not only an offence to the State but a wrong to an individual. If a man neglect to register the birth of his child, he is punished for his negligence, and the matter ends. If he assault another person, and tear his clothes, he is punished for his breach of the Queen's peace, and he is also liable to make compensation for the mischief that he has done to the person injured. But it is the same sanction, and arises out of the same breach of duty, although the sentence may impose both punishment and compensation, and whether that sentence be pronounced in a superior court with the aid of a jury or by a justice of the peace in the exercise of his summary jurisdiction. There is a kind of intermediate case where a breach of the law has been committed but no specified person has sustained any special damage. Such is the case of nuisance. The law enacts that no person may do on a highway any act inconsistent with the lawful use of such highway by the public. Some person sets up on the road a dangerous obstacle. For this act he may be prosecuted and punished; but the prosecution must be conducted by the Crown, and no person who has not sustained any special damage can sue. If, however, any person by reason of such obstacle were thrown from his horse and hurt, he might recover damages from the wrong-doer whether the Crown had previously interfered or not.

Particular Duties. § 5. The third great class of duties is that of relative particular duties, or, as they are called in Roman law, Obligations. They differ from absolute duties because they relate to some person for whose advantage they are imposed. They differ from general duties because the person to whom they so relate is not indefinite but is ascertained at the time when the duty takes effect. Thus their characteristic is that they operate only between the parties to them and do not bind any other persons. They arise either without the consent of these parties or with such consent. That is, as I have already explained, an obligation, like every other legal duty, arises by the command of the State, but this command may be given either directly or indirectly. It may be imposed either expressly by the State itself or by the agreement of the parties acting under the authority of the State. Accordingly, obligations are either Non-consensual or Consensual. Non-consensual obligations are usually called quasi-contracts. They are not contracts, and have nothing in common with contracts except the fact that in each of the two classes the duties are of the same kind. The prefix *quasi* is frequent in Roman law, and seems to have indicated merely an historical fact, namely, that the obligations to which the term was prefixed were introduced by the Prætor, and were not known to the *Jus Quiritium,* or old common law of Rome. The force of the term seems to be that a certain class of obligations have a like legal effect to that which they would have had if the parties had entered into a recognised form of contract upon the subject-matter.

Non-consensual Obligations.   Non-consensual obligations are not very numerous. They are, as we shall presently see, distinguishable on the one hand from implied contracts and on the other hand from those secondary obligations which arise from a breach of duty. They are further distinguishable from the obligations which belong to special conditions, that is which belong not to all persons who have casual dealings with each other but to those persons who stand towards each other in permanent and recognised relations. These are persons in the domestic and semi-domestic relations, such as husband and wife, parent and child, and the other relations artificially formed upon the like model, and persons who pursue certain occupations which the law for its own purposes thinks fit to regulate, such as common carriers, innkeepers, and public officers. In respect of all these persons absolute duties, as we have seen, exist ; but the particular duties which are imposed upon them in the exercise of their occupations are exclusively incident to their special conditions. It is not easy and it is hardly worth while to classify the non-consensual obligations properly so-called. They seem to be consequences of the principle* that except by agreement no person may be enriched at another's expense. Thus they include admission by one of a claim due to another upon the statement of an account; the payment by one of money which the other ought to have paid ; the acquisition by one of money which ought

---

* *Jure naturæ æquum est neminem cum alterius detrimento et injuria fieri locupletiorem.* — Dig. XVII. 206.

to have belonged to another ; the dealing with property found ; the forbearance of one who has property in another's hands to pay the lawful demands of that other ; and the great doctrine of estoppel. A typical example of this class of obligations is the recovery of money paid in mistake, a transaction of which the precise nature seems to have much perplexed * the Roman institutional writers. In this case, and in similar cases, it is customary to say that the law implies a promise to repay. Such a promise is a mere fiction. The case is not one where an agreement, though not expressed in words, may fairly be inferred from the conduct or the relation of the parties. The nature of the payment in mistake negatives the intention of either party to make any agreement to restore what had been given absolutely. But no such fiction is required. Two men had certain dealings, and to the result of these dealings the law thinks fit to attach the character of an obligation.

There is another class of non-consensual obligations. In addition to those which arise from contract and from the direct operation of law, obligations also arise *ex delicto*, that is from a breach of duty, whether general or particular. I have already said that delictal obligations, or rights of action as they are more generally called, are merely secondary, and are intended to give effect to some antecedent command. They thus form a connecting link between substantive law and procedure. They are ancillary to the one. They presuppose the other. But the primary obligations, those which spring from contract and from the quasi-contract, exist anterior to any breach and irrespective of it. They are original and unconditioned commands of the State, whether given directly or indirectly, and may have and are intended to have their full effect, although no right of action upon them has ever accrued.

Consensual Obligations. Consensual obligations form the largest and the most conspicuous portion of modern law. They are formed, as their name implies, by agreement between

* Justinian, Inst. III 14, 1. Ib. 27, 6.

the parties. One man promises another that he will do some act or observe some forbearance. This promise or its equivalent the law under certain conditions compels him to perform. Usually the parties exchange promises, the promise of each being the consideration for the promise of the other. I have already explained the nature of an agreement, and I shall in a subsequent chapter discuss the subject of contracts. I shall therefore in the present place merely mark the precise position of this body of law, and invite attention to two points that seem to require notice.

The first of these points relates to what are called implied contracts. These contracts do not present any structural peculiarity. They differ from other contracts only in their mode of proof. Sometimes the existence and the terms of a contract are proved by the express declaration, in whatever form, of the parties. Sometimes they are proved not by words but by conduct. Sometimes they are proved partly by one and partly by the other. When the contract or any part of it is inferred from the conduct or the circumstances of the parties, it is said to be implied. But whether the evidence by which it is supported be direct or be inferential, the contract is still a contract and nothing but a contract. A man enters a shop, orders goods, and directs them to be sent to his house. No word passes between him and the polite shopman on the subject of price. No one doubts that the person who thus ordered the goods is bound to pay their value. He has made an implied contract; that is, from his conduct a promise to pay may in the circumstances of the case be reasonably inferred. Such a contract is essentially different from the quasi-contract of which I have spoken. An implied contract is a true contract. A quasi-contract is not a contract at all. Implied contracts and quasi-contracts are not two varieties of contract. The former is a contract with a particular mode of proof. The latter is not subordinate to contract but is co-ordinate with it, and the two together form the two divisions of obligations.

The second point to which I have referred is the relation of contracts to general law. One maxim of law declares that private agreements do not derogate from public right. Another maxim asserts that the terms of the agreement conquer the law. These maxims, in spite of appearances, do not conflict. No agreement can indeed become a contract if it be inconsistent with the law of the land. But the law often makes provisions or draws inferences with respect to men's conduct in the management of their affairs where the parties themselves are silent. These provisions may be altered and these inferences may be rebutted by the express stipulations of the parties. To this extent and no further it is true that the contract conquers the law. The command of the law in such cases always in effect contains some such provision as "unless it appear that the parties otherwise intended." Substantially, modern law leaves all such matters to the discretion of the parties interested, and only interferes when they are silent and some rule becomes necessary. If the parties do not like the rule which the law provides, they have only themselves to blame. They might have made any arrangement they thought fit, and they failed to do so. We shall find as we proceed the application of the same principle to the devolution of property after death. A man may by his Will dispose of his property at his discretion. If he fail to make a Will, the property cannot be left without an owner or be made the subject of a general scramble. The law therefore interposes, and lays down rules by which the succession of intestate estates is determined.

First Principles of Legal Duties. § 6. The difference between duties imposed for the purposes of the State and duties imposed with the consent and for the convenience of individuals seems to suggest some important differences as to the foundation of

law. Some writers deny that jurisprudence has any claim
to scientific rank. In their view, law is a mere collection of
rules more or less arbitrary which represent the current
views of expediency. In such circumstances all that the
jurist can usefully do is to arrange in some orderly and
coherent fashion the heterogeneous mass. Others, on the
contrary, hold that jurisprudence is the science of justice ;
that as political economy is based upon the desire for
wealth, so the sentiment of justice is the rock upon which
is founded the science of law. A third class, dissatisfied
with the preceding explanations, and exaggerating a newly
discerned truth, look to custom as their initial force,
and regard all jural phenomena as essentially historical.
None of these views seems to me to be wholly correct ;
and yet, so far from being antagonistic, they are each
of them partially true. It is idle to contend that justice
is concerned in settling the limits of the close season
for game or in prohibiting the issue of bills of exchange
under twenty shillings. Neither is there any better foundation for the proposition that the doctrine of general average
in the case of marine disasters or the doctrine that a
trustee is not to profit by his trust is the result of some
temporary convenience. Nor can we attribute to custom
the Acts relating to public health or the series of judicial
decisions which have within the last half-century established
the law of domicil and the law of railways. Law is in
truth a great function of national life. It is the result of
many factors. Among these factors each of the forces I
have mentioned—the sentiment of justice, the conviction
of utility, the force of custom—holds a prominent place.
If justice be not the basis of all our law, it is the basis
of that great body of law which determines the reciprocal
duties and rights of men in their mutual dealings. When
rights are enjoyed, when obligations are accepted, justice
is supreme. But justice has no place in determining the wants
and the wishes of the State. These are matters of policy

and discretion, constantly shifting, just as the wants and the wishes of individuals shift according to the circumstances of the case. It is in this part of our legal system that the principle of utility finds scope. Of custom I need not now more particularly speak. My present contention is that absolute duties rest mainly upon expediency, and obligations upon justice ; and that general duties, since they relate partly to public policy and partly to private right, are governed not by one of these principles exclusively but by both. It must not, however, be forgotten that in these complex affairs no force acts altogether apart from other forces, and that reaction and interaction are in constant operation. It has been well observed* that " nothing in law springs entirely from a sense of convenience. There are always certain ideas existing antecedently on which the sense of convenience works, and of which it can do no more than form some new combination."

* Sir H. S. Maine's Ancient Law, 233.

CHAPTER V.

THE THEORY OF LEGAL SANCTIONS.

Analysis of
Sanction.
§ 1. The term sanction is used by the Roman lawyers* to denote "those parts of the laws whereby penalties are imposed upon those who have contravened the laws." If the word penalty be taken to include all disagreeable consequences of whatever kind, this old definition implies all the points which are essential to the idea of sanction. There is the contravention of the law, or, in other words, the breach of duty. There is the evil conditional upon the breach, and which arises only when the breach has occurred. Further, the entire provision is a part of the law ; and it is a part which is merely ancillary to the preceding part. The conditional evil is imposed not for its own sake, but with the intention and for the purpose that the prescribed duty shall be performed. Finally, effect is given to this intention by making the breach of the duty more disagreeable to the person upon whom that duty is imposed than its observance. The duty is not merely that an act shall be done or a forbearance observed, but that it shall be done or observed by the person to whom the command is given. There are indeed cases where the State directly interferes, and does, at the expense of the wrong-doer, the act which he ought to have performed. Even in these cases its interference assumes such a form as to make the offender feel that it is prudent to avoid such costly help. Thus a sanction is not necessarily mere physical force. It is the application to the commandee's will of any painful stimulant with the intention of thereby regulating his conduct. But although a sanction differs from physical force, it depends upon the expectation that, if need be, overwhelming physical force will ultimately be used. The law, as I have already observed,

* *Ideo et legum eas partes quibus pœnas constituimus adversus eos qui contra leges fecerint sanctiones vocamus.*—Inst. II, 1, 10.

provides means for bringing to bear upon any offender the collective physical force of the community, and it provides no means by which he can avoid or encounter that force. When the entire force of the society to which he belongs is turned against any individual, and, most of all, when the moral feelings of the community go with that exercise of force, resistance is hopeless, and no alternative remains but submission or ruin.

It thus appears that a sanction is a part of the law, and that it is an accessorial and not a primary part. It is conditioned upon a breach of duty. Its object is to prevent such a breach. With this intent it applies to the offender, without his consent and against his will, some painful influence. It does not directly persuade him to obey, but it makes him uncomfortable if he disobey. Finally, the enforcement of a sanction is possible because the command is issued by the State, and because the power both physical and moral of the State immeasurably transcends the power of any individual citizen.

Position of Sanction in relation to Command. § 2. I have said that a sanction is a part of the law to which it belongs. The precise position of sanctions, however, or, in other words, the true place of criminal law in a code, has given rise to some difficulty. Some think that they are a division, but a distinct division, of substantive law. Others rank them with procedure. The latter view is clearly incorrect. The penalty is necessarily different from the machinery used for enforcing it. The former method is possible, but it would involve the needless and consequently dangerous repetition of the duty. An offence consists of a breach of duty according to its several kinds. The statement of the breach consequently involves the statement of the duty. The two elements, the duty and the consequence of its breach, form part of the same command. They should consequently be inseparable. A sanction, therefore, ought not to be divided from its duty, but should be placed in close proximity to it. The typical form of enactment is, I think, somewhat to the following effect :— " No person shall (with such and such an intention, or in other specified circumstances, if any) do such and such an act, or observe such and such a forbearance. If any person offend herein, he shall be liable to such and such punishment; (*or*) he shall make compensation to the person injured; (*or*) he shall both suffer such punishment and make such compensation, *as the case may be.*"

The passage I have above cited from the Institutes shows —and the general usage of Roman legislation confirms the view—that in the opinion of the Roman jurists sanctions belong to substantive law, and not to procedure. That such is also the doctrine of English law is proved by the rule against retrospective legislation. Where an Act of Parliament appears to conflict with existing arrangements, the presumption,* in the absence of express words to the contrary, is that its provisions were meant, if they relate to any existing duty or right, to be prospective only, but if they relate to matters of procedure to be both prospective and retrospective. The most stringent application of the rule is in the case of penalties. When a man has committed a crime he is tried, not by the rules of procedure which existed at the time when the crime was committed, but by those in force at the time of his trial. But it would be difficult to persuade Parliament to enact, and still more difficult to persuade the judges that Parliament meant to enact, that such a man should suffer any heavier punishment than that which the law had attached to his offence at the time when such offence was committed. " It is always to be remembered, says Lord Macaulay,† that retrospective legislation is bad in principle only when it affects the substantive law. Statutes creating new crimes or increasing the punishments of old crimes ought in no case to be retrospective ; but statutes which merely alter the procedure, if they are in themselves good statutes, ought to be retrospective. To take examples from the legislation of our own time, the

---

* Wright *v.* Hall, 30 L. J. Ex. 40.   † Illst. V. 42.

Act passed in 1845 for punishing the malicious destruction of works of art with whipping was most properly made prospective only. Whatever indignation the authors of that Act might feel against the ruffian who had broken the Barberini vase, they knew that they could not, without the most serious detriment to the commonwealth, pass a law for scourging him. On the other hand, the Act which allowed the affirmation of a Quaker to be received in criminal cases allowed, and most justly and reasonably, such affirmation to be received in the case of a past as well as a future misdemeanour or felony."

Thus both theory and practice concur in determining the true legal place and function of sanction. It is that part of every law which provides for the enforcement of that law. It has nothing to do with procedure. It does not constitute a department of law analogous to but distinct from the duties which it enforces. But it is inseparably attached to those duties; and wherever a duty is commanded, a sanction appears, or ought to appear, at its side.

The Choice of Sanctions. § 3. The particular form of sanction which should in any case be adopted is not a matter for jurisprudence ; it depends upon practical considerations respecting which the Legislature alone can determine. On some aspects of the question, however, I may offer a few remarks, partly because certain deductions from jural principles seem to be applicable, partly because erroneous views on the subject are popular, and partly because the true nature of a sanction can thus be placed in a clearer light.

We have seen that the sanction is ancillary to the primary command, and that its function is to secure the performance of the prescribed duty. From these principles several consequences follow. In the first place, the excellence of a sanction depends upon its success. Whatever means will in the circumstances of the case insure obedience to the law is a good sanction. Whatever means fail, from whatever cause, to produce this result is not a good sanction. In this case, as in so many others, the terms good and bad are relative. There can be no such thing as a universal sanction, just as there can be no such thing as a universal medicine. Every sanction is merely an adaptation of means in varying circumstances to obtain a certain end. Nor, on the other hand, is any sanction absolutely bad. The price necessary to be paid for the attainment of any legislative object may be indeed too dear; but this circumstance proves the badness, not of the sanction, but of the command. If it be assumed that the desired object must at all risks be secured, we must not complain of the means, however painful, by which alone that object can be accomplished. Therefore, before a law is made, its framers will do well to sit down and count the cost thereof. It may, for example, be desirable to abolish heresy, and it is possible to do so ; but if the execution of a law to this effect involve the extermination of the largest and the best portion of the population, the prudence of issuing such a command needs to be reconsidered. In the second place, sanction implies pain. Pain is in itself an evil. An evil ought not to be needlessly inflicted. Consequently, a sanction, although it must be sufficient for its purpose, ought not to be more than sufficient. In other words, the best sanction is that which insures obedience to the law with the least possible amount of suffering. Thus, if a sanction be inadequate, the pain which it occasions is simply wasted ; if it be excessive, the superfluous pain admits of no justification. Further, when, either from excess or from repugnancy to public sentiment or any similar cause, a sanction fails to obtain general sympathy and support, it becomes practically inadequate. Thus too severe a penalty defeats its own object ; it cannot be steadily enforced. A sympathy for the offenders is generated. The law fails in the certainty of its administration, and the severity of the punishment* actually gives encouragement to crime.

* For a striking example, see Macaulay's Hist. IV. 23.

The State's Theory of Punishment. Another consequence of the principles to which I have above referred is that the sole concern of the State in matters of sanction is the regulation of men's conduct in the desired manner. The State, from whatever motive, chooses that certain acts shall be done or certain forbearances observed. It secures this object by punishing disobedience. If there be no disobedience, there is no punishment. Whether the obedience arises from mere terror or from any higher motive the State does not inquire. It is the regulation of conduct, not the regulation of motives, with which it is concerned. Consequently, its aim in punishment is merely the enforcement of obedience and not the moral reformation of the offender. So long as any person outwardly conforms to the law, the State has no concern with his moral condition. When he breaks the law, it punishes him not by way of discipline but by way of prevention and of example. The administration of criminal law is one thing, and moral and religious education is another thing. They aim at different objects, even though to a certain extent and in certain circumstances they employ similar means. I do not contend that when the State has under its absolute control convicted felons, *servos pœnæ*, it does not thereby incur a moral responsibility not merely for the physical but for the moral needs of these unhappy men. Prison discipline affords ample room for a prudent charity and a reasonable philanthropy. But in the choice of its sanctions the law regards the welfare not of the criminal but of those innocent persons whom that criminal has disturbed or endangered. As the law does not provide for the comfort of the offender, so it is not influenced in its treatment of him by its abhorrence of his crime. In such matters the law proceeds without a trace of feeling and upon a settled policy. It desires to effect a specific object, that is to regulate men's conduct in a certain manner. Consequently, it regards not the moral character of the offence but the danger of the example. . A comparatively light punishment may be sufficient to deter the actual offender from a repetition of his offence. But if the offence be one which, from its nature, other persons are likely to commit, the safety of the public requires a more striking example. It may seem hard that a man should be punished not according to the quality of his own act but according to the probability that persons whom he has never seen will commit similar acts. The reason is that the State does not and cannot even attempt to deal with every man according to his absolute deserts. It merely provides for the safety of society. "The extent, it has been observed,* of the danger and alarm created by any violent acts depends primarily upon the motive by which they appear to be inspired. Thus robbery is more generally dangerous than revenge, because he who robs one man would probably rob another, while a person desires to be revenged on those only whom he believes to have injured him; and robbery is dangerous generally, although the robber may not have formed the intention of committing more than one robbery." Thus we can understand some apparent anomalies in our criminal law that often occasion much animadversion. A man, it is sometimes said, may beat his wife into a jelly and escape with perhaps a week's imprisonment. A man who steals an old coat may go to prison perhaps for a year. Hence the inference is drawn that the law regards property with much more favour than it regards the life and limbs of its poorer subjects. The true reason of the difference, apart from mere errors in administration, is that the temptation to violence is much less than the temptation to steal. An assault in a fit of passion or even from revenge does not go beyond the individual who has caused the irritation. But in felonious assaults upon women or in assaults with intent to rob the motives are not evanescent but permanent. There is, consequently, the risk not only that the offender may repeat his offence towards some other victim but also that other persons may follow his example.

* Mr. M. Bernard's *Neutrality of England*, 110.

§ 4. The sanctions for the breach of those duties **Sanctions to Absolute Duties.** which directly affect the State are exclusively in the discretion of the Legislature. Offences of this class were originally the only subject-matter of criminal law. Like every private person in archaic society, the State ascertained its own interests and redressed its own wrongs. When an injury was done, the person wronged or his next of kin as he could or as he thought fit smote the aggressor. The extent of the punishment rested upon the feelings of the injured party, whether that party was the State or was an individual, and upon the modifying influence of custom. In disputes between individuals the interposition of the State* was invoked not by the injured person but by the wrong-doer—not to prevent or to punish crime but to limit revenge. When the wrong was done to the State itself, no such interposition was possible. The State dealt with the offender exactly as in each particular case it thought fit. Gentler manners, and a more assured position, and a greater experience in the adaptation of punishments to the purposes they were meant to serve, have in the course of many centuries mitigated archaic ferocity.

I do not propose to narrate the odious history of punishment. I shall merely describe those punishments which our law now uses. These are very simple and very merciful. At all times and in all circumstances death is the "*ultima linea rerum*," the extreme penalty that man can inflict upon man. In the earlier part of this century the English law is said to have recognised not less than 230 capital crimes. But at the present day death is inflicted in only a few cases, and then in its least painful form. In England death punishment is now restricted to the cases of treason and of murder, and of attempts to murder in certain aggravated circumstances. In Victoria it is also imposed for rape, robbery with wounding, and in some other cases—the total amounting to ten. The necessity of protecting women who are left defenceless and without

* See " The Aryan Household," 437 *et seq.*

help in remote country districts, and the temptation to bush-ranging which the circumstances of the country and the presence of escaped or liberated convicts in the days of transportation afforded, produced this severity in our legislation. In practice, however, it is only in cases of exceptional atrocity that the extreme sentence is carried into execution. Flogging is also used as a punishment, chiefly in cases of sexual offences, but its amount is strictly limited and its infliction is carefully regulated. The maximum amount in this country is 150 lashes administered with the ordinary cat in equal portions at three different times. The principal form of punishment is imprisonment. The severity of the infliction is increased by hard labour, by the wearing of irons, and by solitary confinement ; but scrupulous attention is now given to the general health of the prisoners and to the sanitary condition of the prisons. The term of imprisonment does not exceed in Victoria fifteen years ; and under the prison regulations the length of the term is, except in cases of serious misconduct in prison, considerably reduced. Solitary confinement too is now used only for very short periods. It may indeed be truly said that the rule on this subject contained in the Bill of Rights is faithfully observed, and that at the present day " cruel and excessive punishments " are unknown.

Sanctions to General Duties. § 5. For breaches of general duties there is, as I have already observed, a double sanction. The wrong-doer is punished for his offence against the State, and he has to make compensation for the damage done to the injured party. There is no logical necessity that this should be so. The Legislature may decline to make any given breach of duty an offence against the State, or may direct that the private wrong shall merge into that done to the public. Thus theft, which with us is one of the most heinous of crimes, was in Roman law a mere tort that sounded in damages. Libel continues to be in theory an indictable offence, but practically the present remedy for it is in ordinary cases a civil action. But in matters of sanctions a line which is constantly becoming more and more definite is now drawn between offences against the State and wrongs done to individuals. In the former case the ultimate remedy of personal restraint, either immediately or as an alternative to fine, is employed. In the latter case the appropriate remedy affects the property only of the delinquent. It was at one time supposed that in an offence against a general duty the party injured could not maintain an action unless the offender had been prosecuted. Under the old law, a conviction for felony, that is for the more serious classes of offences, involved forfeiture to the Crown of the felon's property. It was therefore useless to recover judgment for damages against a man who had no means of paying them and no possibility of acquiring such means. But forfeiture is now abolished ; and it is settled that the two remedies, the one civil and the other criminal, are concurrent and distinct.

Compensa- Where a breach of general duty causes loss to
tion. an individual the remedies are simple. Sometimes the law requires the defaulter to perform specifically his duties, or to restore the actual property that he wrongfully detains. Sometimes it requires him to abstain from certain acts which there is reason to believe that, contrary to his duty, he intends to do. More frequently it directs him to make compensation to the other party for the loss that he has occasioned to that party. This loss, however, must not be indirect or the result of some preceding consequence. " It were infinite, as Lord Bacon* observes, to consider the causes of causes, and their impulsions one of another," or to seek to unravel the inextricable intermixture of social causation. The law therefore limits its interference to cases where the loss is the immediate direct and reasonable consequence of the wrong-doing. These commands are enforced either by imprisonment, or in the case of damages by the seizure and

* Max. Reg. 1.

F

sale of the property of the wrong-doer, or of so much of it as is needed to produce the requisite amount and the costs of recovering it.

The selection of the standard by which in any particular case the amount of compensation should be measured is often a matter of difficulty. Some general rules, however, are now sufficiently ascertained. Where there is a wrong, if that wrong have not occasioned any actual loss to the complainant, the damages will be merely nominal ; if there be real loss, the damages will be substantial. Where the loss is pecuniary, the damages will be proportionate to such pecuniary loss. Where the pecuniary transaction involves any aggravating circumstances, or where the injury is not a matter of money but relates to the person the feelings or the character of the party injured, such reasonable compensation may be awarded as in all the circumstances of the case the jury thinks fit. In such personal wrongs, if the facts disclose fraud violence cruelty malice or other improper motive, the damages may be exemplary. It is probable that this last rule is included under the one next preceding it, and that exemplary damages should be regarded merely as a reasonable exercise of the jury's discretion in circumstances of aggravation. The expression exemplary damages savours too much of punishment ; and although the case approaches the line that divides the sanction of public wrongs from the sanction of private wrongs, it seems desirable to retain in such cases the principle of compensation, even though the compensation be measured with a liberal hand.

Sanctions to Particular Duties. § 6. When a man refuses or neglects to perform his contract, the appropriate remedy is apparent. The law should compel him either to carry out his engagement according to its tenor or to pay all the damages that result from its breach. Accordingly, the two ordinary remedies for breach of contract are specific performance and the action for damages.

The latter remedy is also used where there is a breach of a non-consensual obligation. Specific performance appears to be peculiar to English equity. Its use was at first restricted to contracts for the sale of land, and was subsequently limited by various rules which the court laid down for its own guidance. I will not inquire into the causes of the late growth and the limited use of this apparently obvious remedy. It is now available in every branch of the High Court in England, and this extension will probably increase its practical importance.

Although these sanctions seem to be those which are appropriate to breach of contract, and although they are in fact generally employed for the purpose, there is no absolute necessity that they should be so used. Other sanctions have at different times been adopted, and traces of them still survive in our law. The Twelve Tables contain the strange provision that an insolvent debtor should be cut into pieces and distributed among his creditors. Whether this rule was at any time carried into actual operation I will not pretend to determine. But the reduction of an insolvent to a condition of semi-slavery until he had worked out the debt was the ordinary remedy at Rome during the Republic, and a like practice may still be found* in some less advanced countries. We ourselves have had until late in the present reign imprisonment for debt, and the practice still survives in Victoria under the thin disguise of what are called fraud summonses. Domestic and agricultural servants too are liable to imprisonment for mere breach of their contract. In England another class of contracts has been by recent legislation brought within the operation of the criminal law. A breach of a workman's contract with a gas or a water company is in certain conditions a punishable offence. It was felt that in the present state of society such companies exercise public

---

* Writing of Cambodjee, Siam, and Laos, a recent traveller says—"Slavery for debt is not, strictly speaking, slavery: it is a temporary loss of liberty. When any one is unable to pay a sum due, he gives himself or one of his children up to the creditor. The slave's labour is reckoned as equivalent to the interest on the debt; but he is not freed until the principal is paid up. If he is discontented with his master, he borrows money and repays him, passing by this simple fact into a new ownership."—De CARNE's Travels in Indo-China, 83.

functions, and that special provision was needed to prevent the inconvenience to the public that the interruption of these functions must produce. The performance of such a contract is therefore assimilated to the case of an absolute public duty.

The anomalous position of servants to which I have referred has given rise to much criticism. On the one side it is described as an invidious piece of class legislation, which was possible only because it was the masters who made the laws. On the other side, such servants are usually poor, and damages cannot practically be recovered from them. Thus, in the absence of any other remedy, their employers would have no means of enforcing their part of the contract. The solution of the difficulty both as to them and as to other persons working under a contract of service seems to be an adherence to the general rule of enforcement. It is true that in such circumstances the remedy by damages is illusory. It is equally true that the State should not punish when it undertakes merely to enforce. But damages are not the only remedy for breach of contract. There still remains specific performance. The servant or other employé may be required to return to his work; and, if he disobey, imprisonment follows of course. Such imprisonment would be inflicted not for a breach of contract but for wilful disobedience to the order of a competent court. A man cannot be reasonably said to be in contempt if he do not pay money which he has not got. But he is usually able to go back to his work for the term of his engagement; and if he can give a reasonable excuse, a certain discretion must necessarily rest with the court. It is true that Courts of Equity have hitherto refused to direct specific performance in the case of personal services. The remedy would perhaps be unsuitable where skilled labour was concerned. Damages, too, in such circumstances, afford adequate redress. In the case of unskilled labour no such difficulty is practically felt, and damages afford, not indeed an imperfect remedy, but no remedy at all. It seems, therefore, to be deserving at least of consideration whether an

.. extension of the principle of specific performance might not in some degree meet the exigencies of the case.

The Sanction of Nullity.   § 7. There is another form of sanction known to the law, but the operation of which is sometimes misunderstood. It consists in the refusal by the State to recognise and enforce a claim or an agreement or an evidentiary instrument of whatever kind. There are forms of conduct which the law does not think fit to visit with the ordinary kinds of punishment, but of which it desires to express its disapprobation. It will not lend its aid to enforce an agreement for the furtherance of such conduct. It will not accept an instrument which is not executed in the manner and with the forms that it thinks fit to prescribe. It will not permit its officers to act where the proceedings by which their interference is invited are irregular. "It is strange, says Baron Bramwell,[*] that there should be so much difficulty in making it understood that a thing may be unlawful in the sense that the law will not aid it, and yet that the law will not immediately punish it." Perhaps the difficulty to which the learned judge refers would be less if attention were directed to the nature of the sanction. To the command prohibiting the conduct in question the law adds a sanction, not in the usual form, but to the following effect :—" If any person offend herein, any contract made by him for or in furtherance of the prohibited conduct shall be deemed to have been made for an illegal consideration, and the earning of money thereby shall not be deemed to be a lawful occupation." Thus, where a man marries during the life of his wife, if he have not known during the preceding seven years that his wife is alive, the man is not punishable ; but nevertheless the act is unlawful and the second ceremony is void. No person may by advised speaking deny the Christian religion to be true. He may not be punishable for a breach of this duty, but he cannot enforce a contract[†] for the hire of a lecture hall for the purpose of delivering an anti-Christian address. The law

* Cowan v. Milbourn, L. R. 2 Exch. at p. 236.   † Ib.

provides no punishment for prostitution, but it will not enforce a contract* for the hire of a carriage to a known prostitute. So where an Act imposes penalties upon persons who are unable to satisfy justices that they have visible lawful means of support, it has been held †that a person who lived by prostitution had no such means, and was therefore within the meaning of the Act.

Nullity in Contracts. The law of contracts furnishes examples of another variety of this class. A contract is an enforceable agreement. When the conditions upon which the law promises its aid are not fulfilled there is no contract, and the agreement is for legal purposes void. One of these conditions is that the object of the agreement shall be lawful. But there are certain contracts of imperfect obligation where the agreement is recognised by the law for some purposes, although the law refuses to enforce it. The object of the agreement is not illegal, but it does not give rise to any right of action. The former case was that of an illegal act which yet had not some of the usual consequences of illegality. The present case is that of a legal act which yet has not some of the usual consequences of legality. Thus a wager is not an unlawful act. If money be paid upon a wager, the person who receives it may lawfully retain it. If a wager be lawfully made in a foreign country, the contract‡ will be enforced in this country. But upon a wager made in this country no action can, as a general rule, be brought. Again, there are certain classes of contracts which the fourth section of the Statute of Frauds requires to be in writing. If the agreement do not satisfy the terms of the statute, no action can be brought upon it. But this provision affects the proof only and not the agreement itself. Notwithstanding that difficulty of proof, the agreement is a true contract. It will be enforced in a foreign country where no such rule of evidence exists. It will be enforced in our own country if the difficulty of proof can be avoided or overcome. Again, the law declines to assist those who sleep on their claims. A

---

* Pearce *v.* Brooks, L. R. 1 Exch. 218. † Reg. *v.* Sayers, 4 W. W. & aB. L. 46.
‡ Quarrier *v.* Colston, 1 Ph. 147.

right of action is consequently barred by the lapse of a prescribed time. But although the remedy is gone the contract
still survives, and a proper acknowledgment will, without any
further consideration, suffice to renovate the faded right.

Nullity   When the law provides any form of pre-appointed
in Pre-   evidence, or directs not only that some act shall be
appointed
Evidence.   done but that it shall be done in some particular
way, it usually enforces its commands by the sanction of
nullity. It refuses to recognise as evidence any instrument
that is not in the prescribed form. It refuses to consider
that any required act has been performed unless it be done
in the regulated way. Of these cases the most important
examples are found, of the former in the law of Wills and of
Contracts, of the latter in the Rules of Procedure. The
advantages of some solemn declaration of intention which
shall express the deliberate will of the testator or of the
contracting party and shall accurately record in a permanent
form that expression are sufficiently apparent. But the
sanction of nullity is open to many and grave* objections. It
is severe; it is indiscriminating; it usually strikes the innocent client and not the offending practitioner; it must be
added that it is hardly reasonable. The evil which it is the
aim of the Legislature to avert is the frustration of the parties'
intention. The means by which the Legislature proposes to
effect that object is the production of the very evil which
it seeks to avoid. Modern legislation has in many cases
adopted a better method. Following in this case, as in so
many others, the suggestions of Bentham,† it usually provides forms which are declared to be sufficient, but of which
the use is not compulsory. Thus forms of this character are
provided for proceedings before justices. Articles of association are suggested to trading companies, but they are merely
suggestions; standing orders for regulating their proceedings
are offered to municipalities, and they may adopt so much of
these orders as they think fit. Or, to take a larger example,
it is left to the discretion of the Colonial Legislatures to

* See Bentham, VI. 65, 518.   † Ib. 521.

adopt all or any of the provisions contained in the Third Part of the Merchant Shipping Act. In all these cases the law supplies models, but declines the responsibility of laying down rules. Where registration is required, the neglect of registration does not invalidate the act. As in the case of the registration of marriage, that neglect renders the person on whom the duty is imposed punishable. In the case of the registration of deeds or of titles a like neglect postpones as between competing claimants the holder of a prior unregistered instrument to his more vigilant rival.

Opposite Errors in Sanctions. Two opposite tendencies, one in the direction of extreme strictness, the other in the direction of extreme laxity, may be traced in the history of the administration of our law of sanctions. Both proceed from the same cause, the defective state of the substantive law and the efforts of the courts to prevent injustice. Under the old savage criminal law the rules of construction in criminal pleading were so strict that the wonder is how even in the clearest case of guilt a conviction could have been obtained. The most trivial clerical error in the indictment was fatal. The result was to a great extent a paralysis of justice. The excessive technicality of criminal procedure acted like Benefit of Clergy in practically mitigating the ferocity of the then existing sanctions. Both expedients doubtless saved many lives, but of the lives so saved not a few were the wrong lives. On the other hand, when the activity of Parliament increased, the limits of legislation were little understood; and it was thought necessary that almost every Act should provide for an infinity of details. The question then continually arose what was to be done if, as of course frequently happened, some of the details were to go wrong. To meet this difficulty the courts invented the doctrine of "directory" enactments—a word which, as Lord Denman* once said, is "the most healing in the legal vocabulary." Where a statute contained a mere affirmative direction without any penalty or any negative words,

* Dwarris on Statutes, lxxi.

it was held that the act to be done might indeed be done in the prescribed way, but that it might also be done in any other way. Such over-legislation is happily rarer than it was in Lord Denman's time. Yet I well remember the consternation produced in the official mind by the discovery that a luckless sheriff had drawn the names of his jury panel from a green box when the Act* of Parliament required that the box should be painted black. There is no subject upon which the judges have complained, and justly complained, more earnestly than upon the neglect of Parliament to state precisely the consequences which it means to follow from the breach of its commands. But when they themselves exercise legislative powers, the judges are worse offenders in this respect than even the Parliament. It may be doubted whether all the *bêtises* in all the statutes have caused so much expense, vexation, and injustice as the sanctionless rules of court. The judges, whether in the exercise of statutory or of common law powers, have contented themselves with giving certain directions respecting the business of their respective courts ; but they rarely if ever provide in express terms for the breach of these directions. The result is that this judicial legislation is perfectly Draconian. The smallest offence deserves nullification ; for the highest offence they can inflict no severer penalty. In recent times attempts have been made to remedy the grievous evils resulting from this system by giving to the judges powers of amendment and other discretionary powers. But these expedients are at the best exceptional in their nature, and involve special application and additional trouble, delay, and expense. Probably a great advance in practical law reform would be effected by the simple course of stating in each rule the sanction which it was intended that its breach should involve. What sanctions the judges can in such cases apply, or what additional powers, if any, they require for the purpose, are questions which I am not concerned to discuss.

* Act No. 19, s. 11.

CHAPTER VI.

THE THEORY OF THE LEGAL OBJECT.

Objects of
Command
are Acts and
Forbear-
ances.

§ 1. Commands, as we have seen, are directed to persons and are meant to control their conduct. But human conduct consists either in action or in inaction, in doing acts or in abstaining from doing them. It follows then that the object of a command, that in respect of which it is given and to which the duty relates, is an act or a forbearance. No metaphysical subtlety is needed to define an act or indeed any other leading term of law. Law is a practical business, and deals with practical matters. When it speaks of acts or of persons or of things, it uses ordinary words to express ordinary ideas. The speculations of the schools therefore never embarrass the legal mind. For all legal purposes an act presupposes a human being. It assumes that he is practically free to do such act or to leave it undone. It implies that he desires a particular end, and that for the purpose of attaining that end he makes certain muscular motions. These motions thus willed, and their immediate and direct consequences, are called, without any minute analysis, an act. Where the determination of the will such as I have described is to abstain from making such muscular motions for any such end, such willed inaction, as it has been happily termed, is called a forbearance. A forbearance differs from an omission, because the former is always intentional and implies a positive volition, although the accompanying result is negative; while the latter term denotes mere inaction without any further connotation. The word act is sometimes used to include its negative, just as in Roman law the obligation "*facere*" includes the obligation "*non facere*." But where the distinction between the positive and the negative notion

is of such great practical importance as it is in law, if there
be an apt word to express the negative notion, it is not wise
to reject its use.

The object* of every legal command is an act or a forbearance. It is not a motive or an opinion or a belief. The
law requires its commandees to do or to leave undone some
external act. It has no jurisdiction over the secrets of the
heart. Acts and forbearances may indeed be qualified by the
state of mind of the person who does or observes them, and
the existence of states of mind may be proved or disproved
by the acts and the forbearances of the person concerned.
But the mind does not move to the word of command, and
the law can directly control only the manifestation of the
will and not the will itself. These manifestations are acts
and omissions whether intentional or unintentional; and the
regulation of them suffices for all the purposes which law
can reasonably contemplate. So long as a man's conduct
conforms to the law, the motives which determined that
conduct concern directly neither the State nor other persons.
So long as his opinions or his beliefs do not lead him to
pursue any conduct which is contrary to law, these opinions
and beliefs have an interest exclusively for himself. It is
true that the law can issue commands upon all these points,
just as it may forbid the winds to rage or the sea to flow.
It may pry into motives. It may render penal certain
opinions or certain beliefs. It may prove their existence by
every means in its power, and it may punish those who hold
them. Of the possibility of such legislation the history of
the world furnishes abundant and melancholy proof.
This question, therefore, may seem to belong not to the
form of law but to its substance. Yet the acknowledged
failure of all such attempts at all times and in all places
points to some universal fact. That cause seems to be the fatal
confusion of the two great factors of human conduct. Over
all that is external, over our acts and our forbearances,
Cæsar has authority, whether he exercises that authority

* Austin I. 873.

wisely or unwisely. But all that is within, the heart
and all its issues of life, owe their allegiance to another
Master.

If we exclude those laws which relate to religious
persecution, no real exception will be found to the
proposition that neither the Roman nor the English law
deals with any other object than acts and forbearances.
" *Cogitationis pœnam nemo patitur* " was the rule* in the
Digest. "So long, said Lord Mansfield,† as an act rests
in bare intention, it is not punishable by our law; but when
an act is done, the law judges not only of the act itself but
of the intent with which it was done." "It is trite law,
said an earlier judge,‡ that the thought of man is not
triable, for even the devil himself doth not know what the
thought of man is." I can call to mind only two apparent
instances to the contrary. In the Roman law it is said
that a freedman who was ungrateful to his patron might be
reduced to his original servile condition. Yet this example
shows how quickly and how certainly the law transmutes a
command concerning a state of mind into a command
concerning acts and forbearances. In the earlier period of
Roman history, the freedman still continued in the *manus*
of his former master, and was subject to the summary
jurisdiction of the *pater familias*. But under the Empire,
when the authority of the State superseded the authority of
the Household, the law in effect provided that if the freedman
failed to do certain specified acts, or to observe certain
specified forbearances, towards his patron, he should be
liable to return to his slavery. In our law the mere
intention to kill the Queen, expressed in words of advice or
persuasion or in consultations for that purpose, amounts to
treason. But this intention must be proved by some overt
act, and thus the offence is practically an attempt to commit
treason.

It is noteworthy that a request and still more an
agreement go beyond the limits of intention, and amount to

---

* VIII. 19, 18.   † See R. v. Higgins, 2 East 5, *per* Lawrence J., at p. 21.
‡ *Per* Brian C. J. temp. Edw. IV., cited by Lord Blackburn, 2 App. Cas. 602.

definite acts. "A solicitation* or inciting of another, by whatever means it is attempted, is an act done." Thus the inciting of another to commit an offence is something more than a mere intent to commit an offence. It is itself an actual offence. Solicitation which is unsuccessful in its result is an attempt to incite. Accordingly the offer of a bribe is punishable, even though the offer be rejected. The same principle applies where there is an agreement between two or more persons to do an unlawful act, whether that act be only the means to an end or be itself the ultimate object. "A conspiracy, it is said,† consists not merely in the intention of two or more, but in the agreement of two or more, to do an unlawful act or to do a lawful act by unlawful means. So long as such a design rests in intention it is not indictable. When two agree to carry it into effect, the very plot is an act in itself, and the act of each of the parties, promise against promise, *actus contra actum*, capable of being enforced if lawful, punishable if for a criminal object or for the use of criminal means."

§ 2. Every command directs either an act or a forbearance. But that act or that forbearance may be limited to the conduct of the commandee or may in its effects extend to some other person. In the former case it prescribes rules of conduct by which, in the exercise of his own will or in his dealings with his own property, the commandee is required to govern himself. In the latter case it prescribes rules by which the relations between members of the same society are regulated. In either case the rules relate to human conduct, and thus the law in prescribing such rules necessarily deals with persons alone. Things, as such, do not directly come within the sphere of jurisprudence. They make their appearance merely as subsidiary to persons. They are sometimes the matters in respect to which persons are required to act or to forbear. But commands are given to men and not to things; and it is to men and not to

Secondary Object of Command.

---

* R. r. Higgins, 2 East at p. 23.   † Mulcahy r. The Queen, L. R. 3 H. L. at 317.

things, whether animate or inanimate, that duties and rights exclusively belong.

Thus in many cases the act or the forbearance which forms the object of the command has reference to some person other than the commandee or to some thing. This person or this thing is sometimes described as the subject of the command. But the terms subject and object are, when contrasted, somewhat perplexing to the ordinary British mind. What is worse, some of the most eminent jurists use these terms in exactly opposite senses. That which Savigny calls subject, Austin calls object. I have therefore thought it prudent to abandon the ordinary distinction, and to avoid altogether the use of the term subject. In its place I have employed the expression " secondary object " ; and although the expression may be open to criticism, I hope that it will be found to have the merit of indicating with sufficient clearness the meaning that I desire to convey.

In absolute duties the act or the forbearance may have no further object; or it may relate either to a person or to a thing, that is to a sensible object, whether animate or inanimate, other than a human being. Examples of the mere act or forbearance without any secondary object are the absolute duties to assist the police when required to do so, or not to carry on certain occupations without a licence, and all the rules concerning public decency and good order. Examples of a thing as a secondary object in the case of these duties are the laws relating to the lower animals, whether as regards their treatment or the modes of dealing with them in health or in disease. But the case where in absolute duties the secondary object is a person requires somewhat fuller illustration. Such illustration is needed, because the confusion is easy between persons who are such objects and persons who are the holders or, as I prefer to call them, the donees of rights. The latter class will be considered in a separate chapter. The former persons are merely those to whom the commandee's conduct relates, and have no independent concern either in the command or in its performance. The most striking examples of the secondary object as distinguished from the donee of a right are found in the law concerning the family relations and in the law concerning the Aborigines. Thus the law forbids any person from kidnapping another's child. In such a case the child is the secondary object of the command, just as a horse would be if the command were not to steal a horse. So, too, the law commands a man to have his child vaccinated, and to have him educated to a certain standard. These are absolute duties which do not generate any right, and in which the child is merely the subject-matter of the command. As regards the Aborigines, the law has imposed upon the general public several duties, of which one though probably not the sole motive was the benefit of these people. But it would be absurd to contend that a blackfellow has a right not to be supplied with liquor when he wants it; or has a right not to have white tramps wandering with him when he desires their company. In this case also the duties, as I have already observed, are absolute; and the Aborigines are not the donees of rights, but the secondary objects of absolute duties.

In relative duties there is a further development of the secondary object. These duties, as their name imports, relate to persons who have an interest in their performance. In other words, the act or the forbearance is not absolute and final, but is done or observed for the benefit of a third party. Acts and forbearances are required not merely as to certain persons or to certain things, but also as to certain recognised advantages. These advantages consist in the undertaking by the State that it will at the request of the persons interested therein enforce the performance of certain duties. In some material respects these undertakings have the characteristics of property. They are in every well-ordered State permanent. They may, if the law by which they have been assumed so permit, be transferred. They may in the like circumstances be transmitted upon death. They are often of very great value.   They are thus suited to become, and they do become, the secondary objects of legal commands.   We have therefore to enlarge our previous description, and to say that such secondary objects, where they exist, are persons or things or rights.

Object may be Unconditional.   § 3. There are many cases in which the act or the forbearance prescribed by law is absolute and unconditioned.   There is no question of circumstances or of consequences, of intention or of knowledge.   Such is the command of the law.   The maxim that requires a *mens rea* has here no place.   Thus the owner of a cart must have his name painted thereon.   It is a plain straightforward command, and the breach of it is easily proved and is duly punished. A tobacconist may not under a certain statute have in his possession adulterated tobacco.   If he offend herein, he is liable to a heavy fine* even though he had purchased the tobacco as genuine, and though he did not know and had no reason to suspect that it was adulterated.   Where an Act of Parliament provides that no person who is not duly licensed in that behalf shall keep in his house more than two lunatics, no defence† on the ground of innocent intentions or of good management or of convenience can prevent a conviction.   In cases of this description the want of knowledge as well as the absence of intention is immaterial.   Thus the offence of bigamy is not conditional upon the knowledge of the bigamist that his first wife was then alive.   That knowledge has indeed an important effect upon the consequences of his offence.   But the prohibition of such a marriage does not depend upon his state of mind.   " In bigamy, it is said,‡ there is no question of guilty knowledge or innocent ignorance.   If A marries B, living his first wife, he is guilty of felony."   So where a man has an intrigue with a woman whom he at the time believed to be unmarried, but who is in reality a wife, he may be sued as co-respondent in a petition for divorce. The prohibition of adultery is not dependent upon the

* Reg. *v.* Woodrow, 15 M. & W. 404.   † Reg. *v.* Bishop, 5 Q. B. D. 259.
‡ *Per* Lord Brougham, 2 Cl. & F. 500.

knowledge of the adulterer. Where a man elopes with a girl under sixteen years of age,* although he believes on reasonable grounds that she is above that age, he is liable to a heavy sentence. In order to support the charge of an assault upon a policeman in the execution of his duty,† it is not necessary to prove that the defendant knew that the person whom he assaulted was a policeman. It is sufficient to prove that the man was a policeman, that he was in the exercise of his duty, and that the assault was then committed. Whether he was in uniform or in plain clothes is not material. The offender must take the consequences of his conduct.

§ 4. In most cases of general duties, and in some cases of absolute duties, especially in public duties, the acts and forbearances which the law commands are limited. It is not necessary and it is not desired to prohibit in every possible case certain acts; acts that in some circumstances and for some purposes are harmless and even useful, may in different circumstances and for different purposes become hurtful. " Some acts, says Baron Bramwell,‡ are absolutely and intrinsically wrong when they directly and necessarily do injury, such as a blow; others are only so from their probable consequences. There is no absolute or intrinsic negligence; it is always relative to some circumstances of time, place, or person. It is not negligent or wrong for a man to fire at a mark in his own grounds at a distance from others, or to ride very rapidly in his own park; but it is wrong to fire near to, and so to ride on, the public highway. The quality of the act is not altered. It is wrong in whoever does it, and so far it is intrinsically wrong. So the act of firing or riding fast in an enclosure becomes wrong if the person riding in it sees there is some one near who may be injured. But the act is wrong in him only for the reason that he knows of its danger. It would not be wrong in any one else who did not know that." Accordingly, duties are frequently qualified either by some external consideration or by the state of mind

Object limited by External Considerations.

---

* Reg. *v.* Prince, L. R. 2 C. C. 154.   † Reg. *v.* Forbes, 10 Cox C. C. 362.
‡ Degg *v.* Midland Railway Co., 26 L. J. Ex. 171.

G

of the persons upon whom they are imposed. External considerations are those of time, of place, of person, of circumstance, and of consequence. Of each of these influences I shall briefly cite some examples.

Prohibition of Time.
Many acts which at one time are lawful are, when they are done at a different time, prohibited. Many acts, too, that at any time are unlawful are visited with additional punishment when they are committed at some special season. Thus game and fish may not be taken during their respective close seasons, although at other times there is no such prohibition. Many acts of ordinary life which on other days are lawful, or which are even commanded, may not be performed on Sunday. The night too is for obvious reasons carefully watched by the law. Thus ordinary housebreaking, that is the unauthorized entry with felonious intent during the day of a dwelling, is punished by imprisonment for a maximum term of five years; but for burglary, that is for a similar entry during the night, the maximum term is fifteen years.

Prohibition of Place.
The influence of place is also notable. I need only refer to the law of the Precinct* in earlier days. At the present day contempts of Parliament or of courts of justice sometimes depend upon their occurrence in the presence of the House or of the court, and are always aggravated by such occurrence. Certain assemblies, otherwise innocent, are forbidden within a specified distance of the Houses of Parliament. Disturbances in churches or in cemeteries are more severely punished than similar acts done in other places. There is a large body of law, partly statutory partly by-laws, which regulates conduct in towns or other populous places. There is also a multitude of provisions which, for the purposes of public convenience decency and good order, prohibit in public places acts with which in other places the law does not interfere. Bathing on the sea shore or on banks of rivers is in itself innocent and laudable, but it becomes a nuisance if it be practised publicly and without restraint. A man may if he please be

* See " The Aryan Household," 222, 357.

drunk in his own house, but in a public place he must not be
even drunk, much less disorderly. He may in his own house
use as much strong language as he likes; but if he do so in
a public place, he commits the offence which the Romans*
called "*Convicium*," and which with us is not unfamiliar to
the police.

Whatever may have been the case in earlier
days, the influence of person very slightly affects
modern legislation. There are indeed various disqualifications and exemptions arising from age, sex, mental incapacity, crime, and alienage. There are also, as I have said,
special regulations for the practice of various occupations
which the law for different reasons thinks fit to control.
But the principal rules of law apply to all persons alike.
The most notable exception is the Prerogative, or that
branch of law which concerns the legal position of Her
Majesty; and yet even here little of the old harshness practically remains. There is also the special protection which
is given in the execution of their respective duties to the
members of the Legislature and to the various officers of the
State. Assaults upon clergymen are more severely punished
than similar assaults upon other people. Old offenders
receive exceptional treatment, and especially that class which
is known to the law as habitual criminals. For some public
offices various qualifications and disqualifications, mostly of
a pecuniary character, some from considerations of public
convenience, some in the nature of punishment, are provided.
Less frequently exemptions are in some cases granted. Examples of the three kinds are found in the Jury Act.† All
persons subject to certain exceptions and having certain
qualifications are bound to serve on juries. The qualifications
for jurors are that they shall be of the age of twenty-one, that
they shall be natural-born subjects of Her Majesty or be
naturalized for a certain term, and that they shall have a
certain property in land or pay rates to a certain amount.
The disqualifications for the office of juror are attaint of

* Inst. IV. 4, 1. † Act No. 560, Part I.

treason or conviction of any felony or infamous crime, uncer-
tificated insolvency, and illiteracy. The persons who are
exempt from the office of juror are too numerous to state
except in very general terms. They include persons over
sixty years of age, persons who are blind deaf dumb or insane,
members of the Executive Council and of Parliament, public
servants, certain professional men, military and volunteers,
masters of trading vessels and licensed pilots, municipal
functionaries and their staff, the editors publishers and
reporters of newspapers, and the household officers and servants of the Governor. All these classes of persons, in the
words of an earlier Act, are " freed and exempted from being
returned and from serving upon any juries whatsoever."

Prohibition of Circumstances. Circumstances also, either as essential to the
command or as matter of aggravation in case of its
breach, modify in various ways legal duties. Thus fishing is
not prohibited, but fishing with nets under a certain mesh involves the forfeiture of the nets and a heavy fine. If a man
be drunk when he is in charge of a vehicle or when he is
carrying firearms, he is, for obvious reasons, liable to a severer
punishment than he would be if he were drunk and incapable
or even drunk and disorderly. So, too, any number of people
may peaceably assemble for any lawful object, but monster
meetings in circumstances likely to cause reasonable alarm in
the neighbourhood are in themselves, and without reference
to the conduct of the persons assembled, unlawful. That is,
acts which are innocent when done by one man or by a few
men may become wrongful when they are done by a great
number. " The number* and the compact give weight and
cause danger."

Acts done at one's Peril. There is another limitation of command which
marks the opposite extreme to that of the uncon-
ditional prohibition. In the latter case the act itself is
altogether forbidden. In the former case the act is not forbidden but certain consequences of it are. In these circumstances a man is said to do the act "at his peril." There is

* Mulcahy *v.* The Queen, L. R. 3 H. L. at p. 317.

nothing unlawful in the act itself; but if its consequences involve any damage, he is answerable for the loss. There is no controversy as to the intention or other state of mind. The question simply is whether a man has caused his neighbour any loss, and, if he have, whether he did or did not exercise such care as in the circumstances the law requires. The varieties of this class are very numerous and very important. They include the use of property, the keeping of animals, the keeping of things, the management of business, personal circumspection, the custody of another's property, the employment of servants and their subsequent conduct. A man may lawfully do all or any of these things, but he must be careful not thereby to cause any harm to his neighbours. Accordingly, the amount of care must be considered which in respect to them he is required to observe. Much trouble has arisen on this subject from the attempt to arrange its details with reference not to the duty but to the breach of duty. But, as it has been said,* "it is more correct and scientific to define the degrees of care than the degrees of negligence." From this stand-point it will be found that the law notices in different circumstances three duties of care. One is when the act in question is in itself dangerous to the public. In such circumstances, the defendant, as I may for shortness call him, is understood to warrant that no damage whatever shall happen except in case of accident in the sense in which this term will presently be explained. The second case is where there is no reason to anticipate danger, but where, if sufficient care were not taken, danger might probably ensue. In this case the duty of the defendant is less strict. He is bound only to take reasonable care, or, more accurately, to see that reasonable care is taken. That is, he or those whom he can control must take such care as in the opinion of the court is in all the circumstances of the case fairly sufficient for the purpose. In the third case the act is not naturally dangerous, nor does it need special attention to prevent danger.

* *Per* Montagu Smith J., Grills v. G. & S. Collier Co., L. R. 1 C. P. 613.

In these circumstances there must be some distinct and palpable carelessness on the part of the defendant either by himself or by his servants. He must have acted with rashness or with heedlessness or with negligence.

Burthen of Proof in Actions for Negligence. The distinction between these cases is practically shown by the difference in their rules as to the burthen of proof. In the first two cases the damage itself raises a presumption against the defendant. He has caused damage, and he is consequently bound to offer and to prove a sufficient explanation. In the third case the burthen of proof rests with the plaintiff. In order to establish his case, he must prove some breach of duty, that is, in the circumstances assumed, some specific act or omission which led to the disaster in question. Thus a man lights a fire in his field, and it spreads and burns a neighbouring house. He must prove that he was not in fault, and he can only do so by proving that some uncontrollable event, such as an unexpected gale of wind, had led to the mischief. A brick falls* from a railway bridge, and hurts a person in the street. The presumption is that, as bricks do not usually fall from well-constructed buildings, the defendant must have in some way failed in his duty as to building or maintaining the bridge. It rests with him to rebut that presumption, and to show that, whatever may have been the cause of the fall of the brick, he had exercised reasonable care to prevent such an occurrence. But where a gentleman's servant † was riding his master's horse through the streets, and the horse, without any assignable cause, suddenly bolted, and, without any fault of his rider, knocked down and injured a person who happened to be passing by, the person injured could not recover damages. The mere fact that the horse bolted was not of itself evidence of negligence ; but negligence, that is the breach of some duty, the plaintiff was bound to prove. Thus a mere mischance, " *merum infortunium,*" as the old books call it, is not a ground of excuse; it never amounted to a wrong.

* Kearney *v.* L. B. & S. C. Railway Co., 4 H. & C. 403. † Manzoni *v.* Douglas, 6 Q. B. D. 145.

Object Limited by Commandee's State of Mind.

§ 5. Of all the limiting conditions of the law the most important are those which relate to the state of mind of the commandee. In the present form of our law these distinctions are for the most part expressed by the adverbs maliciously, negligently, and knowingly. No words are more familiar in our criminal courts than these and a multitude of similar adverbs with meanings more or less vituperative. There seems to be now a universal consent that the word "malice" and its paronyms, words which have probably been forced to do harder duty than almost any other words in our tongue, should altogether disappear from the language of law. In the case of malice, apart from the absurd extensions of the word, there is an incurable ambiguity which the not very happy distinctions of malice in law and malice in fact have been unable to overcome. Malice in its ordinary sense denotes a motive; and in its technical sense it denotes both the presence of intention—a word which I shall presently explain—and the absence of justification. Negligence, too, is affected with ambiguity; in its popular sense it means a state of mind,[*] and in its technical sense it means a certain department of law, the law namely of negligent as distinguished from malicious wrongs. Since, however, the perversion of the term is only technical, the word may still be used in its proper sense, but not without caution. We are indebted for the solution of the difficulties connected with this question to the masterly analysis of Austin. "Without a single metaphysical subtlety, says J. S. Mill,[†] there cannot be a more happy example than he here affords of metaphysical analysis." This analysis[‡] seems to be now, at least in its leading features, universally accepted. It is therefore unnecessary to repeat the investigation that has once for all been successfully completed, and to remove difficulties that happily are now obsolete. I shall therefore content myself with a reference to Austin's work,[‖] and shall, without repeating his arguments, state briefly the substance of his conclusions.

---

[*] See Mr. Markby's Elements of Law, 107-110.   [†] Dissertations and Discussions, III. 232.
[‡] See Mr Markby's Elements of Law, 106.   [‖] Lect. xix.-xxi.

Intention. Where a man does or deliberately omits to do any act, he either adverts to the consequences of his conduct or he does not. Where he adverts to these consequences and expects or might reasonably expect them to follow, he is said to intend the act or the omission. It is not material whether he wishes the consequences to follow or not, or whether he regards them as ends or merely as means to an end. Equally immaterial is the motive for his conduct. It is enough that he adverts to the consequences, and expects or might reasonably expect their occurrence.

Rashness. Where a man does so advert to the consequences of his contemplated act and expects that they will not follow, if that expectation be formed without reasonable grounds, his conduct is described as rash. The law is meant for rational beings and not for fools ; and it consequently assumes that men foresee the ordinary consequences of their conduct. Rashness thus involves three elements. It implies an advertence to the consequences. It implies a belief that these consequences will not occur. It implies that this belief was formed unreasonably, that is without such care as the person who formed it was required by law to take.

Heedlessness. Where a man does a certain act and, contrary to his duty, does not advert to the consequences of his conduct, he is said to be heedless. He takes no heed to consequences of which it was his duty to take heed. It is not as though he adverted to these consequences and disregarded them or foolishly thought that they would not happen. Heedlessness denotes that in circumstances in which circumspection was required the man acted without any thought upon the matter at all. Where the conduct consists in an omission, that is where an act which ought to have been done is left undone without any thought of the consequences of such omission, the omission is generally called laches or negligence. Laches has by high authority[*] been defined to be "a neglect to do something which by law a man is obliged **Negligence.** to do." Negligence, so far as it is applied to a state of mind, appears to be used in a very wide sense, and to be contrasted with intention. In this sense it would include not only negligence in the limited sense of laches but also rashness and heedlessness. Negligence differs from heedlessness, because the latter implies an act, and the former, as I have said, is confined to omissions. But it is of the essence both of heedlessness and of negligence that the act or the omission is contrary to a legal duty. That duty is negative in the one case and positive in the other, conditions which are necessarily inverted when the duty is broken. Heedlessness implies a duty of forbearance. It is unlawful action without thought. Negligence implies a duty of action. It is unlawful inaction without thought.

Recklessness. There is a term in this series which Austin has not investigated but which deserves some attention. That term is recklessness. Recklessness does not express any independent state of mind. It denotes the absence of interest or concern with which the actor adverts to the consequences. It is therefore merely a variety of intention. The actor considers the consequences and expects them, but is indifferent whether they happen or not. He does not desire them; he does not dislike them. He simply cares nothing about them. The presence of such likings or aversions, or their absence, does not enter into his consideration. But the act is positive, and therefore the state of mind is not negligence. The actor adverts to the consequences, and therefore it is not heedlessness. He does not expect, wisely or unwisely, that the usual consequences will not in that particular case follow, and therefore it is not rashness. Nothing therefore remains but intention; and the intention remains unchanged whether the actor did or did not desire the consequences, or whether he felt no wish either way upon the subject.

For the purpose of illustrating these states of mind, let us take the case of the master of a ship. He scuttles his ship on the high seas. This act is evidently intentional, and he is punishable accordingly. Or in making a voyage from

England to Australia he goes very far south. He knows that in doing so he is likely to meet ice, but thinks without sufficient reason that he will escape it. If disaster happen, he will be liable for rashness. Or, without thinking what he is doing, he lights his pipe and throws the match into some combustible material. His ship takes fire, and he is guilty of heedlessness. Or he gets drunk, shuts himself up in his cabin, takes no observations and gives no directions for the proper working of his ship. She runs ashore, and the captain is guilty of negligence. Or, desiring to make his trip in the shortest possible time, and quite indifferent to the fate of himself his ship his cargo his passengers and his crew, if only he can make his run a few hours sooner than any other captain has hitherto made it, he carries on all his canvas in stormy weather. In such a case he will justly be held to have been reckless.

Other cases may easily be put. A story is told that some men were standing at the door of an hotel in the Far West of America. A stranger was approaching the hotel. One of the group, an expert with the revolver, made a bet that he would hit the stranger on the third button of his waistcoat. He hit him accordingly and the man died. No one can doubt that that sharp-shooter, although from the nature of the case he had no ill-feeling towards his victim, was guilty of murder. An actor in that country is said to have lately wished to imitate the exploit of William Tell. Accordingly, he put an apple on a boy's head, and fired from the whole length of the stage. The boy was killed. The marksman was guilty of manslaughter. He meant to hit the apple, not to shoot the boy; but although he foresaw the possibility of the misfortune, he rashly assumed that it would not occur. A party of volunteers goes out for practice near a road, and a man passing along the road is shot. This is heedlessness. A pointsman on a railway does not turn his points at the proper time, and a collision ensues. He is guilty of negligence. Or a squib is thrown into a crowd, and it strikes a man in the eye and blinds him. The person who threw it cannot be said to have acted from want of thought, but he was reckless of the consequences of his act.

Motive. "A motive, says Austin,* is a wish causing or preceding a volition. A wish for something not to be obtained by wishing it, but which the party believes he shall probably or certainly attain by *means* of those wishes, which are styled acts of the will." Motives and intentions are thus distinct. The former relates to what precedes the act, the latter to what follows it. Motives indeed may be and often are evidence of intention. A man is more likely to advert to the consequences of his act when he has some liking or some aversion to it than when he is altogether indifferent. But men may intentionally do acts which they sincerely regret. The choice of the less of two evils is a daily occurrence. A surgeon when he operates intends to inflict pain, that is he adverts to the pain that is likely to follow from his act and expects it ; but his motive is the benefit of his patient, and he deplores and seeks to minimize the suffering that he causes. Further, the moral quality of a motive has no connexion with the expectation of consequences. One man takes the property of another without his consent. He foresees that his act will deprive the owner of the enjoyment of that property. He thus intends that consequence, and he intends it whether his motive be the relief of his starving mother or the gratification of his own profligate pleasures. Except as evidence of intention, the law rarely concerns itself with motives. It is not to the causes of the act but to its consequences, not to the moral condition of the actor but to the results of his conduct upon others, that the State gives its attention.

The difference between motive and intention, and the nature of recklessness, were illustrated in a case that was lately considered in the English criminal courts. A man named Martin† put an iron bar across the doorway of a theatre at Leeds at the close of the performance, and then turned out the gas on the stairs. A panic ensued, and several

---

* I. 423.   † The Queen *v.* Martin, 8 Q. B. D. 54.

persons were seriously injured. Martin was indicted for unlawfully and maliciously wounding. The Recorder of Leeds,
before whom the case was tried, directed the jury to
consider whether the prisoner did the act " as a mere piece of
foolish mischief," and told them that if they thought so they
should acquit him. The prisoner was found guilty, and on
appeal the conviction was affirmed. It was pointed out that
the direction of the learned Recorder was clearly wrong.
" A man acts maliciously when he wilfully and without lawful excuse does that which he knows will injure another."
The affair was probably meant as a practical joke; but if such
jokes cease to be laughing matter, the perpetrator must take
the consequences. There may have been no malevolence, no
ill-motive towards any of the sufferers. But Martin acted
intentionally; he expected the consequences, and he knew
that these consequences might be serious. He did not
indeed desire the result, but he was simply indifferent
to it. Whether the people were or were not hurt, it was
the same thing to him. The learned Recorder saw that
the motive was not wicked but foolish. He failed to see that
it was not the motive with which the law is concerned, but
the intention and its consequences.

It is noteworthy that the terms rashness, heedlessness,
negligence are dyslogistic. They imply that the conduct of
the person to whom they are severally applied is contrary to
his duty. They correspond respectively to the eulogistic
terms prudence, vigilance, and circumspection. Like all
other terms of this class, they have a composite meaning, and
express at once a matter of fact and a judgment upon that
fact. In ordinary use, no more fruitful source of fallacy
exists than this class of equivocal words. But for legal purposes, if only we take the trouble to make the necessary
analysis, this peculiar connotation is convenient. The eulogistic terms indicate the duty ; the dyslogistic terms indicate
the breach of that duty. Thus these terms which we are
considering involve, as indeed all others of the same class

involve, three distinct implications. There is an act or an omission. This act or omission takes place in a given state of mind. This state of mind in reference to such act or omission is contrary to law. Such states of mind are not in themselves offences. They are severally an element in an offence. They qualify acts and forbearances ; and acts and forbearances so qualified are objects of legal command.

Knowledge. There is another state of mind of which the law takes frequent cognizance. This is knowledge. It has been said that without knowledge there can be no transgression ; and the maxim* *mens rea* is a commonplace with lawyers. I have already shown that knowledge is not an essential ingredient in a legal offence ; that in many cases the law thinks fit to declare a duty of which knowledge forms no part ; and, consequently, that the maxim to which I have referred must be received rather as a rule of interpretation than as a principle of justice. Nevertheless it is not disputed that knowledge is an important element in the greater part of our criminal law. In all cases the terms of the duty furnish the true test of its presence or its absence. The duty may be peremptory or may be qualified, and the corresponding result appears in its breach. In other words, the command sometimes is unrestricted, and sometimes is limited to cases where the act is done with a knowledge of the material facts. The once familiar *scienter* indicates the distinction with sufficient plainness. Its adverbial form shows that it merely qualifies the act ; and the frequent disputes as to the necessity for its presence show that it was no mere formal term. Thus, in speaking of an indictment for the possession of a die for coining, Chief Justice Bovill† said, "There is nothing in the act to make the intent any part of the offence ;" and added, " I agree that under the word ' feloniously ' a guilty knowledge must be shown, that is that the accused person must have knowingly done what is made an offence by the Act." The duty created by the statute was thus irrespective of knowledge ; but the epithet " felonious " at common law

---

* *Actus non facit reum nisi mens sit rea.* † Reg. v. Harvey, L. R. 1 C. C. at p. 89.

implied, at least in the absence of evidence to the contrary, that a guilty knowledge existed. In some cases knowledge is really equivalent to intention. It means only the condition of mind in which the person adverts to the consequence and expects it, or at least thinks that it is likely, or at all events that it is not unlikely, to occur. Probably it is in this sense that the doctrine of the *mens rea* has found such general acceptance. In other cases the question of knowledge is practically a matter of evidence. In these cases the duty does not arise until a certain state of facts is brought to the knowledge of the commandee, in other words, until he has notice of them. On the assumption that knowledge is necessary, the question is whether, as a matter of fact, it exists. But the possession of the means of knowledge is only evidence of the possession of actual knowledge. That evidence, like all other evidence, varies in its cogency according to circumstances. If a man were under a duty to know a certain fact, the presumption is that he performed his duty and made himself acquainted with it. If he had in his possession or within his reach the means of obtaining the required information, that presumption is greatly increased. If the matter were within the ordinary experiences of life, he would not be allowed to affect ignorance. If it were a matter with which he was not bound to acquaint himself, and if another person were interested in his becoming aware of the facts, such other person would be required to show that he did in fact call the commandee's attention to the particular circumstances—that is, that in the strict sense of the word he had given the commandee notice. Thus, in questions as to knowledge, there are two classes of questions, one of law and the other of fact. One is, what are the precise terms of the duty which requires knowledge? The other is, what is the evidence that the party did or did not possess that knowledge? Thus the duty of a man as to the keeping of animals that he knows to be ferocious is a proposition of law. It has now been settled that a man keeps such animals at his peril; that is that the act of keeping them is not forbidden by law, but that he is answerable for any damage they may occasion. If he keep a tiger, and damage ensue, no proof of knowledge is required. The law presumes that every person knows the savage nature of the beast, and will not listen to any disavowal. If he keep a dog that does mischief, he may prove that he was not aware of the dog's temper. But if it be proved that the dog is habitually fierce, the owner will not be allowed to escape his liability by alleging that the dog was always gentle to him, and that he had never heard of his mischievous propensity. He had the means of knowing all the facts about his dog if he had chosen to have used these means.

Object Limited by Joint States of Mind. § 6. There are some other states of mind which play no small part in law, but which differ materially from those which we have hitherto considered. They are not limited to an individual, but express certain mental conditions that are jointly applicable to two or more persons. Of these the principal, and that which appears to underlie all the rest, is consent. Consent implies a plurality of persons, a common design, and an agreement to give effect to that design. It is not now material to consider the evidence for consent, or to inquire how far consent is proved by acquiescence or by mere silence. If the fact of consent be admitted, that consent gives in dealings between parties its colour to the transaction. Its presence or its absence marks the difference between the ordinary course of business and of life and the wrongful interference with person or property. In private relations no man who has consented to any wrong done to him can maintain a claim for damages on account of that wrong. *Volenti non fit injuria.* But it is otherwise with breaches of public duty; no consent can excuse disobedience to a plain command of the law which was intended not for the benefit of any individual but for the general good. If one man kill another with that other's consent and at his request, it is murder. Two prize-fighters cannot upon a charge for an assault plead leave and licence, although as between themselves such a defence might be sufficient in an action for damages. In some cases the law refuses to recognise a capacity for consent, as in lunacy or infancy, or in certain circumstances in the case of young children. Where it is permitted, consent may be given before, at, or after the act in question. Where it follows the act, it is usually called ratification.

It must be observed that a consent, however reluctant, is a true consent. Life is made up of a balancing of conflicting advantages and disadvantages. Too frequently indeed the disadvantages exclusively are present, and the competition assumes the form of a choice of evils. Nevertheless, such a choice, however painful it may be, is a true choice. " *Coactus volui*" are the words of the Digest ; and the Father of Gods and men anticipated this judgment when he surrendered to the vengeance of Herê the holy Ilion* "willing though with unwilling mind." There may, however, be a consent which is not genuine. It may have been obtained by imperfect information; that is where certain facts which ought to have been disclosed have been wrongfully withheld. It may have been extorted by violence or threats. It may have been procured by deceit. But the consent which the law recognises must be full and must be free. The person consenting must have at least sufficient information to enable him to form a correct judgment, and that judgment must not be disturbed by coercion. He must be in a position to say intelligently and freely his yes or his no. If he be not in that position, the words of consent are mere idle sounds. The difficulties, however, are much greater where a true consent has been given but has been procured by deceit. I ought rather to say, since the moral element is not essential, by the misleading silence or the misleading statements or the misleading conduct of the person who procures that consent.

Deceit.   It has for thousands of years been a topic in ethical treatises whether and how far a seller's reticence of facts

---

* ἑκὼν ἀέκοντί γε θυμῷ.—Iliad IV. 43.

which are within his knowledge but are not within the
knowledge of the purchaser is justifiable. In this respect
the moral code doubtless applies a much stricter standard
than the law. So far as English law is concerned, it
declines to make the vendor liable for anything beyond
intentional concealment. He must not speak a falsehood,
and he must not act a falsehood ; but in ordinary
circumstances he is not required to volunteer a statement.
The purchaser must take care of himself. This rule has its
exceptions, although they are not numerous. In certain contracts which are known among lawyers as those *uberrimæ
fidei*, that is in contracts for marine and fire insurance but
especially in the former, in contracts for the sale of land,
and in contracts for the sale of shares in companies, the
omission to state any material fact, even though there may
not have been any fraudulent intention, vitiates the transaction.
The rule as to false representations is naturally much more
stringent. We must exclude from its operation mere expressions of opinion, and mere eulogistic expressions, the
babble of the auction room as they have been called, which
do not deceive and are not likely to deceive any rational being.
A representation means a positive and deliberate assertion as
to a matter of fact. Whether the person who makes it knows
the statement to be false or rashly believes it to be true, or
is merely reckless and does not believe that it is either true or
false, is a matter which, although it may affect his character,
does not concern his legal responsibility. If the statement
be false, and if damage thence ensue, and if it were intended
that the person injured should act upon that statement, the
person who made it is liable. That which the law forbids
is the damage, whatever it may be, which arises from the
unlawful concealment or the false representation. It is concerned with the intention, not with the motive. That motive
may be fraudulent, it may be innocent, it may conceivably be
even laudable ; but in every case the result is the same. The
old distinction between moral fraud and legal fraud arises

H

merely from the use of the dyslogistic term fraud. Fraud of course comes within the rule ; but the rule applies, not to cases of . moral obliquity, but to cases of loss wrongfully caused. Hence, when innocent persons were treated in the same way in which they would have been treated if their motives had been fraudulent, an attempt to distinguish the cases was made by the use of the expression legal fraud. "I do not understand, said Lord Bramwell,[*] legal fraud. To my mind, it has no more meaning than legal heat and legal cold, legal light and legal shade. There never can be a well-founded complaint of legal fraud, or of anything else, except where some duty is shown and correlative right, and some violation of that duty and right. And when these exist, it is much better that they should be stated and acted upon than that recourse should be had to a phrase illogical and unmeaning with the consequent uncertainty."

A recent case,[†] although its results were merely negative, illustrates these principles. A man named Hobbs brought to market some diseased pigs. This proceeding was contrary to the provisions of an Act of Parliament, and he consequently became liable to a prosecution. He made no statement as to the health of the pigs, and was asked no questions on the subject, but sold them in the ordinary course to a man named Ward. The pigs infected not only the other stock belonging to Ward but also his land, and caused considerable loss. For this loss Ward brought his action. But it was held that Hobbs was not bound to disclose the state of health of the pigs, and that he had not made any representation concerning them. It was true that he had committed an offence, and so was liable to criminal proceedings. But to establish a case of fraud it must be proved that something was done with intent to deceive. It is not enough to show certain conduct not done with that intent but which might have such a consequence. Hobbs had made no false representation ; he had concealed nothing which the law required him to disclose. Nor did the law imply in his contract of sale any warranty that the pigs

* Weir *v.* Bell, 3 Ex. D. 243.   † Ward *v.* Hobbs, 3 Q. B. D. 150.

were sound. He certainly had done an illegal act ; he had done an immoral act ; but he had not infringed any right of the plaintiff. Judgment was accordingly given for the defendant.

Collusion. The term collusion is frequently used in connexion with fraud. There is, however, a difference between them. Fraud may be the act of a single offender. But collusion implies accomplices. Collusion is a species of consent, and denotes an agreement between two or more persons to do, with intent to deceive, an act which is otherwise not unlawful. It is consequently of near kin to conspiracy. The latter term denotes an agreement to do an unlawful act. But in collusion the act in itself, and without reference to the intent, is not forbidden. It is the intent that gives to it its colour. That intent is always, as I have said, to deceive. The word means etymologically to play together, and then, according to an expressive metaphor, to play into another's hand. The term is, I think, usually applied not to words but to acts. We speak of collusive proceedings in a court of justice, of collusion in getting up a petition for divorce, of collusion in obtaining evidence, of collusion in giving or withholding a certificate. In most cases, collusion seems to amount to a sort of compound fraud. In either case its analogue may perhaps be sought in those acts which, though inoffensive when they are done separately, become mischievous when they are done by a number. But, however this may be, it has always been a maxim of Courts of Equity that, as Lord Hardwicke* expresses it, "in all cases where a legal right is acquired or exercised by fraud or collusion contrary to conscience, it is the office of this court to enjoin it or decree a compensation."

A contractor made a contract with a waterworks commission for the construction of a reservoir and other works to the satisfaction of the engineer of the commission. Disputes arose, and it was, among other things, alleged that the engineer in collusion with the commission improperly withheld his certificate. Upon this part of the case Sir W. F. Stawell, C. J., delivering† the judgment of the Supreme

* Garth *v.* Cotton, 1 Wh. & Tu. L. C. 481.
† Young *v.* Ballarat Water Commissioners, 5 V. L. R. at p. 544.

Court, used the following words :—" Two persons actuated by different motives may yet entertain the same intent and fraudulently combine to obtain the same object. The engineer may in this case have been anxious to postpone the responsibility of passing as complete works in which the searching hand of time might point out defects; and the defendants may have been in a condition to render the immediate settlement of this debt undesirable : both, from different motives, may have entertained the same object and intent, namely, the postponement of the certificate to the prejudice of the contractors and thus the gaining of time. The mere fact of several persons entertaining a common intent or being desirous to gain a common object does not, however, prove a combination between them, although their community of object may render that combination more probable. . . . . As soon as the works were completed to the knowledge of both the defendants and their engineer, their retention of the moneys due was a fraud on the plaintiffs, and a fraud of which both the defendants and their engineer were aware. He professes his readiness to do the act requisite to enable the plaintiffs to receive payment, if the defendants will only direct him to do so in the mode he wishes. The defendants, aware of this readiness, decline to give the special direction for which the engineer asks, and having previously given a very plain direction decline to enforce it. Thus both may not inaptly be described as playing into each other's hands." These observations suggest several remarks. In the first place, the distinction between motives and intention is carefully pointed out. In the second place, it is shown that different parties acting each under different motives may pursue a common intent. Thirdly, the presence of a common intent is not of itself sufficient to prove combination. Fourthly, combination is proved from the conduct of the parties, and that conduct must in effect amount to a "playing into each others' hands." Lastly, such a combination may properly be called collusion.

CHAPTER VII.

THE THEORY OF IMPUTATION.

Construc-
tion of Legal
Commands.   § 1. When the legal command has been ascertained and its consequences defined, its interpretation awaits consideration. I do not refer to the rules of legal hermeneutics, that is to the application for legal purposes of those rules of construction by which the meaning of written instruments is ordinarily ascertained. But the extent of the command—the precise conduct which it requires and the persons to whom it applies—is sometimes less simple than is at first apparent. Where an act is prohibited, does the prohibition apply to the completed act only or to the act in what may be called its inchoate state? Again, acts are often merely means to an end. Is it the intention that the prohibition should apply to the end itself, or only to some particular method of obtaining that end? Further, a legal command assumes the presence of a commandee, and such commandee, so far as we have hitherto seen, appears as an individual. But what if there be several such commandees? The act to be done or the forbearance to be observed may well be single, but a plurality of persons may be concerned in its execution. What then is the position of the persons thus related? Sometimes also it happens that one man is held answerable for the conduct of other persons over whom he has control. It is obviously important that the conditions and the extent of this vicarious liability should be accurately determined. Nor is this all. The legal command is limited in its operation by other commands or provisions of the law. An act which generally is forbidden may be justified by the existence of certain circumstances of which the law takes notice ; and, consequently, the breach of the command, which otherwise would have been an offence, ceases, in these circumstances, to be an act of disobedience. It may be also

that the law recognises certain extenuating circumstances; and, although it does not withdraw its prohibition, it yet relaxes its sanction. The act is still wrongful, but the wrong may be excused. These matters may be described as forming the grounds of imputation—that is the conditions upon which in any breach of duty the legal sanction is applied to any individual.

Attempts. "The intention, says Austin,[*] coupled with an act tending to the consequence constitutes the *corpus* of the secondary delict, styled an attempt." That is, a person attempts to commit an offence when, with the intention to commit it, he does an act or observes a forbearance which immediately tends thereto. Such an attempt the law prohibits, and visits with sanctions that vary according to the nature of the case. A tendency[†] towards a given result means the existence of a cause which, if it were to operate unimpeded, would naturally produce that result. When, therefore, a man pursues any conduct which, in the absence of any disturbing force, would produce a certain offence, and when he does so with the intention of committing that offence, he is guilty of an attempt to commit it. The source from which the interruption proceeds is not material. Thus, a man was proceeding to set fire to a hay stack, and lighted a match for that purpose. He perceived that he was observed, blew out the match, and ran away. It was held that he had attempted to burn the stack. He had the intent; he had done an act which, if uninterrupted, would have naturally given effect to that intent. He consequently came within the terms of the law; and the subsequent alteration of his purpose, from whatever motives it may have proceeded, did not alter the offence which he had then actually committed.

* I. 481.

† "These facts are correctly indicated by the expression *tendency*. All laws of causation, in consequence of their liability to be counteracted, require to be stated in words affirmative of tendencies only, and not of actual results. In those sciences of causation which have an accurate nomenclature there are special words which signify a tendency to the particular effect with which the science is conversant. Thus *pressure*, in mechanics, is synonymous with tendency to motion, and forces are not reasoned on as causing actual motion but as exerting pressure."—Mill's Logic, I. 455 (3rd. ed.).

His attempt was complete, although the act which he meant to perform was merely inchoate.

This definition of an attempt presents a curious omission. A pickpocket was found with his hand in a gentleman's pocket. He was prosecuted for an attempt to commit larceny. There was no doubt as to either the fact or the intent. But the pocket happened to be empty. The man had stolen nothing, and he could have stolen nothing, because there was nothing to steal. The act, therefore, was not one which, if uninterrupted, would have led to the perpetration of the offence ; consequently the pickpocket was acquitted. The force of the reasoning cannot be denied, although the conclusion is obviously lame and impotent. But if it be desired to escape from this conclusion, there must be a change in the law. Such a change the Commission of English Judges on the *Indictable Offences Bill* 1878 advise, although their amendment is conched in terms which may perhaps seem to darken wisdom. The object would probably be accomplished if in Austin's definition there were added to the words " an act tending to the consequence" some such words as " or which the person doing such act believed so to tend." The presence of the hand in another's pocket with a larcenous intent did not in the circumstances tend to theft ; but the offender believed that it did, and for that act done in that belief and with that intent it is reasonable that he should be punished.

Evasions. It is a maxim that where any conduct is prohibited the prohibition is deemed to extend to any means, direct or indirect, by which the prohibited object may be attained. As the law must be construed so as to confer all the powers necessary for giving effect to its commands, so it must also be construed in such a manner as to give effect to its prohibitions. Probably no better examples of the mode in which the law deals with fraudulent devices can be found than the judgments of some of the great Admiralty Judges. Thus, under the old navigation laws, it was a rule of maritime law that in time of war a neutral could not carry on a direct trade between one of the belligerents and its colonies from which trade he was in time of peace excluded. A trade from the colony to a neutral country was lawful, and a trade from that neutral to the mother country was equally lawful. If, then, by calling at a neutral port the voyage could be divided, the unlawful whole might be resolved into two innocent parts. But the courts always rejected all such artifices; and, when the voyage was really continuous, disregarded all arrangements for disguising its true character by a mere interruption of the transit. In an appeal in a case of this sort, where goods had been landed at the neutral port and then reshipped, Sir William Grant, M.R.,* in the course of a very able judgment, made the following remarks :—"The truth may not always be discernible ; but when it is discovered, it is according to the truth and not according to the fiction that we are to give to the transaction its character and denomination. If the voyage from the place of lading be not really ended, it matters not by what acts the party may have evinced his desire of making it appear to have ended. That those acts have been attended with trouble and expense cannot alter their quality or their effect. The trouble and expense may weigh as circumstances of evidence to show the purpose for which the acts were done ; but if the evasive purpose be admitted or proved, we can never be bound to accept as a substitute for the observance of the law the means, however operose, which have been employed to cover a breach of it. Between the actual importation by which a voyage is really ended and the colourable importation which is to give it the appearance of being ended there must necessarily be a great resemblance. The acts to be done must be almost entirely the same—the landing of the cargo, the entry at the custom-house, and the payment of such duties as the law of the place requires, are necessary ingredients in a genuine importation ; the true purposes of the owner cannot be effected

---

* *The William*, 5 C. Robinson, 385.

withont them. Bnt in a fictitions importation they are mere voluntary ceremonies which have no natural connexion whatever with the purpose of sending on the cargo to another market; and which therefore would never be resorted to by a person entertaining that purpose, except with a view of giving to the voyage which he has resolved to continne the appearance of being broken by an importation which he has resolved not really to make."

The Codex * of Justinian contains a passage which has been thonght to provide that every act done with intention to evade the law is in itself an offence. I donbt whether this be the true meaning of the passage, which seems to me not really to go beyond our own law. At all events our law is more moderate than upon this interpretation was the edict of Constantine. It does not prevent any person from avoiding the provisions of an Act of Parliament so as not to come within its scope. In such cases the question always is whether, npon the true construction of the statute, the law has or has not in that specific instance been violated. Each case, therefore, depends npon its own circumstances. Bnt in construing the statute the question seems to be whether its intention was to prohibit a certain course of conduct or only a certain method of proceeding. In the former case all indirect means are forbidden. In the latter case, a person may attain his object if only he avoid the forbidden means. A man is bound to obey the actnal commands of the law; bnt he is not under any duty to give effect to objects which some persons think that the Legislature wished to enact, and for which in fact it made no provision.

Accessories before the Fact. § 2. In the administration of the criminal law mnch trouble was at one time cansed by the distinctions of principals in the first and in the second degree and of accessories before the fact. These distinctions have ceased to have any practical effect, bnt so far as the principles on which they rested were founded npon reason they still

* I. 14, 5.

require some explanation. Where an offence has been committed, the person who actually commits that offence is not the only person to whom the law attaches liability. The like consequences extend to every person who with unlawful intent does any act which forms part of the offence, and to every person who aids or abets in the offence or in any part of it, and to every person who employs, counsels, or procures any other person to commit it. All these persons without distinction are held to be guilty of the offence in question, and no difference exists as to the degree of their punishment or to the character of the offence or to the method of procedure. When Lady Shrewsbury,* in the disguise of a page, held the Duke of Buckingham's horse while he fought with and killed her injured husband, she, as aiding and abetting the murderer, was in contemplation of law as guilty of murder as he was. Where a person tells a child of five years old to bring him money belonging to the child's father, the child, by reason of its age, is innocent; but the man who incited the child to the wrongful act is guilty of theft. Further, a person who incites to an offence any other person is responsible for every offence which such other person commits in consequence of such incitement, and which the inciter knew, or must be supposed to have known, to be its natural consequence. The soliciting, that is the attempt to incite a person to offend is also criminal, even though such attempt be unsuccessful. Such solicitation is itself an act, and such an act, if it be done with a criminal intent, is punishable. It is not necessary that the incitement be individualized. When Herr Most urged the readers of his paper to murder, he was justly held to be guilty of an attempt to incite to crime not less than if he had addressed his exhortations to each one of them individually and by name.

Accessories after the Fact. Where any person with intent that the offender may escape punishment receives, comforts, assists, or conceals any person whom he knows or believes to have

---

* Macaulay, Hist. of Eng. II. 318.

committed any offence, he is said to be an accessory after the fact to that offence. Except in the case of a married woman who acts in this manner towards her husband, or by her husband's direction towards his friends, such conduct is punishable. The rule is sufficiently simple, but in the existing state of the law its proper expression is embarrassed by practical difficulties. There are no accessories after the fact in misdemeanours. This relation is confined to felonies. But the old distinction between felonies and misdemeanours has long been felt to be useless and inconvenient. The distinctive characteristics of felonies are disappearing, and some misdemeanours are now punished with greater severity than some felonies. The Commission of English Judges have advised that the distinction should be abolished, and there seems to be a general concurrence of opinion in favour of this course. But on the assumption that all crimes are in future to be prosecuted by the same procedure, some substitute for those crimes which are in the existing law described as felonies must be found. The same difficulty arises in other incidents both of felony and of misdemeanours, especially arrest without warrant and the right to bail. The opinion of the English lawyers varies a good deal on this subject. In Victoria the difficulty is increased by the circumstance that our system of prison administration differs from that in force in England, and, consequently, that as between the two countries there is no common measure of punishment. The system which is pursued in Victoria of giving to the judge a wide latitude in punishment prevents the application of any rule derived from the nature of the sanction. Manslaughter and attempt to murder have a common maximum punishment, but no person would regard the two offences as in all circumstances equally blameworthy. Some offences too entail not only the ordinary kind of punishment, but also certain disabilities. This is a distinction which cannot be abandoned. The Legislature has rightly desired to mark in a special manner certain offences for public reprobation. It is difficult and probably needless to describe with sufficient exactitude this class of offences by general terms. Each separate offence can best be dealt with upon its own demerits. It may, as it occurs, be described either as a crime, or as an indictable offence other than a crime, that is as a misdemeanour, or as an offence to be dealt with by justices. In these circumstances, the rules as to accessories and to the other incidents of felony can easily be applied. Crimes will take the place of felonies; and where it is desired to give the power of arrest without warrant in other cases, special provision can be made in the description of the particular offence.

§ 3. Where, with a common intent and for mutual assistance, several persons engage in an unlawful undertaking, and where, in pursuance of the common intent, any one of them commits any offence which is the probable consequence of their illegal undertaking, all the confederates are guilty equally with the person who commits the offence. It follows, therefore, that in such circumstances there is no need to identify the actual offender. If the offence be committed by any one of the whole number, this fact is sufficient to support a conviction of all or of any of the rest. Thus, several young men* went out together for rifle practice. They had one rifle among them, and its range was a mile. They set up a mark at about four hundred yards from some houses, and, without further notice or precaution, commenced to fire. A ball, by whom fired no person could tell, killed a little boy from one of the houses, who had climbed into a tree. On this state of facts it was held that every member of the party was guilty of manslaughter. They all had the common intent, namely, to shoot at the mark. They all assisted each other. They all were engaged in an unlawful pursuit, namely, the use of firearms with a total want of proper circumspection. The result was the natural consequence of their conduct in the circum-

Community of Liability.

* Reg. v. Salmon, 6 Q. B. D. 79.

stances. Accordingly, each of the party was as much liable for that result as he would have been if he had fired the shot. If, in these circumstances, the boy had been only wounded, and if damages were sought for the injury done to him, all the members of the party would have been severally liable for the amount of damage that any one of them had caused. Nor would they, as between themselves, have any right of contribution. Every wrong-doer is liable for the full consequences of his conduct, and the law will not help him to diminish his burthen.

Vicarious Liability.
§ 4. The general principle of justice which governs men's responsibility for their conduct has two branches. One is that, subject to certain specified grounds of defence, every man is answerable for his own acts and his own forbearances, or for those which he has ordered. The other is that no man is answerable for the conduct of any other person. To the latter proposition, however, there are certain exceptions. These are cases of vicarious liability. They arise from an application of the former part of the rule. If a man be liable for the orders that he gives, it must be understood that when he gives to another person a general authority to act in any matter on his behalf, he, in effect, orders every act and every forbearance which, in pursuance of such authority, that other person has done or observed. He may not have ordered any particular act, but he has ordered the performance of a certain class of acts. For the consequences of the execution of the order he is responsible. His liability is not confined to mere contracts. He must answer for all the wrongful acts and omissions of his representatives in the execution of his orders. According to a principle to which I have had and shall have occasion to refer, a man employs servants, as he collects physical forces, at his peril. He may have as many persons to aid him in his business as he thinks fit; but he is deemed to warrant* the public against all unlawful damage arising from the conduct

---

* Burtonshire Coal Co. *v.* Reid, 3 Macq. H. of L. Cas. 206.

of these persons, in the course of their employment, while they are engaged in his business. Accordingly, where a man employs servants or agents or other assistants, he is responsible for their conduct, whether intentional or negligent, in that capacity, to the extent of the authority with which he has invested them. He must answer for all the consequences of the exercise of their discretion, whether that exercise be wise or whether it be foolish. So long as a servant or agent is employed, and as the person so employed acts as such, and within the course of his employment if he be a servant, or if he be an agent within the scope of his agency, the employer or the principal, if he could himself have lawfully done the class of act in question, is bound as to the manner of doing it by the conduct of his representative.

This responsibility exists even though the servant or agent may, without the knowledge of the third party, have received special instructions not contained in the instrument giving the authority, or, in the absence of such an instrument, not to be reasonably inferred from the nature of the obligation. Hence a man may be and often is bound by acts done contrary to his express desire. Such instructions affect the relations between the employer and the employed, but they in no way concern third parties. A stranger is not bound to inquire as to the existence of any private instructions. It is enough for him that a proper authority in terms sufficiently wide for his purpose exists; and on the strength of that authority he deals, through the persons possessing it, with the principal. It is not his fault if that principal have reposed his confidence in an untrustworthy or incapable representative. This doctrine applies not only to breaches of contract or to wrongs done by one party to another, but also to the performance of absolute duties. Thus an old gentleman* was the owner of a quarry on the bank of a navigable river. He was unable personally to superintend the work, but he gave to his men directions that the refuse should be disposed of in a particular way. They disregarded his directions, and

* Reg. v. Stephens, 1 L. R. Q. B.

let the refuse fall into the river. The navigation, consequently, was obstructed, and the owner of the quarry was indicted for a nuisance. He urged that he had no knowledge that the nuisance existed, and that it was caused entirely by the disregard of his directions. But these excuses were ineffectual. His duty was to take care that his work should be so conducted as not to obstruct the navigation. The navigation was obstructed, and it was no defence to say that he had employed disobedient servants. He was consequently found to be guilty of an offence which other men had committed without his knowledge and against his will.

Its Conditions. There are in effect three conditions of vicarious liability. There must be the relation, whether permanent or temporary, of employer and employed. The person employed must act in his capacity as such, and not upon his own account. In such action he must keep within the course of his employment or the scope of his authority, as the case may be. In the first of these three cases, an employer is not liable for any damage done to a mere volunteer who at the request of the ordinary workmen joins them in their work, and in doing so meets with some mischance. Where an employer obtains temporary assistance from any person, and no other relation of service exists between them, the employer is liable for the actual orders he has given to this assistant, but for no more. The law does not raise any implication beyond the terms of the particular order. The man is employed for a particular definite purpose, and not for a general class of acts.

Thus,* where the chairman of a public meeting directed the removal of some persons who were causing a disturbance, and the stewards and their assistants dragged out the wrong man and injured him in doing so, it was held that the chairman was not liable. "There is, said the Court, no such pre-existing relationship as exists in the case of master and servant, and there is, we think, no ground for extending by implication an express authority limited in its terms. The

* Lucas v. Mason, L. R. 10 Ex. 251.

disturbance which gave rise to the defendant's words took place in the presence of those who acted upon them. They were nearer to the plaintiff than was the defendant, and if in doubt might have referred to the defendant for further instructions. It does not therefore seem to us that there was any evidence which should have been submitted to the jury' of a general or implied authority going beyond the limit of that which was created by the express words used, or of any authority to the persons ordered to bring the disturbers forward to exercise a discretion as to who were disturbers."

As regards the second case, expressions are used in several judgments—among these is one by Mr. Justice Willes, which I shall presently cite—from which it might seem that the acting of the servant in his master's interest is a condition of the master's liability. But "it* is not by any means universally true that every act supposed to be done for the interest of the master is done in the course of his employment. A footman might think, and rightly, that it was for the interest of his master that he should get on the box and drive the coach ; but no one would say that to do so was in the scope of the footman's employment, and that the master was responsible for the wilful act of the footman in taking charge of the horses." I think that the idea which these words, as to the master's interest, were meant to convey was that the action of the servant must be in his capacity as such. This requirement is not the same as that of acting within the course of his employment. A servant may do an act which is in the usual course of his duty, but he may do that act not for his master's purposes but for his own. He may, as we shall presently see, drive his master's horse and cart, which he is employed to drive, but he may drive with it upon his own business and to his own destination. He is acting in the course of his employment, but he is not acting in his master's interest, that is in his capacity as a servant.

As regards the third condition that I have mentioned, the liability of the master extends to all the acts of his servant

---

* *Per* Blackburn J., Limpus *v.* London General Omnibus Co., 32 L. J. Ex. 34.

or agent done as such and within the course of his employment or the scope of his authority. It is not confined to his
lawful acts. A servant cannot indeed without his master's
consent bind his master by his punishable offences. If he
were expressly authorized to commit such an offence, the
contract of service would be void for illegality. If he were
not so authorized, that is if the agreement were that he
should do certain lawful acts, the perpetration of any
criminal act would in most cases be out of the course of his
employment. But where in the course of his employment,
that is in the execution of his ordinary duty, the servant
commits any wrongful act or makes any wrongful omission, the master is liable. Thus a newspaper proprietor
employs a printer to print and publish his paper. If the
publisher publish a libel, the proprietor is responsible. He
did not authorize him to publish that particular article,
much less to publish any defamatory matter ; but he did
authorize him in general terms to publish the paper, and if
in the execution of that work other persons be injured, he
must bear the consequences. Although his liability in this
respect is now considerably modified, he is still criminally
responsible for such a libel on the same principle that the
old quarry-owner was prosecuted for obstructing the navigation of the river. In like manner, where one omnibus
obstructed another, and a collision ensued, the company of
the offending driver had to pay damages, although the act
was wrongful, and although it was done in direct disobedience
to the company's instructions. The driver was employed,
not only to drive, but to obtain traffic in competition with
other vehicles. If in endeavouring to effect these objects he
wrongfully crossed another omnibus, such an act was in the
course of his employment. Had he been successful, his
company would have profited by the extra fares. As he
failed, they had to bear the loss of his wrong-doing.

The rule in such cases is sufficiently clear. It is often,
however, difficult to determine whether any given act is or is

I

not within the course of the employment or within the scope of the agency. It may be doubtful whether the actor was a servant, or, if he were, whether he was acting in the particular matter for his master or for himself, or, if he were a servant, and were acting as such, whether his acts were within the scope of his employment. The answer to such questions must depend upon the circumstances of the particular case, the express terms of the authority given or the implication arising from the ordinary course of business in similar circumstances. The working of the principle will best be understood by actual examples.

A Mr. Henlock* employed a labourer to clean out a drain on his land. This labourer was not in Mr. Henlock's service, but was a working man in the neighbourhood. He finished the work without any assistance or without any directions from Mr. Henlock, and received five shillings for his services. But it appeared that in the course of his work the labourer took up part of an adjoining highway and replaced it in an improper manner and with insufficient materials. A horse passing along the highway fell through this damaged place and was injured. The owner of the horse sued Mr. Henlock for damages. It was contended, but without success, that the labourer was an independent contractor ; and it was held that he was acting as the servant of the defendant and under his control, and, consequently, his master must pay for the damage which his bad work had occasioned.

A wine merchant † sent his clerk with his horse and cart under the care of his carman to deliver wine and bring back empty bottles. On their return the clerk asked the carman to drive him to a place in a different direction, where he had business of his own. The carman did so, and, when they were about two miles from the stable, injured a man by his negligent driving. The injured man sued the wine merchant. But although the accident happened by the fault of his servant, and although that servant was at the time performing his ordinary duty, the defendant was not held to be

---

* Saddler *v.* Henlock, 24 L. J. Q. B. 138.   † Story *v.* Ashton, 4 L. R. Q B. 476.

liable. The carman was acting not for his master but for himself. He was driving his master's cart, but not on his master's account. He had in effect set out on a new and independent journey, and for what he did or omitted to do on that journey the master was not responsible.

A man named Poulton* brought by railway a horse to an agricultural show at Salisbury. According to the railway arrangements, horses were, if unsold, to return free on production of a certificate. Poulton produced his certificate, had his horse placed in a box, procured a ticket for himself, and travelled by the same train. At the end of the journey the station-master demanded the fare for the horse; and when it was refused arrested Poulton and kept him in custody for half-an-hour, when he telegraphed to Salisbury and was answered that all was right. Poulton brought an action against the company for false imprisonment. Under the Railway Act, the company is entitled to arrest any person who refuses to pay his fare, and to detain any goods for which the carriage is unpaid. If, therefore, the station-master had arrested Poulton under the belief that he had not paid his fare, when in fact he had done so, such an act would have been within the scope of his employment, and the company would have been liable for it. But in this case he arrested the man for a charge alleged to be due upon the horse. If such a charge were really due, the remedy was the detention of the horse until the money was paid. This arrest, therefore, was " an act out of the scope of his authority, and for which the company would be no more responsible than if he had committed an assault or done any other act which the company never authorized him to do."

I may add the following observations by Mr. Justice Willes† :—"The general rule is that the master is answerable for every such wrong of the servant or agent as is committed in the course of the service and for the master's benefit, though no express command or privity of the master be proved. That principle is acted upon every day in running-down

---

* Poulton *v.* London and South-Western Railway Co., 1 L. R. Q. B. 534.
† Barwick *v.* English Joint Stock Bank, 2 L. R. Ex. at p. 265.

cases. It has been applied also to direct trespass to goods, as in the case of holding the owners of ships liable for the act of masters abroad improperly selling the cargo. It has been held applicable to actions for false imprisonment, in cases where officers of railway companies, entrusted with the execution of by-laws relating to imprisonment and intending to act in the course of their duty, improperly imprison persons who are supposed to come within the terms of the by-laws. It has been acted upon where persons employed by the owners of boats· to navigate them and to take fares have committed an infringement of a ferry, or such like wrong. In all these cases it may be said, as it was said here, that the master has not authorized the act. It is true he has not authorized the particular act, but he has put the agent in his place to do that class of acts, and he must be answerable for the manner in which the agent has conducted himself in doing the business which it was the act of his master to place him in." ·

Although the master may be liable for the servant, or the principal for the agent, the cases cannot be inverted. No duty that is cast upon the master extends to the servant. No duty of the principal binds the agent. They are merely the elongated hands of their employer. Their acts are his acts : but his acts do not concern them. When therefore a man avowedly acts in a representative character which he really holds, his conduct is that of his principal and not of himself. He cannot of course thus evade any absolute or any general duties. No agreement between any two persons can justify or excuse either of them in a breach of the law. But there are some offences of a minor nature,* police offences as they are sometimes called, in which the justices have by statute a discretionary power of dealing with the master alone and of dismissing the case against the servant. These exceptions are not very numerous, and are not practically very important. They can scarcely be said to affect seriously any principle of law.

* The Police Offences Statute 1865, s. 34.

Justification. § 5. Exculpation which is the negative form of Imputation comprises the principles of justification and of excuse. In the former case there is no true disobedience, but only an apparent conflict of duties. In the latter case the law recognises the offence, but exempts the offender from punishment, if not from all the consequences to which he is liable. Justification takes place on several grounds. The first is where a man, in obedience to an express command of the law, does an act which the law generally prohibits. All the persons engaged in the administration of justice do, in the performance of their ordinary duties and as part of those duties, acts which in other circumstances would be grave offences. It is but an extension of the same principle to allege that where the law gives to any person any power, the reasonable exercise of that power within its limits, whether express or implied, is, in the absence of intentional misconduct or of culpable inadvertence, a sufficient defence. Further, the law requires the service of its citizens in the preservation of the public peace and the prevention of crime ; it therefore arms these citizens, when they are so engaged, with all needful immunities and powers. The law also recognises the natural impulses of self-defence and recaption, whether the attempted wrong relates to a man's own person or to the persons of his household or to his house or to his property. In all these cases the general command is deemed, even though no express words to that effect are employed, to be subject to the foregoing exceptions.

Collision of Commands. For the purposes of the present work a lengthened discussion of these principles is unnecessary. Their details may be left to the practical lawyer. Two matters only need further notice. One of these matters is the nature of the command which justifies the breach of another command. Where a person in authority over others gives them a command which is contrary to law, which command are they to obey? The law forbids murder. But the law also commands with equal energy a soldier to execute the orders of his commanding officer. If, then, a commanding officer order an act

which the law regards as murder, how is the soldier to govern
himself? Theoretically, the difficulty is met by the assumption that the commands which the soldier must obey are lawful
commands. But as military acts do not admit of delay, and
as legal advice is, from the nature of the case, unavailable,
the suggested limitation is of little use for practical purposes.
It would be dangerous to infringe the fundamental rule
that every man must know the law and obey it. It is
a blot upon our law that a' soldier, who is ordered to fire
upon a dangerous mob, should have, even in appearance, to
elect between the risk that he may be hanged for murder and
the risk that he may be shot for mutiny. In this difficulty
the course suggested by the Commission of English Judges
seems to be the safest. They observe that the question
practically arises in relation to the suppression of riots.
They propose, therefore, to make a change, but to limit such
change to this particular class of cases. According to this
view, the soldier would be authorized in the suppression of
riots to follow without ·hesitation the orders of his superior
officer if these orders be not manifestly illegal. What might
fairly be considered as a manifestly illegal order would be a
question which the judge would have to decide. Thus, in the
case which in practice is of most frequent occurrence, a
definite choice is made between the conflicting duties; but
the exceptional principle is restricted to these narrow limits,
and within these limits the danger of any public inconvenience
is hardly appreciable.

Command
implies
Power.   The other matter which I propose to notice is
the maxim which declares that every command of
the law includes everything that is essential to the performance of that command. This maxim is not restricted to
public duties. It applies to all transactions between parties.
Every grant and every contract implies, so far as the grantor
or other promisor is competent to give it, a power to do
everything without which the transaction would be ineffectual. In the case of the direct commands of the law, an

implied power arises only where its existence is essential to the object of the law. If that object can be otherwise accomplished, no power is implied. The advantage of the possession of such a power is not material. The question is not whether its existence would be convenient, but whether it is essential. Thus, Colonial Legislatures, since they have not inherited the privileges of the Imperial Parliament, have, in the absence of any express legislative authority, to rely upon the powers implied in their constitutions. These powers enable them to remove any person who obstructs their proceedings, because otherwise they could not properly exercise their functions. But although the power of removal is thus essential to them, the power of punishment for such disorders is not essential. " The right* to remove for self-security is one thing, the right to inflict punishment is another thing. The former is all that is warranted by the legal maxim that has been cited, the latter is not its legitimate consequence."

If the power be well given, questions may arise as to its exercise. It must be exercised in the manner prescribed, and not beyond the extent prescribed. It is not sufficient that the proposed object should be somehow attained. It must be attained by the precise method that the law commands and not by any other method. If a sheriff who was ordered to have a man hanged were to cause him to be shot, the sheriff, although the practical result would be substantially the same, would not be able to justify on a charge of murder. The limit, too, of the power is plainly marked. Nothing more must be done than the exigency of the case actually requires. An assault is unlawful. The moderate correction of a schoolboy is not an assault. But to beat a boy for two hours with a heavy stick, as an intelligent schoolmaster once did, is not moderate correction. This excess vitiates the whole proceedings. The plea of moderate correction is met by the facts disclosing excess, and thus the original illegal character of the assault remains

* Doyle *r.* Falconer, L. R. 1 P. C. C. 328.

unaffected. Where a person enters a house with the house-master's leave and subsequently misconducts himself therein, his entry does not become unlawful, and he is answerable only for his subsequent misbehaviour. But where the entry is made under the authority of the law, the subsequent misconduct relates back to the entry. It is evidence of the unlawful intent with which the entry was really made, and the offender is treated as a trespasser *ab initio.*

Exercise of Statutory Power. Where any power which the law whether expressly or by implication confers is likely in its exercise to be hurtful to any other person, the donee of the power must take care that its exercise shall cause as little harm as is consistent with its proper execution. There is, however, an important distinction in this matter. In ordinary circumstances, a man who uses any dangerous or offensive thing must either warrant the safety or the convenience of the public, or must at least be able to prove that he has taken reasonable precautions. But where the law authorizes him to use any such thing, his responsibility is placed on a much lower level. " When the Legislature* has sanctioned the use of a particular means for a given purpose, that sanction carries with it this consequence—that the use of the means itself for that purpose (provided every precaution which the nature of the case suggests has been observed) is not an act for which an action lies independent of negligence." Thus where a railway company is empowered to run locomotive engines, it is bound to take reasonable precautions against the emission of sparks; but if it do so, it is free from any liability for any mischance thence arising, and the burthen of proof that there was negligence rests on the plaintiff. But where a Railway Act† empowered a company to make and maintain a railway passable for wagons and other carriages only, and the company ran on its line a steam locomotive engine, and sparks from their engine set fire to a hay stack, a very different rule was applied. The legislative authority was wanting, and

---

* Vaughan *v.* Taff Railway Co., 20 L. J. Ex. 247, *per* Cockburn C. J.
† Jones *v.* Festiniog Railway Co., 3 L. R. Q. B. 733.

therefore the ordinary rule continued in operation. Consequently, upon an action brought for the damage done by the fire, the defence that the company had taken all reasonable precautions to prevent the emission of sparks was not allowed, and the plaintiff recovered damages.

Excuse. § 6. Of those persons who are excused from all the consequences of the offences that they have committed, or who are at least dispunishable for them, the first class consists of those whose intelligence, whether from their tender age or from disease or from congenital weakness, is defective. To a certain extent also the relations of married life are admitted as an excuse, and a wife is dispunishable not only for injuries done by her during marriage to her husband's property but even for concealing her guilty husband and assisting his escape. Nor will the law concern itself about microscopic wrongs. If it appear that no substantial injury has been committed, the proceedings may be brought to a summary conclusion. **Mistake.** Other grounds of excuse are found in mistake, consent, or accident. When a man lawfully and honestly acts in the reasonable belief that a state of facts exists which, if it did exist, would justify his conduct, the law will not punish him merely because the facts were not such as he had supposed. A mistake, however, as to law, that is as to substantive general law, not as to the particular rights of any individual, or, as the Romans would have expressed the idea, "*ignorantia juris inter omnes non inter partes*," is not a ground of excuse. Such a rule is necessary for the transaction of legal business; and if any individual case of hardship arise, recourse must be had to the Prerogative of mercy. Practically, the rule, when limited as is above stated, does not work so harshly as might perhaps have been anticipated. It is surprising how quickly and how widely a knowledge of the general law and of any important changes in it becomes diffused.

Consent.   With respect to consent, the rule is clear that no consent on the part of any person can affect the operation of any duty which the State for its own purposes thinks fit to impose. On the other hand, it is equally clear that no person can impose on any other person any new duty without that other person's consent. Consent, therefore, has no ' place in absolute duties. In obligations it is essential. In general duties its presence or its absence depends upon the terms in which the duty is expressed. The act of taking another's property is not in itself and without regard to the circumstances of the act the subject of legislation. If it be done with the owner's consent, it is ordinary business ; and if it be done without his consent, the State will interfere. A surgeon may grievously wound his patient if the patient consent to the operation ; but he must not seize a man against his will and amputate his leg merely for the love of his art, and because he thinks, perhaps rightly, that the case was suitable. for amputation. The consent which the law recognises implies two conditions. In the first place, it must be given freely, that is without any coercion. A consent obtained at the point of the bayonet is not a consent, but a mere form of words simulating consent with which the mind of the speaker never really went. Thus we may suppose that in time of war a merchant ship is attacked by a hostile man-of-war, and, since resistance were useless, surrenders. While the enemy is bringing her into port an opportunity occurs, and the prize makes her escape. His former consent to the capture does not affect the rights of the shipowner. The captor *" lupum auribus tenet."* His authority over his prisoner depends not upon that prisoner's promise to submit but upon his own power to enforce that promise. Coercion must, however, be distinguished, as I have already observed, from what has been called a " grumbling consent." The latter implies a conflict of opposing motives, and the deliberate adoption after more or less hesitation of one particular course. In the second place, a lawful consent implies a full knowledge of all the facts material to enable the person who consents to form a right judgment upon the matter. Thus, when a person waives a right, that is consents to something to his disadvantage, he must understand the effect of what he is about to do. So it is where a man commits a crime by means of an innocent agent. A man induces an attendant to give poison to a sick person on the assurance that the drink so administered is medicine. He is guilty, but the attendant is innocent. There was a consent, indeed, to give a certain drink, but there was no consent to give poison.

In cases of contract these simulated consents again meet us under the titles of mistake and of intimidation. But there is a third case which is less clear. There may be a true consent, but that consent may have been obtained by deceit. Fraud renders a contract voidable; that is it affords ground for the rescission of the contract by the person deceived on the discovery of the fraud. But where a general duty is imposed, that is where an act is prohibited under penalties without the consent of the party injured, if such consent be actually although fraudulently obtained, does the offender come within the terms of the law? On the one side it is urged that criminal law must be construed strictly. On the other side it is plain that the offender would thus take advantage of his own wrong, and would escape the consequences of one offence by the commission of another. In such cases there has been much dispute, and sometimes perhaps some straining of the law. The remedy consists in a proper statement of the duty. Where any act is forbidden without another person's consent, if it be desired to render punishable the frauds to which I have referred, the addition of the words " or with his consent if it be obtained by fraud " will remove the difficulty.

Accident. Another ground of excuse is accident. Accident in this sense means* an event arising from some physical or political agency or some social convulsion, which could not be

* Austin I. 493.

foreseen, or, if foreseen, could not by any reasonable precaution be prevented. It implies the action of some unexpected and resistless external force, whether human or animal or elemental. Thus an earthquake or a hostile invasion is an accident, and no person in the absence of an express contract to the contrary is liable for any damage thence resulting. So, if a man light a fire in his field, he is liable for any damage that may be done to his neighbour by the spread of the fire, even though he had taken ample precaution to confine it to his own ground. But if a sudden tempest arise, and by reason of such tempest the fire be driven beyond his boundaries, he will not be liable, for the tempest was an accident in the sense I have above described. If, however, from the circumstances of the climate he might reasonably have anticipated such a change of weather, the theory of accident is refuted, and he will be liable for the damage which he thus had reason to expect. Sometimes the word accident or mischance is used in a different sense. It implies an act done by the party himself, but done without intention or in some cases without knowledge. Thus a man in a skirmish at night* throws a spear and kills his wife's brother. Such an act is said to be a fatal chance, but it would not amount to an excuse in law. King Oidipus intentionally killed an old man who had given him some provocation, but he did not know that this old man was his father. He was not guilty in any reasonable sense of patricide, that is he did not kill his father knowing him to be such. But it could not be successfully contended that Oidipus was not guilty of manslaughter.

* See the ballad of " Alice Brand " in " The Lady of the Lake."

CHAPTER VIII.

THE THEORY OF LEGAL RIGHTS.

The Meaning of Right. § 1. So far I have treated of the simplest forms of commands and duties. A somewhat complex form now presents itself. Where a command requires not only that a duty shall be performed, but that that performance shall be for the benefit of some definite person or class of persons, a new relation arises. This relation exists not only between the commander and the commandee, but between the commandee and the party in whose favour the duty is imposed. This third party has an interest in the performance of the duty; and, in the event of a breach of that duty, the commander undertakes to notice his complaint and to interfere on his behalf. The relation thus established is called a right. When several such relations are mentioned, they are called rights. A right, therefore, is a relation which arises in certain species of commands. The characteristic of these species does not depend upon the person who issues the command; and, consequently, the relation may exist whether the commander be the State or any other competent authority. But in all other cases save the commands of the State rights seldom occupy any conspicuous position. For all practical purposes it may be alleged that rights are peculiar to law. It is at all events certain that legal rights, and those only, have attained any considerable development; and it is of legal rights and none others that I shall now treat.

Rights occupy in jurisprudence a similar position to that which value holds in political economy. Both rights and value are a part, an important part indeed, but still only a part, of their respective sciences, and each has been mistaken

for its whole science. As political economy has been called
the science of values, so jurisprudence has been supposed to
be the science of rights. In each case the error of the limitation is proved by the fact—which I trust that the place of
this chapter in the present essay tends to establish—that
the discussion of either science may proceed* a long way with-·
out any inquiry in the one case into rights or in the other
case into values. There is also another and a more unhappy
point of resemblance. The importance of a precise definition
of each word is extreme, and yet each word is hopelessly
ambiguous. In the case of political economy it is, with care,
possible to avoid altogether the use of the misleading term ;
but in jurisprudence this expedient, the only sure one, is not
practicable. We must accept the decision of that autocrat
of language common use, and employ the words that it prescribes, however spoiled for our purposes they may have
become. Yet, probably, the most serious obstacle to clear
conceptions of the first principles of law is the obvious
confusion and the bewildering associations of the word
right.

Right, in its earliest form, is an adjective, and is equivalent
to straight. In its secondary use it becomes a laudatory
epithet, indicating that the conduct or the opinion to which
it is applied conforms to some standard to which the speaker
expressly or by implication refers. From this adjective the
abstract substantive " right " is formed, and denotes such a
conformity. But since different standards of conduct exist
for different purposes, and since conformity to one standard
is not necessarily conformity to another standard, it follows
that the same conduct in the same matter may, if it be
measured by different standards, be at once both right and
wrong. Such an absurdity may be avoided by an express
statement of the standard to which reference is made. If the
question be one of morality, we may speak of moral right.
If the question be one of politics, we may speak of political
right. But the original substantive "a right" with its plural

* See J. S. Mill's Political Economy, I. 525.

" rights " is distinct from the substantivized adjective " right." A right has nothing to do with conformity to any standard, legal or moral or other. It denotes a peculiar legal relation. This relation is altogether independent of the rules of morality or of abstract justice. It depends exclusively upon the law. It is in the fullest sense the creature of the law. The law makes it, the law may unmake it. It arises from the law, it is controlled by the law, it expires with the law. Where in any case the law, whether wisely or unwisely, whether sinfully or piously, imposes upon any person a duty for the benefit of another person, it thereby creates in that other person a right; and it in effect undertakes that this expectation which it has thus authorized shall not be disappointed.

Sir William Blackstone furnishes a striking instance of this confusion. He says* that as " municipal law is a rule of civil conduct, commanding what is right and prohibiting what is wrong, it follows that the primary and principal objects of the law are rights and wrongs." This inference, which forms the basis of Blackstone's great work, rests upon a mere verbal puzzle, the confusion, namely, between moral right and legal right. If in the above passage the word right means legal right, the conclusion is a truism; and the contention is that, as law commands what is legally right, things that are legally right are commanded by law, and so form its subject-matter. If in that passage the word right means moral right, then no inference can be drawn; and the assertion, apart from the form of the argument, is notoriously untrue. But if the word rights be taken there to express a certain legal relation, the absurdity will be still more glaring. The contention would in that case be that, as the law commands conformity to a rule, whether legal or moral, a certain class of legal relations must be the principal object of the law. Of a similar class is Hobbes' famous paradox that no law can be unjust. All such dicta rest on a mere equivoque, a similarity in sound between two words and a dissimilarity

* I. 122.

in their sense. They stand on the same level as the celebrated puzzle of the horse chestnut and the chesnut horse.

There is another phase of this verbal confusion. A man does a certain act because he thinks that it is right; that is, because he thinks that his doing so is conformable with the moral law ; in other words, because morally it is his duty to do so. To him, therefore, right means duty. The two terms are equivalent. It is right because it is his duty. It is his duty because it is right. In this sense the word right means moral duty. At one time, in our language, right had in relation to law a similar meaning. Even still among the less educated classes we sometimes hear the expression—an expression which three centuries ago was used by good writers—that such and such a man " has a right " to be punished ; that is, that his punishment would in the circumstances of the case be conformable to law. In like manner, the Roman *jus*, like the Roman *obligatio*, included both duty and right; and the fact that *jus* has usually, and, in the older sense of the term, accurately, been translated by " right " has caused a greater confusion of legal thought than would to those who have not reflected upon the power of words over thoughts appear at first sight possible. But in matters of law right in its modern sense and duty are not coincident but contrasted. They reside not in the same person but in different persons. A man has a right when another person is or when other persons are under a duty which is beneficial to him. A man is under a duty when the law commands him to act or to forbear in a certain manner or under certain conditions. That duty, however, does not, as we have seen, necessarily presuppose a right ; . and where a right is implied, it rests in another person, and not in the person upon whom the duty is imposed. From the legal stand-point, a man does a certain act because he has a right to do it ; he has such a right because the law gives it to him ; and this right consists

in and is bounded by the proper performance of a legal
duty by another man or by other men.

§ 2. There is little difficulty in the analysis
of a right. A right is a certain consequence
of one kind of command. To a right, therefore, all that
is true of command in general applies. Its characteristic
differences consist in the circumstances that the command
is given for the benefit of some definite person other than
the person on whom the duty is imposed ; and that, in the
event of a breach of this duty, the person to whom the
right is given may apply for and obtain from the authority
that created the duty its enforcement or other appropriate
redress. Each of these characteristics—the desirability of
the right, and the vocation of its donee to defend it—requires
consideration.

As a command and its correlative duty imply two
parties, so that variety of command which connotes a right
implies three parties ; but the third party must be in reality
such. He cannot be either the commander or the commandee. It would be unreasonable to command a man to
fulfil some duty towards himself; and to authorize him, if he
failed therein, to complain to the State, for the purpose of
having himself compelled to do that which he of his own
accord might have and ought to have done. There may be
a self-regarding duty, but a self-regarding right is absurd.
Nor, again, can a commander be supposed when his command is broken to complain to himself, and to set himself
in motion to procure for himself redress. He usually enforces
obedience in a less round-about fashion. It is true that in
this country the sovereign, that is the Queen, has rights and
is subject to duties ; that these rights and duties are frequently under the consideration of courts of justice ; and
that the tendency to assimilate these public rights to private
rights is continually growing stronger. But the explanation
is that with the progress of society there is a differentiation

K

in the State ; that practically the State in its legislative capacity is one juristic person, and the State in its administrative capacity is another such person. In English law, the difference between the Queen and the Queen in Parliament is clearly marked. In republican governments, an abstraction, under the style of the State, or the People, or some similar title, is made to serve a similar purpose. This problem, however, although it still exercises jurists not a little, has no practical importance. Whatever names are used to express the distinction, the person who has the right is always regarded as different both from the law which creates the right, and from the maker of that law, and from the person against whom that right avails.

Right and Power. The word right has sometimes been applied, and that by high authority, in a sense inconsistent with the foregoing remarks. Austin,[*] although he insists upon the presence of the third party as essential to a right, speaks of the right of a judge or of a policeman to deal with an offender. J. S. Mill,[†] although he was the first, I think, to point out that a right is always supposed to be desirable, is inclined by a stretch of language to include in it, as Austin does, the exercise of official functions. I need not stop to discuss how far such an extension is consistent with the usage of language. Whether it be so or not, the right of the judge is plainly a different thing from the right of the party in whose favour he decides. It is convenient to appropriate a separate term to each separate notion. Accordingly I propose to speak of the lawful exercise of official functions as a power ; and to limit, as Mill suggests, the term right to those cases where the legislator intended to promote by its creation the advantage of the party upon whom it is conferred.

The distinction between a power and a right was some years ago considered in the English courts[‡] in the following circumstances. A returning officer, in mistake of his duty, refused to receive a vote at an election. The voter was

* See I. 415.   † Dissertations and Discussions, III. 230.
‡ Pryce v. Belcher, 4 C. B. 866.

disqualified and not entitled to vote. He brought an action against the returning officer. It was held that although the plaintiff had the *power* in this way to compel the returning officer, under the apprehension of a prosecution, to put his name on the poll, he had not the *right* to do so; that in doing so he acted in direct contravention of the Act of Parliament, the terms of which were express that he should not be entitled to vote, and that the rejection of his vote did not amount to a violation of anything which the law considers a right. In this case the term power is not used in relation to official conduct, although if the acts of the returning officer had been within his duty, he might be properly said to have had the power of rejecting the vote. The application of the term to the plaintiff may seem perhaps somewhat unusual, but the general nature of the case is apparent. The returning officer was in the performance of an absolute public duty ; for the proper exercise of that duty he was criminally responsible to the Crown. But every official is also responsible to every individual to whom in the exercise of his office he causes, either by his action or by his inaction, special damage. In other words, every person has a legal right to the services of every officer in the manner and the circumstances prescribed by law. In this case the plaintiff, Pryce, sustained no special damage by the rejection of his vote, because he had no vote. He could not, therefore, maintain any action for the breach of a right which did not exist. He could merely, as one of the public, acquaint Her Majesty with the alleged misconduct of one of her officers. To any such well-grounded complaint Her Majesty is always ready to listen, and she is free to deal with them as she thinks fit. Pryce, therefore, had the power to give such information, that is he might lawfully do so, but he had no right in the matter. The Crown had never undertaken to act upon his information, and the punishment of the returning officer was not directly beneficial to him.

K 2

The person towards whom the duty is to be performed is not necessarily the person who has the right. In other words, where the duty relates to a person, that person may or may not be the donee* of the right. The prescribed act or forbearance may be done or observed towards a person who is neither the commander nor the commandee, and who derives no gain and sustains no loss from the transaction. Thus the law forbids any person to take from her father's possession any other person's daughter who is under a certain age. In this case there are not three but four parties. There are the commander, the commandee, the father, and the daughter. If in the circumstances the father be deprived of his daughter's services and so sustain loss, he will be entitled to recover damages, because he has a right to those services whatever be the daughter's age. But if he have not sustained any loss in this respect, the case is different, because the duty is different. No man may deprive another of the services of his child ; but no man may, whether there be services in the question or not, take away another's child of tender years. The latter duty involves no right. It is not imposed for the benefit of the father. He has no right of ownership in the child, and merely exercises certain powers for her welfare. Nor do the wishes or the dislikes of the girl herself form any part of the question. The law holds that she is not of an age at which a true consent can be given. The duty is therefore imposed as a matter of public policy. Thus the girl, whether the father has or has not a right to her services, has herself no right in the matter. She is merely the *res*, the secondary object of the prescribed forbearance. So in the case of a contract, it is a well-known rule that, except in a particular class of cases, none but the parties have any rights under it. If A agree

---

* I use this expression, in preference to the misleading "subject of a right," on the analogy of the familiar phrase the "donee of a power." The latter phrase is indeed used when the donor is a specific individual, while the donee of a right implies that the donor is the State. But in selecting a name which is urgently needed, and which somehow has never found a place in our language, save in the form of a doubtful periphrase, I thought that it was no disadvantage that the name should suggest a truth which it is material to remember and very easy to forget.

with B to do something respecting C, B only, and not C, can in general enforce A's obligation.

The second characteristic may be briefly expressed by the proposition that upon the breach of the duty the donee of the right only may sue the wrong-doer. Simple as this proposition seems, it includes several matters that call for notice. In the first place, it implies that the duty is enforced not by the party but by the State. No man may take the law into his own hands. Of the motives which led, if not to the commencement, yet certainly to the continuance and the development of political organization, one of the strongest was that that organization afforded the means of terminating the fierce and unceasing quarrels of households and of clans. Every well-developed State therefore insists upon retaining the exclusive control of all branches of the duties which it commands, whether these duties do or do not generate rights, and whether they have been imposed for the convenience of the State or at the request of the parties. No subject is of greater historical interest than this. For my present purpose it is sufficient to say that "the law* of England appears both in spirit and in principle to prevent persons from redressing their grievances by their own act." The State appoints its proper officers to hear and determine all claims, and when any claim has been established to carry it into effect. But no man can now decide his own dispute, or can execute a judgment that he has lawfully obtained.

It also follows that rights are enforced upon the complaint only of the party injured. It is of the very essence of a right that, if the duty be not fulfilled, the donee of the right may invoke the assistance of the State. But, if he do not choose to seek help, the State will not volunteer it. It will not permit any other person without proper authority to make such request. If the injured party himself think it worth his while to apply in the proper manner and to the proper court, the State will redeem its promise ; and will,

---

* *Per* Pollock C. B., Hyde *v.* Graham, 1 H. & C. 593.

unless the applicant be himself in default, enforce the duty
which it had imposed. But the donee of the right may
waive or disclaim his right, or may be so remiss in urging it
that he deserves no further consideration, or may have
misconducted himself in the business. In all such cases the
State declines to entertain the complaint.

Right and   It also follows that a right is something different
Liberty.   from the absence of a restrictive duty. A right
implies a positive not a merely negative idea. It connotes
a duty imposed upon some person of which another person
is authorized to require the enforcement. But the mere
relief from a duty does not necessarily give to a person a
right to do the act which was previously forbidden. It is
true that he may lawfully do such act, and his conduct
will accordingly be right or lawful ; that is, he will not
on that account be liable to any sanction. It does not,
however, follow that he has a right, or that any duty which
the State will enforce has been imposed for his benefit
upon any other person. The destruction of the duty on
which a right depends is indeed fatal to that right, but it
does not confer a new right upon the person who is freed
from the restraint. He is to that extent liberated from
control, but no other person is thereby bound. Thus in a
comparatively recent volume of the *Edinburgh Review* * the
following startling proposition is laid down :—" If the
sovereign made a law that A.B. should be at liberty to cut
off the head of any person he met in the street, A.B. would
have precisely the same right to do so as to be paid his
debts." The difference between these two cases is this—in the
former case the homicidal act of A.B. would be a matter
of indifference to the law; it would not be murder or even
manslaughter, but would be excepted out of the operation
of the law that now provides for the punishment of these
crimes. In the other case the law would compel the debtor
to fulfil his obligations. A.B. could not obtain the assistance of the court to compel his victim to submit to his

* cxlv. 408.

blow; but he could obtain that assistance to compel his debtor to pay his debt.

There are thus three kindred terms between which it is needful to distinguish. These are liberty, power, and right. Liberty means the absence of legal interference, whether such absence be general or partial, and usually with the connotation that such interference is unreasonable or otherwise objectionable. Power means the doing of an act in pursuance of some command given by the law, whether peremptorily or by way of discretion, which act would in other circumstances be unlawful. A right implies the interference of the law, on the complaint and at the request of some person for whose benefit a duty has been imposed, for the purpose of enforcing that duty. Thus a man is at liberty to lay any wager that he thinks fit; but the law, though it does not forbid him from doing so, will not assist him in obtaining payment of the amount that he wins, and will not compel him to pay the amount that he loses. A man has the power to arrest offenders in certain cases; and so may assault and may restrain of their freedom persons whom in other circumstances and without the express permission of the law he could not lawfully touch. A man has a right to proceed in the proper court against his defaulting debtor, and to recover the amount of the debt by the compulsory sale, through the sheriff, of that debtor's goods.

Burthen-
some Rights
and Profit-
able Duties. We have seen that rights and duties connote respectively a benefit and a burthen. The former are granted for the advantage of the donee. The latter presuppose a course of conduct which in their absence would probably not be pursued. But time, which changes all things, sometimes reverses this connotation. A right may become burthensome. A duty may become advantageous. A property which once was valuable may be so depreciated that it will not pay the mortgage with which it is charged. A condition in a lease to build, which at one time was reluctantly accepted, may prove, for the lessee, a very fortunate undertaking. Examples of such burthensome rights and of such profitable duties sometimes occur in our political history. Thus the bishops claimed the right, in accordance with the canons of the Church, to withdraw from the House of Lords in cases of impeachment when judgment of life or limb is in question. " This, as Hallam* observes; once claimed as a privilege of the Church, and reluctantly admitted by the State, became, in the lapse of ages, an exclusion and a badge of inferiority." In like manner, on the other side, in the early days of political representation, electorates regarded the duty of sending members to the House of Commons as a grievous burthen, and, whenever opportunity offered, eagerly sought to escape from it. The residents in these electorates in like manner struggled long and hard to avoid the calamity of being included in what we should call the electoral roll. But at the present day localities constantly clamour for representation, and the electoral franchise has appropriated that name almost to the exclusion of every other franchise. Every man too is required by law to serve, either as a Peer of Parliament, if Her Majesty needs his services, or as a member of the House of Commons if he be elected thereto. But it has not been found necessary, at least in modern times, to put into operation the penalties by which those duties are enforced.

Analysis of a Wrong.　　§ 3. Wrong is the contrary of right, and a wrong is the contrary of a right. The same ambiguity therefore which affects right exists in wrong. As the former term means conformity to a standard, so the latter term means nonconformity to a standard. Consequently, unless the standard be ascertained and recognised, all reasoning on the subject of right and wrong is mere waste of words. In the case of legal rights and legal wrongs, as a right means that a relative duty is obeyed or is likely to be obeyed, so a wrong means that a relative duty has actually been broken. A right exists before a breach

* Const. Hist. IL 412.

of the duty ; but a wrong does not arise until the breach
has occurred. A wrong, therefore, like a right, is simply a
legal relation. But these relations are co-ordinate. They
result from a common duty. A wrong is not the violation
of a right, but the violation of a duty. It is true that the
former expression is ordinarily used; but that expression is
a mere abridgment, and, like other abridgments, becomes
misleading. It is merely a metaphor to say that a right,
which is only a relation, is broken. It is the duty cast upon
the party to whom the command is given—the act that is
to be done or the forbearance that is to be observed—that
is disobeyed. So long as that duty is performed, all is well,
and no difficulty arises. When that duty is not performed,
the donee of the right is entitled to seek legal redress. Thus
a right has no independent existence. It denotes merely
a certain course of proceedings taken by its donee upon the
breach of a certain species of duty. When, therefore, we
speak of the violation of a right or of its infringement, we
really mean the violation or the infringement of a duty in
respect of which a right exists, so far as such violation or
infringement affects the donee of the right. When such a
duty has been so broken, a wrong has been done to the donee
of the right, and for that wrong the law will find a remedy.

Even at the expense of some repetition, I may be
permitted to bring together all the parts of a command
of the State which involves rights and wrongs. The State
commands its Subject to do or observe for the benefit
of a Third Party some act or forbearance. Thereupon
that Subject comes under a duty, and this duty the State
will, if need be, enforce. In these circumstances the Third
Party has a right ; that is, he may enjoy the advantage resulting from the performance of the Subject's duty, and he may
complain to the State if that performance be intermitted.
So long as the Subject continues to perform his duty, all is
well. The State is satisfied with his conduct. The Third
Party enjoys his right. No unpleasantness arises. But if

the Subject become disobedient, a new set of relations is introduced. The Subject incurs the displeasure of the State, and is liable to punishment or other painful consequence. The Third Party no longer enjoys a right, but sustains a wrong. For this wrong the Subject is liable to make some appropriate reparation. Liability means that, upon proper proceedings being taken and proper proof adduced, a court of competent jurisdiction may order the offender to suffer suitable punishment or to make suitable amends, or both to suffer punishment and to make amends, as the nature of the case requires. When the disobedience concerns the State alone, it is usually called a punishable offence, or in more serious cases a crime. When the disobedience affects the donee of a right, it is usually called a wrong. The term offence appears to be a general name, and to include both crimes and wrongs. Thus every command produces or may produce two sets of relations. One of these is normal and the other is abnormal. If the command at once accomplish its object, there follow from it obedience, enjoyment of rights, freedom from legal molestation. If it do not directly accomplish its object, there follow from it disobedience, wrongs, legal proceedings and the painful consequences that such proceedings involve.

Classification of Offences.   Every offence is a breach of duty. Every breach of duty either is punishable or is not punishable. Punishable offences may be prosecuted either by indictment or other like proceedings which we need not now consider, or before justices of the peace in the exercise of their summary jurisdiction. Indictable offences, as they may be called, are of two kinds. They are either crimes or misdemeanours. Misdemeanour is a general name for all indictable offences other than crimes. Crimes are a species of indictable offences. They have certain characteristic incidents that attach to them upon charge and upon conviction. Where a man is charged with any crime, he may be arrested without warrant, and he is bailable not as of right but only at the discretion of the court. In other cases, unless special statutory authority be given, a warrant is always required ; and an accused person, upon the production of sufficient sureties to a reasonable amount, is bailable as of right. Where a man is convicted of a crime, he incurs in addition to the punishment specified for the offence certain disabilities. He cannot sit in Parliament or in any Municipal Council. He cannot exercise any Parliamentary or Municipal franchise. He cannot hold any office under the Crown or any public employment. He cannot serve on any jury. If he be an office-holder or a pensioner in any form, his office or his pension or other allowance is forfeited unless he be pardoned within two months from his conviction or before his office be filled. Further, his rights of maintaining action and of dealing with property and of making contracts are suspended during his term of punishment, and his property is placed in the hands of a curator. None of these consequences follow a conviction for a misdemeanour.

Whether any given offence is a crime or a misdemeanour is a question which depends upon the terms of the law by which that offence is created. I have already observed that no general rule on the subject is available, except the obvious one that those offences are described as crimes which appear to the Legislature of the day to be the most dangerous in their character, and, consequently, the most in need of repression. Offences over which justices have summary jurisdiction are, if we speak in the same rough way, those of a less grave character. Of these too it must be said that the jurisdiction of the justices, whatever may be the character of the offence, depends entirely upon express statutory grant. In some cases such jurisdiction is given in circumstances which otherwise would amount to a crime, and in all cases where their jurisdiction is not distinctly taken away, the superior courts exercise a concurrent authority. Where in the opinion of the justices any charge appears to be of a serious nature, they are bound to abstain from adjudication and to send the case for trial. But those minor varieties of

serious offences with which they usually deal are not
regarded as crimes, and practically no superior court interferes with their proceedings in any smaller breach of the law.
Thus the tendency to differentiation in criminal procedure is
well marked.   The minor offences are heard and determined
by justices.   The graver offences come before the superior
courts.   The differences of procedure in these courts according to the nature of the offence no longer exist.   But a clear
line is drawn between those ordinary aberrations to which
all men are in a greater or less degree liable and those
darker offences from which the moral sense of the community
revolts.

Crimes and Torts.   § 4.   We can now appreciate a distinction which
has caused much trouble to jurists, that, namely,
between crimes (in the wide sense) and torts.   The distinction
is less important than the discussion upon it might seem to
indicate.   In practice no person is either aided or embarrassed
by it.   In theory it is altogether useless as a basis for any
classification of law.   It presents, however, certain features
which require explanation.   It does not arise from any
difference in the gravity of the offences that these two words
respectively imply.   Such a difference does indeed generally
exist, but it is not necessary.   A slander, for example, is
morally worse, and its pecuniary consequences may be more
serious, than the neglect to register a young dog within the
first half of January.   Yet the former is only a tort, and
the latter is a punishable offence, although it is dealt with
by an inferior court.   Nor is the difference one of procedure alone.   These differences, that of gravity and that
of procedure, sufficiently distinguish indictable offences and
those less serious offences in which justices of the peace have
a summary jurisdiction.   They mark sufficiently at least for
practical purposes the subdivisions of one class of breaches
of duty.   But as between the classes of these breaches there
is a further difference.   They differ not only in degree and in

procedure, but also in the character of the duties which are broken and in the sanctions for such breach.

The governing principle is, as we might expect, the nature of the duties. If the duty broken be absolute, the consequence is a punishable offence. If it be particular, the consequence is a breach of contract or other obligation. If it be general, the consequence is a tort or both a punishable offence and a tort. In all these cases the sanction is different, the person who sets in motion the law is different, and the procedure is different. The breach of an absolute duty is followed by punishment; the penalty is enforced by the Crown, and the complaint is determined by those tribunals and those modes of procedure which we call criminal. The breach of a particular duty is now followed by compensation or other appropriate remedy. The person who sets the law in motion is the donee of the right. The case is heard and determined in the manner and by the courts which, in contradistinction from those that are called criminal, are called civil. The breach of a general duty is pursued in both or either of the above methods. If it be pursued in the same manner in which it would be pursued if the duty broken were absolute, the case is regarded as a punishable offence. If it be pursued in the same manner in which it would have been pursued if the duty broken were particular, the case is regarded as a tort. Whether it be pursued exclusively in the one way or in the other depends upon the terms of the law by which the duty is created. But, as general duties imply two parties interested in their performance, namely, the commander, that is the State, and the donee of the right, the breach of such a duty affects both of these parties; and thus the same offence may be treated both as a wrong to the State which deserves punishment and as a tort by which special damage is caused to a particular person. Thus, defrauding the public revenue is a punishable offence. In some of its forms it is punished by fine and forfeiture inflicted either by the Commissioner of Customs or before justices. In other cases it is an indictable offence, and is punishable on conviction before the Supreme Court by imprisonment for a long term with or without hard labour. Disorderly conduct in the streets is a punishable offence—not a very heinous one, it is true, but still such an offence. One man agrees to buy property from another man, and then refuses to perform his part of the agreement. That person has broken his contract, and is liable at the suit of the other party to damages or to a decree for specific performance, according to the circumstances of the case. Two men have a dispute as to the ownership of goods, and one of them takes or retains property which really belongs to the other. Such an act does not amount to a crime ; but the person who has done so is guilty of a tort, and is liable to damages. A man fraudulently and without colour of right takes property which he knows to belong to another. He is guilty of the crime of theft, and will be sent to prison probably with hard labour. But this offender has also by his wrongful act caused damage to the owner of the property; and for this tort he is, in addition to his punishment, liable to make to that owner compensation.

The Incl-dents of a Right. § 5. There is a distinction between absolute and relative duties that is of primary practical importance. As the generality and consequent simplicity of absolute duties render them the typical examples of law, so the greater complexity of relative duties and the additional legal relation that they imply give to them the largest share and the most conspicuous position in every legal system. Absolute duties, and, so far as they result in punishable offences, relative duties, are limited to the actual person upon whom the duty is imposed. The design of the law is to regulate conduct ; and since a man's conduct is limited by his life, the rules which are meant for its regulation have no place after his death. No liability therefore for any punishable offence descends under any modern legal system to the legal representatives, whether real or personal, of the offender. For the like reasons, no person can transfer a duty which from its nature is personal and to which the transferee is already himself liable. But the case is otherwise with rights. When the person who is to perform a relative duty is ascertained, there is no reason why the claim of the donee of the right should not be transferred, or should not devolve upon his representatives after his death, or should not during his life be dealt with as a security for the performance of his obligations. These incidents of rights have always been acknowledged ; and thus there has arisen an immense body of law which is distinct from the law concerning duties. The principle applies to all classes of rights, whether they are *in rem* or *in personam*, that is whether they avail against the world or against some specific individual, or, in other words, whether they relate to a general or to a particular duty.

The difference which I have thus described arises from the very terms of the command. The typical form of such a command might be expressed in some such words as the following :—"No person shall do such and such an act, or observe such and such a forbearance : and this duty shall be deemed to be imposed for the advantage of such and such a person, or of one of such and such a class of persons, his heirs executors administrators and assigns." The first clause creates the duty; the second clause constitutes the right ; the addition to the second clause of the words of succession and of transfer mark the extent of that right. These words provide, in certain contingencies, new donees of the right. If such a command contained the first clause and no more, the duty would be absolute. If it stopped at the name of the donee of the right, it would create a right, but a right which was personal and intransferable. Thus rights are restricted to the original donee, or they are not so restricted. Of the latter class the rights of ownership are the most prominent example.

The former class may be illustrated by the right of an officer to the enjoyment of his office. The rights thus given require regulation ; and these regulations form the largest and most intricate portion of law. They relate to ownership and its varieties ; to obligations, in which, under modern law, rights and duties are so intertwined that they cannot be conveniently separated ; to the transfer of rights, whether it be absolute as by way of sale, or conditional as by way of security ; and to their devolution after death.

The difference between these restricted and unrestricted rights is expressed in the maxim usually cited as " *Actio personalis moritur cum persona.*" As the definition of a personal action can hardly be other than an action whose existence is extinguished with the existence of the plaintiff, Austin,[*] although his language is characteristically emphatic, seems justified in asserting that "this wretched saw is a purely identical proposition." Mr. Poste[†] happily conjectures that the word *personalis* is a mere copyist's mistake for *pœnalis*, a mistake I may add which might easily arise when the abridged form (*p. lis*) was the same for each of the two words. When it is thus amended, the maxim is no truism, but states a very important doctrine, although not the doctrine which in its ordinary form it is cited to support. It in effect declares that where a breach of duty involves "*pœna*," or punishment, as its consequence, such duty is deemed to be limited to the original person upon whom it was imposed ; and therefore that the consequences of such breach cannot upon that person's death be transmitted to his legal representatives.

There is another incident of right which deserves attention. In every country the law attaches as a condition to its assistance in enforcing rights the requirement that that assistance shall be sought with reasonable despatch. It is a matter of public policy that controversies shall not be indefinitely prolonged. It is not conducive to the successful administration of justice that State demands should be made when the circumstances out of which they arose have been

* II. 1013.   † Gaius, 493.

forgotten, and when the necessary evidence is no longer available. New interests too are in constant growth, and present continually increasing obstacles to the free treatment of disputes that are but a few years unsettled. The length of time which may be reasonably regarded as a bar to litigation varies in different countries, and with respect to different transactions in the same country. The principal difference consists in claims relating to immovable and to movable property respectively. In early Rome the periods were two years and one year. In England, where the term of prescription for real property has recently been reduced, the same proportion is now adopted, and the periods are twelve years and six years. A claim upon a deed may be enforced at any time within twenty years. Special periods are in some cases fixed by exceptional legislation. But the general rule is that no action can be brought after six years.

It must, however, be observed that this rule of limitation applies only to rights and not to duties. Lapse of time forms no excuse for punishable offences. In some cases, indeed, where the offence is not of a serious nature, certain limits within which legal proceedings must be taken are specially provided. Thus, proceedings for offences against the laws relating to Sunday observance must be taken within ten days, and proceedings for offences relating to the licensing of theatres must be taken within three months, from the date of their occurrence. The jurisdiction of justices is limited to twelve months; but that limitation affects only the competency of the particular court, and not the liability of the offender. Practically, however, it operates as a limitation to those minor offences. But, except in such cases, lapse of time forms no excuse for the breach of absolute and of general duties. Probably this is the true version of, at least in its modern sense, the maxim " *nullum tempus occurrit regi.*" An express statute now deals with the proprietary rights of the Crown. But in criminal cases time is no bar.

L

Governor Wall, to mention but one well-known instance, was hanged for murder eighteen years after the event for which he suffered. So, too, and for the like reason, the Statute of Limitations does not apply to breaches of express trusts. If in such cases the lapse of time were to afford protection, a right would not be secured, but a fraud would be rewarded. The State may impose what terms it thinks fit for the exercise of its powers to enforce obligations. But it never encourages the successful efforts of undetected wrong. Justice is often slow of foot, although she seldom fails ultimately to overtake the criminal that seems so far before her.

The Collision of Rights. § 6. Sometimes there occurs a real or apparent conflict of rights. The rights which the State guarantees in one case may be or may seem inconsistent with the rights which it guarantees in another case. Not unfrequently the inconsistency is merely superficial, and disappears when the true extent of the rights guaranteed is understood. The State does not undertake to insure people against loss ; but provides that they shall enjoy their rights, whatever these rights may be worth. Thus *damnum sine injuria* is a well-known legal phenomenon. One man has a flourishing business ; another man sets up a similar business beside him, and attracts all his customers. The first man sustains much harm, but no wrong. He may exercise his own right, but that right does not include any duty upon his neighbour to forbear from exercising his corresponding right. Similar though often more difficult applications of the same principle occur in regard to the management and use of property. A man may build his house as high, consistently with the public safety, as he likes, and may make in it whatever windows he thinks fit. His neighbour may build a wall higher than the house, and may thereby block all the householder's lights. Each may seriously inconvenience the other, and each may use his right for his own protection. But, in the absence of any duty upon the one party not to overlook his neighbour's ground, or upon the other party not to obstruct his neighbour's light, the mere circumstance that the exercise of an admitted right causes inconvenience or even loss to another does not afford sufficient grounds for the interference of the law. So, too, the unauthorized pollution of a clear stream is to the riparian proprietor below both injury and damage. The pollution of a stream* already made foul and useless is injury without damage. The pollution of a clear stream by a person who is lawfully entitled to pollute it is damage indeed, but is not injury, since it involves no ground for legal complaint. In like manner one man may own the surface of a field, and another may own the minerals beneath that surface. In the absence of any agreement or of any right of entry or of working, neither of the two can win the minerals. The one cannot reach them; the other may not touch them. The owner of the surface cannot meddle with property that is not his. The owner of the minerals cannot trespass upon another's land. Sooner or later their common needs usually bring them to terms, and the law leaves them to make their own arrangements. Again, while land remains in its natural condition, its owner may use it in any reasonable way. If by reason of such use his neighbour sustain any damage, the landowner is not responsible for it. But if he bring upon the land anything whatever that was not naturally there, and if damage thence ensue, he is liable for the consequences of his act. Thus,† when from natural causes water accumulated in a mine, and drained thence into another mine at a lower level, the owner of the mine on the rise was held to be blameless. But when, in similar circumstances, the water was not accumulated naturally, but was pumped up to the higher level, although that operation took place for the better working of the mine, and in the ordinary course of proper

* *Per* Fry J., 5 Ch. Div. 772.
† Smith *v.* Kenrick, 7 C. B. 515. Baird *v.* Williamson, 15 C. B. N. S. 376. Rylands *v.* Fletcher, L. R. 3 H. L. at 341, *per* Lord Cranworth.

mining, the owner of the mine on the rise had to pay damage for the loss occasioned by the overflow. In all such cases the test is whether there has or has not been a breach of a duty. The question is not whether a man may do some act, but whether he is bound so to do it as to avoid certain consequences.

It sometimes happens that two rights clash ; that one is practically the stronger of the two ; that this difference of strength is recognised by the parties, and that the weaker of the two accepts the inevitable. A result is thus produced which is often called privilege, but which is not so much a matter of law as a matter of prudence. Thus it is the right of the subject of a neutral nation, notwithstanding the war, to continue his trade with the belligerents or either of them. It is also the right, so far as a right may be said to exist in international law, of either belligerent to prevent any goods that are likely to benefit his enemy in his military operations from coming into that enemy's possession. Accordingly, when any such goods have a hostile destination, the other belligerent may, without risk of offending the neutral's sovereign, seize and confiscate them, although they belong to a neutral. But the sale and carriage of such goods are not unlawful either by the municipal law of the neutral or even by the so-called Law of Nations. As to the former point there is no room for doubt. As to the latter, it must be observed that the power of seizure for contraband of war goes only to the goods, and not to the ship; and also that it ceases to exist when the goods have reached the hands of the purchaser. The right of the belligerent is merely to stop the goods, not to punish otherwise than by their loss the carrier. There is no duty upon the neutral to forbear from selling or from carrying these or any other goods. But he does so at his peril ; that is he knows that the other belligerent, in the exercise of his right, may seize the goods, which the neutral, in the exercise of his right, may carry or may sell to his enemy.

The same principle explains a well-known rule in constitutional law. The House of Commons may make grants to the Crown ; the House of Lords may, if it think fit, reject or alter these grants. But the House of Commons insists that its grants shall not be altered, and the House of Lords habitually abstains from altering them. Such forbearance the House of Commons calls a privilege. But it is really a matter of discretion, and not of right. There is no legal duty on the House of Lords such as that which exists in Victoria to forbear from altering every word in every Appropriation Bill that comes before it. Nor does the fact that that House invariably coincides in opinion with the House of Commons on such matters give to the latter House any prescriptive right. The Crown has never rejected an Appropriation Bill ; but no one supposes that its legal right to do so is barred. There is no pretence of adverse enjoyment. Thus the so-called privilege is simply the resultant of two conflicting forces.

CHAPTER IX.

RIGHTS *IN REM* OTHER THAN THOSE OF OWNERSHIP.

Division of Rights.
§ 1. We have seen that relative duties are either general or particular, that is that they apply either to all persons indefinitely or to some definite or ascertainable individual. The rights which these duties generate follow naturally the same principle. Rights, therefore, avail either against all persons indefinitely or against some specified person. When the compass of a right is indefinite, when, as the phrase is, it avails against the world, it is called a right *in rem*. When its compass is limited to a particular person, it is called a right *in personam*. The meaning of the latter expression is apparent in its unabridged form—a right *in personam certam*. The meaning of the phrase *in rem* is less obvious. The Roman jurists do not mention by name either of these classes of rights, but they applied this principle of division to actions. In an *actio in rem*, the original form of procedure was a wager between the parties that the thing in dispute was the property of the plaintiff; and the *formula* or order of reference, as we should call it, did not specify any contrary claim by any specified claimant. In an *actio in personam*, the allegation was that the defendant named in the proceedings was under some duty to the plaintiff. Hence the phrases readily acquired the respective meanings of "in general" and "in particular"; and the Civilians applied them in this sense to rights. That is, *jus in rem* meant a right which ought to be enforced by an *actio in rem;* and, in like manner, *jus in personam* meant a right for the enforcement of which an *actio in personam* was the appropriate remedy. In the absence of any recognised English equivalent it is convenient to accept these phrases as terms of art; and to use them as such in the sense already indicated, without

any attempt at a translation, which can hardly fail to be misleading.

Although the classical jurists do not use the expressions "*jus in rem*" and "*jus in personam,*" the ideas which these phrases denote pervade the Roman law. "*Jus in personam*" is, of course, "*obligatio.*" "*Jus in rem*" seems to have been expressed by the word "*jus*" alone. Such, at least, is the meaning of the word in such passages as* "*placet enim ejus rei judicem jus facere,*" "*jus facit hæc pronuntiatio.*" It is noteworthy that the Romans do not seem to have distinguished by separate names the duty and the right. Both "*jus*" and "*obligatio*" express equally these two ideas. "*Jus*" with them meant law (*In omni jure: omne jus quo utimur*); that is, both the right and the duty. "*Obligatio*" included both parties, as well him who received as him who performed. By some strange chance the meanings of these two words have, in our language, undergone a curious transformation. We habitually translate "*jus*" by right without the corresponding notion of duty. But obligation always means with us a duty to the entire exclusion of the right.

These rights *in rem* and *in personam* have nothing in common with the division of property into real and personal. Real property means land and freehold interests in or arising out of land. In other words, it denotes both the object and the extent of ownership. Property is real which relates to land and to an indefinite quantity of interest in that land. Property is personal when it does not relate to land, or when, if it do so relate, it relates to a quantity of interest below the standard. Hence the well-known distinction between Chattels Real, that is interests in land less than freehold, and Chattels Personal. The word personal is also used in law with another meaning. When it is applied not to property but to persons, it means that a duty is imposed upon, or that a right is given to, some person for reasons peculiar to himself, and is consequently not capable of transfer or of devolution. I shall again have occasion to notice these two

* Dig. XXV. 3, 3; XXX. 1.

kinds of property. At present I only desire to observe that the resemblance between their names and the names of the rights which we are considering is merely accidental.

Division of Rights in rem. Rights *in rem* may be arranged according to the objects of the commands from which they spring. These objects may be both primary and secondary, or primary only. In every command the act or the forbearance which is its object may have reference to some thing or to some person, whether he be or be not the donee of the right, or to some right. It may, on the other hand, have no such reference, in which case it does not imply any secondary object. There are thus four leading divisions of rights *in rem*, namely, rights concerning things, rights concerning persons, rights concerning other rights, and rights to mere acts and forbearances. To the first class belong rights of ownership. The other three classes may, for the present, be grouped together under the title of rights other than those of ownership. The following are examples of them. The right against assault is a right where the secondary object is a person, and is also the donee of the right. The right against any infringement of marital or parental authority is a right where the secondary object is a person, but is not the donee of the right. A right of way is a right in which the secondary object is a right *in rem*. A right to the undisturbed benefit from a contract is a right in which the secondary object is a right *in personam*. The right to the support of land or buildings by adjacent land or buildings is a right where there is no secondary object. These rights *in rem* other than those of ownership will occupy our attention in the present chapter. The rights of ownership demand separate consideration.

Rights where Secondary Object is a Person. § 2. Rights *in rem* concerning persons include all those rights relating to the body of the donee of the right, or to his feelings, or to his family and his home, or to the benefits that he expects to derive from his contracts. It is needless here to examine these rights in detail. They are involved in the duties with which they are connected, and a statement of these duties sufficiently explains the corresponding rights. The right of a man to his reputation is nothing more than the general duty of all other men to forbear from defaming him. The right of a man to his liberty is in effect only another form of stating that all other men are under a general duty to forbear from detaining him. All that it is now material to say of these rights is that where any person sustains any loss by any breach of a general duty, he may recover compensation from the offender without regard to any punishment which that offender may in addition to the payment of the compensation have to undergo. The rights respecting the Home are usually regarded as belonging to property. The violations of them are both in the existing statutes and in the proposed English Criminal Code placed under the head of Larceny. They are, however, of a different class. They are the modern form of the old law of the Precinct, itself the continuation of a principle* which meets us everywhere in the archaic customs of our race. For this aspect of this class of rights there is express judicial authority. Speaking of an action for a trespass in a dwelling-house, Lord Denman, C. J.,† says :—" Rights of action of this sort are given in respect of the immediate and present violation of the possession of the plaintiff, independently of his rights of property : they are an extension of that protection which the law throws around the person ; and substantial damages may be recovered in respect of such rights, though no loss or diminution in the value of the property may have occurred."

These rights usually correspond to negative duties; that is, the duty to which they relate is a duty of forbearance. Cases, however, occur where this duty appears in a positive form. The law sometimes provides that, for the benefit of a particular class, some act shall be done. If this duty be neglected, any person of the protected class who

---

* See "The Aryan Household," 222.   * Rogers r. Spence, 13 M. & W. 6SL

sustains injury from the neglect will have a right of action.
Thus, when an Act of Parliament directed that the master of
a ship should carry certain medicines for the use of his crew,
and the captain of a particular ship failed to do so, a sailor who
was ill and suffered from the captain's neglect was held to
be entitled to recover damages. Such cases, however, are
rare; for the law, as we have already seen, never gives such a '
direction except in the case of persons who, like the sailor,
are, from the nature of their position, dependent upon the
commandee, and are unable to provide for themselves.
Where, however, an absolute duty is imposed, that is where
the object of the duty is to effect some public purpose, and
not to benefit a particular class, no such right arises. Cases
of this kind, therefore, are really questions of construction,
and depend upon the true meaning of the particular statute.

Although the right depends upon the terms of the duty,
and it is with the former rather than with the latter that
this chapter is directly concerned, the present place is convenient for some observations upon the extent in certain
cases of the duty, and consequently, even though less obviously, of the right. Thus it is strictly true that a man has a
right not to be murdered. In the early history of our law
murder sounded in damages. The appeal of murder, as it
was called, was an action brought against the murderer by
the next of kin of the murdered man; and was a different proceeding and had a different object from that for the breach
of the King's peace. But to ascertain the limits of such a
right the exact extent of the duty must first be determined.
The term murder is ordinarily used to express several distinct
offences. Cases frequently arose which obviously deserved
punishment, but which were not within the then accepted
definition of the offence. It was not easy to change the
terms of the rule. It was not safe to venture upon a precise
written definition, lest cases might be excluded which were
not foreseen or not sufficiently expressed. The operation of
change also was necessarily slow. In these circumstances,

not merely did the immediate offender often escape punishment, but the law was left in an imperfect condition for an
indefinite time. It is not then a matter for surprise that in
this case, as in many other cases, the judges sought to amend
the law by straining it. They introduced remedies which the
Romans would have described by the prefix "*quasi*," and
which our lawyers called "constructive." The proper form
of amendment would have been an accurate statement of the
duties in question. But such a statement could not at
that time be obtained. The courts therefore relied upon
what has been called the "elasticity" of the common law,
and included under the old name a variety of separate
offences. Thus murder comprises at least nineteen cases of
homicide where there is neither justification nor excuse.
The precise definition of all offences depends upon the definition of the duties of which they respectively imply the breach.
The rights of third parties also follow the duties. These are
questions which in their details belong to practical lawyers,
and hardly fall within the scope of a treatise like the present.
It is not my purpose to define each duty or each right to
which such duty gives rise. It is enough to call attention to
the fact that such definitions do in fact exist, and that in a
well-ordered statement of the law they must find their place.

§ 3. Where a man has a right to any enjoyment, the law guarantees to him the free exercise
of that enjoyment, and prevents, at his request,
all other persons from interrupting such exercise. This
right includes not only enjoyments of the person or of the
family on the one hand, and of ownership on the other hand,
but all other enjoyments and expectations of which the law
takes notice. In this last class of cases the subject-matter
or secondary object of the right is another right. The class
comprises all "*res incorporales*" except such as immediately
arise out of ownership. Its principal divisions are privileges,
offices, and franchises. In each of these divisions the donee

Rights where Secondary Object is a Right in rem.

of the right has a right *in rem* to the undisturbed exercise
of his privilege or of his office or of his franchise, as the
case may be. Such a right does not consist in his power
of acting. That power he already possesses as a physical
fact before the interposition of the law. But his right arises
from the duty of forbearance imposed in his favour upon all
other persons, and consists in the interference of the State,
upon his complaint, to enforce that duty. It is similar to
the rights which protect his personal security or the enjoyment of his property. The objects only to which these rights
severally refer are different.

Privileges.   By the term "privileges" I mean those commands
which consist in a general prohibition of some act except in the
case of a favoured person or class of persons, or in an exclusive permission to such a person or class to do some act that
would otherwise be unlawful. The positive class, to which
the name privilege is usually restricted, includes the various
kinds of copyright, patents for inventions, offices, franchises, and trade marks. When the privilege assumes a
negative form, it is called an exemption or an immunity.
Examples of the negative class are exemption from service
on a jury, or from liability to arrest, or to judicial proceedings,
or to execution upon judgments. Both forms of privilege are
sometimes combined, as in the well-known formula which
gives to Colonial Legislatures "powers, privileges, and immunities" not exceeding those held and enjoyed by the Commons House of Parliament. The word privilege, or rather the
expression Privilege of Parliament, is also used to express
the whole body of Parliamentary law. In earlier times, the
word in this sense was equivalent to Prerogative, and then the
records speak indifferently of the Privilege of the Crown and
of the Prerogative of Parliament. These privileges resemble
ownership, because they imply a right *in rem*—a general
duty of forbearance in respect of their subject-matter, and a
corresponding right in the donee thereof which avails against
the world. They differ from ownership, because the

secondary object of ownership is a thing ; but a privilege has no special secondary object, and involves only a general for-bearance. In the case of privileges, the double form of the proposition in which a right is asserted comes conspicuously into view. The privileged person may do the specified act ; no other person may do that act. The right, indeed, is in most cases not expressly granted, because the liberty to act usually remains with the privileged party as it was before the supposed legislation. But the practical effect is that he alone retains that liberty, and that all other persons are placed in respect thereof under a negative duty. Certain conditions must, indeed, be fulfilled before these rights are established ; but these are in effect investitive facts, and concern the manner of the creation of the right, and not its compass when it has been created.

Offices. Offices differ from mere employments. The latter are matters of obligation only, and give rise to duties and rights *in personam.* But offices imply duties not only *in personam* but also *in rem.* Where any person has been duly appointed to an office, he has a right in his office similar to that of an owner in his property. No person may take another's office, or may disturb him in its exercise, or without lawful authority deprive him thereof. There may also be estates in an office analogous to those ordinarily granted in respect of property. Offices may be hereditary, as the offices of Champion and of Earl Marshal are in England at the present day. They may be held for life as bishops hold, or during good behaviour as judges and some other officials. They may be held for a term of years, as the President of the United States and as members of Parliament hold. Or they may be held during pleasure, which is the tenure of the great majority of Her Majesty's servants in her various services. The characteristic features of such offices are that their creation must be by the Crown, whether by Prerogative or by Act of Parliament; that they must be substantive and not merely temporary ; and that their functions must affect the public, or at least a large number of the public. If these conditions be fulfilled, the employment, whoever the employer may be, will be an office; if they be not fulfilled, it will be only an obligation. The rank, the emolument, and the patron are immaterial. The bellman and the hog-ringer of a parish have been held* to be public officers. A parish clerk or a sexton is as much an officer as an arch-bishop. The rights of the manager of the Barings or of the Rothschilds depend upon the terms of his contract, in the same manner as the rights of a carpenter or of a plumber. At the present day the difference between offices and property is well marked. Offices now have the character of personal trusts. They are never granted beyond the life of the grantee, and rarely, at least in civil offices, beyond his good behaviour. They cannot be assigned. Even the right of nomination is not now saleable, except, by a strange and we may hope temporary anomaly, in the case of ecclesiastical advowsons.

Franchises. Somewhat akin to offices are those rights that are commonly called franchises. These are the liberties and free customs of Magna Charta and of our other early records. A franchise has been defined to be a part of the Royal Prero-gative in the hands of a subject, a definition that I suppose implies the grant by the Crown of certain rights *in rem* which the law recognises. One class of examples is dig-nities. The peerage is a franchise. So is knighthood. So are academic degrees. The right of voting for members of Parliament has taken almost exclusive possession of the name franchise. But the word denotes a number of miscellaneous rights which seem to agree in the following points:— they are rights *in rem;* they are of a public character; and they are usually, if not invariably, restricted to particular persons or classes. Most of the old franchises have become obsolete. No person now seeks a grant of free fishing or of free warren or of a fair or of a market. But a grant by the Parliament † of Victoria to Henry Hopwood of the right to levy certain tolls on a bridge over the Campaspe is a

---

* Rex *v.* St. Nicholas, 10 B. & C. 852.   Rex *v.* Whittlesea, 4 T. R. 807.   † Act No. 30.

franchise; and the statute remains, although the property in the bridge has passed to the public.

Certain industrial rights of this description have recently obtained recognition. These are trade marks, trade names, and goodwill. A trade mark has been described* as an intangible object of ownership ; that is, according to the nomenclature which I have used, it is a right *in rem* other than that of ownership. It is the exclusive right which the manufacturer or the vendor of any commodity acquires to place upon his goods or upon the vessels or packages which contain them some individualizing mark. Such a mark implies as against him a warranty that the goods have been really manufactured or sold by him, and that they are of the quality that he usually manufactures and sells under this description. The illicit use of a trade mark is not only a fraud upon the public, but is a wrong to the true maker or vendor. By a false representation it deprives him *pro tanto* of his market and of the fair results of the reputation which he has earned. An extension of the principles of the trade mark is the trade name. As the one relates to the actual products of an industry, so the other relates to the name under which the industry is carried on. A man may call himself by any name, real or imaginary, that he thinks fit. For trade purposes, although not for any other purposes, the law will recognise an exclusive right to such a name. When, therefore, a man leaves any business, he may sell to another person permission to use the style or title under which that business was previously conducted. In such a case the law will prevent either him or any stranger from using, in circumstances likely to produce deception, either that or any similar style for the conduct of that business.

The trade mark and the trade name have been thus recognised because experience proves that they respectively command a considerable money value. The like reason applies to the case of goodwill. These three rights usually go together. A man who takes the business of another

---

* Prof. Holland's Jurisprudence, 154.

naturally takes the right of using the old name and the old brand. They do not require in this place any lengthened notice. The rights are generally determined by express stipulation. It now suffices to say that, upon the occurrence of the proper investitive facts, there arises against all the world a duty to forbear from using the trade name or the trade mark so acquired, or from interfering otherwise than' by free competition with the goodwill of the business. The rights thus established are assignable and descendible; they may be transferred by the donee during his life, and upon his death they pass to his legal representatives.

§ 4. Where the secondary object of a command is a right *in personam*, a right *in rem* in certain cases arises. I do not now refer to those cases where a contract produces a status, such as that of marriage; or where it operates as a conveyance, as in the sale of chattels; or where it creates new interests in the property by transferring some of the singular rights of ownership, as in bailments or in the tenancy of land. But where a man enters into an obligation, or contemplates such an act, he thereby brings into operation even as regards strangers a command of the State. In other words, the liberty of making a contract and of enjoying the advantages thence resulting is a subject which the law notices, and in respect of which it imposes a general duty and consequently grants a corresponding right. Therefore, although it is true that the terms of the obligation are effectual between the parties to it and none others, it is also true that. the creation of such obligations and the performance of them impose duties of forbearance upon strangers to the contract. Such strangers are not interested in the actual obligation, but they are required not to interfere with the capacity of making it or with its results.

There are, I think, five general duties that come under this class, and of course five rights *in rem* which each man in

Where the Secondary Object is a Right in personam.

respect thereof enjoys. In the first place, every man may enter into any lawful agreement that he thinks fit, and no other person may molest or obstruct him in the exercise of this right. Hence any attempt to prevent one man from undertaking to work for another or to render him any service, or any molestation of the workman while so working or on account of such work, is illegal. It follows that any agreement or incitement to commit any such illegal act is also an offence. Secondly, a man is entitled to the possession of all the evidences of his contract. This right would, indeed, ordinarily apply to him merely as being the owner of the property or other material on which the instruments were written. But it is idle to refuse to recognise any difference between a Bank of England note for £1,000 and the inappreciable scrap of flimsy paper on which it is printed. It seems to be more truthful and more convenient to place in a separate class all valuable securities, whether title deeds or negotiable instruments or documents of title, and to make suitable provision for their protection. This result is practically attained by providing that for the purposes of the criminal law valuable securities shall be deemed to be movable property. But they are not really property, and to call them so is only to revive the old confusion between *"res corporales"* and *"res incorporales."* The paper on which they are written is indeed property, although its value is proverbially infinitesimal. But that which the paper evidences is not a right *in rem* but a right *in personam.* The common law therefore rightly held that choses in action were not subjects of larceny, although it erred in not giving them the necessary protection. That object is attained by imposing for the theft of the documents a commensurate penalty. In the third place, there exists a general duty to forbear, not merely from any interference with the liberty of entering into an obligation, but also from any interference with the liberty of declining to do any such act. If one man by force or threats compel another person against his will to

M

execute an instrument which creates as against him a legal obligation, the person who so acts is justly punishable for his conduct, without regard to the validity or the invalidity of the instrument thus improperly obtained. The like result follows in our fourth instance, that is in cases where there has not been any compulsion, but where the consent of the person who executes the instrument has been obtained by fraud. This case is usually classed with obtaining money under false pretences, while the former class appears to be associated with robbery or similar offences. But both of them seem to be varieties of the same offence, namely, the inducing a person against or without his free consent to incur the burthen of an obligation. The last of these cases is the right to derive the full benefit that results from any obligation to which the donee of the right is a party, and the corresponding duty to forbear from obstructing or intercepting any such benefit. That is, where there is a contract between two parties, a third party may not for his own advantage induce one of them to break his agreement. This principle seems to have been long accepted as regards servants, in whose case it was derived immediately from the Statute of Labourers, but was probably a survival of far older memories. It was not, however, until 1853 that its wider application was recognised. Two theatrical managers* in London quarrelled about a *prima donna*. The great songstress had made an engagement with one of them. His rival induced her to break her engagement and to join his company. The injured manager sued his too successful competitor, and recovered damages. But the case seems to have been regarded with much doubt † in the profession, although, as I have always thought, upon insufficient grounds. After more than a quarter of a century, the question was again‡ raised, and the authority of the former case has been maintained. It is now settled that no person, with intent to injure another or to make profit at his expense, may knowingly procure a person under any contract to that other to break his engagement.

---

* Lumley *v.* Gye, 2 E. & B. 216.   † See Sir W. R. Anson on Contract, 108.
‡ Bowen *v.* Hall, 6 Q. B. D. 333.

Rights in
rem where
there is no
Secondary
Object.
§ 5. Rights *in rem* also arise where there is no secondary object. In such cases the law, as we have seen, imposes upon the commandee the simple duty of forbearance. He is to refrain from certain acts, without regard to any person or to any thing or to any right. Were it not that there is a party who has an interest in enforcing the command, the duty might seem to be absolute. Such a party, however, does exist, and the prescribed forbearance amounts to a general duty in his favour. Of these rights there are two classes, those relating to duties of veracity and those relating to duties of diligence. There is nothing in the rights to veracity, as distinguished from the duties of veracity, that requires special attention. The description of the one is in fact the description of the other. The case of diligence, however, is somewhat different. In this case the duties practically consist of a restriction upon preceding rights *in rem*. As a general rule, a man may use and manage his own property as he likes. He is also the sole judge of his own business and of his own conduct. But these wide statements need considerable limitation. They all are subject to the maxim that directs a man so to use what is his own as not to injure what is his neighbour's. Austin* indeed speaks with contempt of this maxim ; but although in its general form it is insufficient for guidance, it marks the nature of the limitation imposed upon the general right. This limitation, when it is regarded from another stand-point, gives the accurate description of the duty. I propose therefore briefly to notice the leading qualifications of this class of rights, or, in other words, the nature of the duty of circumspection, or, to use a name more familiar to legal readers, of Diligence.

When it is said that a man may do what he pleases with his own land, the expression needs some explanation. The word " land " must be taken to mean land in its natural condition, with all its natural incidents and advantages as nature produces them.† With that land in that condition

---

* II. 823. † See Bryant r. Lefever, 4 C. P. D. 172.

the owner may deal as he thinks fit, but not without a further restriction. He may do with it any act that is necessary to its common and ordinary use according to its circumstances and its situation. He may not, for example, make bricks* so near another man's dwelling as to amount to a nuisance, even though the land be well suited for the purpose, and though the operation be carefully and skilfully performed. Further, in exercising his right, he must take reasonable care to prevent discomfort to others in respect of time, place, manner, or degree. Although the law does not favour the "*vota delicatorum*," it is careful to secure for every person exemption from undoubted nuisances. No business therefore may be pursued which there and then interferes with the enjoyment by any other person of the ordinary and reasonable comforts of human existence. If, however, a man alter the condition of his land, if he erect buildings upon it, or if he bring upon it any animal or any. thing that was not naturally there, he does so at his peril. That is, as I have before explained, he may lawfully do so ; but if any damage thence result, he is responsible. If a man excavate his land, he must so conduct his operations as to leave a sufficient support to the adjacent land in its natural state ; but although he is bound to support his neighbour's land, he is not bound to support his neighbour's buildings. He may keep his premises in any state that he pleases, but he is subject first to the provisions of the law relating to the public health and to the public safety, and next to the condition that he is not to maintain a dangerous trap for his visitors. He may employ any servants or labourers that he likes, but he is responsible for any damage done by them in the course of their employment. He may have in his possession any animal that he knows or has reason to believe to be dangerous ; but he must keep it safely, and if it escape and cause damage, he must bear the loss. In other words, we must use our property in its altered condition, and we must carry on our business, and we must regulate

* See Bamford *v.* Turnley, 31 L. J. Q. B. 286.

our conduct, when such use or business or conduct is naturally dangerous or offensive, with such diligence that nothing short of some physical catastrophe or some suspension of law can excuse any resulting damage. On this subject the courts speak with marked emphasis. " The person, said the Court* of Exchequer Chamber, whose grass or corn is eaten down by the escaping cattle of his neighbour, or whose mine is flooded by the water from his neighbour's reservoir, or whose cellar is invaded by the filth of his neighbour's privy, or whose habitation is made unhealthy by the fumes and noisome vapours of his neighbour's alkali works, is damnified without any fault of his own ; and it seems but reasonable and just that the neighbour who has brought something on his own property which was not naturally there, harmless to others so long as it is confined to his own property, but which he knows to be mischievous if it gets on his neighbour's, should be obliged to make good the damage which ensues if he does not succeed in confining it to his own property. But for his act in bringing it there no mischief could have accrued, and it seems but just that he should at his peril keep it there so that no mischief may accrue, or answer for the natural and anticipated consequences. And upon authority this, we think, is established to be the law, whether the things so brought be beasts or water or filth or stenches."

Where, however, the proceeding in question is not in itself dangerous, but is likely to become dangerous if proper care be not used, the duty of the person by whom or under whose direction that proceeding takes place is less extensive. In these circumstances, he must, in the event of a casualty, show that reasonable care has actually been taken ; and if he can establish this fact, he is exonerated from all liability. The burthen of proof, indeed, rests with him. A misfortune has happened from his conduct or that of his servants, and he is therefore required to give a satisfactory explanation of the event. It is not enough for the purposes of such an

* Fletcher r. Rylands, L. R. 1 Ex. at p. 280.

explanation to prove mere personal diligence. The only ground of excuse is that reasonable care has been taken in the matter. In the absence of such care, the law does not stop to apportion the blame among the parties concerned. It is the duty of the owner or employer or other principal person that such care should be taken; and if from any cause or by any person it be not taken, he is liable. In other cases, as we have already seen, the responsibility is still slighter. Where the proceeding is not dangerous either absolutely or upon certain contingencies, a man is only liable for a misfortune when it can be positively proved that he has shown some want of ordinary care or circumspection. Thus a customs officer,* in the exercise of his duty, was on the premises of the London Dock Company, and, as he was passing under a doorway, some bags of sugar fell upon him from a crane which was fixed over the doorway. It was held that since in the ordinary course of things such an accident does not happen to persons who use proper care, the accident itself afforded, in the absence of explanation by the defendant, evidence of the want of such care. In such a case _res ipsa loquitur._ In other cases, however, the facts are less eloquent. Thus,† a horse strayed. upon a highway where a child was playing. He kicked the child in the face and seriously injured him. An action was brought against the owner of the horse. There was no further evidence, but it was not alleged either that the child was in fault or that the horse was vicious. In these circumstances a verdict for the plaintiff was set aside. It is not enough to prove the casualty. It must further be shown that that casualty was due to some breach of duty by the defendant.

Where the damage done is within the ordinary or probable consequences of the wrongful act or omission, it is not material whether the injury has or has not been caused by the intervention of any third party. Thus a man named Chambers‡ used for athletic sports a field abutting upon a road. The British public were in the habit of climbing on

---

* See Scott _v._ London Dock Company, 34 L. J. Ex. 220.
† Cox _v._ Burbidge, 32 L. J. C. P. 89.   ‡ Clark _v._ Chambers, 3 Q. B. D. 327.

his fence to obtain a gratuitous view of the games. To prevent this annoyance, Chambers, although his doing so was unlawful, put a *chevaux de frise* across the road. Some person, without his knowledge, removed a part of this structure, and placed it upright on the footway. On a dark night, one Clark, without any want of care on his part, while walking along the footway, ran against this obstacle and injured his eye. It was held that for this injury he was entitled to recover damages from Chambers, although if the *chevaux de frise* had been left where Chambers had placed it the accident would not have occurred. Again, a railway company,[*] in a very dry season, employed men to cut the grass and trim the hedges on the sides of their line. The men left the trimmings in heaps near the line for fourteen days. A spark from a passing engine ignited one of the heaps. The wind was high, and the fire spread, and ultimately burned a house at some distance. It was held, though not without differences of opinion between the judges, that these facts disclosed a *primâ facie* case of negligence against the company.

To these rules there are some exceptions. They do not apply to cases of contributory negligence, that is to cases where the damage has been caused by the negligence or other misconduct of the person injured. Nor do they apply where the person injured might by the exercise of ordinary care have avoided the injury. Nor do they apply where the person injured has been guilty of some breach of duty which has occasioned the damage. These defences may, however, be rebutted. They are insufficient when the act causing the damage might have been reasonably expected to produce some mischief. They are insufficient when the person who does the mischief might with ordinary care have avoided it. Nor is it contributory negligence if a person while doing a lawful act voluntarily and not in an unreasonable way expose himself to the danger and incur damage thereby. Nor is it contributory negligence where the wrongful act causes

[*] Smith *v.* London & S. W. Railway Co., L. R. 5 C. P. 98.

such serious inconvenience that the other party may reasonably endeavour to get rid of it, and does so by an act not obviously dangerous and executed without carelessness. If in such circumstances he sustain damage, he may recover compensation notwithstanding his own share in causing the misfortune.

The subject is too large and too much immersed in matter ' to admit of any adequate illustration in these pages. I may, however, cite one or two cases. A gas company laid down a defective pipe, and an escape of gas took place. A gas-fitter was sent for and incautiously approached the place with a lighted candle. An explosion ensued, and considerable damage was done. It was held that, notwithstanding the misconduct of the workman, the company was liable. Its negligence was of a nature likely to cause some damage, and the consequent responsibility was not removed by the intervention of another person. There is another case which in these discussions is often cited. A man hobbled his donkey, and turned him out to graze on the highway. A cart without its driver came at a rapid pace along the road. The poor hobbled donkey could not get out of the way in time, and was run over and killed. His owner brought an action against the owner of the cart. There was no doubt that the donkey ought not to have been turned out to graze on the highway. But it was held that this impropriety did not excuse the want of ordinary care, and that for the consequences of such negligence the owner of the cart must pay; and so the manes of the donkey were appeased.

In the foregoing cases, as compared with other rights *in rem*, the position of the duty and of the right is inverted. In those other cases of rights *in rem* the right is in the specific individual, and the duty avails as against the world. But in the class noticed in the present section the duty avails against the individual, and the right is in all other persons. There is a duty upon the individual owner of land not to use it in a way likely to injure his neighbours, and upon a householder not to permit his house since it is under his control to become a base of hostile operations against the public, and upon the owner of a dangerous animal to keep it in safe custody. All these are duties of forbearance imposed for the benefit of the public upon a specific individual. Only that individual is liable to the duty; but the right to procure the enforcement of the duty is vested in the public indefinitely, or rather in such one of an indefinite number of persons as is ascertained by the event. In the ordinary cases, the duty is of all to some. In the cases which we have now been considering, the duty is of some to all.

CHAPTER X.

THE RIGHTS OF OWNERSHIP.

The Analysis of Ownership. § 1. Many attempts have been made with but little success to define the right of ownership. The cause of this failure is not difficult to trace. There is no such single right. Ownership is merely a collective term denoting the aggregate of several independent rights. It has no meaning other than the sum of its component parts, and it admits of no other definition than an enumeration of these parts. Little difference of opinion exists respecting this enumeration. The rights which collectively constitute ownership are the right to possess, the right to use, the right to the produce, the right to waste, the right of disposition, whether during life or upon death, and the right to exclude all other persons from any interference with the thing owned. In the language of the Civilians, *dominium* includes *jus possidendi*, *jus utendi*, *jus fruendi*, *jus abutendi*, *jus disponendi*, and *jus prohibendi*.

All these rights may, in the case of the same object, either co-exist in the same person or be enjoyed in varying degrees by different persons. In the former case there is full ownership. Subject to the provisions of the general law, the full owner may do what he likes with his property during his life, may bequeath it to whom he pleases on his death, and may effectually exclude all other persons from dealing with it in any way or in any circumstances. If he have less than the full ownership, if he can exercise some but not all the rights that I have mentioned, he has a limited ownership of some kind ; and he may or he may not have the full ownership of his interest, whatever that may be, in the property. But it is not of these differences that I now speak. I propose to describe the nature and the extent of what may be called the singular rights of ownership.

Jus possidendi. Where any person has the established physical control of any property he is said to have the detention of that property. Where any person detains property with the intention of keeping it for the use not of himself but of another, he is said to have the custody of that property. Where, either personally or by a custodian, he detains the property with the intention of keeping it for his own use, he is said to have the possession of that property. Thus a solicitor who keeps his client's papers until his bill of costs is paid has the detention of these papers. A clerk who receives money on account of his employer has the custody of that money. The charterer of a ship has during the term of his charter-party the possession of the ship. So under the old law* the freeholder had possession of his land. The termor for years under him held possession *nomine alieno* in contradistinction to the possession *nomine proprio* of the freeholder : in other words, he had the custody of the land. A bailiff had no possession, but merely the detention. The livery of the termor was a transfer of the possession, but a livery by the bailiff was absolutely without effect.

Detention does not merely mean actual physical prehension. It denotes the power of exclusive access to the object and the power of exercising over it control at pleasure. A man has the detention of a thing when it is in his house or on his land. If goods be left in his house, if a wreck be washed up on his sea frontage, if a bird be shot on his ground, if iron be found at the bottom of his canal, the house master or landlord has the detention of those goods or of that wreck or bird or iron. Such detention must be complete, that is it must not be evidently transitory. Its continuance may of course be precarious, but the physical control must be at least for the time established. The statement of this rule is easier than its application. The amount of control which the law requires is merely matter of degree. The line of establishment may therefore be differently drawn,

* Butler's Note on Co. Lit. 330 b.

according to differences of time or of place or of circumstance. Thus in captures* both in the Roman law and in our Admiralty Courts, the fact of possession at any given time is often important and often doubtful. Many attempts have accordingly been made to find some definite standard. The Roman rule, to which our courts seem inclined to lean, is that the adverse possession is complete where the captive has been brought "*infra præsidia hostium*," into some place of safe keeping whence escape cannot reasonably be expected. Another rule, said to be derived from the hunting customs of the Langobards, takes as its standard twenty-four hours' uninterrupted possession. Similar cases arise in relation to the capture of wild animals. But whatever difficulty its application may involve, the rule itself is clear. The detention must be established. Upon any sufficient indication of the detainor's intention, detention will become possession. There must, however, be reasonable proof of the intention. Most of the difficulties on this subject are really questions of evidence. If property be delivered to a servant for his master, such delivery will amount to possession by the master. If property be found in a man's house, the natural presumption, subject of course to rebutting evidence, is that it is there with his knowledge and his consent. If property be enclosed in other property, and in that state accessible to the person who has the detention of that other property, it is reasonable to suppose that the possession of the two things coincide. But if it can be shown that the house master never suspected the existence of what was in his house, or that the arrangements with the bailee of the enclosing chattel excepted all dealings by him with its contents, there will be no possession either of the house master in the one case or of the bailee in the other. Thus†‡ a roll of bank notes to the value of £55 was dropped in a shop. A person who had business in the shop picked up the roll before the shopkeeper knew that the loss had taken place. The finder delivered the notes to the shopkeeper for

---

restoration to the owner. But after proper advertisements the owner could not be found. At the end of three years the finder claimed the notes, and offered to pay the costs of the advertisements. The shopkeeper insisted that he was entitled to keep what had been found in his shop. It was held that the notes never were in the custody of the shopkeeper, and that they were not within the protection of his house before they were found, as they would have been if they had been intentionally deposited there. Consequently the claim of the first finder prevailed, and was not affected by the circumstance that without any intention to abandon that right he had given the notes to the shopkeeper for a specific purpose which had failed.

The intent in possession may be either indefinite or specific. A person may possess property merely for his own use and without reference to any other person or to any limiting condition. Or he may possess it with the intention to restore or transfer the property upon the occurrence of some particular event. That event may be the payment of a given sum of money, or the discovery of the real owner, or the demand of that owner or other person for whom the property is held, or the expiration of the time, or the fulfilment of the purpose for which the possession was allowed. In the meantime the conditional possessor may defend his right against a stranger as successfully as he could do if his possession were absolute.

The right to the immediate possession of property has always been regarded as a principal right of ownership. In earlier times the two ideas, that of ownership and that of possession, were inseparable. The possessor seemed to be the owner. The owner without possession did not appear to be an owner at all. It was at a late period of social advancement that the two ideas were sundered, and that possession was considered in its separate form. Even still possession remains and must remain as the foundation of the exercise of all the other rights of ownership. The first step which a man must take who desires to use any property or its fruits, or to deal with it at his pleasure, or to exclude others from interfering with it, is to acquire possession of it. The difference indeed between the owner and the possessor is rather personal than relative to third parties. Both of them exercise the same rights. But in the case of the owner these rights avail against the whole world, and do not admit within their legal limits of any dispute. In the case of the possessor they avail against the whole world except one party, and their exercise is subject to that party's claims. Hence possession has always been evidence of ownership—in some cases conclusive evidence, in all cases presumptive. Hence, too, delivery of possession is evidence of a change of ownership, and in earlier times was essential to such a transaction. In the case of land alone the rule is, or rather seems to be, different. The mere possession or occupation of the land itself affords no evidence of ownership. At the most it throws the burthen of proof upon the claimant. The seisin, however, of the freehold, which as we shall presently see is a very different thing, is not less operative than the possession is in the case of a chattel.

Where a person possesses property with the consent of its owner, he may be said to have consensual possession. Where he possesses the property without or against such consent, his possession may be described as adverse. Adverse possession brings with it a peculiar right. In early Roman law this right was called *usucapion*. In our law it is called by a name in itself to us unmeaning, yet having a history—prescription. When a man has been in adverse possession for a certain time, his possession ripens into ownership. Not only are the claims of the original owner barred, but all his rights in the property are effectually transferred to the possessor. But whatever may be the relations between the owner and the possessor of any property, the possessor has against third parties all the rights of ownership. He is entitled to retain his possession against every one except the true owner ; and no person other than that owner can call him to account for any exercise of any right of ownership. If he be deprived of the property, he may recover the specific thing or full damages for its loss. He may maintain an action. for any injury done to it or for any interruption to his enjoyment. Even in this case of land, if no question of title be raised, prior possession, as between two rival possessors, is sufficient. A like observation applies to cases of custody or even of detention. A person who detains or has the custody of any property is said to have a "qualified" or a "special" or a "limited" property therein, by which he -is able to maintain an action. These expressions, not otherwise very intelligible, really mean that whatever may be the obligations of the holder of any property in respect thereof, he may always defend his rights in it against any stranger ; unless indeed he avowedly be a mere agent, in which case his acts are not his own but those of his principal.

Jus utendi, fruendi. The right of use and the right to the produce are sometimes described as being merely the less and the greater that includes it. They are, however, distinct. The permissive use of property differs, on the one side, from possession, and on the other side from the right to the fruits or produce of that property. Such a use is a case of custody, in which the custodian, while he avowedly holds the property for another, uses it with that other's consent for his own purposes under more or fewer limitations. Thus the master of a livery-stable may be the owner of a mare ; his groom may have the custody of her for his master's purposes ; a customer who hires her for an afternoon has the use of her for that period and for the purpose to which his contract applies. And a fourth person may, under some special agreement, be entitled to receive her foals. In many cases the two rights, the *jus utendi* and the *jus fruendi*, are combined; and the Roman "usufruct" was really equivalent to our estate for life. Although the usufruct was called a servitude, it was altogether different from a modern easement. It was not in the nature of a charge or burthen upon land, but was in fact a "dismemberment" of ownership, the fragment of an ownership of which the larger portion belonged to another.

Jus abutendi. The *jus abutendi* is generally described as including the power of alienation. Whether the word does or does not bear this wide meaning, I shall not stop to inquire. In any case some further analysis is needed, and is easily effected. The right of abuser seems to correspond with our right of waste. The person who enjoys it may entirely destroy the property, or may change its form, or may abandon his claim to it. He may, in short, not merely use the property without restriction, but his manner of use may be such as to involve its entire consumption. The property after he has dealt with it may, so far as physical laws permit, cease to be anything; or it may for the time cease to be property. In the former case it has no longer a visible individual existence : in the latter case it has no longer an owner. In our law waste has not so wide a sense : it means merely a change of form, whether for the better or for the worse, in the property. A change of pasture land to arable land, or of arable land to building land, would, in a legal sense, be waste. In popular language the word is always used dyslogistically, but it is not necessarily so specialized in law. It there means such a change in the form of property, irrespective of any change in its value, as, in the interests of the remainderman or reversioner, a limited owner is in the absence of some special authority not allowed to make.

Jus disponendi. The right of disposition applies, as I have said, either to transactions *inter vivos* or to matters of succession ; but it is in the former aspect only that I have now to consider it. It sometimes happens, as the Institutes * observe, that an owner cannot part with his property ; and that a person who is not the owner of property can, nevertheless, alienate it. The examples which

* II. 8.

Justinian gives are the *dos* or separate estate of a wife, the property of a ward, and unredeemed pledges. To these may now be added the powers which under our law trustees possess, and the powers of appointment given in settlements and in Wills. The power of sale in the case of pledges is, as the Institutes above cited point out, really a case of agency. The nature of the original contract gives by implication to the pledgee a conditional power of sale; that is, · it authorizes him on a certain contingency to act as the agent of the pledgor for the sale of the pledged property and for the disposition in a specified manner of its proceeds. The *dos* is among us represented by property settled upon a married woman to her separate use without power of anticipation. This case is the most distinct instance in our law of the separation of the right of alienation from ownership. That right is habitually much favoured, and is regarded as in some sense a necessary incident of ownership. It has been felt that it is contrary to public policy that one generation should fetter the discretion of another. Our courts have consequently been steadfast in their refusal to support any contrivance which tended to a perpetuity, and astute in escaping from every legislative movement in that direction. " All of them, says Lord Coke * speaking of these contrivances, have two inseparable qualities, to be troublesome and fruitless."

But the natural contest between the living and the dead— the wish to use property as present exigencies require, and the wish to control our own even from the grave—has long been waged with varying success. As the result of a protracted conflict, a compromise seems to be now accepted. Land can be tied up for any number of lives in being and for twenty-one years, or in certain contingencies for a few months longer, after the death of the survivor. Even in this case modern legislation distinguishes between the land and its price, and large powers of sale are given to executors and to trustees of settled estates. In the case of personal property,

* 10 Rep. 113 *b.*

N

accumulations are permitted for a term not exceeding twenty-one years from the death of the grantor.

Jus prohibendi.   The rights I have enumerated form in their aggregate the positive idea of ownership. They state the powers which, within the limits of the general law, an owner may exercise over his property. But ownership has also its negative aspect. Like many other propositions which at first sight appear to be simple affirmatives, ownership is found on closer examination to contain not only an affirmative but a negative notion. An owner may do to his property or in respect of it all those acts I have mentioned. No other person may do to that property or in respect of it any such act. Along with the idea of legitimate power there is also the idea of a general duty of forbearance. Nor is this all. There is the idea both of the duty of forbearance and of the right by which the owner is enabled to enforce that duty. All these ideas—the power of the owner, the duty of forbearance upon all other persons, the right of the owner to seek legal redress for any breach of that duty—combine to form the "*jus prohibendi,*" or right of exclusion. This right seems to be the most characteristic of all the rights that concern property. No person regards himself as the owner of any property unless he can exclude all or nearly all others from its enjoyment. The first step in the acquisition of property is, as we shall presently see, appropriation or reduction into possession. The very term possession, the " sitting in front "* of a thing, connotes exclusion and a readiness to enforce it. A man may have only a limited interest in any property, and yet, if it be exclusive, he is the owner of that interest. The reason is that the notion of exclusion implies the general duty of forbearance. All the other elements belong to the secondary notion, that of the right. They are important to the owner

---

* Writing of the preposition προ-τί, πρό-ς, πρόσ-θεν which is found in Sanskrit as *prati* and in other languages, Curtius says, " We may regard *port* (Umbrian *pur*) as the Latin representative of this preposition, occurring with different phonetic modifications in *pol-lingo, por-ricio, pos-sideo, pô-no* (for *posino*)."—Greek Etymology, vol. 1, p. 355.

and to those who claim through or under him. But all men are bound.to notice the existence of ownership in whatever degree or in whatever form it may exist, and to forbear from doing any act inconsistent therewith. This is the forbearance which the law guarantees, and this is consequently the primary notion that presents itself to the mind when it regards the phenomena of ownership.

Like the other rights of ownership, the right of exclusion admits of a separate existence and of different degrees. The most notable instance of the separation of this negative right from its positive companions is the case of a trust estate. A mere trustee has practically neither the possession nor the usufruct nor the use of the trust estate, nor the right of converting it, nor the right of disposing of it. All these rights belong to the persons beneficially interested. But the trustee has the right of exclusion. His duty is to keep the property safely, and to see that it is applied to its proper purposes and to none other. In the latter aspect he has certain relations with his *cestui que* trust. In the former aspect he appears before the world as the owner of the property, the visible representative of the right of exclusion.

Of the degrees of exclusivity, or, as it may be said, of the exceptions to the general rule of exclusion, a good illustration is found in rights of way. I select this instance in preference to licence or any form of permissive use, because, while these are almost always consensual, the rights of way are often adverse. The essence of such a right is not that the owner is bound to do any act, but that he has to submit to some act done to his property by others. That is, his duty consists in a forbearance to exercise in the circumstances supposed his right of exclusion. The extent to which he is required to observe this forbearance depends upon the circumstances of the case. The duty may vary from a mere personal obligation to a duty towards the whole community. In other words, the right of way may be either a private or a public right. One individual may have a right of way over another's ground for himself alone. Another may have such a right for himself, his family, and his servants. A third may have such a right by way of easement; that is the right may be vested, not in any specified individual, but in the owner for the time being of a certain tenement. These rights too may be for mere footways or for cattle or for vehicles or for all these purposes. Various persons may have these rights or any of them in the same property. Finally, the right of way may be a highway, and may be exercised at all times and in all circumstances by all Her Majesty's subjects. In a highway the ownership of the soil is vested, not in the Crown or in any public body, but, subject of course to the right of way, in the owner or the owners of the adjacent land. In all these cases the principle is the same. There is no division of ownership, but there is a greater or less restriction on the right of exclusion. It is noteworthy, too, as indicative of the popular feeling that exclusion is the essence of ownership, that in the case of property abutting upon a road, although the law declares the owner of the adjacent land to be the owner of his half of the road, even though that road was never granted to him, no such person ever supposes that he has or is supposed by his neighbours to have any special interest in the road. He cannot keep other people off it, and he consequently never regards it as his property.

Possession. § 2. Three expressions relating to possession need to be carefully distinguished. These are possession, the right to possess, and the rights of possession. Possession means that state of facts coupled with an intent which in the next preceding section I have endeavoured to explain. The right to possess means the right to acquire and to keep possession of property which at the time is not in the actual control of the donee of the right. The rights of possession mean the rights to which the fact of possession gives rise. These rights are the right of retaining and recovering possession ; the right of action for any disturbance or deprivation of the possession against any person except the rightful owner; and the right in certain circumstances of acquiring the full ownership against even the true owner by uninterrupted adverse possession for a certain length of time. Thus, when a man has purchased goods, he has before he takes them away the right to possess. When he takes them, or, as it is said, has reduced them into possession, they are in his possession. When they are thus in his possession, the rights which arise from possession come into operation, and he can enforce these rights as the occasion may require.

Hence a serious confusion in the use of the term possession has arisen. That term is used to express indifferently one or more of the three meanings I have mentioned. Sometimes it means the mere fact of taking and holding for one's own use, a notion which our forefathers expressed by the now obsolete word *nam*, and which we call in relation to land* occupation, and in relation to movables taking or converting or some equivalent term. Sometimes it means a right to take present possession otherwise than by way of mere permissive use. This is usually called constructive possession. Thus, a person who has bought goods but not removed them may maintain an action against any person who has converted or damaged them. He has acquired the ownership and consequently the right to presently possess them; and for the infringement of this right the law gives a remedy. Sometimes possession includes both these meanings as well as either of them, a notion which mercantile men sometimes express by the form $\frac{and,}{or,}$ and which the Romans† expressed by the word *utrumque*. There are some smaller ambiguities, such as the use of the word possessions in the plural, to which I need not especially refer. The difficulties with which the subject is thus beset are increased by the singular fact that no formal treatise exists upon the English law of possession. Some recent treatises on jurisprudence have chapters of greater or less merit upon

* See Rex *v.* Inhabitants of Eatington, 4 T. R. 177.
† See Savigny on Possession, 247 *et seq.*

the subject, but even in these works the question is not discussed with the fulness customary in other branches of our law. Savigny's great work has long been familiar to English readers, but its practical application is still obscured, partly by the ambiguities I have stated, and partly by those to which I shall presently direct attention. "Upon the English law of possession, says Sir Nathaniel Lindley,* there is not to the writer's knowledge any work, good, bad, or indifferent. The doctrines upon this subject are only to be found by wading through a mass of cases upon the old possessory actions, ejectment, trespass, trover, and larceny; and, as in some actions the plea of not possessed puts in issue the right to possess and not the mere fact of possession, it is necessary to be careful not to be misled by the decisions relating to the evidence admissible under that plea. The very few remarks made by Blackstone in his Commentaries are very unsatisfactory, for not only has he attributed no definite meaning to the word possession, but he has constantly confounded together rights so very distinct as a right to possess and a right of possession, *i.e.*, flowing from possession."

Seisin. These are not the only troubles to which the subject of possession gives rise. Another matter of still greater importance is the confusion of possession with *seisin*. The term *seisin* is generally taken to mean the actual possession of land. In some cases, as in the old maxim of *possessio fratris*, the two words are regarded as synonymous. But the notions of *seisin* and of possession are fundamentally distinct. *Seisin*† means the possession, not of the land, but of the fief; that is, in the language of the older books, of the inheritance or the freehold. Where lands of inheritance were granted to any person, and out of this inheritance various estates were carved, all these estates were regarded as parts of a single whole. The present and the expectant interests composed one fee. Of this fee the immediate tenant of a freehold interest was the ostensible

---

* Introduction to the Study of Jurisprudence, cxvii.
† See Butler's Note on Co. Lit. 266 b. 1 Hayes on Conveyancing, 12.

holder, and upon his fidelity and his vigilance the continuance of the fee as a whole depended. He represented the whole fee. He rendered to the Lord the proper services in consideration of which the grant had originally been made. He defended the possession against strangers. He kept the property intact until the time came when the expectant grantees should acquire the possession. In other words, he was, in addition to his own interest, substantially a trustee to preserve the rights of the remaindermen. But in the days of fiefs, trusts were unknown. The *seisin* consequently governed the title, and the tenants in expectancy therefore sympathized in every disturbance of the freehold. From such a state of things several important consequences followed. The disturbance of an actual *seisin* was a disturbance of the rights of all the remaindermen. If the person who had the *seisin* repudiated the rights expectant on him and claimed an adverse possession, he evidently acted contrary to the duty of his office and to the confidence reposed in him, and he forfeited his estate accordingly. It followed also that the *seisin* as thus understood could never be even for a moment in abeyance. From this fundamental rule were derived the corollaries that no freehold could be limited to commence at a future day, and that a particular estate must always be in existence to support remainders. Moreover, on every transfer by the immediate freeholder of his interest to a stranger, a public delivery of the possession, known by the technical name of *livery of seisin*, was, for obvious reasons, necessary.

Seisin is thus a far more complex term than possession. It includes occupation or the actual possession of the land. It includes also the right to the present possession of the land. But it further includes a series of duties in addition to these rights. It implies a duty to protect the expectant interests, if any; a duty to perform the services due upon the fee; a duty to secure the property against trespassers. Finally, it includes the rights of the expectants or remaindermen to their future possession. Both the doctrine of *seisin* and still more the rules deduced from it still continue, although the state of society out of which they arose has long ago disappeared. The result is that the law of possession as applied to land is in an extraordinary degree perplexed and obscure. Thus it is a common saying that the possession of the tenant is the possession of the landlord. Where the tenant holds merely as the servant or agent of the landlord, the maxim, according to the ordinary principles of representation, is of course true, although as against a mere trespasser the tenant has a right which he can enforce. Where the tenant holds otherwise than in a representative character, the landlord is not really in possession, nor can he maintain any action for any cause other than an injury to his reversion. But the tenant or any person claiming through him is not allowed while he is in possession to claim that he holds by any title superior to that of his landlord. Further, the possession of the tenant is sufficient to maintain the *seisin* of the freehold undisturbed. If, however, other circumstances be favorable, the tenant may acquire a title under the Law of Prescription. In such a case the landlord by his own laches loses his rights, and the possession of the tenant is deemed to become adverse from the time at which it is held that such laches commenced.

Property. § 3. There is a serious ambiguity in the word property. Sometimes it means the right over a thing. Sometimes it means the thing over which that right exists. We speak both of our property in a horse and of a horse as our property. Nor is this merely a popular error. It infects even elaborate* legal works. The two ideas need expression, but it is a source of constant confusion to express them by

---

* Thus in the " Criminal Code (Indictable Offences) Bill," introduced into the House of Commons, 1878, the work, as it is understood, of so eminent a lawyer as Mr. Justice Stephen, the following curious sentence (sect. 102) occurs—" *Obtaining property by* a false pretence is obtaining with intent to misappropriate it anything capable of being stolen from any person by persuading him to transfer such *property as he may have in it* to the offender," &c.

the same term. There is the less excuse for this practice because we are fortunate in having an unequivocal word to express the right. That word is ownership. We have also received for that purpose from the Romans the term dominion; but as that term has in some measure a political sense, and is in its general meaning unfamiliar, it seems prudent to adhere to its Saxon equivalent. I shall therefore always use the word "ownership" to express the right *in rem* over property, and the word "property" to express the thing which is owned.

Property has yet another ambiguity. It usually means a thing over which the right or rather the assemblage of rights which we call ownership exists. But it is also used to express every object of any right *in rem*. The term is often used as a collective noun of the widest sense. "All my property" means not merely all my objects of ownership, but also all my valuable rights *in rem*, whether of ownership or not, and not unfrequently all my rights *in personam*. But ownership does not include all rights *in rem*, and property does not include the objects of all such rights. Ownership is one variety of rights *in rem;* and property is the material object or thing to which that particular variety of right *in rem* applies. Ownership is indeed the most usual and the most important of these rights ; and since there is of necessity a general resemblance between all rights of the same class, it is not surprising that the term should have received an undue extension. Thus trade marks have been described as property. They have indeed many points in common with property, but they have also conspicuous points of difference. There is the same fundamental distinction between them as that which exists between *Res corporales* and *Res incorporales.* The former is an actual thing, the latter is a mere right. Ownership and a valuable right *in rem* are not equivalent expressions. The latter is the wider of the two. Accordingly, a new and more general term has now almost established itself. For "property" in

the general sense to which I have referred we now speak of
"estate." It would be a great advance in jurisprudence if
we were habitually to confine the word property to things,
and the word ownership to rights *in rem* over things. We
might then, in the absence of any specific name, designate
as "valuable rights" all rights *in rem* which are *in com-
mercio* other than those of ownership, and as "estate" the
aggregate of our rights of whatever kind they may be.
Rights arising from obligations might be called "choses
in action"; and "valuable securities" would mean all documents which form the title or evidence of the title to any
property or to any valuable right or to any chose in action.

What Things may be Property. Assuming, then, property to mean the thing
over which ownership exists, I proceed to inquire
what things may be property, or, in other words, to enumerate
those classes of things in which, contrary to its general
practice, the law does not recognise ownership. In the first
place, when we speak of property as a general name for
things that are owned, we must take the word "thing" in
its strict sense as exclusive of persons. Happily, our law
and the law of nearly every civilized State does not now
recognise any rights of ownership over human beings. The
family rights are of a different character, and the true
meaning of slavery is that the slave is property in the same
sense as a thing. The next exception is that of those things
which do not admit of appropriation. The sun shines and
the rain falls alike upon the just and upon the unjust. The
wind bloweth where it listeth. The sea is the highway of
nations. The land indeed may be appropriated, but not
the scenery that it contains. The great invisible forces
of nature also rarely admit of appropriation. In those
cases, however, where what we may call the storage of
force is possible, ownership is recognised. We thus arrive at
our third exception, that, namely, of forces which are capable
of appropriation but are not in fact appropriated. While
such things are unappropriated they are not property. When

they have been reduced into possession, and so long as they continue so, they become property. Thus gas in ordinary circumstances is not property; but when it is confined in pipes it becomes property, and can be stolen. Running water is not property; but when it is taken out of the stream and is accumulated in reservoirs, it becomes property, and has all its incidents. Wild animals are not property until they are lawfully reduced into possession and unless such possession continue. When they are killed by any person, and fall upon the land of another, their bodies may be reduced into possession by the landowner, and thereupon become his property.

Offences against Property.
The complexity of the law which relates to offences against property is well known. That complexity has been justly attributed to the fact that this branch of the law has been framed from a consideration of the offence only, and without regard to the theory of ownership. "It is impossible, says Sir James Stephen,* to understand the provisions of the Larceny Act without a knowledge of the doctrines which it presupposes; that is to say, the doctrine as to the definition of theft and as to things capable of being stolen. The definition of theft turns on the doctrine of possession, and this is unintelligible except in relation to the doctrine of property." The law of theft and of its cognate offences is indeed a remarkable instance of the practical inconvenience of that system of jural arrangement which classifies law not by its duties but by their breach. Regarded from the stand-point of duties, the subject does not present any particular difficulty. The duties which we owe to others in respect of their property may readily be enumerated. We are not to interfere with our neighbour's right to possess. We are not to interfere with his actual possession. We are not to hinder him of the rights which flow from the fact of his possession. We are not to deprive him either wholly or partially of the use of his property or to disturb him in its enjoyment. We are not, by slandering his title, to prevent him from selling

his property to the best advantage. We are not in any way to interfere with any property which we know to belong to another who has not authorized such interference. These rules apply to cases of detention and of custody as well as of possession. So far as strangers are concerned, the duty is unlimited, and takes no notice of the shares into which the ownership of the property may happen to be divided.

In all the cases I have mentioned the law gives a civil remedy, whether by restitution or by damages or by injunction or otherwise, for any injury that the proprietor has sustained. But in certain cases it proceeds further, and deals with the offences criminally. The cases with which it so deals are theft and mischief, that is, the unlawful taking of movable property or its destruction or damage. Of mischief I shall not now treat, and my remarks will be confined to theft and its cognate offences. The offence of theft consists in the conversion, in certain circumstances, of another's movable property. Conversion implies two things, the dispossession of the former possessor and the adverse possession of the converter. The questions of which I have already treated thus arise in relation to possession. A servant receives money for his master, and without giving it to him absconds with it. How can he be said to convert property which by its owner's consent was in his hands and had not yet come into his master's possession? Hence arose a separate offence called embezzlement, and an infinite display of legal ingenuity, not always perhaps to the advancement of substantial justice, ensued. Thus* where a man sent his servant with a cart to fetch coals, and the servant sold the coals and kept the money, it was essential to determine whether the misappropriation took place before the coals were put into the cart or after that event. In the former case the offence was embezzlement ; in the latter it was larceny ; and of course a conviction for the one crime was ineffectual if the facts really amounted to the other. In other words, the question for trial was, not whether the prisoner did or did not steal the coals, but whether he stole them

* Rex v. Reed, Dear. 257.

at oné particular moment or at another. Similarly, another separate offence was developed, that of larceny as a bailee, or, in other words, theft not by a servant but by an agent of property of which he had the consensnal possession. These three offences, theft, embezzlement, and larceny as a bailee, imply respectively the conversion of property without the owner's consent. But what if the owner consented indeed, and if his consent were procured by fraud or were given by mistake or were extorted by intimidation? This difficulty presents itself in more than one part of our criminal law where the want of consent is essential to the offence. In the case of offences against property it gives rise to the offence of obtaining property under false pretences, and greatly increases the practical difficulties arising from the distinction between theft and embezzlement. All trouble is removed by a slight alteration in the definition of the breach of duty. That definition in effect provides that no person with a certain intent may convert another's property without the owner's consent. To this proposition there should be added the words " or with his consent if it be obtained by fraud or by mistake or by intimidation."

The character of theft varies according to the circumstances in which it has been committed. Theft with violence or with threats of violence is called robbery. Robbery, again, has various forms, as it is or is not attended with wounding or with personal violence or with the use of arms. To the general provision as to theft there is one curious exception. A groom, contrary to orders, gave to his master's horse a feed of his master's corn. This man was prosecuted for larceny. He was found guilty, and it seems difficult to frame any definition of theft which would not include his case. But common sense revolts against such a result, and Parliament has interfered expressly to prevent it. Such an interference can only take the unsatisfactory form of declaring that a certain logical consequence from certain premises shall not be accepted. Our law both of theft and of mischief has grown up in the most fragmentary manner. Its natural confusion has been much increased by the extension to many such offences of the jurisdiction of justices of the peace, and by the very perplexing form in which many of our Acts introduce this jurisdiction. Probably in no part of the law could the amending hand without any material alteration of substance be applied with more advantage than to the law of theft.

Modes of Ownership. § 4. Since ownership is thus composed of a number of distinct rights, and since these rights are necessarily vested either absolutely or with some restriction in some person or persons, ownership presents itself under one of five forms. All the rights of ownership may be vested at the same time and without any qualification in one person. This is full ownership. It implies the unrestricted and present enjoyment of these collective rights by a single person for an indefinite time to the whole extent of their legal compass. But the ownership may be limited in any one of four ways. The collective rights may be held for a limited time, or may be jointly held by two or more persons. Some only and not all the rights of ownership may be enjoyed. Or the rights, whether collective or singular, may be held by two or more persons, not jointly but in succession. That is, limited ownership includes interests of limited duration, condominion, rights *in re alienâ*, and successive interests. Of full ownership nothing more needs be said except that under that term I include estates in land in fee simple. It is true that under the old system of tenure land was regarded not as the subject of ownership in the same sense as a chattel is owned, but the estate in it was deemed to be a right *in re alienâ*. The dominion or full ownership rested in the Crown, and the grantee held merely an estate or limited interest. But no practical consequence now follows from this distinction. The incidents have either been repealed or replaced by other rules. Except as to the limitation of future estates, there is now no substantial difference between the ownership of an acre of land and the ownership of a bale of wool.

Separate Exercise of Rights of Ownership. Each of the singular rights which collectively constitute ownership may be enjoyed separately or in conjunction with one or more of the other rights. Thus the lessee of property has its possession, although he has not its ownership. A person who hires chattels for a temporary purpose has the use of these chattels, although he has not their possession. The purchaser of a growing crop may be said to have the right to the produce of the land, although he has neither its possession nor its use. The lessee of minerals has a right of abuser, even though he may have no other right whatever to the surface. A secured creditor has the right of sale to enforce his security, although the ownership and even the possession be in another. The right of exclusion without any of the other rights is found in a mere trustee, as, for example, the trustee of a church. In like manner ownership may exist less by one or more of the singular rights. Thus the reversioner has the ownership but not the possession, "*nuda proprietas deducto usufructu.*" A trustee has the ownership but not the use. A tenant for life may exercise all the powers of ownership except sale and waste. Even the power of exclusion, though it can hardly be entirely removed, may be restricted in the case of particular persons or of a particular purpose, as when an owner has to submit to a right of way whether private or public. Such rights are for the most part rights in another's property or rights which exist in combination with rights *in personam.* In either case a further opportunity will arise of considering them and also future interests. I shall now notice those modes of ownership where the enjoyment of the collective rights or of some of them is limited in its duration or is divided among a plurality of owners.

Limited Interests. Those interests of which the quantity is less than that of full ownership are estates tail, for life, for years, or at will. Estates tail are a mere accidental growth

in the history of real property. They may now be barred
by a simple disentailing deed, and therefore can hardly be
regarded as a substantial interest. They have run their
course, and I will not encumber the present inquiry by
their unprofitable learning. Estates at will are practically
absorbed in tenancies from year to year in the case of land.
In the case of personal chattels they are called bailments,
and in each case they have in the absence of any special
agreement their own rules. Substantially, therefore, there
are now but two forms of inferior estates—for life and for
years. It may be said that whether in land or in chattels
these interests are now governed by the agreements of the
parties. It is only where the contract is silent that the law
interferes with its implied conditions. Everywhere tenure
has given place to contract.

Condo-
minion.   Condominion is probably the oldest form of
ownership. In its archaic form there was no notion
of shares. The *familia* or property of the household was held,
not by any artificial or juristic person, but simply by all the
interested parties without distinction and without division.
So old is this mode of ownership that it has been entirely
forgotten in our law ; and this oblivion is so complete that
when co-ownership meets us in India or in other tribal
societies, it has been a cause always of embarrassment and
too often of unintended wrong. When the State, even in a
rudimental form, appears, this tenure shows signs of decay.
The Twelve Tables provide a special form of action for
dividing the *familia*. In later times the rule has become
settled that no person shall remain a co-owner against his
will. Our law now recognises two classes of co-proprietors,
joint tenants and tenants in common. The difference between
these classes relates only to succession, and is in fact determined by the terms express or implied of the original grant
or other foundation of the interest. In the case of joint
tenants, the limitation is in effect to all the tenants and to
the survivors of them and to the legal representatives of the

last survivor. In the case of tenants in common, it is in effect to each of the tenants and his legal representatives. Thus, in the former case,there is a direct connexion of interest between the tenants ; in the latter case there is no community of interest, but only a mechanical juxtaposition of property. There is a community of property, but not a community of ownership. In the absence of any express provision to the contrary, every case of condominion is now construed to create a tenancy in common. This tenancy requires no special illustration ; if I must give one, it is the ordinary tenancy of partners in the partnership property. Of joint tenancy a good illustration is found in the once popular system of Tontines. Where annuities are granted to a number of persons and their survivors or survivor, the share of each annuitant is divided upon his death among the survivors. The amount payable always remains the same ; but the division is continually decreasing, until at length the whole amount becomes the property of the longest liver.

Rights in Another's Property. § 5. There are certain rights that are usually known by the abbreviated phrase *jura in re*, and that are fully described as *jura in rem in re alienâ*. They are, or at all events belong to, the " *res incorporales*," the " *ea quæ in jure consistunt*," of the Roman jurists, the incorporeal hereditaments of English law. The examples which Blackstone enumerates are advowsons, tithes, commons, ways, offices, dignities, franchises, corodies or pensions, annuities, and rents. I am not concerned to defend this enumeration. It sufficiently illustrates the nature of the rights in question. Perhaps in modern law it might be sufficient to speak of easements, licences, public rights of way, whether by land or water, franchises, and annuities, or other charges. When two or more persons have different interests in the same property, the matter may be regarded under different aspects. We may look at the quantity of interest of the smaller holder, or we may look at the diminution of the enjoyment

o

of the larger holder. The former is the stand-point of our law; the latter is that of the Romans and of their descendants. Accordingly, that part of the law which we describe as treating of modes of ownership or limited interests the Romans called the law of servitudes or burthens upon property. There are certain other rights *in re alienâ*, which, although they are equally with the larger interests rights *in rem*, our law agrees with the Roman law in regarding not as estates in land but as burthens upon it. Of these rights one is that class of " real servitudes," or *servitutes rerum*, which we call easements.

It is of the essence of a modern easement that it should relate to two tenements ; that is, that one tenement, usually called the servient, should be subject to a certain burthen for the benefit of another or dominant tenement. This proposition means that the owner or occupier for the time being of the servient tenement is legally bound either to forbear from excluding the owner or occupier for the time being of the dominant tenement from doing certain acts in relation to the servient tenement, or, as the case may be, to forbear, for the advantage of the dominant owner, from exercising over his own servient tenement certain ordinary acts of ownership. The easements which are now most important are rights of way, rights to water, rights to light and air, and rights of support to lands or buildings. They express, in fact, the rights that arise between neighbours, whether in the country or in town, for the more convenient use of their respective houses and lands. Thus a man may not excavate his own land in such a manner as to deprive his neighbour's unburthened land of its natural support ; or, where there is a right of way, he may not prevent that neighbour from passing over his field. How these rights are acquired and lost I shall presently consider. I shall now merely observe that there cannot be created in any tenement any easement or other interest which at the time of its attempted creation the law does not recognise ;[*]

<hr />

[*] Hill *v.* Tupper, 2 H. & C. 121.

that a man cannot have an easement on his own property; that easements are indivisible ; that they consist* in forbearances, not in acts; that these forbearances cast a duty upon the owner or occupier of the servient tenement; and that he has no right in the easement or in its exercise. The right belongs exclusively to the dominant owner or occupier. Thus, where a man† has an easement for the use of water, and has for many years used large quantities of the water, if he discontinue such use, and the surplus water consequently overflow the servient tenement, the owner of the latter tenement cannot compel the dominant owner to resume his former consumption, and so relieve the overflow, or to make compensation for the damage done.

The duties which easements imply are duties of forbearance. But there are interests in another's property, although they are not easements, which are positive, and imply not forbearances but acts. Some of these rights arise directly from contract, and I shall therefore postpone their consideration until I treat of the combinations of rights *in rem* and *in personam.* Others, which have a different origin, are called in the technical language of our law *"profits à prendre."* They denote the duty of paying to the donee of the right, or at least of placing at his disposal, a certain part of the property or of its produce. To this class belong tithes, the various rights of common, quit rents, and similar charges. But most of these are now either obsolete or obsolescent; and the examples which are of present practical importance are charges upon property, whether of capital sums or by way of annuity, and whether the property be real or personal. Such charges practically amount to a distribution in a particular way of the proceeds of the property. The person entitled to

---

* The maxims of the Roman law are—
 (a.) *Nulli res sua servit.*
 (b.) *Servitutem non ea est natura ut aliquid faciat quis, set ut aliquid patiat r rei non faciat.*
 (c.) *Servitus servitutis esse non potest.*

† Mason r. S. & H. Railway Co., L. R. 6 Q. B. at 587.

the charge has no right of user or of exclusion in the thing owned. To him the property is merely in the nature of a security for an amount of money due to him, and he has substantially nothing to do with the ownership.

Easements are limited in their operation to some particular tenement; that is, they are, in the language of the law, appurtenant and not in gross. It is said that subsidiary interests in gross may be created in land by means of licences. But a licence can hardly be now regarded as a true interest in land. It really amounts to no more than the permission of a trespass. "It makes an act lawful which without it had been unlawful." Such licences have certain well-marked peculiarities. They are revocable at the pleasure of the grantor. They are not exclusive either against the owner or against other persons. They transfer no interest. When the grant of a licence is coupled with an interest, the instrument is not a licence but a lease, and should be pleaded as such. It seems indeed impossible to put a licence higher than a right *in personam*. A ticket to a racecourse or to a theatre is evidence of a licence to enter that course or that theatre at the specified time and on the specified conditions; but the licence may be at any moment revoked, and the remedy, if any, sounds in damages.

Beneficial Interests. § 6. Where one person is the owner of property, he is sometimes required to exercise all his rights of ownership, not for his own purposes but for the benefit of another person. The rights of that other person are in such circumstances called the beneficial interest. The duty of the nominal owner is called a trust. These beneficial interests follow the rules of ownership, and are formed upon similar principles. But they rest upon the personal duty* of the trustees, and are enforced by personal proceedings against

---

* "An use (*i.e.* trust) is a trust or confidence which is not issuing out of land, but as a thing collateral annexed in privity to the estate and to the person touching the land (Scil.), that *cestuy que use* shall take the profits, and that the ter-tenant shall make estates according to his direction. So that he who hath an use hath not *jus neque in re, neque ad rem*, but only a confidence and trust, for which he hath no remedy by the Common Law, but his remedy was only by *subpœna* in Chancery."—Lord Coke, Chudleigh's case, 1 Reports 120 a.

these functionaries, and not by any action *in rem*. They
arose probably from a desire to evade the provisions of the
Statutes of Mortmain, which prohibited the alienation of
land to the Church. The method of evasion was simple but
effective. Since a direct grant to the Church would, under the
statute, be void, a grant was made to a third party for the
use of the Church. If the third party were faithful, all went
well. If he were not faithful, redress was sought in the
courts. The Courts of Common Law regarded such a use,
for so it was then called, as illegal. It was not only
contrary to the Act but repugnant to the preceding part
of the grant. They consequently held that the third party
was the full owner of the property without any qualification. Recourse was then had to the Court of Equity.
The Chancellor was more troubled by the breach of good
faith than by the formal difficulties in the terms of the
grant ; and, himself a dignified ecclesiastic, he thought that
a statute which was meant to injure the Church deserved
no special assistance from him. He had therefore little
hesitation in dealing with the state of facts I have described.
He acknowledged the conclusive authority of the Courts of
Common Law upon a matter of freehold right. He admitted
that, in accordance with their judgment, the third party was
owner in fee, and that he could deal with the land in whatever way he pleased. But the Chancellor added that
conscience and good faith required the third party to exercise his discretion in a particular way. He might do with
the property as he pleased, but it would be well for him if
he should please to do his duty. Whatever his legal rights
might be, he was morally bound to give effect to the trust;
and this moral obligation the court now directed him to
perform. If he declined to obey the Chancellor's order, he
was guilty of contempt, and went to prison until he attained
a better state of mind. If he sought the aid of the Common
Law Courts, he was told that they could do nothing for him.
They had already decided in his favour the controversy as to

the ownership of the property. They had no jurisdiction to interfere with the orders of the Chancellor on questions touching good faith and conscience. Much less could they interfere where there was a contempt of a court of co-equal rank. The third party had thus no choice but to purge his contempt and submit to the Chancellor's order. In this way a double jurisdiction was established ; and under favouring conditions the equitable interest prevailed over the legal estate. This is not the place to narrate the history of that struggle. I shall only notice briefly certain of its aspects.

The relations of the trustee and of his *cestui que* trust are merely obligations. They arise out of the contract of the trustee and the grantor. These obligations, however, generate a right *in rem*. The interest of the *cestui que* trust is a right which avails against the world. It is a maxim that equity follows the law, and the beneficial interest was therefore moulded according to the ordinary rules of ownership. The *cestui que* trust had, with some trifling exceptions, the same powers of dealing with the property that he would have had if he were in possession of the legal estate. Thus this beneficial interest is really a *jus in re alienâ*, but of the strongest form. It is a right in another person's property, but that right is so extensive as practically to smother the rights of the nominal owner. I have already indicated the position of the trustee. He has all the rights of ownership save one. He has not the right of user. There is against him a perpetual usufruct, which extends to every part of the property, and to every transaction with it, and to every interest arising out of it. Further, the beneficial interest is distinct from the *Fidei commissum* of the Roman law. The latter was in substance a mere contract of agency, of which the Emperor Augustus* was induced to grant specific performance. Nor did it operate *inter vivos*, but only in respect to testamentary dispositions. When a Roman testator gave certain property to Lucius, on the understanding that Lucius was to transfer it to Titius,

* Inst. II. 23, 1.

and Lucius accepted the property on these terms, this was in fact an agreement between the testator and Lucius, which the latter, if he had once accepted it, was bound to perform. If he failed to perform it, the matter was of such a nature that the interference of the law was easy and was consistent with justice. It could compel Lucius to make the conveyance that he promised ; and his duty was complete as soon as he transferred the property according to the tenor of his agreement. Such a duty is very different from that of an English trustee. Trusteeship follows the analogy not of a contract but of an office. It may involve for an indefinite period active duties and unceasing responsibilities. The *Fidei commissarius* was a mere conduit-pipe. The trustee has important and onerous duties resembling those performed by a public officer, and exercises certain powers which are needed for the due performance of his functions.

Future Estates. § 7. If we assume that the rights of ownership or some of them exist in any case, a further question arises as to the time at which their operation is to commence. Both the vesting of a right and its enjoyment may be postponed, or the right may vest but its enjoyment may be delayed. These deferred rights or enjoyments must be distinguished from mere executory contracts. The latter are simply future obligations, and take effect only between the parties. But the interests of which I now speak are rights *in rem* relating to ownership which are either contingent or postponed. The Roman law did not recognise such rights. In the later law conditions and time* were admitted in contracts, and were of frequent occurrence in legacies. But the law of property was founded upon possession, and to the Roman mind possession always meant present possession. "Occupatio" was something that a man did, and not something that he merely intended to do. Further, the necessity for the "Heres" or actual owner in possession, who could perform the all-important "Sacra,"† was not less imperative in Roman law

* See Mr. Hunter, Roman Law, 408. † Gaius II. 55.

than the necessity of the tenant of the fee, "the champion*
of the seignory and the guardian of the tenancy," was to our
ancestors. The furthest advance that the Romans made in
the direction of divided ownership was to treat all minor
interests as *jura in re alienâ*, or, as we should say, as burthens
upon property. The nations whose laws have been derived
from those of Rome have generally followed this example.
In the case of chattels, a like rule prevailed in our Common
Law. The reasons which Blackstone† assigns for this rule
are not very cogent, but the fact remains that no future estate
was recognised in personalty. This rule was relaxed in the
case of Wills. In other cases no question practically arises,
since from considerations of convenience and of safety future
interests in chattels are arranged by the intervention of
trustees. But it is otherwise in the case of land. The
Common Law has always recognised the division of the fee
into separate successive estates. As it deals with estates in
fee and with limited estates, so it also deals with Settled
Estates, that is with both estates in fee and limited estates
simultaneously. The reasons for this deviation from the
Roman practice were doubtless feudal. I shall not now
attempt to offer any more definite explanation. For our
present purposes we must be content to accept the recognition
of Future Estates as an ultimate fact. It rested upon the
doctrine of seisin. Together with the doctrine of trusts, it
forms the characteristic feature of English law. It has
survived to the present day, and upon it, as a recent learned
writer‡ observes, "depends all the intricacy of limitations
occurring in the settlement and distribution of land."

The expectant interests in property which our law recognises are called Reversions and Remainders. They arise where
the full ownership is divided between two or more persons.
The reversion means the interest of the grantor that is
expectant upon the determination of the interest in possession
which he has granted to another person in his property. A
remainder means the limited expectancy of some person other

than the grantor. Thus, if land in fee be limited to one man for life, and on his death to another in tail, the first grantee has a possessory estate for life, the second has a remainder in tail, and the grantor has the reversion in fee. Where a remainder is limited to a person not yet ascertained, or to a person upon a condition precedent which may not happen until after the determination of the particular estate, the remainder is said to be contingent. We have seen that by the rules of seisin the fee could never be in abeyance. Consequently no freehold interest could be limited to commence at a future day. Every remainder therefore must depend upon some particular estate. Every contingent remainder therefore must vest before or at the determination of the particular estate, and not after that event. But a lease for years could be granted for a future day. Such an interest, or as it is technically called, an *interesse termini*, is really* an executory contract as to the possession, and is, as I have already said, an obligation only and not a right *in rem*.

It would be vain here to attempt even the slightest notice of the immense mass of learning relating to future estates in land. The mere fact of their survival is evidence that they are suited to our social requirements. In all our projects of real property reform, no proposal for their abolition has so far as I am aware been seriously entertained. Attempts, very cautious and still incomplete, have been made in England† to get rid of the preceding particular estate. But any real reform in this direction must begin at the beginning. It is a delusive and dangerous system to alter the consequences when the cause is allowed to remain. The doctrine of seisin and the rules immediately derived from it ought to be abolished; and future estates should either be dealt with exclusively by way of trust or be directly limited, subject only to registration and to the law against perpetuities.

* Mr. Leake, Dig. 50.   † See 40 & 41 Vict. c. 33.

CHAPTER XI.

THE ACQUISITION AND THE EXTINCTION OF RIGHTS *IN REM.*

Occupancy.   § 1. Rights of ownership may be acquired in property which previously either had no owner or had some owner. In the latter case the new rights may arise with the consent of the former owner or without his consent. Consensual acquisition is in effect transfer whether partial or complete. It is the conveyance of an old right, not the creation of a new right. I shall presently have occasion to discuss the doctrine of transfer. I now speak only of the commencement of a right which did not previously exist. Such a commencement may arise either by the appropriation of unowned property, or by so dealing with the property of another as to acquire therein without his consent a proprietary interest. The case of *res nullius,* or unappropriated objects, is very old and very simple. It is merely the reduction into possession of an ownerless thing. It contains three elements. The thing must be without an owner. It must be brought within the physical control of the claimant. This proceeding must take place with the intent upon his part to hold and use it for his own purposes. In the case of chattels such an appropriation is called finding, or the right of the first finder. The finder takes possession of the thing; but as possession avails against every person except the true owner, and as by the hypothesis no such owner in this case exists, the possession and the ownership coincide. In the case of land this mode of acquisition was called by the Roman lawyers "*occupatio,*" a word still of high significance in international law. Its principles and its practice seem to have been familiar to every branch of the Aryan race. Any person or body of persons might occupy any unappropriated land, that is, land which was not within the recognised boundaries of any clan, and thereby the title of the occupant to that land was established. In modern times this rule is subject to an important limitation. All land occupied by any citizen of a State beyond the boundaries of that State is deemed to be occupied for and on behalf of that State. Thus since all land within Her Majesty's dominions is held from the grant of the Crown, and since all land acquired by her subjects outside those dominions, and not forming part of the territory of any other sovereign, is acquired for Her Majesty, the doctrine of occupancy has in our country become practically obsolete. A curious survival of it lingered to the time of Charles II. in the case of a lease for lives upon the death of the lessee, but even this survival is now forgotten. Still there are occasions in which this dormant doctrine wakes into unexpected activity. It operates in the case of Crown lands, not indeed against the Crown, but against all subsequent comers after possession has been taken. The old squatting tenure of the Australian colonies,* before the occupation of the Crown lands was made a matter of legislation, rested upon the same principles as that upon which Australia was claimed for the Crown of England, or upon which our Aryan ancestors laid the foundation of the European nations.

Things Found. The class of *res nullius* is wider than I have above indicated. It includes not only those things which never had an owner, but those which once had an owner and have lost him. The typical form in this species is Treasure Trove. Treasure in this sense is defined † to be "an old deposit of valuable property the memory whereof does not exist, so that it has now no owner." Property so circumstanced the Romans divided in equal shares between the finder and the owner of the soil. In our law all such property goes to the

* See Curlewis *v.* Campbell, 4 Shadforth's Reports, 3.
† " *Thesaurus est vetus quædam depositio pecuniæ cujus non extat memoria ut jam dominum non habeat.*"—Dig. XLI. 1, 31.

Crown. But it sometimes happens that valuables are found elsewhere than in the earth, and that no owner appears to claim them. In such cases the difficulty is to prove that there is no person who has the right of ownership or at least of prior possession. The duty of the finder is sufficiently plain. He must take reasonable pains to discover the owner. If, after he knows or might with reasonable diligence ascertain the owner, he appropriate the property, he is guilty of theft. But where no title exists, there are often disputes as to priority of possession. I do not speak of those cases where the ownership can be distinctly traced, and where consequently the representative of the true owner claims by a superior title against the possessor. Thus, a bureau* belonging to an old lady went after her death through many adventures and upon many voyages, and ultimately was found to contain, in a secret drawer, a considerable sum. Her executor was the true owner of that money, even though he knew nothing of its existence and though he had sold the bureau. But where there is found in some repository valuable property of which all trace of ownership has disappeared, the question becomes one of prior possession. I do not know that this question has been decided in the English courts, but it appears to have been dealt with in America. A man bought a safe, and afterwards sent it for re-sale to another person, to whom he gave permission to keep his books in the safe until it was sold. This bailee found in a crevice of the safe some bank notes. No person had suspected their existence or could trace their history. A dispute as to their respective claims arose between the man who found the notes and the owner of the safe, and the latter brought an action for the recovery of the notes. The courts refused to compel their restoration. A very able American writer † from whose book I have taken this case insists that this decision is wrong. I cannot concur in this view, although I agree in Mr. Holmes' criticism on the remarks of Sir James Stephen on this subject. In my opinion

---

* Cartwright *v.* Green, 8 Ves. 405.   † Mr. O. W. Holmes, " The Common Law," 225.

the question is whether—all claim of ownership being excluded—the owner of the safe had at any time possession of the notes. If he had, he did not part with it. This possession remained after he sent the safe for sale as it had existed before that event. But he could not have possession without the intent to possess, and he could not have that intent with respect to an object of which he confessedly did not know the existence. In his case the *factum* and the *animus* were never conjoined. When he had the fact, he had not the intent. When he had the intent, he had not the fact.

Abandonment. Possession continues without any renewed effort of body or of mind until either lawfully or unlawfully it comes by some external means to an end, or until the possessor voluntarily relinquishes it. Dispossession may arise from the terms of the grant under which the possession was obtained, or from the judgment of a court of competent jurisdiction, or from re-entry or re-caption by the true owner, or from some merely wrongful act. These matters do not now require our special consideration. But of abandonment something more needs to be said. Abandonment is the contrary of possession. Like possession, its nature is complex; like possession, it implies both a fact and a state of mind. But this fact and this state of mind are the negatives of those which in possession are characteristic. As possession implies the detention of a thing, so abandonment implies the discontinuance of that detention. As possession implies the intention to apply the detained thing to the possessor's own use, so abandonment implies the intention not to apply it to such or to any use. Where an intention of this kind has once been put into effect, the abandonment is complete; and cannot, according to the ordinary rule of election, be revoked against any subsequent possessor. Thus, if a man were intentionally to throw away his old clothes, and another person were to find and take them, it would not be competent for the original owner to allege that he had changed his mind and to insist upon their restitution. In such cases the mere absence of detention is not a proof of an intent to abandon. Such an intention must be shown by means of a reasonable inference from the conduct of the party in all the circumstances of the case. Thus, to take the favorite example upon this subject of the Roman jurists,* a man who has a summer pasture in the mountains and a winter pasture in the plains, does not abandon either of them, although each of them is left vacant for half the year. The nature of such a case rebuts any presumption to which the fact of absence might give rise.

Usucapion. § 2. When possession is adverse and continues for a certain length of time, it ripens into ownership. This rule, which the older Romans called usucapion, and we, after the example of the Romans of the Empire, call prescription, appears in every system of European law. It is subject to variations, which affect not the principle but such details as the length of the time and the kind of the property. Thus under the Twelve Tables—for the later Roman law established a much longer term—the usucapion of land took effect in two years. In England the period is by a recent Act† twelve years; in Victoria it is fifteen years. In early Rome the term for movables was one year; in England and in Victoria it is six years. But in this respect the law of the two last-mentioned countries presents a notable peculiarity. The six years mark the time at which the right of action is barred, but the law is silent as to any change of ownership. I am not aware of any express decision on the subject. Mr. Markby,‡ a very competent authority, states that the general opinion of the profession holds that in this case also the ownership passes. In the case of a contract to which the Statute of Limitations applies, it is familiar law that the obligation survives, although the remedy is barred. Nor, again, is it doubtful that a man may recover his property when and where he can peaceably do so. If then a horse of which there had been adverse possession for more than six years were to stray into

---

* See Savigny on Possession, 272.
† 37 & 38 Vict. c. 57, s. 1.   ‡ Elements of Law, 209.

its former stable, would the original owner, although he could not have maintained an action for it, be entitled to retain the animal that had thus returned into his possession? If he be so entitled, there are two kinds of prescription, differing not in their conditions only, but in their result. If he be not so entitled, there is one mode of acquisition by user, and the varieties of that mode are merely superficial.

The answer in my opinion depends upon the true legal theory of prescription. Why should adverse possession transmute the ownership? The theory of acquiescence * rests upon what, in most cases, is a mere fiction. The theory of positive law merely states the fact, but offers no explanation. The phenomenon is universal, and cannot therefore be attributed to mere imitation or to an accidental coincidence of policy. It must have some jural foundation. I venture to suggest that this foundation is the principle of abandonment. We have seen that a possessor may abandon his possession by ceasing to detain the property with the intention of relinquishing his interest therein. If his abandonment be complete, he cannot change his purpose to any other person's loss. This intention is of course a matter for proof. For many reasons the law thinks fit to prescribe a certain period which shall be deemed to be conclusive evidence of the intention to abandon. I have said that in early Rome this period was fixed at so short a term as one year and two years. .But in this case the law went further : it determined the period of discontinuance which was sufficient to break the user. Possession for the whole of the year was not considered necessary. If there were a substantial compliance with the law, it sufficed. What then was a substantial compliance, or, in other words, what amounted to a usurpation, a breaking of the settled course of possession? To this question the Twelve Tables fix in certain cases the "*trinoctium,*" the term of three days and nights, as a "usurpation" or fatal breach in the continuity of possession. To me then it appears that the fixed term of

* See Dalton r. Angus, 6 App. Cas , *per* Lord Blackburn, at p. 818.

adverse possession is pre-appointed evidence as to the intention of the original owner. If during the whole term fixed by the law he took no effectual means to recover his property, he was estopped from any subsequent assertion of his claim. In these circumstances the possession became in effect that of a *res nullius.* The possessor was entitled to hold against the world save one, and that one could no longer claim. Thus the possession and the ownership again coincide. In this view the explanation of the English rule of the limitation of actions as to chattels is readily understood. The lapse of six years in the case of chattels is conclusive evidence of the abandonment. The barring of the right is one mode of expressing this presumption of law. The same presumption may also be expressed by declaring the ownership to be transferred. Both these provisions amount to this, and no more than this, that the lapse of the six years raises a *presumptio juris et de jure* as to the intention in discontinuing the possession.

Accession. § 3. It sometimes happens that one person deals with the property of another as if it were his own, and that the circumstances of this dealing are such that the law will recognise one of the two as the owner of the altered property. This mode of acquisition is called accession. It occurs where two or more properties of different owners, or the labour of one and the property of the other, become so intermixed that they cannot be separated, or can be separated only at an unreasonable cost. Two questions thus arise. The first is, who is the owner of the joint whole? The second is, what compensation, if any, is the loser entitled to receive? These questions arise or may arise in every case. But the various forms of accession* group themselves under the several heads of the accession of land to land, of movables to land, of movables to movables, and of labour to movables.

The case of the accession of land to land is simple, and rests upon principles of its own. Where the increase or the

* See Mr. Hunter's Roman Law, 129.

diminution is imperceptible, where, in a word, each addition cannot be identified, the identity of the land which receives the accession is not altered. Consequently the possession of the added land vests in the possessor of the original land; and as the former owner of that added land cannot prove his right to any specific portion of the alluvion, he cannot enforce against that possessor his superior right of ownership. Thus the possession and the ownership coincide. Where, however, the shifted property is recognisable, no change in the ownership is effected. If the Po or the Ganges cut off from one bank a considerable portion of ground and carry it across to the other side, the ground so removed will remain the property of its former owner. Where the river entirely changes its course, and leaving its old bed passes through land which originally was dry, the result is that the owners of the original channel are freed from a burthen. They are no longer subject to the rights of way, if any, or to other rights affecting the water. On the other hand, the owner of the land through which the new channel runs must bear the burthen which in the natural course of things comes upon him. Every person must in effect take his land subject to such changes whether for better or for worse as the order of nature brings with it.

The accession of movables to land depends upon a different principle. It is substantially a case of transfer, and it is governed by the leading principles of that doctrine. The question is one of intention. If the owner of the movable intended that it should become a part of the land, the incorporation will be held to have taken place. The movable will cease to have a separate existence. It will be treated as part of the land, and will pass with it. Certain persons may indeed have in certain circumstances as against the owner rights of separating the two objects, and thus of dissolving the connexion. But while that connexion continues the complex object is an immovable. As a general rule, the presumption in this class of accessions is in favour of the

P

intention to incorporate. When one man with his eyes open[*] spends his money on another's property to which he knows that he has no claim, he must take the consequence of his folly. At all events the burthen of offering a sufficient explanation rests with him. He may show that there was wilful silence on the part of the landowner or conduct which was equivalent to a consent. He may show that he has taken possession of the land under an expectation created and encouraged by the landowner that he should have a certain interest therein; and that on the faith of such expectation, and with the knowledge of the landowner and without any objection from him, he has expended money upon the property. In the former case, the landowner will be estopped from asserting his title to the land. In the latter case, the landowner may be compelled to give effect to the expectation in such manner as in the opinion of the court the circumstances of the case may require. There are, however, certain presumptions[†] of law as to the intention so to incorporate the movable with the land. When the thing is accessorial to the use of the land, or where it cannot be removed without substantial injury or disfigurement to the land or building, or where the attachment has been made with a view to the enhancement of the value of the property or for its permanent improvement, the intention to incorporate is sufficiently shown. On the other hand, it is presumed, in the absence of some expression to the contrary, that no intention to incorporate exists in the case of trade fixtures and their accessories, and of tenancies of houses and parts of houses. In these cases the attachment of the movable to the immovable affords no evidence of intention to transfer the ownership of the former; and the landowner therefore, if he have any claim, must furnish some direct proof in its support. In the case of agricultural fixtures in Victoria, if they have been erected by the tenant with the landlord's written consent, they may be removed; but the landlord is entitled to one month's notice of removal, and may during

* Ramsden v. Dyson, L. R. 1 E. & I. App. 129.   † The Queen v. Lee, L. R. 1 Q. B. 256.

that time exercise over them or any of them a right of pre-emption.

Of the accession of movables to movables the Roman law supplies two examples. One is the accession of writing to paper; the other is that of painting to canvas. In the former case it was held that where a man wrote on paper or other material which he in good faith believed to be his own, he could refuse to give it up unless he were paid for the writing; but that if he retained the paper he must pay its value. If, however, the owner of the paper got possession of it, there was no remedy against him. If the writer knew that the paper belonged to another person, he had no claim. On this subject the English law follows the law of Rome. Thus questions have sometimes arisen between vendors and purchasers of land, where important opinions were written by counsel for the purchaser upon the margin of the abstract of title furnished to him by the vendor. "If, says Lord St. Leonards,* the purchaser obtain a private opinion for his own information, and allow this to be inserted in the margin of the abstract, he throws into the general heap that which otherwise would have been his own private property; and the vendor must have the abstract with all the observations when it was last sent back by him to the purchaser's solicitor, and all subsequently written on it, except the opinions of counsel procured by the purchaser for his own private information. It will be referred to chambers to report what is private, and this part must be erased from the abstract; or without a reference the purchaser may erase what was procured for his own private information, the erasure being made on affidavit." In the case of pictures, the same principle has not always been regarded. The Roman jurists held, although not without considerable difference of opinion, that the canvas was merely accessorial to the picture; and that the ownership of the former consequently followed the ownership of the latter. For this deviation from the ordinary rule no satisfactory reason† has been assigned. The difference in

* Vendors and Purchasers (13th ed.), 356. † Gaius, II. 78.

value on which the Roman jurists rely between the painted and the unpainted canvas is not, or at least may not be, greater than the difference between the written and the unwritten sheet. For mere commercial purposes there is a considerable difference between a blank sheet of paper and the same paper when inscribed with the verses of Mr. Tennyson.

The fourth case of accession is called by the Romans "*specificatio,*" or the making of a new article by the combination of two articles of different ownership. Where one man mixes his property with the property of another man in such circumstances that the identity of each of the component parts is lost and that a *tertium quid* is the result, who is the owner? For the proper answer to this question we must distinguish. If the intermixture be made with the consent of both parties, both parties will be the owners of the result in common, and in proportion to their respective shares. If it be made by the wrongful act of one of the parties, the Roman law gives the ownership indeed to the innocent party, but allows to the wrong-doer compensation for his property. The English law* is more rigorous, and as it seems rightly so. Under its provisions the whole property goes without any account to the innocent party, and the wrong-doer must bear the loss which his own misconduct has occasioned. But this rule does not apply to those cases where the property of each party can be distinguished, or where the quality of both articles is uniform and the quantity is known. Thus, if a man, whatever may be his intent, mix together two bags of flour of the same brand, the owners would be regarded as tenants in common of the heap, and would be entitled each to his own share. For practical purposes the property of each owner remains distinguishable. In such circumstances the costs and charges of effecting the division would probably fall upon the person who caused the commixture.

* 2 Bl. Com. 405.

Crown Grants. § 4. We have thus considered the mode of acquiring a title where the property had not previously an
owner or an owner recognised by the law. We have also
considered the like case where the property had a recognised
owner, but that owner did not consent to any change of
ownership. There is yet another case which requires attention, the case, namely, where the property has an owner,
but that owner is the State. For the case of such property
the rules of prescription did not, until a comparatively
recent period, provide. Even the modified form of prescription against the Crown hardly requires in this place
special consideration. For all practical purposes it may
be said that the only mode of acquiring a right to such
property is a Crown grant. Bocland, or the booking of
public land to a private person, is found at a very early
period in our history. It was substantially a form of
charter, its chief peculiarity being that it was made by
the King with his Council of Wise Men. Without discussing matters of merely antiquarian interest, it may be
shortly stated that, as the result of a protracted series of
changes, Her Majesty is now in effect the trustee of all
the property of the State. Such an arrangement is highly
convenient. It provides a definite owner both for all public
property and for all property where no lawful individual
owner is found; and it further provides that such property
shall be duly administered for such purposes and in such
manner as Parliament may direct. Where by any means
any individual becomes entitled to any such property, it is
conveyed to him by a grant from Her Majesty. We shall
see hereafter how such grants are made in the case of successions upon death. In dealing with living persons, the
Crown has exceptional powers in respect to personal property; but it is chiefly in the case of land that its grants are
practically important. Such grants are the foundation of
all titles to real estate, and, especially in new countries, to
many important interests in land for mining, pastoral, and

other purposes. The grantee may transfer the whole or any part of his right as he thinks fit ; but the foundation of the right itself, the ultimate fact in conveyancing, is the Crown grant.

Three points in relation to Crown grants require attention. The first relates to their form, the second to their construction, the third to their repeal. A Crown grant is made under the Great Seal, either of England or of that part of Her Majesty's dominions in which the property is situated, and is signed by Her Majesty either under the sign manual, or in a colony by the Governor as her agent. The issue of a grant under the Great Seal involves a series of elaborate checks* which are intended to guard against fraud or mistake, but which it is not needful here to enumerate. It is sufficient to say with Lord Coke " such was the wisdom of prudent antiquity that whatsoever should pass the Great Seal should come through so many hands to the end that nothing should pass the Great Seal that is so highly esteemed and accounted of in law that was against law or inconvenient ; or that anything should pass from the King anyways which he intended not by any undue or surreptitious warrants."

In the construction of private instruments, a liberal interpretation is applied where such an interpretation is needed to give effect to the true intention of the parties. If there be any ambiguity in the terms of the instrument, the words are construed against the person who uses them, that is, the grantor. But in Crown grants opposite rules prevail. The interpretation is strictly literal. The presumption is always in favour of the Crown. The grantee gets what the very words of his grant lawfully give him and no more. If therefore these words be incorrect or insufficient, the loss falls on the grantee. This strictness was especially observed when it was upon the suit of the grantee that the grant was made ; and accordingly it is usual in the grant of franchises to insert in the charter words importing that the grant is

* See " The Government of England," 94.

made from the special favour, certain knowledge, and mere motion of the Sovereign. In such circumstances the rigour of the construction is somewhat relaxed. But I do not think that such relaxation is admitted in the case of property. Thus if land be granted to a man and his heirs male, an estate which the law does not recognise, such a grant, if it be private, will be amended according to the nature of the instrument in which it occurs. If the instrument be a deed, the grantee will take an estate in fee. If it be a Will, where the rules of construction are less severe than in other cases, he will take an estate in tail. But in the case of a Crown grant* the grantee will take no interest at all. The law will not take upon itself the task of remodelling Her Majesty's grant; and that which in the supposed case Her Majesty has actually granted has no legal effect. It may have been that this distinction between Royal and private grants had its origin in a leaning by its own courts towards the Crown. But it now serves as one of many much needed securities to protect the weakness of the public trustee and his liability to imposition against private rapacity and greed.

It is also a rule that, if the Crown be mistaken or deceived in its grant, or if the grant be informal or be contrary to the rules of law, such grant is absolutely void. That is, a grant of this description is not merely voidable, but has not the effect which was intended or any similar effect. It follows, therefore, that where the pretended grant is cancelled all derivative titles which depend upon it fall along with it. The innocent purchaser must look for his remedy to the original erring grantee. Thus, where Crown lands have been by any means unduly acquired, contrary to the provisions of an Act of Parliament, the proper mode of redress is not a resumption of grants or any indirect legislative action, but the order of a court of competent jurisdiction to rescind the grant either upon *scire facias* or upon an information in Equity.

* 2 Black. 348.

§ 5. Rights in another's property may arise by grant, testament, or prescription. The two former cases are merely modes of transfer. They are the carving of a smaller out of a larger interest ; and as they necessarily depend upon the terms of the instrument that creates them, they require no special notice. It is otherwise with prescription. The difficulty here arises from the extension to mere rights or *res incorporales* of the principles of possession which apply to *res corporales* or things. Prescription, as we have seen, arises where one man has for a certain period the adverse possession of another's property. But possession* and property denote something tangible. The possession of a right is a metaphorical expression. We can possess a thing or an animal or even a person ; but we cannot possess, in the ordinary sense of the term, a jural relation. Rights of ownership, however, may be divided, and rights *in rem* other than those of ownership may arise. The enjoyment of such rights needs regulation, and for their disturbance remedies must be found. In such circumstances it was natural to look for guidance to the established rules of property, even though the new cases were of a class for which those rules were never designed.

The distinction I have thus indicated was expressed in the Roman law by the term Quasi-possession. The word itself rarely occurs in the classical jurists. Its use indeed seems to be limited to a single passage† of Gaius. But the ideas which it conveys were under various forms of periphrasis sufficiently familiar. The jurists were aware that the expression under any form was not accurate, but they used it in the absence of any specific name. They meant by it, as Savigny‡ observes, "nothing else than the exercise of a *jus in re*, which stands in the same relation to the actual *jus in re* as

---

* *Possideri autem possunt quæ sunt corporalia.*—Dig. XLI. 2, 3. *Nec possideri intelligitur jus incorporale.*—Ib. 3, 4.
† IV. 139.   ‡ On Possession, 131.

true possession stands to ownership." The phrase was, however, unfortunate. It seems to suggest that the right in question is merely a modification of possession, when from the nature of the case the two rights must be distinct. It is indeed probable that in this case as in so many others the prefix "quasi" points to an historical* difference, although the force of this contention is somewhat weakened by the consideration that possession is itself a Prætorian term, and therefore that quasi-possession can hardly indicate the usual contrast between Prætorian and Quiritarian law. Quasi-possession was doubtless of later growth than possession, but the development was, I conceive, in each case distinct. I think that possession and quasi-possession are really applications of the same principle to different circumstances. Quasi-possession is not subordinate to possession, but is co-ordinate with it. It is not a mere form or consequence of possession, but the two are varieties of a common principle. They severally imply the exercise of the right, but the right is not the same in each case. In the case of things such exercise is called possession. In the case of rights it has no specific name, although by a false analogy and by an unwise extension of the name it is sometimes called quasi-possession. Thus possession is the actual exercise of the right to possess. Quasi-possession is the actual exercise of the right, whatever it may be, to which the quasi-possessor lays claim.

When possession exists, that is, when the right to possess is actually exercised, the rights of possession, of which prescription is one, take effect; and after they have been exercised for a certain time, those legal consequences which we call prescription ensue. In other words, the claim of right becomes a right. That which was once disputable no longer admits of dispute. The investitive facts are complete, and the law recognises the claim. Neither the person at

* Mr. Hunter's Roman Law, 217.

whose expense the right is claimed nor any stranger may interfere with the exercise of the right. The circumstances in which quasi-possession gives rise to a similar result may be briefly stated. The right claimed must be actually exercised. It must be exercised as of right *tanquam sui juris*, that is, "*nec vi* * *nec clam nec precario*," but in the avowed assertion of a distinct claim. This exercise must be known to the other party, and he must have acquiesced therein. This exercise and this acquiescence must have continued as between the parties themselves or their representatives for not less than twenty years. If all these conditions be fulfilled, the claim is established and the right is recognised and enforced. But, as I conceive, no right can arise unless and until the term of prescription be actually completed. How far these principles apply to all rights other than those of ownership it would not perhaps be safe at present to pronounce. It is certain, however, that they apply to easements.

Rights which have been acquired by use may be lost by the discontinuance of that use. If, therefore, a person who is not under any legal disability fail to exercise a right *in re alienâ* for a period of twenty years, he will be held to have relinquished his right. The same result may of course be obtained by express disclaimer at any earlier time. In the case of easements, extinction of the right also takes place when both the dominant and the servient tenements come into the hands of the same proprietor for his own use. A man cannot have an easement in his own property; the greater right includes and absorbs the less. In such circumstances, therefore, the easement merges in the ownership. Various other causes have also the effect of extinguishing easements. They belong, however, to the learning of that special subject, and do not seem to be necessary for the illustration of any general principle.

* See *per* Blackburn J., L. R. 6 Q. B. at 584.

**The Acquisi-
tion and
Extinction
of Rights
in rem other
than those of
Ownership.**

§ 6. The learning as to the acquisition of rights *in rem* other than those of ownership divides itself into two parts. That acquisition either does or does not depend upon the presence of special investitive facts. There are cases where the occurrence of certain events is necessary before the right can take effect. There are cases where, beyond the fact that the donee of the right is a member, whether permanent or temporary, of the community or actually has the secondary object of the right, no particular event is required. A man has a right to his personal security, to his freedom, to his reputation, so soon as he becomes a member of the community. He has a right to the society and the control of his family, and to the enjoyment of his property, and to the benefit of his contracts, so soon as he has a family to control or property to enjoy or contracts from which he may hope to benefit. In these cases no investitive facts, or rather no special investitive facts beyond those implied in the very statement of the case, are necessary for the acquisition of his right. Such rights have been called natural,[*] an epithet misleading indeed, but which may perhaps sufficiently indicate the negative facts of their origin. They have also been described as "inalienable," and by various other eulogistic terms which savour of the stump rather than of philosophic analysis. I trust that their true character is now sufficiently apparent. They are the rights which correlate certain classes of General Duties and nothing more. I have nothing to add to what I have already said of those rights. They arise when the donee becomes a member of the community, that is in ordinary cases when he is born. They continue until he ceases to be such a member, that is until he dies or is expatriated or has forfeited them or some of them by his crimes.

The other cases of rights *in rem* find their origin in enjoyment. As the enjoyment of property means its possession,

[*] See Austin, II. 592.

so the enjoyment of a non-proprietary right means its exercise. A man pursues some particular conduct—in certain circumstances the law will create in his favour a general duty of forbearance, either with or without certain conditions precedent. These conditions when they exist constitute the investitive facts of each case. Thus a man makes and uses a certain invention ; he then obtains by a specified procedure a grant from Her Majesty of letters patent, which forbid other persons from using during their continuance the invention. These letters must be registered in the proper public office in a certain prescribed way. Such grant and such registration are the investitive facts of the exclusive right of the patentee. In other cases, as in copyright and trade marks, no grant is required ; simple registration without anything more secures the desired right. But that right depends in the first instance upon the actual use. The registration is introduced for the purposes of public convenience, and is the condition upon which the use is rendered exclusive. In goodwill the use is recognised by law without any requirement of grant or of registration. In all these cases the foundation of the right is the use. This use is acknowledged and protected by the law ; and the law gives its recognition and its protection either unconditionally or upon conditions varying with the circumstances of each case.

The cases of offices and of franchises are somewhat different. In them the rights depend directly upon the grant. But even with offices the exercise of the right is essential. It follows the grant, which in other cases it precedes. The position of the use and of the right is merely inverted. Except where the service is an absolute duty, in which case the term office in its ordinary sense is hardly applicable, the grant of an office is ineffective until it has been accepted by the grantee. Nor is this all. Investiture, or something equivalent to investiture, is needed. That is, the grant is issued and the office in pursuance thereof formally conferred ; and in addition thereto the officer on his part does some act in his official capacity which indicates both the acceptance of his new duties and the exercise of his new rights. In franchises the grant alone seems necessary, but the disuse of the right would usually be evidence of its relinquishment. In some cases where the franchise is created or is regulated by statute, some condition precedent is frequently imposed either upon the acquisition of the right or upon its exercise. Thus in the Australian universities degrees can be conferred in the first instance only after examination. A degree actually conferred in contravention of this provision of the Act of Incorporation would doubtless be void. A member of Parliament cannot act as such until he has taken the oath prescribed by law. If he fail to take that oath, he does not cease to be a member, but the exercise of his rights is materially curtailed.

Res Corporales and Incorporales. It may perhaps be convenient if here I briefly state the leading points of difference between what the Romans called "*res corporales*" and "*res incorporales*," or, as I have called them, the rights of ownership and other rights *in rem*. Most of what I am about to write is mere recapitulation; but in certain respects I shall have to anticipate. Where a "*res corporalis*" is a "*res nullius*," that is, where a subject of property or thing capable of appropriation has no owner, possession and ownership coincide. Where a subject of property has an owner, the possession and the ownership may be divided. This result may take place where the several rights are successive or where they are simultaneous. In the latter case the possession may be adverse or consensual. Adverse possession for a prescribed number of years is conclusive evidence of abandonment by the owner. The possession therefore of the adverse possessor ripens into his ownership, and thus the possession and the ownership are again combined. Consensual possession arises by, and is equivalent to, according to the circumstances of the case, either transfer or the creation of some minor interest in the property. But where there is a grant of the right to possess, there must either be an actual delivery of the physical possession, or the instrument by which the transaction is effected must be registered in the manner prescribed by law. "*Res incorporales*," or rights *in rem* which do not relate to subjects of property, comprise four classes—rights in another's property, letters patent offices and franchises, copyright trade marks and goodwill, and beneficial interests. Rights in another's property are acquired by consent, express or implied. Express consent is in such cases evidenced by a grant. Implied consent is evidenced by the exercise of the claim to the knowledge of the owner, and without his consent and without his effectual opposition. Letters patent offices and franchises all emanate from the Crown, and are acquired by grant and acceptance. From this class copyright trade marks and goodwill differ, because they are not derived from any grant, but are acquired by the exercise of the right and, except in the case of goodwill, by registration. Beneficial interests are created either by contract or by grant and acceptance. In dealings with them, notice of such dealings must be given to the person whose actual right it is sought to affect, although his assent is not required.

CHAPTER XII.

RIGHTS *IN PERSONAM.*

Rights aris-
ing from
Contract.
§ 1. In treating of relative general duties I
have been able, not indeed in all cases but in some
of considerable importance, to discuss separately those duties
and the rights which they imply. In treating of relative
particular duties this distinction is less important, and in
some cases is in fact impracticable. I have sufficiently for
my purpose described non-consensual obligations. I shall
now—without any attempt to distinguish between objects,
which, although their stand-point is different, in fact
coincide—examine more closely than I have already done
the obligations and the rights which arise from contract.

I venture to repeat the substance of what in a previous
chapter I have said of obligations. They apply not to all
persons but to certain determinate individuals. Like all
other duties, they arise from the command of the State ; but
that command is given sometimes directly, sometimes indirectly. In some cases the State of its own will and for its
own purposes thinks fit to impose upon some ascertained or
ascertainable person in reference to some other such person
certain duties which do not extend beyond the parties concerned. In other cases the State permits two or more parties
to regulate their conduct in their own way. It merely
enforces under certain conditions the rules which by mutual
agreement they have made for themselves, or, if they will
not make their own rules, it prescribes the terms on which
it is assumed that their dealings take place. These enforceable agreements are called contracts.

Contracts contain two classes of elements, of which
classes one is permanent and the other is variable. The first
class is essential to the idea of contract, and no State has

enforced or is likely to enforce any agreement in which these elements are not found. The other class varies at different times and in different countries, and its elements are matters rather of local practice than of general principle. The former class includes the parties, their intent, the genuineness of their agreement, the character of the subject-matter of that agreement, and the extent and duration of the obligation thence resulting. The other class relates to the presence or the absence of any special form or of any consideration, and to the modes of proof or other rules of procedure which the courts of each country think fit to require. Each of these classes needs examination.

The Permanent Elements of Contract. § 2. To every contract there must necessarily be two or more parties. A man cannot make a binding agreement with himself, at all events not such an agreement as modern law will notice. Thus, where an insurance company* had two departments under separate management, one for fire business the other for granting annuities, it was held that the one department could not make a valid contract with the other department. In like manner, where a man† borrowed money from a fund in which he and others were jointly interested, and covenanted to repay the loan to the joint account, it was held that such a covenant was nugatory, and that the law knows no means by which a man can undertake to pay himself.

In every contract the parties must be definite. An obligation, as its name imports, denotes a *vinculum juris*, a specific legal relation between two or more parties. In other words, the right arising from a contract is *jus in personam certam*. The law does not allow the voluntary creation of general duties. Two specific persons or groups of persons may in relation to certain specified conduct enter into contracts. But an agreement which affects to bind others than the parties and those who claim through them is ineffectual. The utmost that in this direction the law allows is that an offer may be made to

---

* Grey v. Ellison, 1 Giff. 438.　　　† Faulkner v. Lowe, 2 Ex. 575.

an unascertained member of a class, as in the case of an advertisement of a reward for information desired ; but no agreement can arise until some particular person who complies with the description has accepted the offer.

In every contract the parties must have a certain intent. This intent is for the creation of reciprocal rights and duties. In other words, contracts relate to matters of business, and not to matters of amusement or of social intercourse. It is this intent which distinguishes a contract from an agreement between colleagues or companions, between the members of a bench of judges, or between the majority at a public meeting. There is the like distinction, and from the like cause, between a business transaction and a transaction for other purposes, between a contract to buy and sell and an agreement to play whist or to read Shakspeare. I do not know that this limitation, although it is necessary for the purposes of analysis, has ever caused any practical difficulty. Men are sufficiently alive to the distinction, and consequently no confusion actually occurs. For theoretical purposes the distinction seems to furnish an answer to the contention that it is not the agreement which gives rise to the obligation. A man, it is said, who acts in a particular way is often held to be bound, although he never intended to be so. But his intention can be evidenced only by his conduct, and in the case assumed* his conduct furnishes conclusive proof of that intention. It is not the actual state of the promisor's mind, but the belief in that state which for practical purposes he intentionally produces in the mind of the other party, that the law regards as material.

Next to the parties and their state of mind comes the actual agreement. This consists of two parts. There is first the consent or concurrence of purpose, the *pactio duorum pluriumve in idem placitum*† of the Digest. There is next

---

* See Sir W. R. Anson, Law of Contract (2nd ed.), p. 10.

† " *Pactum autem a pactione dicitur (inde etiam pacis nomen appellatum est) et est pactio duorum pluriumve in idem placitum et consensus.*"—II. 14. 1. 2. This passage, or a part of it, is sometimes cited as a definition of " consensus." But the subject is clearly " *pactum.*"

the mutual signification of that concurrence. In other words, the agreement must be genuine, and the fact of its existence must be proved. Of its genuineness I will not now speak. The marks of reality will best be understood when we inquire into their absence. The signification of the intention practically reduces itself to some form of question and answer. The stipulation of the Roman law—*"Spondesne? Spondeo"*—apart from the use of any technical term is the typical form. One party offers, the other accepts. In the bilateral contract the process is repeated with the parties inverted. But words, much less any set form of words, are not necessary. A nod from a bidder in an auction room and the consequent fall of the hammer may constitute, without the utterance by the bidder of a syllable, a complete offer and acceptance. Where the negotiation is conducted by correspondence, questions of much nicety often arise. It is strange that after so many years, and in a country where exchange never ceases, the law of England on some of these questions is still unsettled. It appears, however, that an offer until it is accepted may be at any time revoked, even though it professes to remain open for a specified period; that an offer is complete when it is posted to the other party; and that it is a sufficient revocation of an offer when circumstances which distinctly imply a revocation have by any means come before his acceptance of it to the knowledge of the party to whom the offer was made.

Every agreement relates to conduct. It is an agreement to do some act or to observe some forbearance. The act or the forbearance may or may not directly concern the parties or either of them, but it is the parties, and they alone, that are concerned in the contract. When the secondary object of the command is a person, those secondary persons* respecting whose conduct or for whose benefit the contract is made are not privy to the agreement. They cannot, as a general rule, sue or be sued upon it. Apart, however, from these considerations, it is not every act or every forbearance

* Tweddle *v.* Atkinson, 1 B. & S. 393.

that the law will recognise as a fit subject for contract. Such act or forbearance must be definite, must be appreciable in terms of money, must be physically possible, and must be not forbidden by law. We have seen that it is of the essence of an obligation that it should affect definite persons. For the same reasons these persons must be affected in a definite way. The *"juris vinculum"* must be precise in its duration and its extent. The contract must show who are the persons whose freedom of action is restrained, and in what particulars to what extent and for what period such restraint is to operate. The subject-matter of the contract must also be reducible* to terms of money ; that is, it must be of some actual value. It is with the serious practical business of life, as I have already observed, and not with its amusements or even its higher interests, that the law concerns itself. It will not therefore notice the neglect to attend a dinner to which the offender has accepted an invitation, or a refusal to keep a promise to dance at a ball with a particular partner, or the omission to take the chair in pursuance of promise at a public meeting, although in each of these cases much vexation and inconvenience may result.

The subject-matter of the promise must also be within the range of physical possibility. The law desires to help the serious arrangements of reasonable men, and not the vain fancies or the idle humours of fools. If, therefore, at the time when the agreement is made, the promise be practically impossible of performance, no legal obligation will be created. If it subsequently become impossible, a different question, and one to which I must subsequently refer, arises. The measure of impossibility is the state of physical knowledge and of the appliances of the day. A promise to touch the sky with my finger is as foolish now as it was in the days of Gaius, but a contract to go from London to Rome in a day is a much less striking illustration of physical impossibility than it appeared when he selected it to Sir William

---

* *Ea enim in obligatione consistere quæ pecunia lui præstarire possunt.*—Dig. XL. 7, 9, 2.

Blackstone. In our text-books impossibility is usually treated in relation to consideration, and the failure of the consideration is assigned as the reason for the avoidance of the agreement. But the principle applies where consideration is unknown. In the Roman law, where the rule of consideration did not prevail, the doctrine of impossibility is expressly stated as characteristic of the stipulation.

Little needs be said on the subject of illegality. No State is likely to enforce an agreement which is contrary to its express commands. Hence the Roman lawyers included in one class illegal and impossible agreements. Such agreements are alike forbidden, the one by law, the other by nature. What acts or forbearances the law thinks fit to prohibit is a question which naturally varies under each system of law. But where any legal prohibition exists, no agreement which is contrary to it or which tends to oppose it can receive any legal effect. Thus a lecturer engaged* for a certain evening the use of a public lecture-hall. Subsequently the owner of the hall ascertained that the subject of the proposed lecture was an attack upon the Christian religion, and was forbidden by a certain Act of Parliament. He accordingly refused to allow his hall to be so used. The disappointed lecturer sued him for breach of contract, but without success. The law, in short, implies in every contract a condition precedent of its legality. If that condition be not fulfilled, the contract is deemed never to have come into existence.

The Variable
Elements of
Contract.
§ 3. The variable elements in contract present themselves under two aspects. One is form : the other is consideration. Of the great struggle between the Formal and the Formless contract this is not the place to speak. It is enough to say that in archaic society some special solemnity or some set form of words, varying according to the custom of each people, was always deemed essential to give validity to a promise. Law, following custom, lent

* Cowan r. Millburn, L. R. 2 Ex. 230.

its aid to those promises and to those promises only in which
the proper word or the proper ceremonies were used. If
these words or these ceremonies were used, the intention of
the parties was unnecessary. If they were not used, the
clearest expression of intention was insufficient. By slow
degrees and from various causes the needs of a growing
society burst the archaic restrictions, and the Formless or
Consensual contract was established. The latter epithet
indeed was not happy. The case is one out of many where
serious error has arisen from that elliptical form of expression in which busy men, themselves perfectly familiar with
the subject-matter, frequently indulge. Every agreement is
necessarily consensual. But the obligations which arose "*ex
consensu solo* " were, for brevity, called consensual in contradistinction to those which required a specific form. The true
distinction is thus indicated by the term that is omitted and
not by the term that is retained. All contracts are consensual, but some are formal and others formless. In English
law the Formal contract survives in the deed or instrument
under seal. Indications are not wanting that the mystic
power of the seal is approaching to its close. Still, although
it is now but the shadow of its former self, the specialty or
deed retains some marked characteristics. It cannot be
directly contradicted. It requires no consideration. It is
exclusively used in certain important transactions. The
obligation arising from it can be released in no other way
than by a similar ceremony. Its term of limitation is much
longer than the term of parol contracts. There are indeed
other survivals, as they seem, of the Formal contract; but
they are rather substitutes for it than the contract itself.
These are contracts by record, which include private Acts of
Parliament, judgments by confession, and recognizances.
The two former classes are not properly contracts, but for
the purpose of giving effect to their real design are so
treated in derogation of their apparent authority. Recognizances are only a peculiar kind of unilateral promise made

to the Crown in the transaction of judicial business. Other Formal contracts have in former times been known to our law, but they are now obsolete. The great bulk of the business of the present day is transacted by contracts which express by any sufficient means the intention of the parties.

The other variable element to which I have referred is one which the Roman law approached but never reached, and which forms the characteristic feature of the modern English contract. This element is Consideration. Except in the case of the formal contracts that I have mentioned, " the law of this country* supplies no means nor affords any remedy to compel the performance of an agreement made without sufficient consideration." In every parol contract therefore, that is in every contract which is not under seal whether it be oral or be in writing, the consideration must be proved. In the ordinary course, that proof is given by the plaintiff; but in the case of negotiable instruments the presumption is, from the nature of the transaction, held to be in favour of the presence of consideration. The burthen therefore of proving its absence rests with the defendant. If, as between him and the plaintiff, he can show that no consideration was given for the making of the instrument or for its indorsement, the action cannot be maintained. Thus the rule of consideration prevails in all contracts not under seal without any exception.

Although the law relating to consideration naturally occupies a large part of the practitioner's attention, the statement of its principles needs be but brief. When it is said that every parol contract must have some consideration, two propositions are implied. The first is that the consideration must be genuine. The second is that the amount of that consideration is not material. If the court were required to decide upon the adequacy of any particular consideration, the law would practically make the bargain between the parties instead of enforcing the bargain which the parties had made for themselves. But whatever may

* Rann r. Hughes, 7 T. R. 350.

be its amount, the consideration must be real; and the question of adequacy may, when the agreement is challenged upon other grounds, be relevant to the good faith of the transaction.

" A consideration, it has been said,* means something which is of some value in the eye of the law." Legal value is thus the test of the reality of a consideration. This expression includes every appreciable benefit accruing to one party and every appreciable burthen or inconvenience falling upon the other party. From this definition several consequences follow. In the first place, motive is not consideration. A man may make an agreement because he wishes that something should be done or because he thinks that it ought to be done. But wishes or opinions, however laudable or sound, if no benefit accrue from them, have no value in the eye of the law. Again, the advantage or the disadvantage must be a matter of business and not a matter of sentiment. In other words, a mere moral obligation is not a consideration. Gratitude, natural affection, honour, are sentiments of too delicate a nature to bear the rude handling of the law. Even a benefit which has been actually received at some previous time is insufficient, because the promisor does not receive any benefit and the promisee does not sustain any inconvenience in return for his promise. Further, a promise to do the promisor's legal duty is not a consideration; nor is a promise to observe a forbearance which he cannot legally or physically observe. It is needless to add that the subject-matter of the consideration must be possible both in law and in fact, and must be sufficiently definite in its terms to admit of being practically enforced. These and similar matters can best be understood by examples with which our text-books abound. I refer to them merely to illustrate the nature of a consideration and the familiar proposition that, where a valid consideration exists, English law will, in the absence of any disturbing influence to the contrary, maintain and enforce a contract.

* Thomas r. Thomas, 2 Q. B. 851, *per* Patteson J.

Void Agree-   § 4. I have mentioned certain conditious all of
ments and
Voidable   which must concur to convert an agreement into a
Contracts.
          contract. Their operation will best be understood
by observing the effect of their absence. Such cases present
a difference. Sometimes the absence of these conditions does
not permit the agreement ever to become a contract. Sometimes the contract is complete, but is liable to be rescinded
if the party injuriously affected by the omission think fit to
do so. In the former case the agreement is said to be void;
in the latter case the contract is said to be voidable. Of the
former class the two main causes of avoidance are mistake
               and illegality. By mistake I mean neither an error in
Mistake.
               expression nor a failure of consideration nor a failure in
performance; but such a want of real consent as vitiates not
only the contract but the actual agreement. Where a man
makes an agreement with one person and thinks that he is
dealing with another person, or where both parties are mistaken as to the nature of the transaction, or where they
severally mean different subject-matters, there is no agreement in the true sense of the term. There is not " *duorum
in idem placitum consensus.*" Thus, a Mr. Jones* was in the
habit of dealing with a man named Brocklehurst. Brocklehurst sold his business to Boulton, and Jones, not knowing of
the change, sent an order as usual to Brocklehurst. Boulton,
without notifying the change, executed the order. A dispute
arose respecting the goods, and Boulton sued Jones for the
price. There was no suggestion of fraud, but it was held
that the plaintiff must show that there was a contract with
himself. This he could not do, because Jones believed at the
time that he was dealing with Brocklehurst, and had never
even heard of Boulton. The plaintiff was therefore non-
suited. *A fortiori* the same principle applies where the
mistake is produced by fraud, but the result follows not from
the fraud but from the absence of real consent.

    Even where there is no difficulty as to the parties, it
sometimes happens that one of them is mistaken as to the

---

* Boulton *v.* Jones, 2 H. & N. 564.

nature of the transaction. This case is not of frequent occurrence, because the mistake is usually caused either by fraud or by the negligence of the person who makes it. If a man* execute a deed which but for his own negligence or heedlessness he might have read and could have understood, he cannot free himself from his obligation by alleging that he did not read it, or that he was misinformed of its contents, or that he believed it to be a mere form. But if there be no negligence, the agreement in such a case of error will be void. Thus the acceptor of a bill of exchange† induced one Mackinnon to indorse it, telling him that it was a guarantee. The bill came into the hands of a Mr. Foster, who took it in good faith for value. The bill was not paid, and Foster sued Mackinnon upon his indorsement. The jury found that in the circumstances of the case there had been no negligence on the part of Mackinnon. It was held that he was not liable. " It is plain, said the court, on principle and on authority, that if a blind man, or a man who cannot read, or who for some reason not implying negligence forbears to read, has a written contract falsely read over to him, the reader misreading to such a degree that the written contract is of a nature altogether different from the contract pretended to be read from the paper which the blind or illiterate man afterwards signs, then, at least if there be no negligence, the signature so obtained is of no force; and it is invalid not merely on the ground of fraud where fraud exists, but on the ground that the mind of the signer did not accompany the signature ; in other words, that he never intended to sign, and therefore in contemplation of law never did sign, the contract to which his name is appended."

Where both the parties intend to deal, and where there is an apparent concurrence of wishes, it may happen that the subject-matter of their agreement has ceased to exist; or that under an ambiguous description each of them means a different thing ; or that the promise is accepted under a

* Hunter *v.* Walters, L. R. 7 Ch. 81.   † Foster *v.* Mackinnon, L. R. 4 C. P. 704.

conception which the promisor knows to be erroneous. In the first of these cases there is no *placitum;* in the other two the parties are not *"ad idem placitum."* If there be no *placitum,* it is not material whether the cause of the failure be physical or legal. It is enough that from whatever cause there is no available subject-matter upon which the " consensus" can operate. Thus, a cargo of corn* was sold which at the time of the sale the parties supposed to be on its voyage from Salonica to England, but which prior to the sale had become heated and was consequently unloaded and sold. It was held that there was no contract, since the thing about which the parties intended to contract had at the time of the agreement ceased to exist. So, too, a gentleman† leased from a near relative a salmon fishery in the west of Ireland. The title to the family property was very complicated; and it was subsequently found that the fishery really belonged to the lessee, and that he was paying rent for his own property. The lease was declared to be void, although in the circumstances of the case relief was granted upon terms.

There may be a latent ambiguity in the subject-matter of an agreement. That is, the description given may equally apply to either of two things, of which one party meant the one and the other party meant the other. Thus, one merchant agreed‡ to buy from another merchant a cargo of cotton " to arrive, ex *Peerless,* from Bombay." There were two ships, each named the *Peerless,* trading from Bombay, and on each of them the vendor had cotton; but the value of the cotton in the two ships differed considerably. Each of the parties meant a different ship, and the result was that no contract existed. The third case I have mentioned may be thus § expressed. Where there is a mistake not as to the subject-matter of the agreement

* Couturier *v.* Hastie, 5 H. L. C. 673.
† Cooper *v.* Phibbs, L. R. 2 H. L. 170.
‡ Raffles *v.* Winchelhaus, 2 H. & C. 906.
§ Sir W. R. Anson, Law of Contract (2nd ed.), 135.

but as to its terms, if one of the parties be at the time cog-
nizant of the fact of the error, he will not be allowed to
take advantage of it ; but the agreement, even though he
made no representation on the subject, will be held to be
void. Thus, where a man wants old oats and buys certain
specific oats,* the seller is not legally bound to tell him that
the oats are not old. But if the seller know that the buyer
thinks that the seller has promised to sell him old oats, and
is selling to him such oats acccordingly, he must either
correct the error or submit to the risk of having the sale
rescinded.

Illegality.   The second cause which prevents an agreement
from ripening into a contract is illegality. There may be a
genuine consent of suitable parties for a definite object ; in
other words, there may be an agreement complete in every
respect ; but the object of that agreement may be illegal, or
the means necessary for its accomplishment may involve
some breach of the law. In such cases no contract is created.
I do not propose to examine in detail the various acts of
forbearance which the law has thought fit to interdict. It
is enough to state the general rule that every agreement is
void which cannot be performed without some illegality, or
of which the object or the tendency is a breach of any legal
duty, or which is made with the knowledge that such breach
is intended and that the agreement is meant to further such
intent. But the effect of such invalidity varies according to
circumstances. Where the agreement consists of several
distinct parts, and is in effect not a single agreement but an
aggregate of independent promises based on independent
considerations, the illegality of one such promise will not
invalidate the rest. Where, on the contrary, the agreement
is indivisible, or where the consideration or if there be
several any of the considerations for several promises is
illegal, the whole transaction is void. In such cases promises are severable, but considerations are not. There are
no means of ascertaining the proportions in which the

* Smith r. Hughes, L. R. 6 Q. B. 597.

different considerations have influenced the promisor's mind. Where in consideration of five shillings a man promises to carry a message and to commit an assault, the two promises can easily be separated; and the good part can be performed, and the bad part rejected as surplusage. But where, in consideration of £5 and of service rendered in committing an assault, a man promises to grant a lease, it is impossible to say how much of the promise is due to the innocent money and how much to the guilty service.

There is a notable difference also between a promise of which the object is illegal and a promise for which the consideration is illegal. In the former case the agreement is merely void, and every subsequent promise in respect of it is deemed to be made without consideration. In the latter case, not only the agreement but also every transaction arising out of the agreement is itself illegal. The practical consequence of this distinction appears in the case of negotiable instruments. Where an agreement is void as being without consideration, a bill of exchange given on account of it is as between the parties ineffectual. If, however, the bill be put into circulation and come into the hands of a *bonâ fide* indorsee, he will not be affected by the circumstance that as between the drawer and the acceptor the promise was merely voluntary; and the ordinary presumption that the transaction was for value will arise. But where the agreement rests on an illegal consideration, the presumption is that there was no consideration, and that the original party, not being able to sue on the instrument himself, transferred it to another to sue upon it for his benefit. The subsequent holder must consequently prove that he received it for value; and his claim may be repelled by the defence that when he received it he knew of the stain on its origin.

Two men,[*] Needham and Jones, made a bet respecting the amount of the hop duties payable in the preceding year.

Jones lost, and gave in payment a bill at two months for
£40 19s. Needham indorsed the bill to Taylor, who indorsed
it to Fitch. The bill was not paid, and Fitch brought his
action. Besides certain other defences not material to the
present question, Jones pleaded that the bill was given in
an illegal transaction. It was held that such bets were not
prohibited by law, but were "mere idle wagers" which the
law would neither enforce nor punish; that the case was
therefore one of want of consideration; that Fitch was a
bonâ fide indorsee; that he must consequently be presumed
to have taken the bill for value; and therefore that his
claim could only be met by proving that he took it without
value. No such evidence was produced, and Jones had to
pay the bill. But if the bill had been given in payment of
a bet upon any game, upon, for example, the result of a foot-
ball match, the result would have been different. It would
then have under the statute been regarded as having been
given upon an unlawful consideration, and no proceedings
respecting it could have been maintained.

Voidable Contracts. There is another class of cases of which the
characteristic is that a consent has been obtained,
but not a true consent. The agreement may have apparently
complied with all the required conditions, but the consent
has been procured by some violent or deceitful or unfair
means. In such circumstances the agreement is not void.
A lawful agreement has been improperly made, and consequently a *primâ facie* contract has been created. But this
contract is liable to be rescinded by the injured party as soon
as he becomes acquainted with the wrong done to him in so
procuring his consent. Voidable contracts differ in some
important respects from void agreements. In the first place,
they are while they last true contracts; consequently all
legitimate dealings with them before their rescission are
valid. Their rescission therefore must be subject to any
such dealings that may have taken place. In the second
place, the right of rescission rests exclusively with the party

injured. No objection can be taken to the contract by any other person. If the injured party elect to affirm the contract, he may do so ; but whatever his election may be, it applies to the entire contract. He may take the whole or he may reject the whole; but he cannot accept what he likes and leave out what he dislikes. In the third place, as the contract is *primâ facie* valid, there is need of some distinct act or notice of intention on the part of the complainant before it can be regarded as rescinded. Fourthly, the remedies in the two cases differ in some respects; and, as I have already said, the rescission must be subject to the intervening rights that may have arisen, and may be even controlled by them.

The cases in which contracts are voidable are those in which the contract has been procured by misrepresentation, whether innocent or fraudulent, by duress, or by undue influence. Of the two former classes I have already had occasion to treat. In each case there is consent, and in each case that consent is not genuine. In the one case it is obtained by falsehood, whether intentional or unintentional; in the other by intimidation. A sort of mixture of the two evils, a mischievous compound of fraud and of duress, is that vitiating element which our law calls undue influence. It is not peculiar to contracts, and indeed is more frequently found in cases of gifts or of testamentary dispositions. When between two parties influence has been acquired and abused, and confidence has been reposed and betrayed, a contract formed in such circumstances may be set aside; and no affirmation of any such contract will be recognised so long as the noxious influence in any degree continues. Many examples of contracts rescinded on this ground may be found in the abuse of their power by confidential advisers, whether spiritual, medical, or legal. But the rule is not limited to any special relations. If the undue influence be in fact exercised, there is sufficient ground for the interference of the court.

Conditional, § 5. During the negotiations for a contract,
Collateral,
and Alterna- statements are often made and promises are often
tive Con
tracts. given which influence the mind of the other party.
Where these statements or promises form part of the contract, they are called Conditions. Where they do not form
part of the contract, they are called Representations. The
question whether any particular statement is a condition or
a representation is a matter of the intention of the parties,
and depends therefore upon the facts of each case. Except
in certain specific contracts—those said to be *uberrimæ fidei*
—representations, as they are not intended to make a part
of the contract, either form, as we shall see, subsidiary contracts, or are regarded as mere idle words, the one-sided
recommendation by the speaker of his services or of his
wares. The untruth of a condition if it be a statement, or
its breach if it be a promise, entitles the party to whom it is
made to be discharged from his liabilities under the contract.
These conditions differ from contingent contracts, in which
the promise depends upon the occurrence of some contingency
and does not come into operation until that contingency has
taken place. The difference between a representation and a
condition depends, as I have said, upon the intention of the
parties, and not upon the relative importance of the subject-
matter. " Parties, said Lord Blackburn,* may think some
matter, apparently of very little importance, essential ; and
if they sufficiently express an intention to make the literal
fulfilment of such a thing a condition precedent, it will be
one ; or they may think that the performance of some
matter, apparently of essential importance, and *primâ facie*
a condition precedent, is not really vital, and may be compensated for in damages ; and if they sufficiently expressed
such intention, it will not be a condition precedent." The
failure of a condition renders the contract voidable at the
option of the promisee. If either in terms or by his conduct
he elect to affirm the contract, the breach of the condition
will give him a right of action for the damage, if any, that he

* Bettini r. Gye, 1 Q. B. D. 187.

has sustained, and no more. In other words, acquiescence in
its breach reduces a condition to the position of a warranty.
Warranties.   In addition to the principal contract, the parties
may also make any collateral and subsidiary contracts that
they think fit. Such secondary contracts are called warranties.
Their breach does not discharge the original contract, but
gives a right of action for the damage that such breach has
occasioned.   The question whether a given agreement be a
condition or a warranty is a matter of construction. " The
intention of the parties* governs in the making and in the
construction of all contracts. If the parties so intend, the
sale may be absolute with a warranty super-added ; or the
sale may be conditional, to be null if the warranty is broken."

We shall best understand these distinctions by an example.
In a charter-party† dated 19th October, 1860, it was agreed
between Messrs. Behn and Burgess respectively that Behn's
ship, " now in the port of Amsterdam," should proceed to
Newport, and there load a cargo of coals and carry them to
Hong Kong. The ship was not at Amsterdam on the 19th,
and did not arrive there until the 23rd. When she reached
Newport, Burgess refused to load the coals, and repudiated
the contract. Behn thereupon brought his action. The
question turned upon the words " now in the port of
Amsterdam." Were these words a part of the contract or
were they mere terms of description? If they were a part
of the contract, was it intended that the presence of the ship
in that port on that day should be a condition the breach of
which would render the contract voidable, or a warranty the
breach of which would be sufficiently compensated by
damages? It was ultimately held that in all the circumstances of the case the words amounted to a condition, and
that by its breach the charterer was discharged from his
obligation to perform his part of the contract.

Warranties may be implied as well as expressed. Thus,
when goods are sold, there is an implied warranty by the seller
that he has a good title. If the goods be sold by sample,

* Bannerman *v.* White, 10 C. B. N. S. 860, *per* Erle C. J.
† Behn *v.* Burgess, 3 B. & S. 751.

there is a further warranty that the bulk is equal to the
sample. If they be sold under a trade mark, there is implied the additional warranty that the trade mark is genuine,
and that it has been lawfully used. It has been said* that
" no warranty is implied at law unless it be founded on reason
or on the presumed intention of the parties, and with a just
regard to the interests of the party who is supposed to give
it as well as of the party to whom it is supposed to be given."
This is doubtless true, but is not specially confined to warranties. A warranty is a collateral contract, and therefore
an implied warranty is an implied collateral contract. In
other words, a collateral contract, like any other contract,
may be proved not by words or by writing, but by the
conduct of the parties and the ordinary course of business.
Implied warranties, therefore, come under the general rules
of implied contracts.

Alternative Obligations. It sometimes happens that an obligation assumes an alternative form. In such cases the
election rests with the person on whom the duty is imposed.
This is indeed a general rule of construction, and is not
limited to contracts. In the case of an alternative legacy
the option rests with the legatee. Such a legacy is not an
alternative duty but an alternative gift, and the intention of
the testator was to benefit the legatee. In the older Roman
law † the duty of paying a legacy out of property which had
in general terms been left to him was in certain forms of
bequest cast upon the heir, and in such circumstances he and
not the legatee exercised the option. By the legislation of
Justinian‡ the old forms of legacies were abolished, and the
gift to the legatee was direct. The *" legatum optionis"* thus
assumed its modern form of an alternative gift. These
alternative duties differ from penalties and from alternative
remedies. Where the law imposes a penalty upon any conduct, it does not give an option to the commandee either to
break the law or to pay the penalty. On the contrary, a
penalty, of itself and without any other words, implies a

* Redhead v. Midland Ry. Co., L. R. 4 Q. B. at p. 392.
† See Ulpian, XXIV. 14.   ‡ Inst. II. 20, 23.

prohibition; and the conduct therefore remains unlawful whether the penalty has or has not been enforced. Where also the duty is single, but there are two or more remedies, the person who seeks to enforce the duty may pursue any remedy that he thinks fit. In this case the duty is not alternative, but the law provides more than one method of enforcing its performance. There is another rule concerning options which is of considerable practical importance. Where with a full knowledge of the necessary facts a person has definitely made his election, he cannot change his mind. In Lord Coke's phrase, "*Quod semel placuit amplius displicere non potest.*" This maxim is only a case of a much wider principle, that remedy which declares that "no man may change his purpose to another's wrong." An example of the more limited form occurred in an insurance* case. Under a fire policy, an insurance company was bound either to rebuild or to pay a certain amount. A loss occurred, and the company elected to rebuild. Before they did so, the municipal authorities, in the exercise of their lawful powers, declared that the house, apart from the effects of the fire, was dangerous, and caused it to be pulled down. The insurance company contended that by this act of a competent legal authority they were excused, or at least that they were entitled to take the other alternative and to pay the money. But it was held that they had made their choice and must abide by it; that the effect of their election was the same as it would have been if they had originally contracted to do that which they elected to do; and that the circumstance that their contract had become more tedious and more expensive than they had anticipated was no reason why they should be released from its performance.

The Dis-
charge of
Consensual
Obligations.

§ 6. Where a contract has been made, the promisor is bound first to maintain the contractual obligation† until the time for performance, if it be deferred, arrive; and, second, to perform his contract accord-

---

* Brown *v.* Royal Insurance Society, 28 L. J. Q. B. 205.
† Frost *v.* Knight, L. R. 7 Ex. 114.

ing to its tenor. Where a contract is made for a future day, if before the arrival of that day the promisor announces his intention of not proceeding with it, the promisee is entitled either to regard the contract as at an end and to commence at once an action for its breach or to treat it as still continuing and to await the arrival of the time for its performance. A gentleman promised to marry a lady after his father's death. Subsequently, while his father was living, he broke off the engagement. The lady sued him successfully for a breach of his promise. If, however, the promisee elect to adhere to the contract, he takes the risk of any event which may in the interval exonerate the promisor. Thus, Reid, a shipowner,[*] agreed with a merchant named Hoskins that his ship should proceed to Odessa, and there take a cargo from Hoskins' agent, which cargo was to be loaded within forty-five days. When the ship arrived, the agent refused to supply a cargo, and told him that he might go away. The captain, instead of treating this refusal as a breach of contract and sailing away, continued to make his demand. Before the expiration of the forty-five days, the Crimean war was declared, and the performance of the contract was thus rendered legally impossible. Reid brought his action, but it was held that, since the contract was treated as subsisting, Hoskins was entitled to the discharge of his contract by the declaration of war.

If the promisor fail to perform his contract, he is liable either to be compelled to specific performance or to make compensation to the injured party. Whether he fulfil his duty or fail in it, the obligation is at an end. In the former case the obligation has discharged its function; in the latter case it is said to be merged in another obligation. For reasóns which I have stated in a previous chapter, I do not think that this supposed creation of a new obligation is correct. The right of action is merely the sanction by which the original obligation is enforced. Such right may be waived, or may be barred by lapse of time, or may be sued upon to judgment. It is then said to be merged in the new

* Reid *v.* Hoskins, 26 L. J. Q. B. 5.

obligation that is assumed to arise out of the record. This statement of the case seems needlessly circuitous. There is only one obligation, that which arises from the contract of the parties. There is an event upon which this obligation becomes enforceable, and there are the legal proceedings by which it is enforced. But from such an obligation, whatever be its precise nature, there are certain grounds of exoneration. There may be a new agreement in substitution for the old one, or events may have occurred which amount to a waiver of the original right, or which practically destroy the contract. I shall not now discuss the rules relating to performance or to breach, and shall only illustrate briefly the principles of exoneration.

The new agreement must generally be made in the same form as that in which the original agreement was made. According to the metaphor of the old lawyers, the legal tie must be loosed by the same formality as that by which it was made fast. This rule has lost much of its importance since the decadence of the Formal contract. It is true that a contract under seal must still be released under seal. But a parol contract may be released by parol, and parol in this sense is not equivalent to oral or verbal. It follows then that where a contract must be in writing, it may be absolutely released by word of mouth, although* a new unwritten agreement cannot be substituted for it, nor will a release be implied from any invalid agreement. The writing is not the agreement, but only the evidence of the agreement. But it is to originate not to terminate a contract that the law requires written evidence. The promisee may of course by his own act waive the completion of the contract or of any part of it, or may deprive himself of his right by preventing the execution of the promise. Thus in a contract † for building a house it was agreed that the work should be finished on or before a given day, and in default heavy penalties were imposed. During the erection of the building, additions were made to the design of such an extent as necessarily to

---

* Noble *v.* Ward, L. R. 2 Exch. 135.   † Thornhill *v.* Neats, 3 C. B. N. S. 831.

delay the completion of the entire work. On the expiration of the stipulated time the owner claimed the penalties. But it was held that there was substantially a new agreement, that the additions to the work and the original restriction as to time were inconsistent, and that the later provisions in effect repealed the earlier. So where an artist* engaged to perform at a concert and was prevented from appearing by dangerous illness, or where a building † was hired for the purposes of a public concert and was burned down before the day for the performance of the concert had arrived, neither the artist nor the owner of the building was held to be liable for a breach of their respective contracts. It was observed that such cases were not within the contract. That is, neither party could be reasonably supposed to have contemplated their occurrence, and consequently no promise was made regarding them. The same principle applies where the promised act or forbearance becomes impossible by operation of law. A lessor covenanted for himself and his assigns that during the term of the lease certain adjacent land then belonging to him should not be built upon. Subsequently, a railway company, under its Act of Parliament, took the land compulsorily, and built upon it a station. The lessee sued the landlord on his covenant; but it was held that the railway company was not an assign within the meaning of the contract.

In all these cases it was competent for the parties, if they thought fit so to do, to make special engagements by which the respective promisors would have been liable. The artist might have agreed to sing, whether he was well or whether he was ill, and in the event of his death his executors would have been bound to pay damages for the non-fulfilment of his contract. The lessor might have undertaken that at all risks the hall should be available on the evening required. The landlord might have promised that in no circumstances should any building be erected during the term of the lease on the adjoining land. But

---

* Robinson *v.* Davison, L. R. 6 Exch. 269.   † Taylor *v.* Caldwell, 2 B. & S. 826.

where such stringent stipulations are not distinctly expressed, the law declines to imply them. If the parties choose to make them, the law will enforce their deliberate agreements, however harsh they may appear. But it will not of its own mere motion compel any man to do what is useless or impossible. It will not therefore adopt a construction which would force a man to render a personal service that he is unable to render, or at least to render profitably. Nor will it force him to prevent or to repair a physical calamity or the operation of an Act of Parliament. Such events are not really excuses for a breach of obligation. They are rather cases in which on a fair interpretation of the contract no obligation had in fact arisen.

CHAPTER XIII.

THE COMBINATIONS OF RIGHTS.

Rights *in rem* followed by other Rights. § 1. We have seen that there are two leading classes of rights, those *in rem* and those *in personam*. Of these two classes there are four combinations. Rights *in rem* may be combined with other rights *in rem* or with rights *in personam*. Rights *in personam* may be combined with rights *in rem* or with other rights of their own class. Such combinations take place when it is desired to give by the use of the one right greater effect to the action of the other. They consist therefore of primary and of accessory rights. The occasions on which this support of rights by other rights is desirable are frequent in business, and the subject is consequently of much importance to the practitioner. In the theory of law, however, they do not require equal attention. The combinations of separate rights which in their simple forms have already been ascertained merely require analysis. " Many a fact or event, says Austin,* which is styled simply a contract is properly a complex event compounded of a conveyance and a contract, and imparting *uno flatu* a right *in rem* and *in personam*."

Where the primary right is *in rem,* its combinations may easily be described. I do not call to mind any case where a right *in rem* has another similar right accessorial to it. But rights *in rem* are sometimes attended by rights *in personam*. This combination is commonly found in transfers. In the ordinary conveyance of land with the usual covenants the same instrument contains a transfer of an existing right *in rem* and the creation of several new obligations. These rights are entirely distinct, and it is merely a matter of convenience that they all appear in the same instrument.

* I. 57.

The transfer of the right *in rem* is the main object; and the contracts by the seller to the buyer that he has a good title, that he guarantees to the buyer quiet enjoyment, and that he will, if required, make further assurance, are subsidiary to the primary purpose. A similar result is obtained in the sale of chattels by means of implied warranties. A man sells to another goods by sample without any stipulation except the agreement as to the price. The bargain and sale transfers the ownership, that is the vendor's right *in rem*. But the law implies from the nature of the transaction collateral contracts on the part of the vendor— that he has a good title to the property, that the bulk corresponds to the sample, that the trade mark, if any, is genuine and is lawfully used, and other promises according to the nature of the case.

Of these rights *in personam* which thus presuppose an existing right another example is found in the contract of indemnity. This contract in effect provides that upon the occurrence of some loss, that is of some event more or less detrimental to the enjoyment of some right, the promisor shall pay to the person who sustains the loss the whole or some stipulated portion of the damage. Two circumstances in this contract deserve notice. First, the contract is conditional; that is the occasion for payment does not arise unless and until the loss has been actually sustained. Second, the contract is one against loss. Consequently the liability of the promisor, although it may equal, can never exceed the damage sustained by the promisee. Further, in each particular case the amount of the damage is the measure of the liability. Again, if the loss be compensated from any other quarter, the promisor is not liable; and if in such circumstances he have paid the amount, he may recover it from the promisee as money paid without consideration. In short, the object of the contract is not to make gain but to avoid loss. In other words, a contract of indemnity is not an aleatory contract. A familiar example of the contract of indemnity is insurance, that is an agreement to hold harmless the insured party against any specified loss, either on sea or as the case may be on land. The contract of marine insurance is said in an Act of the reign of Elizabeth to be "of immemorial antiquity"; it existed therefore by the custom of merchants long before it was regulated by the Legislature. Insurance against disaster by land is of later origin, and seems to have been at its commencement limited to cases of fire. In recent times it has received considerable extension, and now applies both to personal risk and to every valuable object. In this contract, at all events in the case of marine and of fire insurance, the assuring party is bound to state with absolute frankness every fact within his knowledge that is material to the risk. This duty is expressed by the rule to which I have already had occasion to refer that insurance is a contract "*uberrimæ fidei.*"

It is needless now to consider the special provisions which legislation has attached to contracts of insurance. It is more material to observe that the forms of insurance which I have described differ essentially from life assurance. They are contracts of indemnity. Life assurance is not an accessorial contract, but an original contract of an aleatory character. "A life-policy[*] never refers to the reason for effecting it. It is simply a contract that in consideration of a certain annual payment the company will pay at a future time a fixed sum calculated by them with reference to the value of the premiums which are to be paid in order to purchase the postponed payment." The operation of life assurance has indeed been limited by statute to cases where the insuring party has some interest in the life of the person insured. But this is a rule of public policy; and, after the contract has been completed, it does not affect the subsequent relations of the parties. Thus, where a creditor effects an insurance upon the life of his debtor, if subsequently the debt be paid and the insurance be still continued and the premiums regularly paid, the company[†] must pay the policy when it becomes due.

[*] *Per* Wood V. C., Law *v.* London Indisputable Life Policy Co., 1 K. & G. 229.
[†] Dalby *v.* London Life Insurance Co., 15 C. B. 365.

It cannot set up the defence that the original debt has been paid, and consequently that the insuring creditor has sustained no loss. The difference between the two classes of contracts also appears in the rule as to misrepresentation. Life assurance is not a contract "*uberrimæ fidei.*" Whether it ought to be so or not is a matter upon which there may be difference of opinion. But as the law now stands it seems to be settled that "untruths* in the representations made to the insurer as to the life insured will not affect the validity of the contract unless they be made fraudulently or unless their truth be made an express condition of the contract."

Combinations of Obligations. § 2. Where the primary right is *in personam*, the accessorial right *in rem* may have reference either to persons or to things. No further division in this respect seems to be practically required. The accessorial right may also be another obligation. In this class therefore three combinations arise. There are contracts which generate rights *in rem* as to persons. There are contracts which generate rights *in rem* as to things. There are contracts which generate accessorial rights *in personam*. To the first division belong contracts of marriage, of service, of agency, and of partnership. To the second division belong contracts of bailment, of carriage, of hire, of security for debt, and of sale. To the third division belong contracts of indemnity, of suretyship, and of negotiable instruments. Each of these classes I shall now separately examine, not indeed with that fulness of detail which a practical treatise on the subject demands, but so far only as is needful to explain its nature and its relations.

Obligations with Accessorial Rights *in rem* as to Persons. The first of these classes includes, as I have said, those contracts which relate not to things but to persons, and which consequently generate not merely proprietary rights but rights affecting the domestic or the industrial relations. These are marriage,

* Sir W. R. Anson, Law of Contract, 140 (2nd ed.).

upon which the whole doctrine of the family depends; service,. which in its modern form of employment is the contract of free labour, as well for domestic purposes as for the numerous objects to which the needs of an industrial community give rise ; agency or representation, which is a special form of employment; and partnership, which is a special form of agency. Marriage is a contract be-

Marriage. tween two persons of different sexes to live together with each other, and with no other person, during their joint lives. This agreement is made either in a specified form before an official appointed by law for that purpose, or in the form customary with some religious denomination before a recognised minister of that denomination. Certain duties in connexion with the marriage ceremony are imposed upon the celebrant. He is required to see that there is evidence that the parties are capable of intermarriage, and that they are of full age, or that, if either of them be under age, the proper consent of the parents or guardians has been obtained. When the ceremony has been completed, he is required to see that it is duly registered. But neither the qualification of the celebrant nor the fulfilment of any of these duties is essential to the marriage. The celebrant, or in some cases the bridegroom, is punishable if the prescribed duties are not performed ; a heavy penalty is imposed upon the celebration of marriage by an unqualified person; but where the parties are innocent no breach of duty by a third party affects the validity of the contract. Every country has its own regulations relating both to the capacity for marriage, to the form of its celebration, and to its legal consequences upon the capacities and the powers of the married persons. But in its main features the law of marriage in all Christian communities is substantially the same, and the relation is fundamentally different from that which in polygamous countries prevails between the sexes.

There has been much discussion on the question whether marriage is a contract or a status. It is, in truth, both. It

is a contract which of itself gives rise to a status. The latter
term is not one which a writer who wishes to avoid ambiguity would willingly use.   But the proposition means that
on the completion of the contract of marriage there at once
arises, both as between the married persons themselves and
as between each of them and all other persons, a large body
of special duties and rights.   These consist mainly in various
modifications of the general law.   Consequently, the law of
marriage is not found in any single chapter of a code, but is
necessarily scattered over different parts.   Some of its provisions come under absolute duties.   Some come under
general duties.   Its origin must be sought in contracts.
Important rules concerning it are found in the succession
to rights.   And the main body of the rules relating to the
proprietary and the personal duties and rights of the married
pair find their place in the law of Special Conditions, in
which they form a separate chapter.

Service.   The contract of service is the modern representative
of one of the oldest of human relations.   That contract has
in recent times far outgrown not only the original status of
slavery, but the domestic relation to which the name service
is especially attached.   I have already indicated the general
duties which prohibit all attempts on the part of an outsider
to disturb this contract, or to interfere with the respective
duties of the parties.   It is not necessary here to consider
the terms and the implications of the contract itself.   I shall
now merely notice, so far as I have not already done, the
liability which a man incurs to third parties for the wrongful
acts of those whom he employs.   We have already seen that
for any conduct of a servant which causes damage to
another, if it be done in his capacity of servant and in the
course of his employment, the master, and not the servant,
is liable.   This rule prevails even though the servant's action
be in direct disobedience to his instructions, and though as
between him and his master he is liable to damages.   In the
development of modern industrial life the contract of service

has received a wide extension. The contractor of the present day is separated by a wide line from the educated slave of Rome. The rule now is twofold. On the one side no employer can shift his personal duty to a contractor, or can by a contract evade the consequences of an undertaking which is in itself dangerous to the public. On the other side, no employer is liable for any damage that may arise from the negligence of a contractor in the execution of work in which but for such negligence no damage would have occurred. I may repeat that the employment of servants is one of those acts which a man does at his peril. In ordinary circumstances every person is liable for his own conduct, for what he has done or forborne or ordered, and not for the conduct of any other person. If, however, for his own purposes, he think fit to bring together and employ servants or other workmen, he is bound to take care that no harm arises to his neighbours from their operations. If the work be in itself dangerous, the employer is deemed to warrant the safety of the public. If the work be dangerous only in the event of carelessness, his duty is to see that reasonable care is exercised not by himself only but by all persons concerned in its performance. Thus, where a man erects* a platform for the purpose of letting seats to view a procession, if it give way and damage ensue, he is liable for the disaster; and no proof of care or trouble upon his part, or that he had let the work to a skilful contractor, or that he had used every conceivable precaution, will exonerate him. A shipowner † employed a contractor to paint his ship. The staging which the contractor erected along the side of the vessel gave way, and one of the painters who was standing on it was severely hurt. He brought his action against the shipowner. It was held that the shipowner owed no duty to the plaintiff. The work was of a nature that if proper precautions were taken involved no danger to the public. The failure in those precautions was due to the contractor, and it was with the contractor alone that the plaintiff had any contract. He had

* Francis r. Cockrell, L. R. 5 Q. B. 501.   † Heaven r. Pender, 9 Q. B. D. 302.

therefore sued the wrong man. A gentleman * kept in his
office a lavatory for his own use. A clerk, contrary to orders,
used it and forgot to turn the tap. The water overflowed and
damaged the room beneath. The tenant of that room sued
the master. But it was held that although the wrong-doer
was a servant, the neglect in question was not in the course
of his employment, and the action therefore failed.

Employer's   A more vexed question still remains. What in
Liability.   the absence of any agreement are the relations
of the master of an undertaking to his workmen? These
relations are obviously of a special character. Where for
his own purposes a man engages in any undertaking, it is
just that he should be bound to exercise the utmost circumspection. He exposes to risks more or less serious strangers
who have no option as to the risk and no concern in the
undertaking. But these conditions do not apply to his
dealings with his assistants. These assistants of their own
free will have joined the enterprise, and take a part in its
operations. They thus accept the risks incident to the
employment which they have entered voluntarily and with
a full knowledge of its consequences. For them the question is substantially one of wages. The character of the
employment—whether it be hazardous and unpleasant or
safe and agreeable—largely determines the numbers of those
who pursue it, and consequently the rate of their remuneration. In these altered circumstances the duty of the
employer is necessarily modified. He is bound to observe
a less degree of circumspection in the one case than in the
other. His duty, too, differs not merely in degree but in
kind. The care which the master of an undertaking exercises for the safety of the public is a general duty; the care
which he exercises for the safety of the workman is a duty
which arises out of their contract. It may consequently
vary indefinitely, according to the terms upon which they
have agreed. But in this contract, as in others, the law
must make provision when the parties are silent—provision

* Stevens *v.* Woodward, 6 Q. B. D. 318.

which may be altered by express stipulation, but which, in the absence of such stipulation, is implied as arising from the nature of the transaction. The question therefore is : What implications are just in a mere contract of hiring where nothing is expressed beyond the amount of wages and the character of the work? As to what may be called the conditions of the undertaking there is no dispute. It has always been held that the master undertakes to exercise reasonable care that these conditions shall be reasonably favorable. He must provide and maintain suitable equipments according to the nature of the work, and adequate supervision. But as to the conduct of the work, as to the behaviour of the men employed in it, his duty is different. He does not deal with his workmen as if they were strangers whose safety he was bound to warrant, but as men who knowingly take part in an enterprise which has its own recognised risks. For his personal conduct and for the directions which he gives he is, of course, liable. For the conduct of his servants to each other he is responsible only so far as the ordinary principles of vicarious liability* apply. According to these principles he is not liable except where the act or default of which complaint is made is his personal act or default, or takes place in obedience to his orders whether general or special, or is the act or default of some agent to whom he has given authority in the matter. It follows then that the proper implication of the contract of service, so far as regards the safety of the workmen, is that the employer shall see that the undertaking is conducted without negligence. That negligence relates to his own conduct, his own orders, and the conduct and the orders of those to whom he has delegated wholly or in part his functions of superintendence and control. If from any negligence as thus understood any harm, without any fault or contributory negligence upon his part, befall any workman, the employer must make compensation to that workman. But if without reference to any rule or by-law any ordinary workman—that is any workman

* See above, page 125 *et seq.*

who is not set in authority over others—injure a fellow-workman, such injury, although it be done by a servant in the course of his service, is yet not within the scope of his employment, and the employer is therefore not responsible for it.

These conclusions appear in substance to coincide with the doctrines of the Common Law as corrected by the provisions of the Act of the Imperial Parliament known as the Employer's Liability Act 1880. It has been held * that the grievance which that Act was meant to remedy was the escape of employers from liability where injury was done to workmen through the negligence of superintendents or other persons having control in the employment. The previous rule was that for injuries caused by one workman to another in a common employment the master was not liable. It seems to have been thought that the common employment was the cause of the duty, and not a mere statement of the facts in which it was applied. Accordingly the rule was extended to cases of superintendence, because, as it was said,† "a foreman is a servant as much as the other servants whose work he superintends." This proposition is certainly true, but it is not less true that the foreman is something more than a servant. He is not only a workman, but he is also, to the extent of his superintendence, the agent of the employer. The Employer's Liability Act—although its meaning may not be at first sight apparent, and although it shows only too plainly the marks of compromise—seems to have effectually but not without some inevitable clumsiness made in the cases of most frequent occurrence the necessary changes. It at least furnishes trustworthy materials by the aid of which a complete statement of the rights and duties both of employer and of employed may be constructed. But the case to which I have above referred decides, what indeed is otherwise abundantly clear, that this Act does not

---

* Griffiths *r.* Earl of Dudley, 9 Q. B. D. 357.

† *Per* Willes J., 33 L. J. C. P. at 335. See Feltham *r.* England, L. R. 2 Q. B. 33.

profess to impose new duties on the employer. It merely alters the rules that in the absence of any agreement* are henceforth to be observed. It follows therefore that the parties may always substitute their own stipulations for the provisions of the Act. The object of the Act was not to found a new rule of public policy, but "to get rid† of the inference arising from the fact of common employment with respect to injuries caused by any person belonging to the specified classes."

Agency. As a man may employ another to do any work or perform any service for his convenience, so the particular service which he desires may be that of representation. He may need and may employ another to incur obligations in his name and on his behalf, or to exercise rights in the same manner and to the same extent as he would have done if he had himself been personally present. Such a power arises out of the contract of agency, and its extent and its duration depend upon the terms of the agreement between the agent and his principal. There are thus the contract with an agent and the contract by an agent. When the former is made, the latter follows in the natural course of events. The contract with the agent exists only between the original parties—the employer and the employed. The contract by the agent introduces a third party, and brings into legal relation two parties who might not otherwise have met. This result is effected by means of the services of an intermediate party who is employed for that purpose, and whose personal responsibility is limited to the proper performance of his intervenient function. Like every other contract, the contract of agency may be not only expressed but implied. Both its existence and its terms may be inferred from the course of dealing between the parties or from the course of dealing

---

* "The effect of it (*i.e.*, The Employer's Liability Act) is that the workman may bring his action in five specified cases, and the employer shall not be able to say in answer that the plaintiff occupied the position of workman in his service, and must therefore be taken to have impliedly contracted not to hold the employer liable. In other words, the legal result of the plaintiff being a workman shall not be that he has impliedly contracted to bear the risks of the employment."—*Per* Cave J., Griffiths *v.* Earl of Dudley, 9 Q. B. D. at p. 366.
† *Per* Field J., *Ib.*

usual between parties in similar circumstances. When the agency has been established, the powers of the agent, so far as regards third parties, continue until the third party has notice of its change or of its termination. The private relations of the agent and of the principal and the confidential communications between them do not concern strangers. They are authorized to deal with the agent as with one possessing all the powers expressed or implied in his commission; and until they have information to the contrary they may continue to deal on the same terms as those on which they originally dealt.

Upon one point as regards the relation of agency to marriage, I may in the present place offer a few remarks. Marriage of itself* does not create any agency. Except in cases of agency by necessity, the agency of a wife exists in the same circumstances, and in none other, as the agency of a sister or of a daughter or even of a housekeeper exists. Where the agency of the wife does in fact exist, it arises either from the direct authority of the husband or by implication from his conduct. As in every other case of agency, the authority so given may be withdrawn at the pleasure of the principal. An express power of agency from the husband needs no comment. Such a power may be implied when the husband has habitually allowed his wife to purchase goods for her own use or for the use of the joint household. The only implication peculiar to a wife is the so-called agency of necessity. It may be that while they are living apart the husband fails to provide his wife with necessaries, that is with the means of maintenance suitable to her condition in life. In such circumstances, if she contract for such necessaries in his name, his silence amounts to consent. The law requires him to maintain his wife, and consequently raises a presumption, which may however be rebutted, that she has authority from him to pledge his credit for the necessaries which he has not otherwise provided. But in either of these cases he may revoke the

* Debenham *v.* Mellon, 6 App. Ca. 24.

implied authority ; and as to any subsequent dealings he may do so without notice to the persons with whom she deals. A tradesman, in fact, deals with a married woman at his peril. He must, however unpleasant such inquiries may be, ascertain what authority, if any, his customer has to pledge her husband's credit. If he can show some authority that may be implied from the husband's conduct, he is of course entitled to notice of the termination of such authority. But apart from such implied authority, he must remember that the wife merely as such is not her husband's agent ; and that any power that her husband may in that behalf have given her he may if he think fit take away.

Partnership. The relation of partnership is only an application of the doctrine of agency. Where two or more persons agree that they or some of them shall carry on business on their common account, such a contract produces certain new relations not only between the parties but also between each of them and the public. Each partner becomes for the purpose of their business the agent of the other members of the firm ; and, whatever may be their mutual relations, binds each of them by his engagements. It is now settled that, as in all other contracts, the existence of partnership depends upon the true intention of the parties ; and this intention may be shown either expressly or by implication. The receipt of a share in the profits or any similar form of payment is relevant but not conclusive evidence to establish the contract. The same principle applies to every person whose conduct is such as to induce in others a reasonable belief that he is a partner. If a man who is not a partner act in any business as though he were a partner, he will be estopped from denying his partnership as against those persons who may have been misled by his conduct. These consequences follow from the actual contract of partnership. It is this contract which of itself gives to the partners

s 2

the power of reciprocal agency. Their case is not that of a power implied by law from the necessity of the case or from the conduct of the persons concerned. Their mutual agency is part of their original agreement, and consequently continues in force so long as that agreement itself continues. The other members of a firm cannot revoke against his will the power of one of their number unless they dissolve the partnership. Such a revocation would be a contradiction in terms. They all have agreed that for certain purposes they all shall be reciprocally agents. While that agreement lasts, some of them cannot bind the rest of their number by a new agreement to which those others are not parties.

Obligations with Accessorial Rights in rem as to things. § 3. The second class of combined obligations is that of contracts which generate rights *in rem* relating to things. This class includes bailments, hire, sale, and the contracts which relate to property given as security for pecuniary loans. The rights *in rem* thus produced belong, except in certain cases of sale, to that division of rights *in rem* which is known as *in're alienâ*. That is, the contract does not generate a right of full ownership; but only what is called a qualified or limited ownership, a partial right in property of which the principal ownership is vested in another. The same idea may be expressed in other words if we say that the rights of ownership are divided ; that the larger portion rests without qualification in one person, and the smaller portion rests temporarily and for a certain specific purpose in another person. Difficult questions sometimes arise as to the precise legal implication of some of these relations when the parties have not fully expressed their intentions. But these questions belong to practical law, and are not essential to the present discussion.

Bailments. In the contract of bailment the owner of goods delivers them to another person for a certain definite purpose.

The mutual rights of the parties are determined by the terms, express or implied, of the contract ; but as against all other persons each of these parties has a well-marked right *in rem*. Each is entitled to enforce against all other persons the ordinary duty of forbearance as regards the property. The reason of this rule is apparent when we consider the nature of the respective rights of the bailor and of the bailee. The former has the ownership and the possession of the property ; the latter has its custody. Each of these rights, when they are separately enjoyed, admits and requires special protection. Subject to such rules as are needed to check multiplicity of actions, both the bailor and the bailee, or either of them, may sue for any wrong done during the bailment in respect of the property bailed. As between themselves indeed the contract prevails ; and in such cases the terms of the contract are rarely expressed at length. Hence the implications in this class of contracts have been much discussed. I believe that the doctrine of the three degrees of care which we have found to govern men's conduct in respect of their personal proceedings and the management of their business will enable us to formulate in an intelligible way the result of the somewhat perplexing authorities on this subject.

The object for which bailments are made is to keep the property, or to carry it, or to work upon or about it. This object may be intended to benefit one of the parties only, or both of them. In other words, we have the usual distinction between what is matter of good feeling and what is matter of business. In every case the bailee is bound to take, to a certain extent, care of the property delivered to him. But the extent of this care and the description of the persons against whom precaution must be taken differ in gratuitous bailments and in bailments for value. The latter class presents two varieties, where the bailee does or where he does not exercise the public function of a carrier.

Where the bailee is a common carrier, the common law has thought fit, from considerations of public policy, real or imaginary, to impose upon him very onerous duties. He, in effect, is held to warrant that the goods entrusted to him shall be carried safely and securely. This duty was not regarded as implied in his contract, but was imposed upon him by law absolutely, as if it were the duty that pertained to the discharge of a public function. Recent legislation has to some extent qualified this rigour; and common carriers are now allowed, in certain circumstances and within certain limits, to protect themselves by express contract. But, subject to these relaxations, the general rule remains that, in the event of any loss, the common carrier can excuse himself in no other way than by proving that the loss was caused by the occurrence of some such untoward physical or social disaster as I have before described under the designation accident. Where the bailee is not a common carrier, but is remunerated for his services, whatever may be the form of the bailment, the law requires that in the absence of any agreement to the contrary he shall see that reasonable care is taken in the performance of the duty he has accepted. This responsibility means, as we have elsewhere seen, not that he personally or any other particular person is to take such care, but generally that such care must be taken, and that he must see that it is taken. Where the bailee is not remunerated, his responsibility is much less grave. In the absence of any special agreement, he is required to keep the property bailed without negligence. That is, the person who sustains the loss must prove that that loss was caused by some breach of duty on the part of the gratuitous bailee. In this case the burthen of proof that negligence existed rests with the plaintiff. Accordingly, where a Tasmanian gentleman* deposited with his bankers in Melbourne for safe keeping a box containing valuable securities, to which he himself had access as he required, and the box was kept in the strong-room of the bank in the usual way, and some of the securities were stolen by one of

* Lewis *v.* McMullen, 4 W. W. & a'B., 1 (Law).

the bank clerks, it was held, and the decision was confirmed[*] by the Privy Council, that there was no evidence of negligence to go to the jury. The mere fact of the loss was insufficient to raise any presumption against the bank, and no further evidence of carelessness was or could be produced. Had the deeds been deposited in such a manner as to give the bank a lien over them for an overdue balance of an account or any other interest, the case would have been different.

Another Victorian case illustrates a different application[†] of the same principles. Mr. Moffat, a wealthy squatter, invited Mr. Bateman, an eminent artist, to visit his country house for the purpose of advising upon its decoration and the laying out of its grounds. During the visit he proposed to drive Mr. Bateman for a similar purpose to another house at some distance. On the journey the king-bolt of the carriage broke, both gentlemen were thrown violently out, and Mr. Bateman was seriously injured. He brought his action and obtained a verdict. But although the Supreme Court upheld the verdict, the Privy Council[‡] reversed the decision. It was pointed out that the case ought not to have been sent to the jury. The mere occurrence of the accident was insufficient to fix upon the defendant any liability. His duty, as a gratuitous carrier, was to carry his companion without negligence ; and no reasonable evidence of a breach of that duty was forthcoming. Thus the common carrier of goods and the gratuitous carrier of a person mark the two opposite extremes of the duties that relate to carriage. The intervening space comprises the ordinary cases of carriers for hire other than common carriers who do not warrant their loads or their passengers, but who are subject to a much more onerous duty than the mere absence of negligence. They are bound to see that reasonable care is taken in the performance of their work, both as regards the quality of the vehicle horses and equipment, and as regards the care and skill of the driver. They are not liable for any latent defect which no care could have prevented and no vigilance could

---

[*] Giblin v. McMullen, L. R. 2 P. C. 317.   [†] Bateman v. Moffat, 5 W. W. & A.B. 140.
[‡] Moffat v. Bateman, L. R. 3 P. C. 115.

have detected. But when any casualty occurs, they are bound
to offer a sufficient explanation of its cause, and to show that
the *primâ facie* imputation which the casualty of itself suggests does not really attach to them.

Negligence
in Bailments.
We have now reached the last step in a generalization of considerable extent. Where in circumstances not amounting to a punishable offence one person
causes damage to another person, a common principle in every
variety of circumstances measures his liability. Whether the
damage arises from the defendant's personal conduct, or from
the conduct of his servants in the course of their employment, or from the manner in which his business is conducted
or his property is administered, or from his want of care
whether by himself or his servants towards the property
of another of which he has accepted the charge, the nature
of his duty is alike. The material question is not the state
of his own mind, but the loss sustained by his neighbour.
Where the law forbids a certain intentional course of action,
the rule is "*voluntas spectatur non exitus.*"* In cases of
negligence this rule is inverted. There, as Lord Bacon†
observes, "the law doth rather consider the damage of the
party wronged than the malice of him that was the wrong-
doer." That a man must use his own without harming his
neighbour, whether "his own" relates to property or to
personal energy or to any form of social activity, is sufficiently plain. In other words, he must observe a certain
amount of circumspection. This amount varies according
to circumstances, and the difficulty consists in determining
that amount and those circumstances. It may be said
generally that, when any undertaking is in itself dangerous,
a greater degree of attention and of care is needed than
in those cases where, with ordinary prudence, danger does
not usually arise. A distinction, too, is made between
business transactions and the · various courtesies of life.
Further, the law notices the habits of the tame animals
that are in daily use, and the occasional difficulty of con-

trolling them. Hence duties of circumspection admit of arrangement into three classes, according as they severally impose in their respective circumstances that strictest form of responsibility which is familiarly known as insurance or warranty, or the exercise of reasonable care, or the absence of negligence. I need not repeat the observations which in the preceding pages* I have made respecting these several subjects. I will only add two remarks. The first † is that, even where the Legislature thinks fit to interpose and to authorize the use of a dangerous force, the result is merely the reduction as regards the person who uses it of the standard of caution from one degree to a lower degree. The other is that, with reference to the immediate subject of the present paragraph, all cases of dealing with another's property, which is lawfully within our control, come within the like rules. Apart from the exceptional case of the common carrier or of an innkeeper, a man may by express agreement undertake, whatever may be the nature of the bailment, to return or to carry safely and securely any chattel. In the absence of any specific agreement on the subject, the law lays down certain rules as between bailor and bailee. In the ordinary case of hire or other business transactions, the duty of the bailee is to see that reasonable care is taken of the property bailed. If he borrow that property for his own exclusive advantage, that is gratuitously, he is bound to restore it safely in any ordinary event. But where the transaction is for the exclusive benefit of the bailor, that is where the bailee undertakes the duty gratuitously, the inversion of the rule follows the inversion of the facts. The bailee is then bound merely to avoid negligence, and unless his negligence be affirmatively proved, his liability is not established.

Loan. Another form of rights *in re alienâ* which is usually classed with bailments is that of rights which arise from loans for use. Such rights do indeed arise from a contract of bailment; but this bailment contemplates the use by the bailee of

---

* See above, pp. 100, 125, 180. † See above, p. 136.

the property bailed, and not its safe-keeping or other treatment for the convenience of the bailor. In this case as well as in the other bailments the difference resting upon the motive of the transaction prevails. The loan may be gratuitous or it may be upon hire. The gratuitous loan, the *commodatum* of the Roman law, implies that the thing lent shall be itself returned in due course; and that the borrower, who alone benefits by the transaction, shall warrant its restoration against the world. The principle is in effect another form of that on which the gratuitous bailee is relieved from all responsibility for the goods entrusted to his care beyond that which results from his own wrongful acts or omissions or those of his servants. He who has the advantage must take the burthen. He who has no advantage is relieved from any burthen except that to which his own misconduct gives rise. There is another case, that which the Romans called *mutuum*, where another thing of the same kind and not the identical thing lent, is returned to the lender. But it is now settled that such a transaction, at all events where* there is any consideration in the contract, is not a bailment but a contract of sale. Thus, where a man deposits money with a bank, whether on a current account or for a fixed term, the transaction, although it is called a deposit, is clearly a loan. Neither the depositor nor the bank intended that the money should be wrapped in a napkin. It was to the advantage of each of them, of the one directly and of the other indirectly, that the money should during the term of deposit be made productive. For this purpose the most convenient course for all parties is to transfer the ownership of the money to the bank, subject to certain obligations as to repayment. That such is the real state of the case is apparent from the nature of the risk. If the money be lost, the loss falls on the bank, not on the depositor. On the other hand, if the bank were to make a large profit by means of the loan, it would not be according to the custom of bankers to share the profit with their customer.

---

* South Australian Ins. Coy. *v.* Randell, L. R. 3 P. C. C. 101.

The ordinary form of loan is of course that for hire. As in every other case of right *in re alienâ,* either the owner of the property or the person who has hired it may maintain an action for any injury done to his interest. It is, however, to the mutual relations of the parties that the main interest in this contract belongs. Its principles are very simple. On the one side, the duty of the lender is to give quiet possession of the thing lent, and to see that it has no defects likely to cause extraordinary risk. On the other side, the hirer is bound to pay the hire, to see that reasonable care is taken of the property, to use it in the manner and for the purposes specified in the contract and not otherwise, and to return it at the appointed time in as good condition, excepting fair wear and tear, as that in which he received it. As regards chattels, these rules are almost universal. But in the case of real property the obligation rests in English law not on contract but on tenure ; and although our law is gradually assuming a more satisfactory form, much yet remains to be done before the law of landlord and tenant is placed on a rational foundation.

Security. Property is often delivered as a security for the payment of money or for the further performance of some obligation. This contract is called pledge. But the name pledge is usually confined to a particular form of dealing, and the contract obviously exceeds the bounds of mere bailment. It is therefore convenient to regard it as a separate contract, and to give it the wider name of security. There is always in such cases the contract to secure the fulfilment of an obligation whether pecuniary or other. There is always, too, the creation of a right *in re alienâ* with regard to some property. Further, this right is conditional in its nature. It takes effect when and only when default has been made in respect to the obligation. Thereupon the reserved right comes into force, but the operation of that force is limited. It secures the performance of the obligation and the payment of all costs and charges incident thereto, but it goes no further. The creditor has a power of sale over the subject-matter of the pledge, but he has nothing more. He may without any further reference to the defaulting debtor sell the property pledged ; but he must return to the owner the balance of the purchase-money, after the debt and its incidental expenses have been fully paid. It is immaterial what form of words is used in the agreement. If it appear that the transaction was in truth not a sale but a mere security for an obligation, the rule "once a mortgage always a mortgage" prevails; and effect will be given to the original intention of the parties, and to that intention only.

Like many other legal institutions, Security has a long and intricate history. That history I do not profess to relate. It is enough that ultimately two principles have become settled. One is that every reasonable facility to the lender for enforcing his rights is equally beneficial to the borrower. The other is that the transaction is a matter not of conveyance but of contract. The right *in rem* is merely accessory to the obligation. But the right *in rem* varies according to the circumstances of each case. Sometimes the security given is the right of ownership, sometimes it is merely the right to possess. At a late period in the history of law a mere appropriation without the conveyance of any legal interest was in certain circumstances found to be sufficient. These are the three forms of security—Mortgage, Pledge, and Charge. In the mortgage the ownership is transferred conditionally and for the purposes of security only. In the pledge the right to possess is similarly transferred, whether the actual possession passes to the creditor or not. The pledgor may continue to have the custody and the use of the pledged property, although the legal possession of it is vested in the pledgee. In the charge neither the right of ownership nor the right to possess nor the actual possession is altered. The property is appropriated to the payment of the obligation; and that appropriation, without the consent of the creditor, cannot be directly or indirectly revoked. The owner of the property, therefore, and every person who, whether by devolution or by transfer, succeeds him in the ownership, holds the property subject to the incumbrance. In other words, the charge must be satisfied before the net value of the property can be finally settled. When the subject-matter of the charge is a beneficial interest or a "chose in action," that is a right to some act which a third party is bound to do for the benefit of the debtor, notice to such third party of the charge is requisite, but his consent is not material. Where the pledgee has the actual possession of the pledged property, he must keep it without negligence, but his responsibility does not go further. There is also implied in the contract as against him a warranty that he will not use the pledge where it is of such a nature that it will be the worse for use, or where by its use it will be exposed to any extraordinary danger. If he fail in his duty in this respect, he will be liable for a breach of his warranty; but a mere impropriety of use is not a ground for a rescission of the contract. The pledgee is liable to an action for any damages which his misconduct may have caused, but the right to recover immediate possession does not thereby vest in the pledgor. Nothing but the payment of the debt is sufficient to maintain such a demand.

Sale. The last of these cases of combined rights is that of sale. Some difficulty arises in the treatment of this subject, because it runs into the matter of the following chapter, and forms part of the inquiry regarding the transfer of rights. But such transfers take their rise in contract. It is therefore fitting—and practical requirements point in the same direction—to discuss in the present place, however briefly, the nature of this agreement.

There is some ambiguity in the expression a contract of sale. It means both the actual contract and an agreement to make that contract. In the former case the right *in rem* at once arises, in the latter case it is only expectant. Thus a contract of marriage, as we have seen, gives rise at once to the status of marriage; but a contract to marry produces merely an obligation which has for its object the formation of the actual contract. A lease of land is a contract which creates various rights and duties between the parties, and also creates certain rights *in rem* in regard to the demised property. But an agreement for a lease is a different thing. In like manner, a contract of sale not merely creates a new obligation, but transfers a pre-existing right *in rem*. A contract to sell, that is a promise to make a contract of sale, does not of itself produce any such effect. The tendency indeed is to diminish by legislation, so far as the nature of the case admits, the results of the distinction. The rule of equity that everything which ought to be done must be regarded as done gives practically in the sale of land the like effect to a contract of sale and to a contract to sell. But in the sale of goods the old distinction prevails, and it is important to understand its operation.

Where two parties agree the one to buy the other to sell some specific thing for a price then actually ascertained, the contract of sale is said to be executed. The contract and the conveyance are in such circumstances simultaneous. The whole transaction is effected at the same moment. In appearance it is a conveyance rather than a contract, for the contractual part is exhausted in producing the transfer. This composite proceeding our forefathers accurately described as a bargain and sale. It requires in this place no further notice, except the remark that the property sold must be specific, and that nothing must remain to be done by the seller for the purpose of ascertaining the exact price, such as completing the thing or weighing measuring or testing it. When in such circumstances the bargain is concluded, the sale takes immediate effect; and the ownership of the property or other interest therein is thereupon transferred. At the same moment and by the same means an obligation for the payment of the price is, unless the contrary intention appear, created in favour of the seller against the buyer..

Where, however, the property is not specific, or where something remains to be done to it or about it, or where otherwise the agreement is not present but prospective, the contract is said to be executory. That is, it is not a sale but a promise to sell. When the time has arrived or the events on which the promise depended have occurred, that which was executory becomes executed. In other words, the promise to sell becomes an actual sale. But in the meantime the ownership of the property remains unchanged. The contract of sale is at most merely inchoate ; and until it is complete it is not the intention of the parties that any transfer should take place. Consequently, when during the interval the property is innocently lost, a question arises as to the incidence of that loss. Thus, a man buys across the counter cloth for a coat; he desires it to be charged to his account and to be sent home. Before the parcel can be sent, a fire occurs in the shop, and the cloth is consumed. In this case the purchaser must pay for the cloth, although it never even came into his hands. But if instead of buying the cloth, he had ordered a coat, and if before he accepted the coat it had been burned, the loss would fall upon the tradesman. *Res perit suo domino.* The owner must bear the accidental loss. In the former case, at the moment of the loss, the buyer was the owner of the cloth; in the latter case the tradesman was the owner of the coat. In such cases a further question sometimes arises. Is the coat property, or does it merely embody work done upon property ? Where labour or skill is expended upon any object, does the skill merge in the thing or does the thing in effect absorb it ? In economic language, is the product* a commodity or a service ? The question is in law by no means an idle one. If the claim be for work and labour, the agreement needs not be in writing. If it be for goods sold and delivered, writing is essential. It is but lately, and after some fluctuation of

* See Senior's Political Economy, 51.

opinion, that this question* has been finally settled. An old lady had occasion to visit her dentist, and, as the result of the interview, ordered from him a set of artificial teeth. Before the teeth were ready she died. Her executors declined either to accept the teeth or to pay for them ; and the dentist brought his action. The defence was that the agreement was for the sale of goods of the value of £10, and consequently ought to have been in writing. This contention prevailed, and it was held that the contract is a sale of goods if it contemplate the ultimate delivery of a chattel. "I do not think, said Mr. Justice Blackburn, that the relative value of the labour and of the materials on which it is bestowed can in any case be the test of what is the cause of action, and that if Benvenuto Cellini had contracted to execute a work of art for another, much as the value of the skill might exceed that of the materials, the contract would have been none the less for the sale of a chattel."

Obligations with Accessorial Obligations. § 4. The third class of combined rights to which I have referred is that of contracts which generate subsidiary rights, not *in rem* but *in personam.* To this class belong the contracts of indemnity of suretyship and of negotiable instruments. A contract of indemnity is a conditional contract by one person to hold another person harmless against the consequences of some liability. It is thus subsidiary to the previous liability and is dependent upon it. The loss sustained is not merely the event upon which the contract is conditioned, but is the measure of damages. If the event in question have occurred, and if compensation for it be made from some other source, the promisor is not liable. If, in ignorance of the fact that such compensation has been so made, he pay the money, he may recover the amount from the promisee. Of this kind of contract the most notable example is fire and marine insurance. Such insurances are contracts to reimburse up to the sum

* Leo *v.* Griffin, 1 B. & S. 272.

specified the insured person for the loss which he may sustain
from the occurrence of the particular event. They are not
wagers that such events will not occur. They are agreements
to defray within a certain limit the amount of loss which if
these events do occur the insured may actually sustain. The
company is not to pay in any case more than the maximum
sum stated in the policy. If the actual loss be less than
that amount, the payment is proportionately less. If the
amount of the damage be defrayed by any other person,
no loss has been in fact sustained, and the company is
consequently exempt from liability. The case is otherwise, as I have said, with life insurance. This is not a
subsidiary but a primary contract. The agreement is not
to replace a possible loss but to make a deferred payment.
In consideration of the present payment during a given
period of a comparatively small premium, the insurer undertakes to pay at an indefinite but ascertainable date a large
sum.

Suretyship, or guarantee as it is often called, is a means
of securing the performance of an obligation by the obligation of another person to perform it on the failure of the
original promisor. So far at least as it guarantees the
repayment of a debt, suretyship is the counterpart* of
mortgage. In both cases the rights are accessorial. In
both cases both the principal and the accessorial duties
and rights arise out of contracts. In both cases the principal
contract is for the loan of money ; and in both cases the
accessorial contract is intended to secure the repayment of
that loan. But the mortgage generates a right *in rem*, while
the guarantee generates a right *in personam*. The latter is
in truth a secondary obligation, of which the purpose is to
secure by some means external to the original promise the
performance of that promise. It is usually intended to secure
the repayment of money, but it may be an indemnity for any
loss caused by the default or misconduct of the person in
question. Thus a man may undertake to pay the debt of

* See Mr. Hunter's Roman Law, 383.

T

another if that other should fail himself to discharge it; or he may agree to indemnify an employer against any loss sustained by the conduct of his employé. Questions arise in matters of suretyship between the creditor and the surety, between the debtor and the surety, and between co-sureties. It is enough in this place to observe that where there are several sureties, if the occasion for the performance of their obligation should arise, the right of contribution, except where the parties are wrong-doers, exists.

There are some other cases which may also be referred to this class. Such are judgment *pro confesso,* account stated, and the *constitutum** of the Roman law. These do not involve the interference of a third party, but merely give to the promisee an additional remedy beyond that which he already possesses. The same remark applies generally to what are called collateral securities. This is the term ordinarily used where some further security is taken in some transaction upon which the usual security, although perhaps to an insufficient amount, has been already given. Sometimes the object is not to eke out an insufficient remedy, but to obtain a more convenient one. Sometimes the collateral contract is available when from some cause the original remedy fails. In all cases, however, the general rule as to securities prevails; and these further rights are in force until the original contract is performed, and no longer. But although I have *ex abundanti cautelâ* mentioned these cases, they are of little moment for our present purpose. They are merely ordinary obligations, which either mark certain stages in a transaction, or which it is convenient to use in a particular way in order to attain some practical object. They do not appear to add any new light to the theory of law.

Negotiable Instruments. § 5. Very different, both in practical importance and in theoretic interest, from the instances I have last mentioned is another class of composite rights *in*

---

* See Mr. Hunter's Roman Law, 337.

personam. I mean the great class of Negotiable Instruments.. These familiar documents are highly complex. They commence with an ordinary contract. They advance by means of indorsement into secondary contracts of suretyship. Finally, they have acquired certain peculiarities of transfer which constitute their most marked characteristic. On this characteristic I shall have to enlarge in a subsequent chapter. At present I shall attempt to explain the nature of the original contract and of the accessorial contract to which it gives rise. A bill of exchange is the most familiar form of a negotiable instrument, and sufficiently illustrates for our purpose the incidents of the entire class. I shall therefore briefly describe its nature. It assumes that one man owes money to another; that he has funds in the hands of a third person; and that he wishes to apply these funds to the payment of his obligation. He accordingly gives to his creditor a written order upon the third party directing him to pay at a specified time a specified sum to the creditor or to his order or to the bearer of the instrument, as the case may be. This instrument, when it is presented to him, the third party, if he be willing to undertake the responsibility, accepts, and signs it accordingly. He thereby undertakes to pay the bill when it becomes due according to its tenor at the place which in his acceptance he has specified; or, if he have not specified any place, at his usual place of business or abode. So far the case resembles that of a delivery order for goods to a bailee, and the acceptance is in fact the bailee's attornment to the new bailor. But the bill when so accepted may be delivered if it be made payable to bearer, or indorsed and delivered if it be made payable to order, to some other person who may be an entire stranger to the original parties. The effect of the mere delivery is a sale of the bill as it stands, or, in other words, an assignment of the obligation arising from the original contract without the creation of any further or other obligation. The effect of the indorsement and delivery is not only to assign the obligation arising

T 2

·from the original contract, but also to create a contract
of suretyship by the indorsee with his transferee that
the acceptor will perform his agreement. Thus every new
·indorsement is a new conditional contract* for indemnity
against all loss directly occasioned by the dishonour of the
bill when it is in due course presented for payment to the
acceptor.

Negotia-bility. The principal feature of such instruments, that in
fact which constitutes their negotiability, is the peculiarity in their transfer. A negotiable instrument is not
merely assignable, for this is a quality which it shares with
all other choses in action, but it passes to the *bonâ fide*
assignee free from all defects in the title of the previous
holders. This peculiarity is a creature of law and not of
agreement. It is confined to negotiable instruments as
recognised by law; consequently no arbitrary addition can be
made to the list of such instruments. Those instruments
which the general custom of merchants has hitherto treated
as negotiable the law now regards as negotiable. Those
instruments which now or hereafter may by a similar usage
be so treated, the courts, if they be satisfied as to the generality of the usage, may also from time to time recognise.
But no individual or no body of persons short of the entire
mercantile community can create a new negotiability. It
has been thought that there is an exception to this rule, and
that in certain circumstances at least a practical negotiability
may be obtained by the mere consent of the parties. There
·are cases in which the transferee has successfully contended
that by reason of a representation to that effect made by the
·original debtor, and of his having bought on the faith of
that representation, he was not liable to any equities affecting
an instrument not otherwise negotiable. The explanation of
these cases is, that in such circumstances the right of the
transferee depends not upon any quality in the instrument
itself, but upon the privity of legal relation that is established between the original contractor and the transferee

* See *per* Brett L. J., 3 Q. B. D. 510.

In other words, the case is one not of negotiability but of estoppel.

Bills of Exchange and Bills of Lading. In negotiable instruments the right *in rem* is accessory to the right *in personam*. The ownership of the paper follows the right arising from the obligation. In this respect these instruments are the opposites to documents of title. In the bill of exchange the ownership of the instrument follows the obligation. In the bill of lading the right to sue on the obligation follows the ownership of the instrument. The reason of the distinction may readily be perceived. The document of title, as we shall presently see, symbolizes and represents the goods to which it relates. The goods are the principal objects in the transaction; and the obligation follows the document because it follows the goods, and the document is in effect the goods. But in the negotiable instrument the right *in personam* is the principal object. The instrument is merely the pre-appointed evidence of that right, and is therefore accessorial to it, as the title deeds of an estate are accessorial to and follow the ownership. Hence the ownership of the paper passes with the possession, and follows the obligation. Thus both negotiable instruments and documents of title are governed by the same rule, though its application varies according to the circumstances of each case. "*Accessorium non ducit sed sequitur suum principale.*" The principal and not the accessory must lead the way. It is indeed probable, as Savigny has suggested, that negotiable instruments owe their effect in no small degree to the fact that they necessarily have a material form. They are in some sense an intermediate step between *res corporales* and *res incorporales*. They are obligations; but it is not difficult to assume that the holder of the document which contains the obligation, indefinite though he might be, is in substance a party to the obligation itself. The instrument itself was a thing; and the thing could be transferred, and in its transfer carried with it the mere rights that were incidental to it.

But these rights so far exceeded the value of the thing, and the latter was so manifestly accessorial to the former, that by a natural inconsistency the thing, as I have said, was held to follow the right. The use of these instruments arose long after the rules of rights *in rem* and *in personam* were settled ; and the law relating to them bears marks of the attempts, . not always consistent, to reconcile the exigencies of social growth and the accepted principles of the jurists.

CHAPTER XIV.

THE TRANSFER OF RIGHTS.

The Analysis of Transfer. § 1. It will help us to ascertain the doctrine of the transfer of rights if we distinguish it from other subjects which it more or less closely resembles. In the first place then transfer differs from the acquisition of rights. Transfer presupposes an existing right. Acquisition implies the creation of a new right. Subordinate rights may indeed be carved out of a wider and older right, and in this sense transfer may be described as a mode of acquisition. But this process is substantially a transfer of part of a pre-existing interest as distinguished from a transfer of the whole of that interest. The grant of the whole unexpired portion of a term of years is held to be an assignment of the lease; but the grant of that portion less by one day is not an assignment, but is the creation of a sub-lease. In such circumstances the original right is merely subdivided into certain component parts, each of which becomes a separate legal object. No new right is acquired; nothing exists which did not previously exist. Only a change, irrespective it may be of the original grantor, takes place by mutual consent in the number of the donees of the right.

In the second place, transfer is not equivalent to alienation. It is a much narrower term. It implies alienation *inter vivos*. The devolution of property after death is a different thing. Such devolution resembles transfer because both of them are forms of alienation, that is because in each case the property of one man passes to another man. But the difference between life and death sets between the two varieties a great gulf; and although the influence of the one may be readily traced in the history of the other, it is prudent even at the present day to adopt in respect to each subject a separate treatment. There is yet a third difference. Transfer is not merely alienation *inter vivos:* it is also a voluntary alienation. It does not include every transmission of a right from one living person to another. It implies the consent of both parties. It is thus distinguished from all conveyances by operation of law. The whole property of an insolvent vests in his assignee as soon as the order of sequestration is made; but this is not transfer in the usual sense. The law sometimes simulates the form of transfer, as when some legal official in pursuance of an order of court executes a conveyance in the name of some party to a suit. Such a proceeding is merely technical. The operative part of the transaction is the order of court, or, in other words, the command of the State through its proper officer. Such a command of itself transfers the ownership without the consent or the apparent consent of the former owner.

Transfer then means the voluntary assignment of an existing transferable object by the owner or the possessor of that object to some other person. There are the two parties. There is the mutual consent. There is the transferable object to which that consent relates. These are the antecedent conditions in every transfer. Where these conditions are present and not otherwise, a transfer, whatever its actual requirements may be, becomes possible. Little needs be said as to the parties. Unless he be subject to some disqualification either general or arising out of the particular transaction, every person who owns or possesses a transferable object may, according to the quantity of his interest therein, dispose of it. Subject to the like restrictions, every person who can make a contract may accept the transfer. Nor is the necessity for mutual consent* less obvious. No man can be compelled to accept from another any right against his will. A transfer does not usually take place unless it be desired by the transferee, and consequently disputes as to his intention seldom arise. But if every

---

* *In omnibus rebus quæ dominium transferunt, concurrat oportet affectus ex utraque parte contrahentium.*—Dig. XLIV. 7, 55.

person were allowed at his own mere will to transfer his rights when they seemed likely to become burthensome, the unfortunate transferee would soon sink overwhelmed, like the treacherous Roman maid, by the fatal gifts of his pretended friends. The third of these antecedent conditions presents greater difficulty than either of the others. Transferable objects cannot be described as readily as we have described the parties and the need for their consent. Whether a duty or a right is or is not transferable depends upon the terms of its creation. It may by these terms be limited merely to the man upon whom it is imposed or to whom it is given. It may be limited to him and his legal representatives. It may be limited to him, his legal representatives and assigns. In the first case the duty or the right is strictly personal. In the second case it survives to the legal representatives. In the third case it is freely transmissible. It is therefore necessary to ascertain the proper limitation in each of the various classes of duties and of rights.

Principle of Transfer. "Nothing, says Gaius,[*] is so conformable to natural equity as that the will of the owner who wishes to transfer to another his *res* should have effect given to it by law. Accordingly, a *res corporalis*, of whatsoever kind it may be, can be delivered, and when delivered by the owner is alienated." This passage, especially when read in connexion with other observations of the great commentator, shows both the principle of the transfer of rights and its method. Whether the subject-matter be *res corporalis* or *res incorporalis*, a right of which the secondary object is a thing or a mere right without any secondary object, the transaction primarily depends upon the will of the *dominus*, or, as I have called him, the donee of the right. To that will, when it has been unequivocally expressed, the law gives effect. For the purpose of securing the right action of the law, proof of the owner's intention is required. In the case of rights relating to a thing, where delivery is physically

---

[*] *Nihil tam conveniens naturali æquitati quam voluntatem domini volentis rem suam in alium transferri ratam haberi. Et ideo cujus cumque generis sit corporalis res tradi potest et a domino tradita alienatur.*—Dig. XLI. 1, 9. Inst. Just. II. 1, 40.

possible, that proof is found in the actual change of the possession of the thing. In the case of mere rights, where delivery is not physically possible, no other means are available except the original method of the Formal contract. Thus the delivery is a means of which the transfer is the end; and the delivery, from the nature of the case, is limited to one particular class of transfers, that in which delivery can physically be made.

" Traditio " or the delivery of a thing for the purpose of transfer, bears a close resemblance to possession and abandonment. Each of these terms implies two parts, an act and an intention. Possession, as we have seen, is the act of detention with the intention of appropriation. Abandonment or dereliction is the act of ceasing to detain with the intention of ceasing to appropriate. " Traditio" is the act of ceasing to detain with the intention that another person should possess. Doubtless, in the history of law, "traditio" belongs to the Prætorian possession; and denotes the change effected by simple delivery which was recognised as lawful by the Prætor, as distinguished from the change of Quiritary ownership which could only be effected by the Bronze and Balance or by the legal contrivance of a fictitious Recovery. It would be easy to trace in minute details the resemblance between " traditio " and " possessio," but at present I shall notice only two circumstances. One is that both of these terms relate to *res corporales* exclusively, and offer no explanation of *res incorporales*. The other is that in both of these terms there is a dangerous ambiguity. As "possessio" was composite and its name was accordingly given to either of its component parts, so " traditio" was similarly used in a double sense. Sometimes it means the transfer of the right ; sometimes it means the delivery or physical change of detention by which in the case of things such transfer is effected.

It follows that, as in possession so also in tradition, the *factum* alone is insufficient. The *animus* also is needed for the purposes of " alienatio." It is not enough to prove that the owner parted with his property. It is equally necessary to show that he intended that that property should go to another, and that that other was willing to receive it. In the language of the Roman jurists, the *voluntas domini* must be attended by a *justa causa*. In our language the intent to transfer must be proved. It is in this proof that the difficulties connected with transfer consist. In general terms, it may perhaps be stated that at the present day every transfer has three requisites. There must be a formal declaration of intention by the transferor. There must be some exercise of his new right by the transferee. There must be some notice of the change of ownership to the public either by the open exercise of his right by the new owner or by some form of public registration. Each of these conditions varies according to circumstances. The evidence of the transferor's intention and the evidence of the transferee's acceptance of his new position are not alike in all cases. Various points of difference must be noted. There is the difference between rights which relate to things and rights which have not such relation. There is the difference between real estate and chattels. There is the difference between direct and beneficial interests. There is the exception to the ordinary rules of proof which the Law Merchant has introduced. There is also the constant distinction between matters of business and free gifts. Of the results of these causes of difference I shall now endeavour to offer some account.

The Transfer of Rights in rem concerning Things. § 2. I have said that transfer implies an exercise of the rights of ownership, or of some of them, by the transferee in his own right with the consent of the transferor. In the case of things the compliance with these conditions is easy. It amounts to what is usually called delivery of possession, that is the placing of the property at the disposal of the purchaser. Some misapprehension has probably been caused by the use of this word "delivery." It seems to imply some action on the part of the original possessor. But the duty of this person is a duty not of action but of forbearance. He is not required to do any act for the purpose of effecting delivery. His duty is simply to permit the transferee to exercise his right. Delivery, in short, means not an active transmission of the property, but a mere consent or permission on the part of its former possessor to its removal by the transferee. We can thus understand the importance that "traditio" or delivery has always held in matters of transfer. It was the most distinct and the most public mode of claiming right over the property with the avowed acquiescence of the owner. It is the act of the grantee that is significant in the transaction much more than the act of the grantor. In support of this view, in the case of things I cite the oldest form of legal transfer—that of the "mancipatio," or, as it is often called, the proceeding by the Bronze and Balance. Its very name, importing as it does the seizure by the strong hand, indicates its nature. It was, in fact, a form of *occupatio* with the consent of the parties who had or might be supposed to have prior claims. As in the latest form of conveying real property we have fallen back on our original starting point, and make every transfer of land practically a fresh grant from the Crown; so in the archaic times a transfer of any of the objects which their custom had recognised as property presented itself to the minds of the men of that day as the reduction into possession of an ownerless object, the former owner being induced to hold his peace as to his claim. The form of the ceremony* tells its own tale. Both parties met in the presence of five† witnesses

---

* Gaius, I. 119, 121.

† In the Roman law the number of witnesses varied according to the nature of the transaction. In Mancipation they were, as stated above, five. In Testaments they were seven. In Confarreation, the Quiritarian form of marriage, they were ten. In marriage by Coemption, which was a mere Mancipation, they were five (Gaius, I. 112, 113). We know that the seven witnesses to the Testament were the usual five, the Libripens and the Familiæ Emptor. The ten in Confarreation (" *præsentibus decem testibus*," Gaius, I. 112) were, I conceive, the five witnesses of the Familia of the bridegroom and of the bride respectively. As to the five witnesses I have stated my views in " The Aryan Household," 129. These views seem to be supported by the ten in the Confarreation, a circumstance which in that book I accidentally omitted to notice.

and of a functionary styled the Balance-hanger. The purchaser thereupon laid hold of the property or its symbol, and
thus made his claim—" I allege that this property is mine
according to the law of the Quirites, and it has been purchased by me with this bronze and bronze-balance." He
then struck the balance with the ingot, and gave to the
vendor the ingot as his price. The action as thus described
is exclusively that of the purchaser. The vendor is merely
passive, and, except that he receives the money, has no more
to do in the proceeding than the witnesses. It is the purchaser who makes his claim, and exercises as of right in the
presence of the former owner his adverse possession. The
vendor acquiesces in the claim, and is thus estopped from
subsequently setting up his former right.

In the old English law we can trace a similar course of
thought, modified, however, by the particular circumstances
of the time. The transfer of land was at one period of our
history not a sale between equals. It was a grant by a
superior to a person who, so far at least as regarded that
transaction, was his inferior, and who was bound by the
terms of their agreement not to pay him once for all a certain
price, but to render him from time to time certain continuous
personal services. In such a transfer there was first a grant
called a feoffment, expressing the conveyance of the property
by the grantor and the terms and duration of the interest.
But this feoffment, although accepted by the feoffee, passed
of itself no estate beyond at most a mere estate at will.
For the completion of the transaction there remained another
part not less essential, namely, the livery of seisin or
investiture. This delivery of possession of the land which
was the subject of the fief was the actual exercise of his
new right by the grantee in the presence and with the
acquiescence of his grantor. It was the essential act of
conveyance, and words were required only to explain the act,
like the *Fiducia* or *lex Mancipii** of the old Roman law, or
if need were, to limit and direct the estates for which it was

* See Gaius, I. 114, 123.

intended that the seisin should be held. Blackstone* indeed suggests that this livery was merely intended to indicate the delivery of quiet possession. But he admits that this is merely a conjecture; and although Blackstone is an acknowledged authority both as to the common law and as to the law which was in actual operation at the time when he wrote, his reasons, whether philosophical or historical, for the existence of these states of the law do not command similar confidence. The examples that he subsequently gives of the ceremony—the transfer in certain cases of the staff, the old symbol of authority, and the entry of the feoffee into the house (where a house was transferred) alone, his shutting the door and then opening it, and admitting the other persons present—point to some definite public act of ownership done by the grantee in presence of the grantor and with his acquiescence.

In Roman law the transfer of *res nec mancipi* was effected by tradition. In less technical language, the latter method of transfer as gradually established by the Prætorian jurisdiction superseded the old mancipation; and in all cases of "*Res corporales*" it adopted for its evidence of intention the actual delivery of possession of the property or of its symbol. In our common law the like process is known as Bargain and Sale, and is the appropriate method for the transfer of personal chattels. I have already said that a Bargain and Sale is what is sometimes called an executed contract. It amounts to a conveyance of the property sold—absolute when the property is reduced into possession, conditional while the price remains unsatisfied and the possession remains with the seller. In the case of an absolute sale of chattels no question arises. The bargain is made, and the sale is complete. In pursuance of the agreement, the property comes into the hands of the purchaser or of his agents. He has without dispute the right to possess. This exercise of that right, the reduction of the property into actual possession, is the natural consequence of the transaction. It is by this

* II. 311.

means that he openly exercises his new right over it. Consequently, the absence of such reduction has usually been regarded as *primâ facie* evidence of fraud. If, notwithstanding a sale, the former owner continue in possession, a fictitious ownership is suggested, and the public may readily be deceived. Some explanation is therefore in such cases necessary. But such an explanation may be given ; and when it has been given, the unfavorable presumption is removed. In other words, the reduction into possession of property in pursuance of an absolute contract of sale is evidence that the new owner has accepted his new rights, and that the former owner has acknowledged that his claims are satisfied. It is the usual and the best evidence that the transfer has been duly completed. But it is not the only means of proof by which the same conclusion may be established.

It forms no part of my present purpose to inquire into the system of conveyancing which has grown up under the Statute of Uses. That system is essentially not merely local but accidental. It is the result of the unexpected operation upon the doctrine of seisin of a particular statute. It is certainly strange that the transfer of real property in English law for the last three centuries and a half should have resulted from an unforeseen consequence of an Act of Parliament which was never meant to produce any such result, which was enacted for an entirely different purpose, and which altogether failed to accomplish that purpose. Another recognised method of transfer in our law consists in a declaration, which in the case of land must be in writing, by the grantor, or by some custodian for the grantor, that he holds the property in trust for the grantee. For such a declaration no particular form is required. Practically, however, men do not care to have their property held for them in trust by their vendors. This method therefore is more frequently found in family arrangements and in gifts than in commercial transactions. I may then in this place state briefly the provisions of the law which relate to the transfer of property without consideration. The law does not refuse to take notice of such transfers, although it is not disposed to show them any special favour.

Transfer   A gift is complete and irrevocable when in addi-
by Gift. tion to the intention of the donor the actual possession of the thing is transferred to the donee; or when the actual possession of the thing is transferred to another person in trust for the donee ; or when the donor has executed a complete declaration of trust in favour of the donee ; or when the transfer is made by an instrument under seal.   In other words, gifts require a " traditio " or its equivalent ; or else the intention of the parties must be expressed in a Formal contract.   If these conditions be fulfilled, the gift will pass the ownership or other interest according to its terms.   If they be not fulfilled, the gift remains revocable at the pleasure of the donor.   But all gifts, and indeed all transfers, are voidable at the option of the party injured, if they be intended to defeat or delay creditors present or prospective.   Under the old law of real property, a gift of land was practically impossible.   It can now be effected by means of registration, but probably not by any other method. Where a gift of a chattel has been made in good faith, if there have been an actual delivery, or if a sufficient trust have been created, or if the gift be made by deed, the gift will be valid.   But the law will not go out of its way to support any mistake in the matter.   Where a man intends to make a gift by delivery, if he fail to do so, but succeed in creating a trust, the good trust will not supply the place of the bad delivery.

Refusal of' I have hitherto assumed that in a bargain and
Delivery. sale everything has been done upon both sides ; that the property has been delivered, and that the price has been paid.   The course of commerce, however, does not always run so smooth.   Sometimes it happens that one of the parties will not give, or as the case may be will not accept, delivery. Sometimes it happens that the buyer will not pay the price.

It is necessary to consider what effect these misadventures produce upon the transfer. Where the seller refuses to give delivery upon tender to him of the price, he commits a breach of his contract; and he is liable to an action for damages, or if the nature of the case admit for specific performance. Where the buyer refuses to accept delivery, the question generally turns on the seller's right of re-sale ; and the answer to the question* depends upon the intent with which the refusal has been made. If it appear that the buyer intended wholly to repudiate the performance of his contract, the seller, if he think fit, may treat such conduct as an offer to rescind, and may accordingly act as if the whole proceeding had never taken place. If such an intention do not appear, the seller cannot by his own mere motion rescind the contract. If he re-sell, he will be liable for breach of his agreement. In the action for such a breach the measure of damages will be the amount of the excess if any of the market price over the contract price ; if there be no such excess, the damages will be merely nominal. He may, however, if there be a deficiency, recover the amount of such deficiency in an action for breach of contract. Substantially, therefore, a re-sale by the seller, as the agent of the buyer or rather as his pledgee, amounts to a practical remedy.

Default of Payment. The other case I have mentioned, that of default of payment, requires more consideration. At first sight indeed nothing can be clearer. Payment is an essential condition of the contract. Until that condition has been performed, that is until payment has been either actually made or tendered, the buyer has no claim either 'to the possession or to the ownership of the property. But in the ordinary course of business goods are often before payment delivered to a carrier for the buyer. If before they reach the buyer he make default, what are the rights of the seller? In such circumstances no change of possession has yet taken place. The "traditio" is merely inchoate. It is true that

* Campbell on Sales, 330.

U

the carrier is the agent of the buyer. Such agency, however, is not to accept the goods but only to carry them. The reality of this distinction is apparent when it is considered that, if the goods were not according to order, the buyer after he had received them from the carrier and examined them might, notwithstanding the carrier's agency, have refused to accept them. While therefore the transit continues, that is while the goods remain in the hands of the carrier as such, the seller has still his conditional possession. He has yet time to insist upon the condition precedent of payment. But when the goods have actually come into the hands of the buyer or of an agent of the buyer duly authorized to undertake their custody for him, the transit is at an end ; the possession has been changed, and the seller has no other remedy than an action upon his contract. Accordingly, if during the transit it appear that the buyer is not able to pay the price when the goods reach him, the unpaid seller is restored to the position in which he stood before the goods left his hands. He must satisfy the demand of the carrier ; but, subject to that charge, he is entitled to resume the control of his goods. The same principle applies when the agreement contemplates an unexpired period of credit. I think, however, that the reason in this case somewhat differs from that in the preceding case. We have already seen that, where the promise is a future act, the promisee is entitled to the maintenance of that promise until the time for its performance arrives. Where credit is given, the promise is that the price or the security which is given for it will be paid on a certain day. If before that day it appear that the promisor intends not to fulfil his promise, the agreement is broken. The promisee may consequently avail himself of his former remedy as if the promise had never been made. That former remedy consists in the exercise of his vendor's right. Thus the contract to give credit is brought to an end by the default of the promisor; and the case returns to the ordinary conditions of a stoppage in transit without any special agreement. I may add, although I shall presently notice the subject more fully, that where goods are represented by symbols, the transfer of the symbol amounts to a transfer both of the possession and of the ownership. Consequently, the right of stoppage in transit does not apply to goods in respect of which documents of title have been indorsed and delivered in the ordinary course of business. The transfer of such goods is governed by the transfer of their symbols.

§ 3. In the Roman law* "*Res incorporales*" **The Transfer of other Rights in rem.** were transferred, according to Quiritary law by mancipation, or by a recovery in a feigned suit before the Prætor; and according to Prætorian law by the Formal contract known by its later name of Stipulation. When the distinction between the soil of Italy and the soil of the Provinces was abolished, all transactions of this class were treated as obligations. They were created by stipulation, and were transferred by novation, that is by a new stipulation made between the transferee and the original grantor. This process, as its name implies, was not, at least in form, the transfer of an existing right; but was the substitution of a new agreement between different parties for an old one. By this expedient, whatever its other consequences may have been, the complications that arise from transfer were avoided. In our law there is a true transfer of such rights. We have therefore to consider by what means effect in such cases is given to the agreement between the parties and to its results as regards the public. In the case of privileges the transfer is easily effected. These rights require registration. They do not come into operation until an entry setting forth certain prescribed particulars is made by the proper officer in a public register. In the same way in which they are created they can be transferred. A memorandum in writing of the transfer signed by the parties or their agents gives the necessary authority to the registrar; and he

* Gaius, II. 2S *et seq.*

U 2

thereupon makes in his book the proper entries indicating the transfer accordingly. Thus the transferee becomes the registered owner ; and the fact that he is so may be ascertained by any person who chooses to search the register. This proceeding resembles the issue of a new grant of land, or the novation of an obligation. The registration is the evidence not so much of a transfer made and accepted, as of the creation of a novated right by the original grantor.

I have written of transfers as if the parties to them were the transferor and the transferee and none others. In practice, however, matters are often less simple. The property may be held either in ownership or in possession by a third party; and the subject of the transfer is then not the whole ownership with all its incidents, but the limited interest, whatever it may be, of the transferor. This is the case of a transfer of a right *in re alienâ*, whether the subject of the transfer be that right itself or be the ownership less by that right. Thus the third party may be a trustee, and may have the full ownership except only the right of use ; while the beneficial interest either in whole or in part may belong to the transferor and be the subject-matter of the transfer. Or the third party may be a bailee having merely the possession or the custody of the property. Or he may simply be a debtor of the transferor, and the intention may be to transfer the benefits of an obligation. In such cases there are four parties whose position must be considered. These are the transferor, the transferee, the third party as I have above described him, and the public. As between the first two parties, the case is merely one of contract. But the third party must know to what person he has to perform his duties ; and the public must know the person whose proprietary rights they are bound to respect. From the nature of the case, such knowledge cannot be obtained from the actual possession of the property. That test is available only in the simplest forms of transfer. But the rule, of which the delivery of possession is, as I have said, only one case—the rule which requires the open and undisputed exercise of the right of the transferee, is sufficient, whatever may be the complexity of the circumstances, for our guidance. Whatever rights may arise between the parties themselves from their contract, the transfer is not complete until notice of it has been given to the third party. Such notice serves a double purpose. It informs the third party of what, for the proper discharge of his duty, it is essential that he should know. It is also the nearest approach to actual possession that the nature of the case admits. It is so, because, like delivery, it is the avowed and formal exercise of the right of ownership, of which exercise the original owner is aware and in which he acquiesces. In the one case, as in the other, the principle of estoppel applies. The result is the same, although the methods necessarily vary.

The Transfer of Rights in personam. § 4. I have said that " Choses in action," that is rights arising from an obligation, are transferable by notice, and I need not repeat the reasons for that form of assignment. Such transferability, however, has been of very slow growth. The Roman jurists would not hear of it. " Obligations," says Gains,* after describing the various forms of transfer, " in whatever manner contracted, admit of none of these things." It was only by a novation, that is by the substitution of a new contract for the former one, that any such object could be effected. At a later period an expedient known as *"cessio actionum"* was adopted. The promisee was allowed to assign his interest, and to constitute irrevocably the assignee as his agent to sue in his name on the contract and to retain for his own use the proceeds of the action. At a still later date, the assignee was allowed to sue, under certain conditions, in his own name. The English Courts of Law and of Equity followed respectively the two last-mentioned rules. By recent legislation, the rule of equity has, with some modification, been definitely established. Choses in action may now be assigned absolutely, in writing, after notice in writing to the debtor, and subject to all existing equities.

There is a class of rights *in personam* of which the transfer is exceptional. This class is that of negotiable instruments. Where such an instrument is made payable to bearer, the right to it passes by mere delivery. Where it is made payable to order, it passes by indorsement and delivery. Indorsement is an order written upon the instrument by its holder in favour of some other person. Sometimes the indorsement consists simply of the name of the writer. The bill is then said to be indorsed in blank; and such a signature is taken to mean an order by the holder in favour of any person who may become its possessor. There are three incidents of this form of transfer. The first incident is that the holder may sue in his own right; and, consequently, that no notice of assignment is necessary. The original promise is made to the drawer or to the person named in his order, or to bearer as the case may be. Consequently, the person mentioned in the order, or the bearer, is a party to the instrument in his own right; and therefore deals with the obligor directly, and not through the medium of any other person. The second incident is that the *bonâ fide* possession, that is the possession of a purchaser for value without notice of any defect in the title to the instrument, is conclusive proof of ownership. Consequently, as we shall presently see, the transfer of a negotiable instrument may in the circumstances above indicated convey to the assignee a better title than the assignor had. In other words, the *bonâ fide* holder of a negotiable instrument is not, like the *bonâ fide* holder of other rights *in personam*, subject to any equities that affect the right. The third incident is the presumption that the transfer of a negotiable instrument, which in its origin was mercantile, was made for valuable consideration. This presumption may be rebutted, but the burthen of proof rests upon the person who denies the consideration. When, however, the title to the instrument has been proved to be defective, the presumption is shifted; and the holder must prove that he received the instrument for value. It will then be a sufficient reply if it can be shown that he was nevertheless concerned in or aware of the damaging circumstances of its title. That is, the holder must show positively that he comes under the class which is excepted from the rule as to bad title; but as the law never presumes misconduct, he has only to prove value, and the proof of a guilty knowledge rests upon the other side.

Negotiable instruments are derived from mercantile usage adopted by law; consequently, an instrument cannot be made negotiable merely by calling it so, or by using in novel circumstances the established forms. A negotiable instrument means an instrument which, by the custom of merchants as it now exists or as it may hereafter exist, is negotiable, and which is recognised as such by the courts. Thus it has been held* that a debenture issued by a company under its seal, and purporting to be payable to bearer, was not negotiable. Its words were inconsistent with its form. An instrument under seal is not assignable by mere delivery unless a contrary usage of merchants be shown; and in the case of the debentures no such usage was alleged.

Documents of title, that is bills of lading and their equivalents, although in some respects they bear a close resemblance to negotiable instruments, must be distinguished from them. Like negotiable instruments, they are contracts; they owe their peculiarities to the Law Merchant or to statutory extensions of that law; they are transferred by delivery and indorsement; they enable the holder to sue in his own right; and they need no notice of assignment. But the contracts are regarded as symbols of the goods to which they refer; and they are in fact contrivances for transferring mercantile rights *in rem* and not mere rights *in personam.* They do in effect transfer both the ownership and the possession of those goods to the holder of the document for the time being. It follows that, when the document has

* Crouch *v.* Credit Foncier of England, L. R. 3 Q. B. 374.

been indorsed and delivered, the transit is at an end; and that since the transit is at an end the unpaid vendor's right of stoppage in transit also ceases. But the rights under a document of title, whether they be *in rem* or *in personam*, are subject to the ordinary rule; and are no greater in the hands of the transferee than they were in the hands of the transferor. The *bonâ fide* holder for value of a document of title* must prove his title. Thus, if a thief were to steal a bill of exchange and a bill of lading, and were to sell both bills to a person who bought them in the ordinary course of business for their full value without any knowledge of the theft, the innocent purchaser would be protected in the case of the bill of exchange, but would have to bear the loss in the case of the bill of lading.

The Avoidance of Transfers. § 5. Since transfer depends upon the consent of the parties, it follows that all the conditions which in discussing contract we found to be essential to true consent should find their place in transfer. Nor is it material whether the transfer takes the form of sale or of gift, or whether the instrument by which effect is given to it be a mere memorandum in writing or a deed. Every circumstance which avoids or renders voidable any other contract will in like manner affect a contract of sale. Every circumstance which thus affects a contract of sale will affect a transfer in pursuance of such contract or a gift made under similar conditions. In the case of voidable contracts it will be remembered that the contract is valid until it has been avoided. Consequently, every *bonâ fide* transfer made prior to its rescission will be supported. But in addition to these causes of invalidity which are common to all cases of consent there are some peculiar restrictions that affect the validity of transfer. Such restrictions are meant for the protection of creditors. A man can transfer that only which he has, and he cannot be said to have property when he is in fact insolvent. When therefore a transfer,

* Gurney v. Dohrend, 3 E. & D. 622.

whether for value or not, is made with intent to defraud creditors, such transfer is voidable at the option of those creditors. Such an intent may be inferred without reference to the transferor's state of mind when the effect of the transaction is in fact to injure the creditors, because every man is supposed to intend the natural consequences of his acts. The most common form of these frauds upon creditors is that of post-nuptial settlements. Such settlements sometimes took a more skilful form. They were made in consideration of marriage, but they purported to secure to the wife and children all the after-acquired property of the settlor. Arrangements of this character were unquestionably convenient for those who enjoyed their protection, but they were less favorably regarded by the creditors who suffered from them. In Victoria, accordingly, statutory provision* has been made both for preventing these frauds and for defining transfers which are made in fraud of creditors. Except in case of ante-nuptial settlements, or of *bonâ fide* sales or mortgages for value, or of post-nuptial settlements of property acquired after marriage in right of the wife, if a man become insolvent, all his transfers during the two years next preceding his insolvency become voidable at the option of his assignee or trustee. The like effect takes place in the case of transfers reaching back five years, unless the parties claiming under the transfer can show that at the time of the transfer the transferor was in fact able to pay his debts without the aid of the property conveyed. Further, every covenant in an ante-nuptial settlement to settle after-acquired property is voidable at the option of the assignee of the insolvent estate, unless the property have been transferred pursuant to the covenant before the insolvency has taken place.

The Strengthening of Titles by Transfer. § 6. I have said, and it seems to go without saying, that no person can give to another a right that he does not himself enjoy. *Nemo dat quod non habet.* Yet there are circumstances in which even

* Act No. 379, s. 70.

this obvious truth requires limitation. A transfer may sometimes convey to the transferee a right greater than that to which the transferor was entitled. I do not refer to cases of mere agency, whether expressed or implied. In such circumstances, the agent does not give that which is not his own ; but his principal gives through the hands of his agent, and consequently it is to the principal and not to the agent that our maxim applies. Nor does the agent cease to be an agent when he acts under a power of sale implied by law. When a pledgee sells a forfeited pledge, he is not less an agent than he would be if he held from the owner a power of attorney for the purposes of the sale. Nor do I refer to the case where, in the course of his duty, a public officer sells some other person's property. Such an officer may by a fiction be said to be an agent appointed by law. Fictions of this kind are, however, needless. It is better to describe the vendor as what he really is, an officer of the law deriving his authority not from the mandate of the owner but from the direct command of the State. It is upon that command and not upon any other basis that such a sale rests. Thus even where the document under which a sheriff sells property is ultimately set aside, yet, if it be not invalid upon its face, his proceedings* will be supported; and the owner of the property will be entitled only to its price, and not to the property itself. I have already shown that where in pursuance of an order of the court, a Master or other official executes a conveyance on behalf of some owner mentioned in such order, the conveyance is merely formal, and the order of the court is of itself and without any conveyance sufficient to effect the transfer. But there are two cases in which the transferee really obtains more than his transferor had to give. One is that of money and the recognised substitutes of money. The other is that of a purchase in good faith for valuable consideration. Both of these cases rest upon substantially the same ground—the exigencies of exchange.

* Campbell on Sales, 72.

In all countries where it exists, the ownership of coined money, of the current coin of the realm as our books call it, passes by mere delivery. Even where coin has been stolen, if it be received from the thief by another person in good faith, the innocent holder acquires a good title. It used to be said that this consequence followed because money could not be ear-marked. It is needless to discuss this foolish reason for good law. The true cause of the exception is now universally acknowledged. Close akin to money in the usage of modern society are negotiable instruments. They owed their characteristic feature to the practice of merchants; and the qualities thus acquired have fitted them to serve as a substitute for coin. A *bonâ fide* holder takes, as we have seen, such an instrument exactly as he takes money, without any concern for the circumstances of its acquisition. From motives of general convenience, negotiable instruments pass freely from hand to hand, the various kinds having indeed certain specific differences, but all agreeing in one point, namely, that the title of the *bonâ fide* holder is unimpeachable. This peculiarity depends upon two conditions; first, that the coin or the paper as the case may be has been taken for value, and second that it has been taken in good faith. The presumption—a presumption which, in the case of coin, is conclusive—is that the circulating medium has been received for value. The second condition is rather negative than positive. In place of saying that the coin or the paper must have been received in good faith, it is more exact to say that it must not have been received in bad faith. Between the two forms of expression there is a very practical difference. The burthen of proof rests upon the person who makes the allegation, that is, in the present case, upon the person who alleges the bad faith, and not upon the person who alleges the good faith. The law never presupposes any breach of duty. It always assumes, until the contrary is shown, that each of its subjects will obey its commands. It has been held* that good faith means the absence of notice

* Cuming *v.* Brown, 9 East 5.

of any circumstance which ought in fairness to have prevented the transferee from taking the property. Bad faith then may be described as the opposite of good faith, and as implying notice of some circumstance* which renders the transaction neither fair nor honest. Against an innocent purchaser in the sense in which I have described him, the court will never give relief. It will never use its discretionary powers to his prejudice. When he has the actual possession of property, the court will, if it be possible, support him in that possession. It is only when two innocent purchasers come into collision, when a difference must be made between rights apparently equal, and one of two innocent persons must bear a loss, that the court will regard other considerations than purchase for value without bad faith.

This rule of the innocent purchaser has, to a great extent, superseded the old doctrine of sale in market overt. It is still law in England that, under certain conditions, a sale of chattels in a market recognised by law gives to the buyer a good title independently of the title of his seller. This rule, however, is strictly local. It is one of those portions of the common law which the English emigrant does not carry with him to his new home; neither in the States of America nor in any colony is the rule in force. The reason is that in none of these countries is there any market recognised by law within the meaning of the English rule. The markets to which the common law referred were markets which were created by charter or which arose by prescription. The markets in the colonies are of statutory origin. Such markets were not those which the law contemplated. It is remarkable that no attempt has been made in any of these countries, so far as I am aware, to revive under statutory authority the common law doctrine. It was probably felt that the rule of the innocent purchaser was in its modern form sufficient. For any deficiency in that rule a remedy was sought in a safer and more modern expedient than the sale in the market. That expedient is the practice of registration.

* Rodger *v.* Comptoir d'Escompte de Paris, L. R. 2 P. C. 393.

The Registration of Transfers. § 7. Registration is used both in the acquisition of rights and in their transfer. It is convenient to consider these subjects together, and what I am about to say will consequently apply, so far as may be, both to acquisition and to transfer.

There are two purposes which registration serves. One is to furnish evidence of the transaction. The other is to afford security to the public in its dealings by giving formal notice of the holder of the right. Under either of these two divisions the various cases of registration seem to range themselves. The former division includes the registration of marriages of births and of deaths ; the registration of deeds; the registration of a multitude of different occupations; and—an instance which, as compared with similar registrations under the laws of other Australian colonies, well illustrates the difference—the registration of cattle brands. The latter division includes the registration of the titles to real property and to interests therein, of bills of sale, of shipping, of patents, of copyrights, of trade marks, and of stocks and shares, whether they relate to public or other debts, or to interests in the different kinds of companies. The fundamental difference between these two divisions appears to be that the right is in the one case independent of the registration, and in the other case is dependent upon it. In other words, registration is in the latter case a condition precedent to the vesting of the right. In the former case it is a duty consequent upon the vesting of the right, and having a sanction more or less independent of it. The difference between the two systems is shown by a comparison of the register of deeds with a register of shares in a company. The register of deeds supplies a list of all the documents which relate to a given estate ; it affords the means of identifying the estate and of determining the title to it. But it does not register the actual title. It only preserves and renders accessible the evidence that a title has been acquired. Under the best possible system of registering deeds, searches must be made, deeds must be perused, and abstracts must be prepared. The investigation of title must still involve in a greater or less degree time and trouble, and consequently expense. A register of shares, on the other hand, shows not merely the transactions by which changes of ownership are produced but the actual changes themselves. It shows not only that the grantor has executed a deed purporting to convey to the grantee certain rights in certain property, but that these rights are actually taken out of the one and are vested in the other. It does not merely preserve in a convenient form the materials for constructing the history of a title, but it establishes the title itself. Each method, however, has its own advantages, and is adapted to its own purpose. The registration of title is adapted for dealings with property or for other rights which admit of transfer. The registration of instruments applies where the object is solely to provide means for future evidence. The registration of marriages is for many reasons highly expedient, but it would be unfortunate if the validity of a marriage were to depend upon the circumspection or the carelessness of the person who celebrates it. A registration of births and of deaths is also desirable ; but a failure to register them cannot alter the facts. In such cases registration is an absolute duty, and is enforced by pecuniary penalties. But where proprietary rights are concerned, the official entries may well be not only sufficient but necessary evidence of title.

The subject upon which the question of registration has been chiefly discussed has been the transfer of land. Experience has abundantly proved the insufficiency for this purpose of a register of deeds. But a sound system of registration of title has not yet been obtained. Many efforts have been made in England with this object, but hitherto without success. In these colonies a different method has been adopted. The Government has undertaken the duty of conveyancing. The Crown grant is replaced on the first occasion of dealing with the property by an instrument called a certificate of title, which passes to its registered holder a Parliamentary title. On every transfer the existing certificate is surrendered, and a new certificate is issued in its place. Up to the present time this method, which is obviously something quite different from a true registration of title, has worked fairly well. But it is wrong in principle, and it has as yet been tried only in small communities. It may reasonably be doubted whether any such Government office can stand the strain which in a large population it would be required to bear. I believe that the true method is to ascertain the conditions of transferability in the case of personal property, and to place land under the like conditions. The principal differences between the two cases are merely legal. These have been for the most part removed in this country, and will sooner or later disappear in England. The natural difference is that land is specific, and that personal property usually is not. One acre of land is not the equivalent of another acre ; but one sum of £100 in shares or debentures is in the like circumstances the precise equivalent of another such sum. This difference could be counteracted, and in a new country very easily counteracted, by taking as the basis of registration the land itself. If a proper map of the country were prepared, and if each Crown grant and each subdivision of a Crown grant were made the unit of registration, land could be transferred as easily, as safely, and as cheaply as shares in a gas company or in a bank, and without the interference of any official other than the clerk in charge of the register. In 1862 a scheme to this effect was prepared for Victoria, and was laid before Parliament by the then Government. The then Registrar-General certified his assent to the details and his readiness to undertake its administration. Unfortunately, the circumstances of the day were unfavorable, and a great opportunity was lost.

CHAPTER XV.

THE SUCCESSION TO RIGHTS.

What Duties and Rights are Descendible. § 1. The question of the succession to rights presupposes an important consideration. Before we determine what persons ought to succeed to the legal position of a deceased person or by what means such successors should be ascertained, we have to decide upon the proper objects of succession. Man, who brought nothing into the world, cannot indeed take anything out of it. All the material objects which belonged to him he must inevitably leave for the use of others. But it does not follow that these others may equally claim all the acts and forbearances, unconnected with things, to which the deceased at the time of his death was, or would if he had survived have been, entitled. We must therefore inquire in what cases of duties and of rights the law by the terms of its commands includes not only its commandee but his legal representatives. In the first place, Absolute duties, whether public or private, are strictly personal. They are imposed for the purposes of the State, and they apply to every subject of the State. Consequently, no advantage could be gained by their survival. The legal representative is already personally liable to them. The dead man is beyond their reach. The same observation and for the same reason applies to General duties, so far as they involve a public and not merely a private injury. The law abhors the blood-feud. It has taken into its own hands the vengeance of the next agnate; and it acknowledges, what the agnate could never understand, that death discharges all such debts. It is the clearest principle of the developed State never to visit the crimes of the father upon the children. It is slow to recognise even actions for wrongs done by the deceased. The general rule is that when at the time of his death the deceased person is liable to any other person for any breach of a general duty, the liability does not descend to his legal representative. To this rule our law makes certain exceptions. The legal representatives are liable when the breach of duty relates to the property of the other person, if the cause of action have arisen within six months of the death of the offender, and if proceedings be taken within six months after the legal representatives have lawfully entered upon their office. The legal representatives also are, without any special limitation, liable for the consequences of the breach of any fiduciary duty which the deceased may have committed, whether the deceased did or did not derive any benefit from such breach.

Subject to the exception that I shall presently mention, the obligations arising from contract always descend to the legal representative. When a man makes a contract, he is understood to agree for himself his executors and administrators, unless the nature of the case negatives the presumption. This presumption is rebutted, or this exception to the general rule arises, where the contract relates to the exercise by the deceased of some personal qualities of body or of mind or to the forbearance of such exercise. It would be absurd that a contract to marry should pass to a man's executors. It would be not less absurd that a contract by a great artist to exercise his art—of Patti to sing or of Millais to paint, of Tennyson to write a poem or of Woolner to make a statue—should be regarded as other than strictly personal. So it has been held that a contract of apprenticeship is discharged by the death of the master, and even the amount of the premium paid is not returnable. On the same principle, a contract to forbear from the exercise of any occupation, as, for example, the contract of a professional man not to practise in a certain locality, affects himself only and not his executors. In all such cases the contract is discharged by death ; and as

X

the executors are not liable upon it, so they have from it no claim upon the other party.

Rights arise in the case only of Relative duties. We are therefore restricted to this class of duties in matters connected with the transmission of rights. In General duties the right to recover damages does not survive to the legal representative of the donee of the right when the cause of action has been some personal suffering, whether physical or mental, sustained by the deceased person. An action for assault or an action for libel cannot be maintained by executors, however strong the case might have been if the deceased had himself been the plaintiff. A man had promised* to marry a woman and broke his promise. She died, and her executors brought an action for damages against the man for the breach of promise to their testatrix. But the action could not be maintained; and the court observed that "although marriage may be regarded as a temporal advantage to the party as far as respects personal comfort, still it cannot be considered as an increase of the transmissible personal estate." To this rule there are exceptions. Where the death of the donee of the right has been caused by negligence, in such circumstances that if he had lived he would have had a right of action against the person guilty of such negligence, the right of action survives for a limited time for the benefit of certain near relatives of the deceased person. The right survives to the personal representatives for the benefit of these relatives; and if the personal representatives do not sue, the persons beneficially interested may, within a further prescribed time, take the necessary proceedings. It has been sometimes said that this is a new right created for the executors. But it is now settled † that it is merely an extension of the original right of the deceased person. Again, in Victoria,‡ where injury is caused by negligence in mining operations, whether the immediate result be fatal or not, the legal representatives may, without any special limitation

* Chamberlain v. Williamson, 2 M. & S. 408.
† Griffiths v. Earl of Dudley, 9 Q. B. D. 363.   ‡ Act No. 480, s. 8.

either as to time or to the persons beneficially interested, recover damages from the owner of the mine ; and the damages are made chargeable upon the mining plant and other property.

But all the proprietary rights of the deceased, all his privileges and other rights *in rem*, all his choses in action, all his valuable securities, in a word his whole estate, whether real or personal, with all its benefits and all its burthens, descend to his legal representatives. In all sub-sisting rights of actions upon contract and for injuries done to the personal estate the executor succeeds without any special restriction. Where the right of action arises upon an injury to the real estate, his powers are limited. In such cases the wrong done must have been committed within six months of the death of the deceased, and the executor must bring his action within twelve months of such death.

§ 2. I have for the sake of brevity spoken of the "legal representative" of a deceased person. This expression, however, includes several terms which mark respectively notable events in legal history. Its full form is " heirs executors and administrators." The executor is the person appointed by the testator himself in his Will to act as his representative in the collection the manage-ment and the distribution of his personal assets. In the absence of a valid Will or of an executor named in such a Will, a competent court appoints an officer called the administrator, who is charged under the direction of the court with the care of the personal estate of the deceased person, whether its distribution is to be made according to law or according to the provisions of the executor-less Will. But the heir was a very different person. He was not a mere trustee, but succeeded in his own right and for his own use not to the personalty but to the real estate of his ancestor. His name*—the taker, a modified form of that of the "herus" or living owner—recalls the earliest

Descent of Realty and of Per-sonalty. (marginal note)

* See Curtius, Greek Etymology, I. 246.

x 2

customs of our race. His history is the history of the greater part of our law. His contrast with the executor marks the momentous distinction between realty and personalty. His presence necessitates two distinct systems of law in all matters of ownership and of succession, and in many matters of obligation. Step by step, during the last half-century, encroachments have been made upon the old prerogatives of the heir, and his position is now far less conspicuous even in England than it was in the days of our grandfathers. In Victoria a bolder advance has been made. The heir has been literally disestablished and disendowed. He no longer takes a beneficial interest in the ancestral property. He does not even survive as a mere trustee. His place knows him no more. Yet we have done this great thing almost in terror. The very Act by which the final change was made is studiously obscure. It was passed almost without discussion. It attracted no notice either on the hustings or in the press. Few persons outside the profession seem even now to be aware of this great legal revolution. Fewer still appreciate its importance, or reflect that by a few words in a merely technical Act* the foundation of more than half our law was taken away. Notwithstanding this removal of the foundation, the superstructure has received little care. The consequential alterations that this great reform involved have not been made. The result is that although this change has facilitated, I might almost say has rendered practically possible, a systematic statement of our substantive general law, that portion of Victorian law which relates to real property is in a state of bewildering confusion. Happily the substantial changes, those in respect of which differences of opinion might exist, have been actually made. All that is now needed is a single sustained effort to clear away the ruins of time.

In these circumstances it would be worse than useless if I were to dilate upon a moribund learning. Nor could I hope to add anything to that immense mass of learning, acuteness,

---

* Act No. 427, *An Act for amending the Law relating to the Administration of the Estates of Deceased Persons*, 1872.

and ingenuity which, after having for so many generations served its purpose, has practically perished for us and will probably soon cease to be studied anywhere. In this country the principle is now established, and in another generation at the most will probably be established in England, that there is no distinction between real and personal estate. As equity has absorbed law, so personalty has absorbed realty. Traces of the old system will doubtless long remain. Where property has been held under any system of law for more than 800 years, survivals of that system will not soon disappear. But substantially the law of Victoria has ceased to make any material distinction of rights as applied to land and to chattels ; and so far as succession goes, it recognises no distinction at all. Even in English conveyancing* the heir is no longer indispensable, and grants in fee simple and fee tail without any words of inheritance are now sufficient. It is scarcely too much to allege, it is quite safe to predict, that the term "heirs," once beyond all other terms a term of art, is not, or in the course of a few years will not be, known to modern law.

Intestacy. § 3. It was I think a theory of Bentham, it was certainly the accepted doctrine thirty years ago, that a testament was the normal mode of determining the devolution of property, and that it was only in the absence of such an instrument that the law interfered with special provisions. The law of intestacy was thus placed on the same footing as the law of contracts, where, as the old maxim says, " *Modus et conventio vincunt legem.*" Since that time our knowledge of legal history has made considerable advance ; and no competent person now doubts that intestacy was the ancient form, and that testaments are a comparatively modern innovation. Yet Bentham's view, historically wrong as it certainly was, expresses with sufficient accuracy† the existing state of the law. It is true that in modern society a testament is the ordinary mode of disposition.

---

* See " The Conveyancing and Law of Property Act 1881," 44 & 45 Vic. c. 41, s. 51.
† See Cooper *v.* Cooper, L. R. 7 E. & I. App. 66. *per* Lord Cairns.

It is true that, at least in English countries, it is in the absence of any such disposition and not otherwise that the law interferes. It is true that the disposition adopted by a Will may be and often is very different from that which in its absence is made by operation of law. But the same results may be obtained by the historical method ; and where no practical advantage is gained by a different arrangement, it seems that the order of our subject should be guided by the known course of legal events.

Two questions meet us at the commencement of our inquiry as to intestacy. One relates to the legal estate; the other to the beneficial interest. Under the old law the heir took the real estate without any external authority, but simply by virtue of his heirship. The personal estate went to the administrator, for what reasons and by what course of events it is needless here to narrate. Under the present law in Victoria the real estate devolves not upon the heir, but upon the administrator in the same manner as it would devolve if it were personalty. The administrator of course holds the real estate in trust for the persons who are beneficially interested. These trusts are in Victoria the same as those in the case of personal estate. That is, the heir does not now take any beneficial interest in the land; but it descends to the personal representative to be dealt with as chattels are dealt with under the Statute of Distributions. The different rules in different countries regarding undevised land are noteworthy. In England the rule of primogeniture, that is the exclusive succession of the eldest son or next heir, prevails; but in the absence of any settlement the owner may dispose by Will of the whole or any part of his land to any person or in any lawful way that he thinks fit. In France the rule is that of equal distribution among all the children, and the law does not permit any testamentary disposition to the contrary. In the more recent British communities, in America, Australia, and India, these opposite methods are combined. The English power of free bequest is retained; but, failing its exercise, the French rule of equal distribution applies.

The actual rules of distribution which in all countries where the English law prevails govern personalty, and in some such countries govern both personal and real estate, are very simple. If a man die and leave a wife and lineal descendents, the widow takes one-third of his property and the remaining two-thirds go to the children or other descendents. If he leave a wife and next of kin, but no lineal descendents, the widow takes half and the other half goes to those who are of kin to the deceased. If he leave a wife and neither lineal descendents nor any kin, the widow takes half and the other half goes to the Crown. If he leave lineal descendents but no widow, the lineal descendents take the whole. When the lineal descendents are in different degrees of kindred to the deceased, the distribution is made *per stirpes*—that is, the grandchildren, whatever may be their number, can claim the shares of their deceased parents and no more. Where the deceased has left neither wife nor children, his property goes to his next of kin. The next of kin may be divided into two classes, those who may be described as belonging to the deceased man's own family, and his remoter relations. The former class includes his father, his mother, his brothers, and his sisters; and where any brother or sister has died, their children if any, so far as relates to the share of the deceased parent. If the father survive, he succeeds to the whole property. If the mother and brothers and sisters or any of them survive, they divide the property in equal shares, subject to the rights of the children of any deceased brother or sister to the share which their parent if alive would have taken. Failing this first class, or near kin, the property is divided in equal shares among those who are in the nearest degree of kindred to the deceased. If a woman die leaving a husband surviving her, the husband takes the whole. If a woman die without leaving a husband surviving her, her property is distributable in the same way as the property of a man who dies intestate without leaving a widow.

General rules of this description are best understood by examples. Let us then suppose that a man dies intestate, leaving a freehold estate worth £10,000 and personal property worth £8,000, after the payment of all his debts. He leaves surviving him a father, one brother, two sisters, four children of a deceased brother, a widow, and two children—a boy and a girl. In such circumstances, under the old law, the wife would be entitled to one-third of the land for her life as her dower ; the son would take the whole of the land, subject to the dower ; the £8,000 would be divided equally between the widow, the son, and the daughter. Under the present law in Victoria, the whole estate, that is the £18,000, would be treated as money; and the widow, the son, and the daughter would take each £6,000. Neither under the old nor the present law would the other relatives take anything. If there were no children, the widow would under the law of Victoria now receive £9,000; the remainder would go to the father, or, if there were no father, would be divided into four parts, one part to each of the surviving brother and sisters, and one in equal shares between the orphans. That is, the widow would receive £9,000 ; the brother and sisters, £2,250 each ; and the orphan nephew and nieces £562 10s. each. If there were no widow, and the surviving relations were four first-cousins and six second-cousins, the four first-cousins would divide the whole amount in equal shares. If there were no first-cousins, the six second-cousins would in like manner take in equal shares to the exclusion of all remoter relatives.

Wills. § 4. An important practical distinction was at one time expressed by the terms Testament and Will. The former term denoted a disposition of personal property; the latter term a disposition of land. The two terms are accordingly coupled in our older books of conveyancing as indicating that the testator meant to deal with both classes of property. The difference has indeed disappeared. Yet, although the law of real property has been absorbed or is in course of absorption by the law of personal property, the term originally denoting the instrument for the devise of land, equivocal as it is, has, with the curious fate which sometimes attends words, superseded the unambiguous term which denoted the instrument for the bequest of chattels. Beyond all other legal questions, the jural interest in the matter of Wills is mainly historical. On this subject much has been said, and something perhaps remains to be said. But it is not with the archaic Will that analytical jurisprudence is concerned. I must leave to others the task of tracing the events which gives to posthumous gifts their present character. The present inquiry must be content to accept as ultimate facts such gifts in their modern form.

The modern Will affords little room for comment. It is mainly a matter of intention, and each case rests upon its own circumstances. In this respect it resembles contract. Contracts and Wills are indeed near of kin. They form, when taken together, the means by which the individual practically makes his own law in his own affairs. The one regulates his conduct as to those affairs during his life ; the other determines the devolution of his property upon his death. The two institutions are thus inconsistent with that archaic society in which both the use and the devolution of property rested not with the House-Father but with the "*Familia*" and the "*Gens.*" Yet, notwithstanding this alliance, there is a material difference between the Contract and the Will. In contract two parties are concerned, and the problem is to ascertain their common intention. The claims of the one necessitates strictness in investigating the claims of the other. But a Will is unilateral. In it there is only one person whose intention is material. The discovery of that intention is the problem of the Will, and the desire to attain this object causes the construction of these instruments to be of necessity lax.

The external conditions of a modern Will may readily be stated. Its contents are known or need to be known to the testator alone. It takes effect upon his death and not sooner. If there be sufficient proof of his intention to revoke, it is revocable at his pleasure until the moment of his death. It creates no duty in the legal representatives above or beyond the duties which relate to the assets of the testator. It must be made with certain formalities. Under English law these formalities have ultimately assumed the following form :— The instrument must be in writing. It must be signed by the testator in such a manner as to show that he intended his signature to authenticate the whole document. That signature must be attested by two witnesses, who must have seen, or at least have had an opportunity of seeing, the act of signing ; and who in proof thereof must in the presence both of the testator and of each other themselves sign the instrument. A document executed with these formalities and no other document is a legal Will ; and effect will be given to its provisions, if they be intelligible, so far as they are not inconsistent with positive law.

Although a modern Will has everywhere the same general features, there is room for considerable variety in its details. Each country may have and usually has its own rules as to the capacity of the testator, as to the formalities of the Will, as to the extent of the power of bequest, as to the capacity of the donees under the Will, as to the manner in which a valid Will may be revoked, as to the time from which a Will begins to operate, as to the time at which and the events upon which persons claiming under the Will may exercise their powers. Our law in these matters is simple. It imposes upon the testator the minimum of restriction. Every person of full age and of sound mind may by his Will duly executed freely dispose from his death of all his descendible rights in any lawful way, and to any person whether related to him or not that he thinks fit. Its principle is uncontrolled freedom of testation within the limits of the general law, and precise rules as to the form of the instrument. On the latter point it admits a few inconsiderable exceptions. Where the testator is blind, some additional forms are for the purposes of security required. For the Wills of soldiers or of sailors hardly any form is needed. Sailors have always been exceptionally treated by the law, partly from their ordinary want of knowledge of the affairs of life upon shore, and partly from the impossibility of obtaining in the course of their vocation proper legal assistance and advice. The relaxation in favour of soldiers rests I think upon a different basis. It seems to be a survival from the times when the Roman Emperors lavished their interested favours upon the greedy and uncertain legionaries. Probably it may claim a still remoter descent from the time when, with the chances of war before him, the Quirite* upon the sudden proclamation of the levy obtained from his fellow clansmen assembled with him under arms those consents for the future government of his household which in time of peace these same clansmen duly met in the special assembly of all the clans would with ampler leisure and more befitting solemnities have granted.

Additions or alterations may be made in a Will by an instrument executed in all respects with the same formalities as the Will itself. Such a supplementary instrument is called a Codicil. The Will and its Codicil are read together, the Codicil in case of conflict, as expressing the later wishes of the testator, prevailing. But a Codicil in this sense is very different from the "Codicilli" of the Roman law. The latter document, to which, just at the time when the authority of the State over the old clan customs had become predominant, the first Cæsar Augustus† gave his sanction, was not a secondary instrument, but was in fact the Formless‡ Testament. It is from this Augustan mode of testamentary disposition, and not from any earlier source, that the modern

---

* Gaius, II. 101.   † Inst. II. 25, 2.
‡ Mr. Hunter's Roman Law, 644.

Will is really derived. Its greater safety and greater convenience soon superseded the old Formal Testament even under its modified conditions ; and by a strange vicissitude of fortune the Testament came to depend for its validity upon its younger rival. A clause was habitually inserted in Testaments providing that if for any reason the instrument failed as a Testament it should be regarded as *Codicilli.* But as the *Codicilli* thus prevailed over the old *Testamentum,* so the modern Will has assumed the first place in testamentary dispositions, and the once triumphant *Codicilli* have dwindled into the merely subsidiary Codicil.

Bequests. § 5. Under the old Roman law the distinction between the Formal and the Formless extended not only to Wills but even to legacies. The peculiar position of the Heres in that law caused further complications. From these difficulties English law is happily free. The executor is simply a trustee whose duty is to carry out the trusts of the Will. In these circumstances the testator has only to express his intentions with sufficient clearness, and the legatee will in due course receive his share. Little therefore remains here to be said upon the theory of legacies. The details of the subject are indeed more than abundant, but they belong to the practitioner. I shall only indicate by way of illustration a few of the leading rules.

I do not propose to treat of the follies or the blunders or the mistakes of testators. I assume that the Will was at the time of its execution rightly made to express the testator's intentions with regard to the facts as they then existed. But various events may occur both before and after the Will comes into operation which may disturb his reasonable expectations. Thus it may happen that at the testator's death something which he had when he made his Will and which he has specifically bequeathed is not in existence, or has ceased to belong to him. It may happen that, whether from an erroneous estimate of his fortune or from a change in circumstances, his assets are insufficient fully to meet the legacies he has given. It may happen that his legatee has died, or has not been born, or has not fulfilled some condition precedent. In all these cases the assistance of the law is required. The testator's intention is still the governing principle, but that intention has to be applied to states of fact different from those which he contemplated.

Sometimes a legacy is given in general terms, sometimes a specific thing is given. If the subject of a specific legacy be not found, or if only part of it be found, in the testator's assets after his death, the legacy is lost either wholly or in part, as the case may be. In the case of a general legacy no such question can arise. The bequest is then made not of a definite thing but of a certain portion of the assets. If there be sufficient assets, the legatee must have his legacy in the terms of the Will. But if the assets prove insufficient, the general legatees must abate, that is, the reduced sum must be divided among them in proportion to their respective interests. In such circumstances, what becomes of the specific legatees? Their gifts consist of certain definite things, and these things and none other they are to have in any case. Therefore the specific legatees do not contribute, but receive their legacies in the first instance ; and the abatement takes place only upon the balance. Thus each class of legacy has its peculiar advantage. The general legacies are not liable to ademption. The specific legacies are not liable to abatement. Sometimes a legacy is given which is in its nature general, but which is to be paid out of a particular fund. Such a legacy is called demonstrative. A demonstrative legacy combines in some degree the advantages of both the preceding classes. It is not liable to ademption, but, if the specified fund be not available, it is payable out of the general assets. On the other hand, if the fund be in existence but the assets be insufficient, the demonstrative legacy is treated as specific to the extent of the prescribed fund. If the fund be exhausted before the legacy is satisfied, the unpaid portion is treated as a general legacy, and is liable to abatement accordingly.

Where the legatee is not in existence at the death of the testator, the legacy lapses ; that is the amount becomes part of the residue of the estate and goes to the residuary legatee, if any.   If there be no residuary legatee, the testator is deemed to have died intestate as to that amount, and the sum is accordingly dealt with according to the law of intestate estates.   But where the legatee was a child or other issue of the testator and has died during the life time of the testator, and has left issue living at the testator's death, the issue take the legacy as if the legatee had died immediately after. the testator.   Where a legacy is given but is postponed to a future time or to the occurrence of a future event, and where after the death of the testator, but before the arrival of the time or the occurrence of the event, the legatee dies, a difficult question frequently arises. Thus, if £5,000 be left to a legatee payable upon marriage or majority, and if that legatee die unmarried at the age of eighteen, what becomes of the legacy ?   Does it sink into the residue, or become undisposed of property, or does it go to the legal representatives of the legatee ?   The answer depends upon the precise terms of the bequest.   If an immediate gift were made to the legatee, and the payment only of that gift were postponed, the gift would have vested in the legatee, and upon his death the property would have passed to his legal representatives.   But if the gift were conditional upon the marriage or the attainment of the specified age, these events, or either of them, would amount to a condition precedent for the vesting of the legacy.   Consequently, if that condition were not fulfilled, neither the legatee nor his representatives would take any interest in the legacy; but it would either fall into the residue or remain undisposed of, according to the circumstances of the case.

I will illustrate these rules also, as I have done those of intestacy, by an example.   Let us suppose that a Will contains the following legacies :— To his son John the testator's Government debentures ; to his son James his freehold house at Ballarat ; to his daughter Mary £2,000, payable out of his bank shares ; to his daughter Frances £2,000 ; and to other general legatees £3,000. Frances dies in the life time of the testator, leaving three children. On the death of the testator it is found that he has left no Government debentures, but that after payment of his debts his assets are as follow—the house at Ballarat worth £2,500, bank shares worth £1,500, and other personal property worth £4,000. In these circumstances John takes nothing ; his legacy was specific, and has been adeemed. James takes the house ; Mary takes the bank shares towards the payment of her legacy, and for the remaining portion has a claim on the general assets. These general assets amount to £4,000 ; the charges against them are—the balance of Mary's legacy £500 ; legacy to Frances £2,000 ; other legacies £3,000 ; total £5,500. All these general legatees must therefore abate in proportion to their respective interests; that is, they are to receive in the proportions mentioned in the will £4,000 instead of £5,500. Frances' legacy thus reduced will be divided between her three children.

Administration of Estate.   § 6. Every Will requires for its execution some person who is charged to give effect to its provisions. Such a person is, according to English law, the executor, or, where the case so requires, the administrator with the Will annexed. In Roman law this duty devolved upon the " Heres " or Heir. But between the " Heres " and either the executor or the Heir of the English law there is a wide difference. The " Heres " differed from the Heir because he was bound to give effect to the legacies contained in the Testament, while the Heir had no concern whatever with the Will. He differed from the executor, firstly because he took the property of the deceased in his own right ; secondly, because he was subject to the legacies for a part and not for the whole of the property; thirdly, because he was liable personally and not merely to the extent of the assets for all the obligations of the testator; and fourthly, because when he was a member of the testator's household he was not permitted to refuse the inheritance. It may indeed be said that in Roman law a Testament was made for the sake of the "Heres" and to ' guide his discretion in the administration of the property of the Household. In English law the original theory of the English Heir as distinguished from the "Heres" was that, while the "Heres" was assumed, not by way of fiction but in very fact, to continue in his own person his ancestor's existence, the Heir derived his interest not from his father but from the gift of the original grantor. The one system implies the custom of the pure-blooded clan, the other system plainly tells of the Comitatus.

The "Heres." Both the "Heres" and the "Heir" agree in this point, that to each of them the notion of a Will in the modern sense is equally abhorrent. Each of them, although from different causes, had a vested interest· in his ancestor's property during that ancestor's life time, and this interest was in no way due to the ancestor's favour. The "Heres" continued the ownership. "*Morte parentis* * *quasi continuatur dominium.*" He stood in the exact place of the deceased *Pater Familias.* Hence he succeeded to the whole of the property of whatever kind of the deceased man. Consequently, no person could be testate as to part of his property and intestate as to another part. The "Heres" succeeded too not only to the rights of his ancestor but also to his duties. He was therefore bound to meet the obligations of that ancestor absolutely, and not merely to the extent of the assets that he received. In other words, the Familia or Corporate Household enjoyed its rights and was subject to its liabilities, whoever might happen for the time being to be its *Pater* or managing director. Further, if the "Heres" was in the *manus* of the deceased *Pater*, that is if

---

* Inst. III. 1, 3.

at the time of the death he was a member of the Household, he could not under the old law refuse the inheritance. The "testamentum" was originally a mere arrangement for providing for the succession on the failure of direct heirs. The " Heres" under a testament held precisely the same position, except as to "legata" or charges upon the estate, as the " *Heres ab intestato*" held. In the course of time two changes were made in his favour. Under the Republic the Prætor allowed to a " Heres " outside the Household a certain time for inquiry before he declared his final acceptance of the inheritance. By the legislation of Justinian, his responsibility was limited to the extent of the assets that he received.

The Heir.   The position of the feudal Heir was very different. He succeeded[*] by virtue of the original grant and according to its form. Hence he did not represent his ancestor. He did not receive any gift from his ancestor's bounty. He was not concerned in any other property of his ancestor than that to which he was heir, or in any of that ancestor's obligations. Accordingly, the maxims to which I have referred of the Roman law had no application to his case. His history was that the grant to him was in course of time construed not to confer upon him an individual interest, but to indicate the quantity of interest which his predecessor held. A grant to a man and his heirs was taken to mean not a separate grant to each of two or more persons, but a grant to one person with unlimited powers of disposition. This doctrine was established before the time of Bracton, and it is not difficult to trace in it the ingenuity of the lawyers. The old custom, however, did not entirely give way. Until the days of the Tudors technical difficulties obstructed the alienation of land by Will. The interests of the Lords were in favour of a strict construction of the " *Charta doni.*" The famous statute " *de donis conditionalibus*" marked the last determined effort to repress free transfer. But as Lord Coke[†] observes, those perpetuities, like monopolies, were

---

[*] See Butler's Note (V. 3) on Co. Lit. 191 *a*.   [†] 10 Rep. 42 *b*, and see 113 *b*.

Y

" born under some unfortunate constellation, for they in so great a number of suits concerning them in all the courts of Westminster never had any judgment given for them but many judgments given against them. And from those fettered inheritances the freeholds of the subject are thereby set at liberty according to their original freedom." The process of emancipation has not been stationary since the days of Lord Coke. But I must not further linger over the shadowy " Heres," and the hardly more substantial Heir. I proceed therefore to the rules that govern the Executor-Trustee.

An executor derives his authority from the Will;

The Executor.

but he cannot except in certain matters of emergency enter upon his office unless and until he obtain the consent of the State. This consent is obtained by the grant of probate of the Will from a court of competent jurisdiction. Such a grant in effect declares that the Will has been duly executed ; that the executor seeking probate has been duly appointed and accepts the trust; and that he is the owner in trust of the estate of the deceased. Upon the grant of the probate, the ownership of the several parts of the estate vests by relation from the death of the testator in the executor. He is allowed twelve months to collect and clear the estate ; and no legatee can enforce the payment of any gift under the Will within that period, or can at any time take any such gift without the executor's consent. The first duty then of the executor is to ascertain the amount of the assets coming to him, to realize that amount, and to pay all the testator's debts. Everything that comes by virtue of his office into the hands of the executor is assets. All assets are liable without distinction for the payment of debts. No legacy of any kind is payable until all the debts have been satisfied. All unsecured debts, whether they be by deed or parol, are payable *pari passu ;* but priority is given to the death-bed and funeral expenses of the testator, to the expenses of obtaining probate, and to wages due for services rendered to the deceased within three months next preceding his death by any labourer, artisan, or domestic servant. When the debts have been discharged, but not sooner, the legacies are payable; and their payment is determined as between themselves by the rules some of which I have indicated. After the payment of all the debts and of all the legacies, the surplus, if any, of the estate is payable to the residuary legatee, or if there be no such legatee to the person legally entitled thereto.

There are, of course, other provisions where the nature of the case does not admit of an estate being wound up so readily as I have assumed. Nor was the process at all times equally simple. But these are the general principles which since the assimilation of real and personal property have been established. They apply not only to executors but to administrators. The latter officers, as I have said, differ from executors since they derive their authority not from the Will but from the appointment of the court. They are, consequently, subject to stricter supervision in the exercise of their discretionary powers than the person in whom the testator thought fit to repose his personal confidence. Subject, however, to this distinction, the executor and the administrator are respectively trustees of the property of a deceased person ; and the trusts which they are bound to fulfil are imposed in the one case by the Will of the testator, in the other case by the direct provisions of the law.

CHAPTER XVI.

THE RECOGNITION OF FOREIGN RIGHTS.

Limits of the Recognition of Foreign Rights.

§ 1. Allegiance and protection are reciprocal. Her Majesty's permanent subjects, as distinguished from the mere strangers within her gates, owe to her allegiance at all times and in all places. In return for this duty, Her Majesty owes to every such subject protection not in her own dominions only but through all the world. So wide an obligation necessitates some explanation; and when the occasion arises, the protection must be granted as against independent States by other agencies than the judgments of the courts. Again, in the use of the sea, which is the highway of nations, rules are necessary for the guidance of Her Majesty's subjects both as between themselves and as regards their conduct towards foreigners. These rules are administered not by the courts of ordinary jurisdiction, but by Courts of Admiralty especially appointed for the purpose and following customs and methods common, or supposed to have originally been common, to the whole family of European nations. Thus in the dealings between States as such the business is transacted through diplomatic agents. In matters that arise at sea, whether as between the Queen's subjects, or as between such subjects and foreigners, the Courts of Admiralty administering the old maritime customs have jurisdiction. I mention here these organs of the State merely for the purpose of exclusion. They form no part of my present subject. It was necessary to distinguish them from a class of cases which at first sight appear to resemble them, but which in fact belong to ordinary law. The courts are often invited to deal with questions where the parties are within the jurisdiction, but where the cause of action has arisen in a foreign country or in some way involves matters relating to foreign rights. It is obvious that in no country is foreign law administered as such. But foreign law may be and is often recognised by national law, and so becomes *pro tanto* a part of that law. The question therefore arises in what circumstances and to what extent this recognition of foreign law takes place. I must premise a brief explanation as to the meaning in this connexion of the word "Foreign." It is not confined to political nationality ; it includes jurisdiction. The phrase which best expresses its meaning is an independent jurisdiction, not a foreign country. Doubtless the origin of the rule contemplated exclusively separate nationalities. France and Spain and Holland were foreign countries, and were sharply distinguished from the dominions of our Crown. It would once have seemed an unreasonable stretch of language to speak of any part of these dominions as foreign to any other part of them. In the present day, however, when the Queen reigns over many self-governing communities in every part of the world, the ordinary government of any one of them is different from the government of any of the rest. It has been judicially decided that for the purposes of which I write the colonies must be treated in the same manner as foreign nations. The following pages, therefore, of this chapter relate not merely to independent political communities but also to the autonomous members of a common State.

There are certain large groups of foreign law which other States do not usually recognise. No State concerns itself with offences against the penal law of another State or against its fiscal regulations. No State recognises any claim which is inconsistent with the accepted maxims of the Customs between Nations, or which tends to produce in its own territory a violation of its own law. Arrangements have indeed been made by treaties between most civilized nations for the surrender upon certain conditions of persons within their territories who are in good faith and upon reasonable grounds charged with the perpetration in the country which asks extradition of any serious non-political offence. Friendly nations, too, will not complain if their subjects be fairly punished by another country for a breach of its smuggling laws, even though the alleged offence may have taken place far beyond the limits of the territorial waters. These, however, are matters of diplomacy rather than of law. Probably it may be said that no State will notice any Absolute duty created by another State, or any Relative duty so far as its breach constitutes a crime, otherwise than at most as a ground for extradition. It is not foreign duties but foreign rights that this branch of law regards. In the case of the colonial or other transmarine possessions of Her Majesty such matters are usually dealt with by Imperial legislation. It is in this way and for the purposes of their external relations that the legislative authority of the Imperial Parliament over all parts of the Queen's dominions is most frequently and most beneficially exercised.

Again, no country recognises any foreign law in the case of immovables, that is of land and of interests in land. All such cases must be determined by the law of the country where the land is situated, whether the matter relate to substance or to form. If a man make abroad a Will respecting English land, that Will must be executed in English form. If a foreigner own such land, he may if he think fit create therein such interests as the English law permits and none other, whatever wider powers the law of his own country may in such cases allow. The reason of this rule is apparent. Where movable property is concerned, the court which has jurisdiction over the person of the owner can by its personal process enforce its decrees. But no such power exists in the case of immovables. As to them the order must go to the executive officers of the country where the land itself is situated. But the courts of one country cannot issue directions to the executive government of another country. On this subject, however, a distinction must be observed. Although they cannot do so directly, courts may indirectly affect a foreign immovable. Where a court has personal jurisdiction over the owner of foreign land, it may in the exercise of that jurisdiction compel the owner so to dispose of or deal with his land as to give effect to any obligation which he may have incurred; and the extent of such obligation is to be measured by the law which the court administers and not by the *lex situs*. But this jurisdiction must not be exercised if the *lex situs* render it impossible for the owner to do that which the court would otherwise have ordered him to do; and the court must be careful not to make its mere personal jurisdiction a ground for determining the right to the ownership or the possession of the foreign land. Thus where William Penn and Lord Baltimore had made a contract to ascertain the boundaries of Pennsylvania and of Maryland, Lord Hardwicke decreed specific performance. Where a bankrupt refused to include in his assets his foreign immovables, it was held* that he ought not to be indirectly coerced by the refusal of his certificate until he complied, although the grant of the certificate was in the discretion of the court.

Further, no court will recognise the remedies or the procedure of a foreign court. When a foreign plaintiff seeks its aid, it will hear and determine his complaint according to its own methods and by its own rules of evidence. It will, if need be, give him such relief as it would give for a like cause of action that had arisen in its own jurisdiction. It will not concern itself about the redress or the methods of procuring redress which the plaintiff might have obtained elsewhere. He comes to Rome, and he must be content to fare at Rome as Rome fares. Whether for better or for worse, he must take the court its powers and its practice as he finds it. But in matters of substantive right, as between party and party, English law recognises, under certain conditions and according to certain rules, the law of the country in which the right arose or in which it was intended to take effect. The most important of these conditions and of these rules I propose in this chapter to consider.

* Cockerell *v.* Dickens, 3 Mo. P. C. C. 133.

§ 2. In considering the recognition of foreign rights *in rem* we are met at the outset by two limitations. The first is that such cases must relate to singular cases of property, and not to what is called a *universitas juris*, that is the devolution of the property of the owner considered as a whole. The second is that such questions must relate to movables only and not to immovables. Questions concerning a *universitas juris* are governed, as we shall presently see, by the law of the domicil. Questions concerning immovables are governed by the law of the place where the property is situated. But the rule as to singular movables, that is movables not regarded as a part of a *universitas juris*, is different. Where their ownership is lawfully acquired or transferred according to the law of the place in which the transaction occurs, such ownership will be recognised by English law. In such cases the question is not whether in the like circumstances our courts would have taken the same view as that taken in the foreign country. The right has well accrued under the law of that country; and the English courts, in the absence of some sufficient reason to the contrary, have merely on the principles of comity to recognise it and give it effect. Thus, a ship* with a cargo of Russian deals sailed from Riga to Hull. She was wrecked on the coast of Norway. The master, although he might have done so, did not communicate with the owners of the cargo, as under English law he ought to have done. By English law, therefore, he was not authorized to act as their agent for the sale of the deals, and the sale was consequently void. Nevertheless, acting upon the Norwegian law, which in this respect is different from ours and justified the course he followed, the master sold with the proper formalities the cargo. The deals were subsequently sent to England, and thereupon the English owner brought trover for them against the purchasers under the sale in Norway. It was held, and the judgment has since been approved and followed, that the sale gave a good title. The right had fully accrued under the law of the place in which the transaction occurred, and such a right must be maintained.

In cases of rights *in rem* other than those of ownership, the general rule is that where an action is brought in one jurisdiction for a wrong committed in another jurisdiction, if the act complained of be a wrong in both these jurisdictions, the action will lie. But the act complained of must have been illegal where it was done, and its illegality must have continued up to the time when the action was brought. Thus an action for trespass* was brought in England against Governor Eyre for acts done under his authority in repressing an insurrection in Jamaica. It was not disputed that the acts in question were offences both in Jamaica, where they were committed, and in England. Before the action was brought, the Legislature of Jamaica had passed an Act of Indemnity to the Governor and to all those who were concerned in the suppression of the rebellion. It was held that this Act was fatal to the success of the action. No man can be found guilty of a wrong which is not a wrong at the time of his trial.

A question arises whether an action will lie in one country for an injury to an immovable in another country. An English steamer† ran against a pier in a Spanish port and did considerable damage. The company that owned the pier was English, and brought an action in England against the steam company. The case was heard by consent, but the court expressed grave doubts as to its jurisdiction. The question is therefore still open. It may perhaps be convenient that such a jurisdiction should exist, but it seems difficult to support it upon general principles. If a man strike another in a foreign country, that act is an assault according to the law both of that country and of England. The parties might have been in England; and if they were, and the blow were there struck, the act would have been an offence in England. But the case of a pier is different. The collision with that pier could not in the nature of things have occurred in England. It does not seem to be enough that a similar act to that which is the subject of complaint is an offence in the country where the action is brought. That very act if it were committed in England ought to be an offence. But such a proposition in the case of an immovable assumes a physical impossibility.

The Recognition of Foreign Rights *in Personam.* § 3. The law relating to the recognition of foreign obligations is at once the most frequent in practice and the most complex of all the cases of foreign rights. The right must, as in the cases of rights *in rem*, be perfect according to its own law. It must also be not inconsistent with our law; that is, it must not arise from an agreement of which the object or the consideration was illegal, or which was made with intent to violate any law in this country, or which contains any material provision tending to infringe in this country the policy of our law. If it comply with these conditions, it will be enforced by the remedies and according to the procedure which our courts ordinarily use. The last two rules are sufficiently plain, but it is not always easy to determine the law which governs a foreign contract. A Russian domiciled in Germany may make in France a contract concerning goods in Holland performable in England. In these circumstances and in others much more complex than these it is necessary to ascertain the general principle which controls such transactions.

This principle appears to be that the interpretation of every such contract and the obligations arising from it are determined by the law of the place* where it is intended that the contract shall be performed. If that place be stated in the contract, there is no room for dispute. If it be not so stated, the intention of the parties must be proved; and for the purpose of facilitating that proof various rules have been established. In the absence of any expression to the contrary,

* Lloyd *v.* Gulbert, L. R. 1 Q. B. 115, *per* Willes J.

the place where the contract is made is assumed to be the place of its performance. Where there are several parties to the contract, each of whom resides in a different country, they are understood to contract each according to his own law. Where there are several places of performance, the law of each place prevails as to the matters to be done therein respectively. Where there is a contract of carriage from one country to another, and the fulfilment of the contract is the whole carriage, the place where the contract was made is also the place of its performance. In cases of affreightment, where there is more than one place of performance, the law of the ship prevails. I cite these rules merely as examples, and not as forming a complete enumeration. Their statement will probably be more intelligible if it be accompanied with a few illustrations. "Thus, says Mr. Justice Story,[*] suppose a negotiable bill of exchange is drawn in Massachusetts on England, and is indorsed in New York, and again by the first indorser in Pennsylvania and by the second in Maryland, and the bill is dishonoured, what damages will the holder be entitled to? The law as to damages in these States is different. In Massachusetts it is ten per cent. ; in New York and Pennsylvania twenty per cent., and in Maryland fifteen per cent. What rule then is to govern ? The answer is that in each case the *lex loci contractus*. The drawer is liable on the bill according to the law of the place where the bill[†] was drawn, and the successive indorsers are liable on the bill according to the law of the place of their indorsement, every indorsement being treated as a new and substantive contract. The consequence is that the indorser may render himself liable upon a dishonour of the bill for a much higher rate of damages than he can recover from the drawer."

Mr. Shand,[‡] a passenger from London to the Mauritius, took a ticket in the usual way in London on board one of the Peninsular and Oriental Company's steamers. The ticket

[*] Conflict of Laws, sect. 314.
[†] Or rather, where the principal is payable. See Westlake, 243.
[‡] Peninsular and Oriental Steam Navigation Company *v.* Shand, 3 Moo. P. C. N. S. 290.

contained a limitation of the company's liability as to the passenger's luggage. This limitation was good according to English law, but was not good according to the French law which prevails at the Mauritius. One of Mr. Shand's trunks disappeared between Suez and the Mauritius. For this loss he sued the company. It was ultimately held by the Privy Council that there was an entire contract of carriage, and that the law of England must govern it.

Mr. Lloyd,* a British subject, at St. Thomas, a Danish West Indian island, chartered the ship *Olivier*, belonging to M.. Guibert, a Frenchman, for a voyage from St. Marc in Hayti to Liverpool, and shipped accordingly a cargo at St. Marc. On her voyage the ship sustained damage from a storm, and put into Fayal, a Portuguese port, for repair. Money was raised for the repairs on a bottomry bond, and the ship completed her voyage. The bondholder proceeded for his money in the Court of Admiralty against the ship freight and cargo. The ship and freight were insufficient to satisfy the bond; and the plaintiff, as owner of the cargo, was compelled to pay the deficiency and the costs. For this amount he sued the owner. M. Guibert, as he was entitled to do by the French law, abandoned the ship and freight, and thus claimed to be freed from liability. But under the English law a shipowner in such circumstances is personally liable without any limitation. The question therefore arose, by which of these five laws, English, French, Danish, Portuguese, or Haytian, was the case governed? It was held by the Exchequer Chamber that in such circumstances the law of the ship prevails.

I have said that for the purposes of recognition the foreign right must be perfect according to its proper law. If it were not so, there would be nothing for our courts to enforce. Two consequences follow from this rule. One is that although the contract may be lawful both according to the law of the place where it was made and of the place where the action is brought, yet, if it were invalid in the

* Lloyd *c.* Guibert, L. R. 1 Q. B. 115.

place of its performance, the right would have no existence, and the action consequently could not be maintained. The second is that if a foreign obligation be complete according to its proper law, our courts, unless it be directly prohibited by our law, will enforce it even though they would not enforce a similar contract made within their own jurisdiction. Thus the sale of lottery tickets is forbidden* by the law of New York, and is allowed by the law of Kentucky. A partnership formed in Kentucky for the purpose of conducting a lottery in that State is lawful both in Massachusetts and in New York, and the contract will be enforced accordingly. A partnership formed in New York for the purpose of conducting a lottery in Kentucky would be illegal in both States, and no action upon it could be maintained in either country. No action could be maintained in Kentucky in respect of a lottery company formed in New York and proposing to operate therein. Whether an action could be maintained in New York by a Kentucky lottery company operating in Kentucky is a question which depends upon the terms of the New York statute. If by that statute lotteries were absolutely forbidden, no such action could be entertained. But if the prohibition were not peremptory, and merely declared all such contracts void, the action would lie, although if the contract had been made in and for Massachusetts it could not have been enforced.

Some words are needed as to the discharge in foreign countries of contracts made elsewhere. Where an obligation is discharged by its proper law, if the discharge actually extinguish the obligation and do not merely affect the remedies or the course of procedure to enforce them, the right is at an end in every country, and foreign courts cannot take notice of that which has no existence. But where the law of a foreign country affects to discharge obligations incurred elsewhere, such a defence will not be recognised in the country where the obligation was incurred unless the plaintiff has directly or indirectly consented to the

* Story's Conflict of Laws, sect. 258 *a.*

proceedings. By Imperial legislation a certificate in an English bankruptcy is a discharge* of all colonial claims, but a colonial certificate has no similar effect in England. An English certificate will not, however, relieve the bankrupt † from any criminal responsibility which before its issue he may have incurred in the colony in respect of any offence committed by him against its insolvency laws.

The Recognition of Foreign Judgments. § 4. The effect of a foreign judgment *in rem* is undisputed. It is indeed only a particular case of the rule that the ownership of a movable depends upon the law of the place where the alleged right was acquired. Where a court of competent jurisdiction in any country pronounces in the lawful exercise of its authority that a particular movable situated within that country is the property of a particular person, there is no doubt that the person in whose favour the judgment has been pronounced has acquired his right of ownership in conformity with the law of that country. But the effect of a foreign judgment *in personam* has been more slowly acknowledged. Before, however, I enter upon the subject, I must premise a distinction. There are two ways in which the judgment of an outside court may be treated. It may be admitted as it were *ad eundem*, and may be accepted as being in effect a judgment of the admitting court itself. Or it may be regarded as a cause of action in which the judgment appears as evidence of more or less weight. The former method is that in use between the superior courts of the different parts of the United Kingdom, and also between the superior courts of the various Australasian colonies. Under certain simple regulations, the judgment of the sister court is registered in the court of the country in which its operation is desired; and thereupon it acquires the like force and effect that it would have had if it had been pronounced by the registering court itself. But this peculiar comity does not extend to other courts, and their judgments obtain recognition in the

---

* See Ellis *v.* McIlenry, L. R. 6 C. P. 228.　　† Gill *v.* Barron, L. R. 2 P. C. 157.

manner I am about to describe. For the purposes of this section, therefore, the word "Foreign" must be taken in a somewhat more restricted sense than that in which it has in the foregoing pages been used.

A person* who has obtained a foreign judgment may either waive it and sue on the original cause of action, or he may sue upon the judgment. If he elect to pursue the latter course, he may do so where the judgment has been given as a judicial decision, and not *pro confesso* or upon an award, in which cases it is regarded as a mere form of contract. The judgment also must be for a sum certain, payable as a settlement of the cause of action; and the defendant must be subject to the jurisdiction of the country whose court pronounces judgment. Further, the judgment, whether it be or be not subject to appeal, must be final, or final until it is reversed; and there must be no valid excuse why the obligation should not be fulfilled. In these circumstances the judgment is conclusive evidence as to its amount, and as to the fact that that amount is due. Some of these rules, however, require some further explanation. Thus, I have said that the defendant must be subject to the jurisdiction of the country in which, not of the court by which, judgment is pronounced; because our courts will not inquire into the competency of any foreign court. It is enough that the jurisdiction is somewhere in the country. The relative positions of the courts of that country is a matter for their own consideration, and not for the decision of a foreign and imperfectly informed tribunal. A person is regarded as subject to the jurisdiction of a country when he owes political allegiance to it, or is resident therein, or has voluntarily appeared in the matter in dispute as a suitor before its tribunal. To an action upon such a judgment the following defences may be offered :—The defendant may deny that there is any valid subsisting obligation. Or he may allege as an excuse for its non-performance that the judgment was obtained by fraud; or that there was wilful and perverse error

* See Westlake, Private International Law, Ch. XVII.

in the court; or that its proceedings showed a breach of
natural justice, that is apparently of the rules for a fair and
impartial hearing and examination of the case which English
courts usually observe; or that the obligation is prohibited by
our law. On behalf of a defendant, a foreign judgment upon
the matter in dispute, if it be final in the country where it
was pronounced, is a conclusive answer to all proceedings
against the person in whose favour it was given. But a
plaintiff who has been refused relief abroad may obtain in
the court in which he sues a different relief upon the
same facts, or the same relief upon different facts, as the
circumstances of the case may require.

The Theory of Domicil. § 5. We have hitherto considered the simple
cases of foreign rights whether *in rem* or *in personam*. We must now examine those more complex cases
which involve the devolution of a foreigner's property taken
as a whole, with its burthens as well as its benefits, or the
rise of a personal status growing out of a contract—in other
words, the law of marriage and of divorce. These rights
depend upon a principle distinct from political allegiance on
the one hand and from a temporary and incidental submission to a foreign authority on the other hand. This principle
is the basis of the law of domicil.

The law of domicil is of very recent* origin. It owes its
development first to the extension of our Indian Empire,
and next to the great increase in locomotion that is so conspicuous a feature of the last half-century. About a hundred
years ago a novel practice began to attract attention.
Scotchmen used to go to India, make fortunes there, and
return to die not in their native country but either in
England or in the Channel Islands, or even on the Continent.
Questions respecting their succession not unfrequently arose;

---

* "The truth is, my Lords, that the doctrine of domicil has sprung up in this country
very recently, and that neither the Legislature nor the Judges until within a few years
thought much of it: but it is a very convenient doctrine, it is now well understood, and I
think that it solves the difficulty with which this case was surrounded."— *Per* Lord
Campbell (1845). Thompson *v.* The Advocate-General, 12 Cl. & F. at p. 29.

and as the movement between different communities steadily increased, a new body of law was gradually established. Perhaps in all respects this law is not yet complete, but it is sufficiently settled to admit of a tolerably correct description.

Every man has in contemplation of law a domicil,* that is a country which he regards as his home. This country, or perhaps we ought to say jurisdiction, is not necessarily that of which he is politically a citizen; but it is that in which he freely and not under the influence of any external necessity elects to live without any definite intention of leaving it. The law of this country determines all questions relating to his personal capacity, to the succession to his property, and to his marriage and its dissolution. It is the law which may reasonably be supposed to have been present to his mind when he contemplated the arrangements for the great governing events of his life. For these purposes, every man at every moment of his life is assumed to have some domicil. At his birth he acquires the domicil of his father or, if he have no father, of his mother. This is called the domicil of origin, and may be replaced from time to time at pleasure by a domicil of choice. But when and as often as any domicil of choice ceases to operate, the domicil of origin immediately reverts. Domicil, like so many other jural phenomena, consists of a fact and of an intention. The former is a particular residence; the latter implies the purpose that such residence shall be general and unlimited. Both these elements must combine, although the order of the combination is not material, to constitute a domicil. If either of them fail, the domicil of choice is at an end, and the domicil of origin resumes its control. A man may accordingly change his domicil as often as he pleases; but in the absence of any domicil of choice or in the interval between two such domicils he resumes his domicil of origin. Thus, an English lady † had married a Frenchman and acquired a French

* Udney *v.* Udney, L. R. 1 Sc. App. 453.
† In the Goods of Raffenel, 32 L. J. Prob. Cas. 203.

z

domicil. After her husband's death she determined to leave
France and to live in England. She accordingly embarked
on a passenger steamer in Calais for London. Before the
steamer left her moorings, Madame Raffenel, who had been
in delicate health, became so ill that she was taken on shore
and soon afterwards died there. She left a will relating to
English property, which was valid by English law but was
invalid by the law of France. Of this will probate was
refused in England. Her intention to change her domicil
was clear, but that intention was not carried into effect.
The French domicil consequently continued and was that in
which she died. If she had arrived in England, she would
upon her landing have instantly acquired an English
domicil. Had she died on the sea, her French domicil would
have been abandoned. Her English domicil, that is her new
domicil of choice, would not have been acquired. Consequently, her domicil of origin—which in this case happened
to be English, but which might have been that of any other
country—would have revived, and her succession would have
been determined by its law.

I shall not pause to consider the circumstances which
under various states of facts constitute the evidence of the
intention necessary in domicil, or the effects upon that
relation of any legal disability. But some difference of
opinion still prevails as to the precise nature of the required
intent. Some authorities hold that the voluntary fixing of
a man's sole or chief residence in a particular country without limitation as to purpose or to time is sufficient. Others
maintain that the intent must go further, and must involve
a distinct purpose both to leave his former domicil and to
submit himself to the laws and government of his new
country. The latter opinion was expressed in the House of
Lords by two law lords of great eminence, and has subsequently been maintained* with much energy by Mr. Westlake. But on the whole it does not seem to have met with
general approval. The question can hardly be said to be

---

* Private International Law, 2nd ed., 205 *et seq.*

finally settled, but the present tendency of legal opinion can scarcely be doubted.

The Appli-
cation of
Domicil. § 6. Where a person dies leaving property in any country, if that property be immovable, no question arises. Such property, as we have already seen, is governed in all respects by the law of the country in which it is situated, and by no other law. If the property be movable, the case is otherwise. If the deceased be domiciled in the country in which his personalty is situated, there is no conflict of laws. But if a mere stranger die in any country having personal property there, his succession will be determined by the law of the country of his last domicil. If the deceased have property within two jurisdictions, the law of the domicil still prevails; but separate probates or letters of administration as the case may be must be taken in each jurisdiction. The probate or administration issued in the country of the domicil is called the Principal; that issued in any other country is called the Ancillary. It is the duty of the ancillary representatives to clear the estate; it is the duty of the principal representatives to distribute it when it is cleared. The ancillary representatives collect the assets and pay the debts within the scope of their authority, and then transfer the net balance to the principal representatives. The principal representatives, who in their own country also perform the duties of collection and of clearing, distribute the aggregate available assets among the parties who by the law of the country of the last domicil of the deceased are entitled thereto, and in the shares which by that law those persons respectively ought to receive. A curious conflict of claims of different sets of representatives sometimes arises. The owner of a line of stage coaches* which plied daily between two towns, one in the State of New York and the other in another State, died. Probates were in due course issued in each State. The question arose to which of the two sets of executors did the coaches and the

* Story, Conflict of Laws, sect. 521.

z 2

horses that were in daily transit belong? The answer is that such property belongs to that legal representative who first in pursuance of the authority under which he acts reduces it into possession.

The questions connected with domicil that have been the most difficult of solution are those connected with marriage and divorce. I shall state as briefly as I can the leading general rules which appear to be deducible from the numerous and not always consistent cases on the subject. The marriage in a foreign country of two strangers, that is of two persons neither of whom is domiciled in the recognising country, will generally be recognised in any other country on two conditions :—first, that the ceremony be duly celebrated according to the law of the country in which it is performed ; second, that the parties be capable of intermarriage. This capacity must exist according to three different laws ; first, according to the law of the recognising country ; second, according to the law of the place of celebration ; third, according to the law of the respective domicils of the parties, unless their incapacity under such personal law arise from some penal law or some law in restraint of marriage generally. Thus, under the law of Portugal* two first-cousins may not without the Papal dispensation intermarry. Such a marriage without such dispensation would consequently be in all circumstances void in Portugal. Nor would such a marriage, if it were duly celebrated in another country where no such restriction existed, be recognised by Portuguese law. Nor would such a marriage, in whatever foreign country it might be celebrated, if both the parties had a Portuguese domicil, be recognised in England. The marriage on this assumption was a nullity by the proper law of the parties, and there consequently was never any right which the English courts could recognise. Nor would such a marriage be valid in England, even though it were duly celebrated in England according to English law, if both the parties had a Portuguese domicil. The parties were by their proper law inca-

* Sottomayor r. De Barros, 3 P. D. 1, 5 P. D. 04.

pable of intermarriage; and it is by their proper law—that is, the law of their domicil—that the English law measures their capacity. But where one of the cousins was domiciled in Portugal and the other was domiciled in England, and the marriage was duly celebrated in England, the marriage is valid in England, although it would not be valid in Portugal. Such an English marriage would doubtless be recognised in this country or in any country which was not subject to the rule of ecclesiastical law which the Portuguese have adopted. A right was duly created in England, and there is no reason in the law of this country or of any country where marriages of this character are not forbidden why such right should not be recognised in the usual way. It follows that two persons may be lawfully married according to the law of one country and not married according to the law of another country. But this state of things, lamentable though it be, is the necessary result from the want of a universal law of marriage.

Questions as to the necessity for marriage of the consent of parents or other specified persons depend upon the terms of the law by which such consent is required. If by that law the consent be a matter of capacity, a marriage without such consent is everywhere invalid. But if the marriage may take place in some form without consent, the consent is a matter not of capacity but of form. In such circumstances, if the marriage be well celebrated according to the *lex loci contractus*, it will be valid in other countries, although probably not in the country where the consent was required. Thus, where two persons* came from France to London with the avowed intent of evading the French law of parental consent, and were married in London, the French courts declared the marriage to be void as having been contracted in fraud of their law. But the English courts, notwithstanding this decision, upheld the marriage. The husband married again, with his father's consent, in France. The wife, who had settled in England, would have been guilty of bigamy

---

* Simonin *r.* Mallac, 2 S. & T. 77.

if she had followed his example. In English law we find an example of consent as a matter of capacity in the Royal Marriage Act, and of consent as a matter of solemnity or form in the history of the old Gretna Green weddings.

In matters of divorce and other matrimonial causes the English courts and those that follow their practice have not jurisdiction unless at the commencement of the suit the parties be domiciled in the country, or if not domiciled be resident therein, not as visitors or travellers, and not having taken up such residence for the purpose of facilitating or obtaining a divorce. On the other hand, these courts will not recognise a divorce decreed by a foreign court unless at the commencement of the suit the parties be domiciled in the country in which the decree is pronounced. The domicil of the wife is that of her husband; but if the husband desert his wife, or otherwise act in such a manner that she is justified in living apart from him, he cannot by changing his domicil deprive her of her right to sue for a divorce or other remedy in the courts of the matrimonial domicil. Thus, a Chinaman married in Victoria a Victorian girl; he subsequently left her, returned to China, and there married again. She followed him to China, but without success. She then returned to Victoria and presented a petition for a divorce.* The divorce was granted, and I conceive that it is in force not only in Victoria but would be universally accepted.

* Ho-a-Mie *v.* Ho-a-Mie, 6 Vict. Rep. 113.

CHAPTER XVII.

THE CODIFICATION OF THE LAW.

The Legal Work of Codification. § 1. We have seen that the law is composed partly of customary rules which have never been authoritatively formulated and partly of statutes. These statutes have been enacted at different times by different persons and in different circumstances, as the exigency of the moment required, with little regard in many cases either to each other or to the Common Law. The consequence is that the law is fragmentary, voluminous, difficult to find, uncertain when found, and altogether beyond the reach of non-professional persons. If by any means it could be so revised and re-written that a single Act of Parliament should contain the whole law on the subject to which it relates, without any material change in its substance, and plainly expressed in ordinary language, such a change would be an unmixed good. It is not indeed the advantage of the change but its present practicability that we need to consider. Apart from what may be called its political conditions, that is the means of passing into law the bill when it is actually prepared, three conditions or sets of conditions must concur for the construction of a successful code. Such success requires a certain development of legislation, a certain intentional application of logical method, and a certain system of legal composition. I do not refer to the qualifications of the actual framers of the code; but I mean that the law should have attained a reasonable degree of permanence, and that the public should be capable of appreciating the advantages in their statutes of orderly arrangement and of perspicuous writing. On each of these conditions I shall offer a few remarks.

Questions of form are out of place while the substance of the work continues undetermined. When men are doubtful what rules it is prudent to adopt, they give little heed to niceties of arrangement. Nor is it possible while the law is seriously unsettled to adapt it to a permanent form. While, therefore, the actual principles of the law are shifting, or while any large part of it is in a state of transition, any attempt at a code can at best be merely provisional. For this reason, Bentham's projects of codification were premature. Most of his reforms have been carried, but it has been in detail and not in a connected form. In the penal law, where the changes were the most urgent, the labours of a generation of reformers were needed to secure uniformity of opinion upon the substance of that law. Even at a later period a great preparatory treatment of materials was necessary. For many years Commission after Commission laboured at the Criminal law. The Acts of 1861, insufficient as they now seem, marked a great advance. These Acts are about to give way to the Bill to consolidate the law relating to indictable offences, which we owe to the exertions of Mr. Justice Stephen and to the labours of the Commission of English Judges, over which, in 1878, Lord Blackburn presided. It may be that even the present generation may see this Bill superseded by a true code. Within the last twenty years much has been done in England by clearing from the statutes the accumulated rubbish of centuries, by consolidating, as opportunity offered, numerous scattered but cognate Acts, and sometimes even by reducing portions both of the Common law and of the statutes into the form of isolated chapters of a code. It is also noteworthy that of late years the judgments of some of the best English Judges have been so framed as to supply an almost complete preliminary treatment of the materials for a formal statement of the whole law upon the subjects with which they have had respectively to deal.

In Victoria the condition of legislation is favorable for an attempt at codification. In 1864 and the following year, the then chaos of Colonial Acts was reduced to order by the exertions of Mr. Justice Higinbotham, the then Attorney-General. Political troubles unhappily intervened, and indeed have, with little intermission, continued almost to the present year; and Mr. Higinbotham failed to obtain the credit to which he was justly entitled. It has been observed* that "the formal amendment of the law is indeed one of the most useful services which can be rendered to the human race, and one which never fails of an ample reward of fame." I fear that this remark is true only of Royal personages, of the Justinians and of the Napoleons, and not of the actual labourers in the field of law. But I write from abundant personal knowledge when I testify to the extraordinary amount of labour and of care that in the midst of many pressing occupations Mr. Justice Higinbotham then personally gave to the work of consolidation, and to the benefits which, notwithstanding a few errors of detail inseparable from such a task, his labours have conferred both upon the public and upon the student of law.

There is another advantage of this class which in comparison with England Victoria possesses. I mean the abolition of the distinction between real and personal property. No person who has not had practical experience of the work of codification can conceive how great a relief this one alteration in the law has produced. I have already had occasion to enlarge upon this reform. I shall therefore merely cite Austin's† remarks as showing at once the character of the evil and the only safe method of dealing with it :—" This needless distinction between real and personal property, which is nearly the largest of the distinctions that the law of England contains, is one prolific source of the unrivalled intricacy of the system and of it smatchless confusion and obscurity. To the absence of this distinction, a cause of complexness, disorder, and darkness, which naught

* Ed. Rev. CXXVI. 349.   . † I. 59.

but the extirpation of the distinction can thoroughly cure, the greater compactness of the Roman system, with its greater symmetry and clearness, are mainly imputable." I may add, as a further advantage in dealing with the Victorian Statutes, that since the time of the consolidation to which I have referred there has, until the present year, been but little new legislation. Most of our recent Acts, too, refer either to companies of some kind or to municipalities, or to the disposition of Crown lands, all of them matters which come under the class of "special conditions," and which consequently do not find a place in a general code. But this advantage is not altogether unmixed. The omission to bring our law up to the standard of the latest English legislation frequently causes to the codifier serious embarrassment ; and under penalty of much useless trouble and the certainty of speedy alterations, the assistance of Parliament must be sought to accelerate some much needed reforms.

The Logical Work of Codification. § 2. "A code of laws, says Bentham,* is like a vast forest; the more it is divided, the better it is known." "Every attempt, says Austin,† to digest the aggregate of the law or to compose a commentary embracing the same subject ought to be preceded by a perspicuous notion of the leading distinctions and divisions. On the degree of precision and justness with which these are conceived and predetermined the merit and success of the attempt will mainly depend. Errors or defects in the detail are readily extirped or supplied. Errors in the general design infect the entire system and are absolutely incurable." The need of the classification of the law is thus apparent. Its difficulty is proved by the fact that after many attempts the work still remains to be done. It is not enough to form such rough and ready groups as may suffice for the immediate needs of the practitioner. The problem is to obtain such a systematic arrangement of the law as will admit of its presentation to the public in a reasonable form. Classifi-

* III. 157.   † II. 985 and 1130.

cation is not only a matter of convenience but a means of knowledge. It is necessary to show not merely the existence of certain parts, but their mutual relation and the places which they respectively hold in a great and organized whole. A complete classification must comply with certain well understood conditions. It must be adequate, that is it must cover the whole subject. It must be distinct, that is its parts must not cross or overlap. It must be natural, that is it must turn upon the most important features of the things classified, so that attention may be fixed upon the leading and not upon the minor differences in the subject. For this purpose, therefore, it must rest upon some ultimate fact, some principle which determines other phenomena and is not determined by them. Such are the rules which modern logic prescribes for classification. Unless these rules be duly observed, all other labour in the direction of codification is merely wasted. The most learned lawyer and the most skilful draftsman can do nothing in this matter without the aid of the "*ars artium.*" I shall state very briefly the mere results of the application to law of this department of logic, as they bear both on the systems followed by other writers and that upon which I have myself worked. If I have been so fortunate as to have found the true method, still more if the sufficiency of that method be proved by actual experience, the story of the time and of the trouble and of the failures which the search for it has cost will not greatly interest my readers.

Austin's Classification. We are now in a position to estimate the value of some of the projects for the classification of law which have at different times been proposed. A classification of which Rights is the basis must necessarily be imperfect. It does not comply with the fundamental condition of adequacy. In other words, it fails to cover the whole ground. Even if the classification be perfect as regards rights, there is a large body of law of which it takes no notice. Rights are only a secondary incident in commands, and belong to a

particular variety of duties. They consequently can never
form a true basis for the classification of law. To this
theoretical objection the test of experience adds its confirma-
tion. Austin's scheme of classification is a conclusive proof
that Rights are an insufficient basis. I do not refer to any
recent criticisms upon his arrangement. But he himself
admits that he can upon his principles find no place for
criminal law. He has to "interpolate" a description of
primary absolute duties, which, as he* says "ought to be
placed somewhere," but for which his narrow system
affords no room. Such an omission is obviously fatal to
his scheme.

Division
of the
Institutes.   The case is still worse when we come to the
"Rights of Things" and the "Rights of Persons"
of our older† lawyers. The Civilians misinterpreted the
language of the Roman lawyers. Hale,‡ singularly clear-
sighted though he was, was in some degree misled by the
language of the Civilians, and Blackstone improved upon
Hale's mistake. These eminent lawyers found in the text-
books of their day discussions on *Jus rerum* and on *Jus
personarum.* They translated these words literally as they
thought, and they wrote about the rights of things and the
rights of persons. They forgot under the powerful influence
of words that rights can exist only in persons; and that consequently the expression "rights of persons" is tautologous,
and the expression "rights of things" is absurd. Their
mistranslation was threefold. They thought that *Jus* meant
a right when in reality it means law. They misconceived
the force of the genitive case, which here is, in the language
of the grammarians, not subjective but objective. Hence
"jus personarum" means the law relating to persons, and
"jus rerum" means the law relating to things. Further,
they mistook the meaning of the word "*res.*" In the
Roman law, as I shall proceed to show, *res* does not mean
in our sense of the term a thing. Thus the ordinary version
of the "jus rerum" is a curious instance of the maximum of

---

* I. 68.   † See Austin, I. 374.
‡ See Austin's tribute to Hale's great merit as a jurist, I. 70.

mistranslation. There are three errors in two words. Each
of the words is wrongly rendered, and their relation is
misconceived.

"The Institutes of Justinian, says Gibbon,[*] proceed by
no contemptible method from persons to things and from
things to actions." The opinion thus expressed has deeply
affected the whole history of law. I do not now propose to
consider whether this method be or be not contemptible.
But I contend that, in the sense in which Gibbon uses the
terms, it was not the Roman method. The Roman jurists
knew that it was not with things in the usual sense of the
word but with persons that law is concerned. They never
used the expression "*Jus rerum,*" but always wrote "*De
rebus.*" What they meant by *res* was the subject-matter of
law. "*Materia juri subjecta*"—"*In quâ jus versatur*"—"*ea
quæ jure nostro afficiuntur*"—"*quæ tanquam materia ei sunt
proposita*"—such[†] are some of the phrases in which they
characterize the term. When they had occasion to write of
a thing in the ordinary sense, they called it[‡] not *res* but
corpus. In this sense of the term *res* the famous expressions "*Res Incorporales*"—"*ea quæ in jure consistunt,*"
are readily intelligible. Consequently the expression "*De
rebus*" means a discussion upon what I have called the
objects of commands, both primary and secondary. The
expression "*jus personarum*" with us means the law relating
to Special Conditions. But our law is territorial, and the
law of early Rome was not territorial but personal. The
title "*De jure personarum*" was consequently a discussion
upon commandees, or the persons to whom the law applied,
a matter[§] of primary importance to the Roman lawyers,
although in modern times it has dwindled into insignificance.
When Gaius,[‖] and after him Justinian, wrote "*Superiore
libro de jure personarum exposuimus, modo videamus de
rebus,*" they intended to convey a meaning which may be

* Chapter 44.   † See Austin, II. 955.
‡ " *Pecuniæ nomine non solum numerata pecunia sed omnes res tam soli quam mobiles et tam
corpora quam jura continentur.*"—Dig. LXVI. 222.   See also Inst. II. 4.
§ See " The Aryan Household," 342.   ‖ II. 1.

paraphrased in some such terms as the following :—" In the former book we have treated of the persons to whom our law applies ; we shall now proceed to consider the objects of the law's commands"—that is, acts and forbearances and those secondary objects to which acts and forbearances relate.

Bentham's Classification. Another scheme of classification — one which Bentham* advocates—finds its basis in offences. It classifies law not by duties or by rights but by sanctions. That is, it regards the fundamental notion of law as not a duty but a breach of duty. The obvious objection to this scheme is that the classification rests not on the command itself but upon something dependent on it. It places the handmaid above the mistress. It makes the principal depend upon the accessory. This classification coincides indeed with the ordinary division of legal proceedings into civil and criminal. But such a division, which has been the result partly of historical causes and partly of professional convenience, is altogether useless for any scientific purpose. At present the criminal law means the law, of whatever description, that is administered in courts of criminal jurisdiction. It includes a description of the offence, of the punishment for such offence, and of the procedure thereon; that is, according to the older and correct expression, of the " Pleas of the Crown." But it is impossible to describe an offence without referring, at least by implication, to the duty of which it is a breach. Further, the duty, as I have already had occasion to observe, exists independently of the offence; and continues even though no offence in respect of it has ever been committed. Thus a sanction, which is only a conditional evil, can never form a basis for classifying those antecedents upon which it is conditioned.

Jus Publicum et Privatum. The last basis of classification that I shall notice is the division by the Roman lawyers of "Jus Publicum" and "Jus Privatum." This division has, as regards modern law, been rejected by Hale, Blackstone, and Austin. Austin† has stated at some length the grounds of

* III. 100.   † Lect. xliv.

his objections; and most other writers, including so competent a critic upon classification as John Mill,* have acquiesced in his argument. In these circumstances I should not have adverted to the subject were it not that a recent writer† of repute has revived the old division. His view appears to depend upon the propositions‡ that the immediate objects of law are the creation and protection of legal rights ; that the creation of rights and the creation of duties are equivalent; that the selection of either of the two as a basis of classification is a mere matter of personal preference ; and that the State can be what he calls "a person of inherence," that is, in other words, that a commander has "a right" to obedience. None of these propositions is consistent with the views that I have in the preceding pages endeavoured to maintain, and I need not therefore discuss any of them here. But as an appeal has been made § in support of this division to "the irrecusable authority of the Roman jurists," I may venture to add that I have elsewhere ‖ attempted to trace the meaning and the history of the terms "Jus Publicum" and "Jus Privatum." If my contention in that place be correct, the difference is one which belongs to the infancy of law; and although it necessarily held a leading place in the Roman text-books, it has no claim to any such position in modern analytical jurisprudence.

Three Departments of Law. From what I have already said, the principle of classification that I propose follows as of course. It was indeed on this account that I have deferred to the present stage of my inquiry the discussion of classification. A complete definition belongs strictly to the end of an inquiry, and not to the beginning. A like rule seems to hold as to arrangement. At all events I preferred that in so difficult and important a case the classification should be the outcome of the discussion and not its guide. The proof of my classification is found in all that I have already said. It cannot, therefore, be alleged that the whole system consists of deductions from certain premises more or less arbitrarily

---

* Dissertations and Discussions, III. 255. † Prof. Holland's Jurisprudence, 91 (2nd ed.).
‡ See *Ib.* pp. 60, 66, 95. § *Ib.* p. 94. ‖ "The Aryan Household," c. XV.

assumed. The matter to be arranged is the general commands of the State. These commands are issued either for their own sake or for the purpose of giving effect to other prior commands. That is, they are either principal or accessorial; or, to use Bentham's familiar expression, they are either substantive or adjective. The substantive commands apply either to all persons who are under the control of the' State, or to some only of such persons. In other words, the Substantive Law is either general or special. Thus there are three leading divisions or departments of law—Substantive General Law, Substantive Special Law, and Adjective Law, or, as we may otherwise call the last two, the Law relating to Special Conditions or classes of persons, and the Law of Procedure. It is of the first of these great departments, and only of the first, that I now write; and the problem is to find for this department of law a suitable ground of division.

Substantive General Law. The Substantive General Law comprises the largest portion of the general commands of the State. These commands create severally duties. These duties are of different kinds. According as they do not relate, or do relate, to the interest of some person other than the person on whom the duty is imposed, they are either absolute or relative. Relative duties are either general or particular. The rights which Relative duties imply, and the power which the State allows to parties of practically making for themselves by their contracts their own law, form another and probably the largest part of legal business. Thus Substantive General Law divides itself into Absolute duties, General duties, Particular duties, and Rights. Duties, therefore, and the rights which some of these duties imply, are the basis of this classification. Since duties and commands connote each other, a division based upon duties necessarily covers the whole subject. Duty, too, is a phenomenon which governs other jural phenomena, and is not governed by them. It precedes sanctions. It includes rights. Thus it complies with all the requirements for a basis of scientific classification. In practice, I think that the result as expressed in the proposed Draft Code will be found to confirm the theoretic expectation.

Law of Special Conditions. My notice of the other two divisions of law, the Law of Special Conditions and the Law of Procedure, must needs be very brief. Neither of them comes within the scope of my present purpose. I shall only show the distinction that exists between each of them and the Substantive General Law, and indicate their leading characteristics. The Law of Special Conditions consists of the special duties and special rights of particular classes of persons. These cases are necessarily modifications, in some form, of these universal duties which I have described ; or, to express the same thought in other terms, are complex cases for which special provision has been made. They consequently find their appropriate place after the statement of those duties whose effect they presuppose. This is what jurists call the Law of Status or of Conditions. It forms a great and miscellaneous body of law, much larger, I think, than text-writers generally suppose, and affording little room for classification. It may be divided into the Law of Public Conditions and the Law of Private Conditions. The former division contains all the special laws relating to the Crown, to Parliament, to the several departments of the public service, to municipal, trading, and other corporations. The latter division probably does not admit of any systematic grouping. It comprises the old " Law of Persons," as it was improperly called—that is, the law of the domestic relations, of marriage, of infancy, of master and servant, and the like. It comprises, also, all the numerous cases where, not for the imposition of a general duty but for the regulation of the conduct of the persons engaged in the business, special legislation has been deemed necessary; such as, for example, among many others, the law of auctioneers, of butchers, of bakers, of carriers, of innkeepers, of soldiers, of sailors, and

2 A

of licensed publicans. To this class also belongs that branch
of absolute duties which is not of universal but of special
application. Such, for example, is the law which relates to
towns and other populous places. Many duties are imposed
upon persons who are residents of particular localities, or
who resort to particular localities, which duties do not concern their fellow-subjects in other parts of the country.'
Such duties, consequently, require a separate treatment, and
find their natural place among the other cases of exceptional
legislation.

Law of   The Law of Procedure to some extent borders
Procedure. upon the Law of Special Conditions. It presupposes the existence of Courts of Justice ; and the creation,
constitution, and powers of such courts belong to that branch
of the Law of Conditions which may be styled Political. But
after such courts have been called into existence there arises
a great body of technical law, which regulates the manner in
which cases are commenced and are prepared for hearing,
the method in which the business of the court is transacted,
the presumptions of proof, and the admission and rejection
of evidence, the conditions upon which, in the exercise of
their discretion, the courts may give or withhold redress, the
incidence of the costs of litigation, the form in which judgments are given, and the process by which they are enforced.
It is not always easy to determine whether a given law does
or does not belong to procedure, but this is merely the
ordinary difficulty as to matters of fact that besets every
division. On some disputed points, however, there have been
judicial decisions. Thus Set-off is a matter of procedure. So,
it appears, is election under a Will. So are the law of Insolvency and the law which regulates the mode in which the
Crown sues and is sued. In like manner the law relating to
the limitation of actions, as distinguished from prescription
or as the Roman lawyers called it usucapion, is mere procedure, and will not be noticed in the courts of a country in
which a different rule of limitation prevails. It is chiefly in

relation to foreign rights that the distinction is of practical importance. Such rights will usually be enforced, but those who apply to a court for aid must be content to accept the procedure and the remedies of that court according to the rules which govern it in its daily course.

It is hardly possible to obtain in any system of legal arrangement absolute precision. The various parts of the law so shade into each other that a sharp line cannot always be drawn. Even where a sufficient line has been obtained, border cases occur, respecting which, in a greater or less degree, doubt must exist. Moreover, in an organic structure, almost every part has more than one connexion, and its place may thus vary with the stand-point. Further, the exigencies of practical convenience sometimes demand concessions, and logical exactitude must give place to utility. This last element of disturbance is most felt when the whole of the law, both the substantive law and the law of conditions and the law of procedure, is not simultaneously codified. This difficulty, however, will naturally disappear when the whole work of codification is complete, and in the course of time most rules will ultimately fall into their proper places. But in a first and a partial and it may be said a provisional attempt some inconsistencies, both intentional and unintentional, are inevitable. "Whoever, says Austin,* reads and reflects on the arrangement of a *corpus juris* must perceive that it cannot be constructed with logical rigour. The members or parts of the arrangement being extremely numerous, and their common matter being an organic whole, they can hardly be *opposed* completely. In other words, the arrangement of a *corpus juris* can only be so constructed that none of its members shall contain matter which logically belongs to another. I the principles of the various divisions were conceived and expressed clearly, and if the necessary departure from the principles were marked conspicuously, the arrangement would make the *approach* to logical completeness and

* I. 67.

correctness which is all that its stubborn and reluctant matter will permit us to accomplish."

The Literary Work of Codification.   § 3. Until the present reign was well advanced the law thought fit to prescribe the character of a legal sentence. Its definition of such a sentence was in effect the whole matter contained in a single instrument. Acts of Parliament were drawn in the manner used in preparing deeds ; and deeds were, with the intent of preventing the possibility of interpolation, written continuously in one interminable sentence, without any division, without any punctuation, and without any contrivance by which in ordinary compositions aid is given to the wearied attention. As a concession to the weaker brethren, the clauses of Acts of Parliament were usually numbered, not I presume in the original documents but in the copies published by the Queen's printer. These numbers were often inaccurate. Thus, the Bill of Rights, the most important law probably in the Statute Book, is, unless its numeration be entirely disregarded, a hopeless puzzle. The clauses themselves, too, were sometimes of an incredible length. One of them,* not by any means the worst of its kind, is still extant in the Victorian Statutes, the Act in which it is found having escaped the hands of the consolidators. It contains 82 lines of print, and each line has an average of about 13 words. A section which professes to describe the nature of a wash-charger in a sentence consisting of nearly 1,100 words and extending without so much as a comma over a page and a half royal 8vo does not economize the brain power of its readers.

I do not undertake fully to account for this terrible style of legal composition. It certainly was to some extent due to the mode of remuneration. Draftsmen were paid by the length of their draft, and money could be made out of the charges for copying per folio. There is no necessary connexion between prolixity and law. Lawyers, as Bentham in reference to the grim formula "*Sus. per col.*" remarked, can

* Act No. 147, s. 40.

write quite as concisely as other men when it suits them to do so. Apart, however, from any deliberate purpose, a professional style was founded under these influences ; and in the most conservative of professions that style was not easily laid aside. Whatever the cause may have been, the fact remained. Mortal man could not write even tolerably if his sentences must be longer than those of a German philosopher, and if his fees depended directly upon his verbosity. In the early part of this reign, an Act of Parliament provided that in the taxation of costs regard should be had in determining the fees for the preparation of deeds to the difficulty of the case and not to the length of the instrument. In 1850, another Act* directed that Acts of Parliament should be divided into sections, and that each section should without any introductory words be deemed a substantive enactment. I know not how far the change may be due to the direct result of these Acts ; but it is certain that after their enactment, with a new generation of draftsmen, the form of Acts of Parliament has shown a remarkable alteration. These Acts are now readable. They are divided into sections of reasonable length. Vain repetitions are carefully avoided. Various contrivances both of the author and of the printer are in common use, and greatly facilitate the comprehension of complicated enactments. On the whole, the form and the style of the best English Acts now leave little to be desired.

Rules of Legal Composition. "The words of a law, says Bentham,† ought to be weighed like diamonds." To every word effect must be given ; for every idea adequate expression must be found. Under the grave risk of possible failure, therefore, a law must contain exactly as many words as are required for its purpose, neither more nor fewer. On the one side, when the subject-matter is complex, brevity is not wit but folly. On the other side, in all circumstances, every superfluous word creates an additional risk in the interpretation. Under such conditions ornament is inadmissible. The one merit in legal composition is perspicuity. Of that kind of writing

* 13 & 14 Vict. c. 21, s. 2.   † III. 209.

Quintilian's remark[*] is especially true. It is not enough
that a good writer may be understood. He must be incapable
of being misunderstood. No rules will make a good writer,
either on law or on any other subject. Yet there are some
minor observances which in legal composition tend to secure
the necessary clearness and to smooth some practical difficulties. They were first pointed out, so far as I know, by the
late Mr. Coode in his pamphlet "On Legislative Expression,"
and I may perhaps be permitted to add my personal testi-
mony that in a tolerably extensive experience I have never
known them to fail. A legal sentence usually consists of a
Case, a Condition, a Subject, and a Predicate. These parts
ought always to follow the order in which I have placed them.
If there be neither case nor condition, the matter is simple.
If there be more than one case or more than one condition,
the additional parts should be introduced in that part of the
sentence which is appropriated to their class. They may
conveniently begin—the case with the word "where" or some
equivalent term ; the condition with the word "if." The
mood and the tense of the verb in each of these parts deserve
attention. The case should always be expressed in the indicative, and the condition in the conjunctive mood. In both
divisions the present tense, and not the future, should, for a
reason that I shall presently state, be employed. The subject
should always be a person, since it is to persons that duties
and rights pertain ; and should be followed by the word
"shall," or if it be desired to express permission by "may,"
with or without the negative as circumstances require. Our
Interpretation Act contains a general provision as to the use
of gender and number, and a like provision should be made for
the inclusion, where need be, of a man's legal representatives.
These simple expedients secure very considerable advantages.
Provisoes, not the least irritating part of the old method, are
almost entirely avoided, and the sentences are framed on the
principle of the Period, the most economic[†] form of writing,
so far, at least, as the attention of the reader is concerned.

---

[*] *Non ut intelligere possit sed ne omnino possit non intelligere, curandum.*—Inst. VIII. 2.
[†] See Mr. Herbert Spencer "On the Philosophy of Style," Essays I. 228.

The ambiguity of the word "shall," which in our language expresses both futurity and command, disappears; and in the description of the case and of the condition, the present tense may well be substituted for the future, as the law is supposed to be at every moment speaking. The use of the general clauses I have mentioned removes the continued interruption to consecutive thought which is caused by the ever-recurring use of pronouns with different genders and numbers, and by the ceaseless but exasperating re-iteration of "heirs executors administrators and assigns." The weariness which these and similar repetitions produce arises from the same cause as that which, even in favorable circumstances, renders comparatively ineffective the loose or non-periodic structure of the sentence. The rules of the Period too should be carefully followed. On this point care is now especially needed, because under the old system the absence of punctuation served to indicate and so to check the tendency towards the loose sentence. Few persons who have not actually tried the experiment would readily credit the influence upon legal composition of the habitual observance of these rules.

The Legislative Work of Codification. § 4. If we assume that the work as I have described it has been sufficiently performed, and that a tolerable draft-code has been prepared, a further and not less important problem arises for solution. By what means is the code to obtain the force of law? It is I think owing in great measure to this difficulty that so little practical effort in the way of codification has been made in England. The work indeed belongs to Government, and does not come within the sphere of private enterprise. In any scientific investigation the inquirer publishes his results. If they be sound, they are accepted by competent students; and their author finds his reward, if not in a substantial form, at least in fame. But in the case of codification it is otherwise. Few barristers who were anxious for their professional position would undertake on their own account the formation of a code. The reason is that the work unless it become law is worthless. However perfect may be its workmanship, it is until it acquires the force of law useless to the profession. It is not law. It is not a text-book. It has a dangerous savour of theory, which solicitors abhor. In the eyes of the public it is a law book, and therefore to be shunned. Publishers do not covet books of great cost and of no sale. No care, no learning, no skill, can prevent this result. Nothing will give value to any draft-code except the authority of the Queen in Parliament. Hence, again, the question meets us—How is that authority to be obtained?

Two obstacles here present themselves. Such a measure ought to be proposed by Ministers. But Ministers are overwhelmed by the ceaseless labours and struggles of the hour; and until some pressure comes upon them from without, they are not likely to undertake such a task. Strong pressure, such pressure at least as Ministers regard, cannot be expected, for the public has long since learned to look upon legal evils as hardships in the ordinary nature of things to which they must only submit as patiently as they may. But even if Ministers could be set in motion, another obstacle well nigh insuperable remains. How could such a measure be got through Parliament? When could time be found for the consideration of a Bill containing thousands of clauses? In what condition would such delicate workmanship emerge from Committee?

There is a passage of Austin* which has attracted much attention, that "the technical part of legislation is incomparably more difficult than what may be styled the ethical, and that it is far easier to conceive justly what would be useful law than so to construct the same law that it may accomplish the design of the lawgiver." With greater moderation and probably with greater truth the most distinguished† of his critics observes that "it will readily be admitted that the two qualifications are different, that the one is no guarantee for the other, and that the talent which

* II. 371.   † J. S. Mill, Dissertations and Discussions, III. 251.

is merely instrumental is, in any high degree of perfection, nearly if not quite as rare as that to which it is subordinate." Such comparisons are always difficult and rarely profitable. But this discussion suggests two practical considerations. One is that a code, or indeed a much less extensive project of law, is, or ought to be, as it has been called, a work of art. The other is that our Parliamentary procedure has been framed not for works of this class but for the despatch of ordinary business, for the ethical part of legislation, to use Austin's language, and not for the technical part. Hence it follows that, on the assumption that a code has been by some means procured, some special arrangements in Parliamentary practice must be made for its reception. It is certainly true, as Mr. Justice Stephen has remarked, that Parliament could no more frame a code that it could paint a picture. Its function is to determine the substance of the law. The form of the law is the province of experts. The consent of Parliament is necessary, and that consent would doubtless be conditional upon the production of proper evidence of careful consideration and revision. This evidence would be supplied by the aid of such competent advisers as the circumstances of the case admitted ; and on the faith of such evidence the consent of Parliament, without any attempt at alteration, might not unreasonably be sought. I do not know of any practical alternative. In this way, and in this way only,[*] can a code be enacted in a country under Parliamentary government.

The Proposed Code of Victoria. § 5. In Victoria the conditions are, at least, not unfavorable to codification. I have already shown that the present state of the law presents considerable

---

[*] " Early this session " (1833) " I " (Lord Campbell) " re-introduced my Bills for abolishing fines and recoveries, for allowing brothers and sisters of the half-blood to succeed one another, for regulating the law of dower, and for fixing at twenty years the period of possession which shall give a right to real property. They quietly passed through both Houses of Parliament without one single syllable being altered in any of them. This is the only way of legislating on such a subject. They had been drawn by the Real Property Commissioners, printed and extensively circulated, and repeatedly revised with the advantage of the observations of skilful men studying them in their closet. A mixed and numerous deliberative Assembly is wholly unfit for such work."—*Lord Campbell's Life*, vol. ii., page 29.

facilities. In a new country the *vis inertiæ*, although far from inconsiderable, is less formidable than in older communities. In the enactment of the Consolidating Acts, Parliament has shown an encouraging confidence. But there was little likelihood that a code would be initiated by any Ministry. The assistance of Government might perhaps in favorable circumstances be expected, but the beginning must be made from without. It seemed too that the time for discussion had passed, and that the time for action had arrived. Enough had been said during the last century about the advantages of a code. It was time that something should be done. The controversy upon the classification of the law was indeed essential, but it ought not to be eternal. The question had advanced so far that its final solution could only be obtained by actual experiment. If a new theory, the theory of duties, were started, the best proof of its merits would be to show that in very fact it answered the purpose for which it was designed. By various means, it matters not how, the necessary conditions for such an undertaking were at length fulfilled. Accordingly, in 1879, a Bill was introduced into the Legislative Council entitled " A Bill to declare consolidate and amend the General Substantive Law relating to certain duties of the People." This Bill, which was intended as a mere experiment, did not include the duties relating to property and did not proceed beyond its second reading. In the following session it was revised and completed, and in this state was passed by the Legislative Council, but was not considered in the Legislative Assembly. In 1881 a similar Bill dealing with Obligations was read a second time in the Legislative Council, but was intentionally not further advanced. These attempts were received with considerable favour both by Parliament and by the public; and at the end of that year Parliament, on the motion of the then Premier, Sir Bryan O'Loghlen, granted £2,000 for the expenses of the necessary revision of these Bills and of others that were in preparation. The Bills were then combined, various additions were made to them, and a Draft-Code* containing the whole General Substantive Law of Victoria was the result. This draft was in June, 1882, placed for revision in the hands of eight barristers,† assisted by two other barristers as secretaries. The work was distributed among them, and arrangements were made for mutual checks and general consultations. The labours of these revisers have not yet ended; but when their work is complete, it is probable that Parliament will be asked to give effect to their recommendations.

This Draft-Code does not profess to include all the law either of Victoria or that is in force in Victoria. It treats only of Substantive Law and omits all matters concerning the Law of Procedure. These matters require separate discussion, and perhaps in the present state of the law are hardly yet ripe for codification. Nor does it include those branches of law which Austin groups under the description of the Law of Conditions, that is those laws which affect none but particular classes of persons, whether public or private. For each of these classes the law is more or less exceptional and peculiar, and consists in various modifications of the General Law which it presupposes. Nor even in those subjects with which is it immediately concerned does the Draft-Code include those Acts of the Imperial Parliament which are made expressly applicable to the colony. Over such Acts the Colonial Legislature has no control, and it consequently has no authority to consolidate them. But subject to the necessary exception of those Imperial Acts, the present draft-code professes to include all the law, whether common or statute, which actually concerns every person in the country. It states the rules of legal interpretation, the maxims that

---

* For the Analysis of Contents of this Draft-Code, see Appendix *infra* page 385.
† The names of these gentlemen are as follow:—Mr. J. Warrington Rogers, Q.C., Messrs. H. P. Walker, T. P. Webb, J. B. Gregory, H. B. Higgins, S. St. John Topp, W. E. Johnston, and T. P. McInerney. The secretaries are Messrs. J. C. Anderson and A. H. Campbell. Owing to the pressure of other professional engagements, Messrs. Higgins, Topp, and Johnston resigned, and were succeeded by Messrs. G. H. Neighbour, E. B. Hamilton, and the secretary, Mr. Anderson.

are observed in the administration of the law, and the parties to the several classes of duties and of rights. It declares the various duties which the State imposes on all its subjects. It specifies the various circumstances in which these duties are broken. It assigns the consequences, whether criminal or civil, due to each such breach; and it incidentally indicates the tribunal which in every such case has jurisdiction. It sets forth the various rights which Relative Duties connote and their respective consequences. It states the nature and the consequences of contracts, and it enumerates the various combinations which in practice obligations assume. It also describes the great incidents of Transfer and of Succession, and it notices the circumstances in which rights that have accrued within other jurisdictions obtain in our courts recognition.

It thus appears that the present Draft-Code includes, so far as they come within its scope, both indictable offences and offences of summary jurisdiction. In this respect it goes much beyond the proposed English Code of Indictable Offences. I do not mean to discuss the comparative merits of these arrangements. It is gratifying, however, to cite in favour of the course that I have adopted the authority of the late Lord Chief Justice Cockburn. In his* letter to the Attorney-General of England on the Criminal Code (Indictable Offences) Bill he thus writes, " It is obvious that the reason for the retention of these sections (*i.e.* certain sections in various criminal Acts not repealed by the proposed Bill) is the intended omission from the code of all offences punishable on summary conviction ; and herein, as it seems to me, is to be found a radical defect which must necessarily mar the completeness of the work, namely, that when dealing with offences its operation is limited to such offences as are the subject of indictment ; but surely whatever constitutes an offence against the penal law should properly find its place in a code which can only be complete if it sets forth that law in its entirety. The offence being

* Ordered by the House of Commons to be printed, June 16, 1879, p. 9.

established, the mode in which, under different circumstances, the offender may be proceeded against, and the punishment which, according to the degree of guilt, may be awarded, should be set forth. It is all important to those who have to administer the penal law in its subordinate departments to have the law before them as an entire and unbroken whole. . . . The offences being, as they necessarily must be, specified, it would occupy but comparatively small space, and cause little additional trouble, to say under what circumstances such of them as it is intended to make the subject of summary proceeding shall be so subject, and what in such case shall be the method of proceeding and the measure of punishment. The statement of the law applicable to the offence would then be complete. Why should the code be limited to 'indictable offences'? What is wanted is a consolidation or code of the law relating to crimes, no matter what may be the method of proceeding applicable to them. Larceny is not the less larceny, assault is not the less assault, malicious injuries to property are not the less malicious injuries—all these offences are none the less within the criminal law because under one set of circumstances they may be fitly dealt with by one mode of procedure, and under a different set of circumstances by another."

The principal source of danger in a work of such magnitude as a code is that of omission. It is probable that with reasonable care the statement of the rules which it contains will in the great majority of cases be exact, or at all events as nearly exact as the existing state of the authorities admit. But no care and no industry can insure that every proposition of law shall be recorded. That man would indeed be rash who would venture to allege that any code contains not only the law but the whole of the law. Fortunately the remedy is simple. It consists merely in not attempting too much or in not seeking an unattainable perfection. It would be dangerous in the highest degree to repeal, as some zealous reformers have desired, the whole Common Law. It is enough to provide that, so far as the provisions of the Code are founded on the Common Law, these provisions shall be deemed to be a declaration of that law as it now exists; and that, where the Code is silent, the Common Law shall remain unaltered. In this way, where it is found that an omission has been made, recourse can be had to the old law; and to that extent matters will continue as they were before the Code. But the largest part of the Common Law, and that part which is in the most frequent use, will have received an authoritative declaration, and acquired a statutory form. With each successive revision of the Code the outstanding portions will gradually decrease in number and in importance, until they are finally absorbed. Thus the old Common Law will meet its natural and its honourable end. It will have run its course. It began in custom; it will end in disuse. When it is no longer needed, it will be no longer studied. In the words of its own maxim, " *Cessante ratione cessat Lex.*"

The Revision of a Code. § 6. In every great change unreasonable hopes and unreasonable fears are alike rife. In the present case, I assume that the fears are either groundless, or that, if they be well founded, the evils are outweighed by acknowledged advantages. But I may say a word of caution as to the hopes. It cannot be expected that any code should be entirely free from error, or that it should supersede the need of professional advice, or that when completed it should last without change for ever. A code is really a book of reference, and has all the qualities of such books. Its merits and its defects can never be known by mere inspection. They can be discovered only by actual and continued use. Further, its defects are positive, and its merits are mostly negative; and attention always* fastens upon the small part that is positive, while the large part that is negative is overlooked. Doubtless in every code errors will exist, and will be from time to time brought into notice. But so long

---

* *Natura humani intellectus magis afficitur affirmativis et activis quam negativis et privativis.*— Bacon, De Aug. Sci. v. 4.

as they are comparatively few and comparatively slight, and so long as they can readily be corrected by amending Acts, there is no reason to complain that this particular class of work is subject to the ordinary imperfections of human labour. Not less vain is it to suppose that in any conceivable state of the law society could dispense with the services of a legal profession. Apart from any question of the orderly conduct of business, law must always involve the application of general rules to complicated states of facts, and such an application is a work of skill. A good code will not get rid of lawyers, but it will enable them to advise their clients with genuine confidence. There is no greater error than the popular belief that lawyers are interested in an obscure and ambiguous state of the law. It is their duty and their interest to ascertain with accuracy their clients' legal position. Whatever enables them to do so with increased accuracy and despatch is clear gain both to their clients and to themselves. A diminished cost of production always tends to increase exchange, just as an increased cost always tends to diminish it. But the sale of legal advice and assistance does not materially differ from other modes of industry.

The vainest of all such hopes is that a code when it has been completed will remain permanently without need of change. Law is an expression of national life, and consequently it can cease to change only when the nation ceases to live. An absolutely faultless code would after sixty or seventy years present a very different appearance from that which it bore when it was enacted. If our law were codified, and were to remain in that state without further amendment, it would probably never revert, not certainly for many centuries, to anything like its present disorder. But some change and consequently some tendency to confusion are from the nature of things unavoidable. The true course, therefore, is to make arrangements for effecting the needful changes with the utmost despatch and with the least detriment to the symmetry of the Code. It is

probable that the most convenient instrument of revision
will, at least in this country, be the Council of the Judges.
Under the Judicature Act, which, while these pages are in
the press, has become law, the Judges of the Supreme Court
are formed into a Council, and are required to report annually
to the Governor not merely on the operation of that Act but
upon all matters connected with the administration of the
law that they consider deserving of notice. This duty, which
is much wider than that imposed in the corresponding section
of the English Act, would furnish a safe and convenient
means for the suggestion, as occasion requires, of the
necessary changes in the Code. These changes might not
perhaps be always made with such rapidity as could be
desired ; but under the influence of such annual reports it
would be safe to reckon upon at least a decennial revision.
If arrangements could be made by which the special care
of the Code should be assigned to some individual judge, or
even to some officer acting under the direction of the judges,
it is not easy to see what further or better machinery for the
purpose could be desired.

APPENDIX.

Subjoined is a detailed Table of Contents, being the introductory portion, of the Draft Code of Victorian Laws, to which in Chapter 17 (pages 378 to 382 supra) reference has been made. Although the Draft Code has been prepared in accordance wi..a this arrangement, the Contents are here given provisionally and subject to alteration in further revision for publication.

A BILL

To declare consolidate and amend the Substantive General Law.

BE it enacted by the Queen's Most Excellent Majesty by and with the advice and the consent of the Legislative Council and the Legislative Assembly of Victoria in this present Parliament assembled and by the authority of the same as follows :—

INTRODUCTORY.

Short title.

1. This Act may be cited as " *The General Code* 1884."

Act declaratory of Common Law.

2. So far as it is founded upon the Common Law this Act shall be deemed to declare upon the subjects to which it relates the doctrines of that law as it now exists.

Extent of Act.

3. This Act shall be deemed to apply to all persons either absolutely or in their mutual relations ; and not (except so far as is herein expressly provided) to any particular classes of persons, or to any special or exceptional relations whether public or private, or to any matter of administrative regulation or of judicial procedure or to Her Majesty's Prerogative.

2 B

Arrange-
ment of
Act.
4. This Act is arranged in Parts Divisions and Sub-divisions as follow :—

PART I.—THE INTERPRETATION OF WRITTEN INSTRUMENTS.

Division 1.—Rules for the interpretation of all written instruments.
Subdivisions.—(*a*) Words ; (*b*) Intention ; (*c*) Implications; (*d*) Computation of distance and of time.

Division 2.—Special rules for the interpretation of Statutes.
Subdivisions.—(*a*) Evidence of intention; (*b*) Remedial and preventive Statutes; (*c*) Permissive and imperative Statutes; (*d*) Enabling Statutes; (*e*) Operation of Statutes upon contracts; (*f*) Repugnancy; (*g*) Form and citation of Statutes; (*h*) Implications in Statutes ; (*i*) Glossary.

Division 3.—Rules for the interpretation of written instruments other than Statutes.

Division 4.—Special rules for the interpretation of contracts.

Division 5.—Special rules for the interpretation of wills.

Division 6.—Maxims of the Law.

PART II.—DUTIES AND RIGHTS AND THE PARTIES THERETO.

Division 1.—Matters of liability.
Subdivisions.—(*a*) Attempt, abetment, and procurement of offences; (*b*) Community of liability; (*c*) Vicarious liability; (*d*) Descent of liability.

Division 2.—Matters of justification.
Subdivisions.—(*a*) Legal commands and powers; (*b*) Preservation of the peace; (*c*) Self-defence; (*d*) Defence of property.

Division 3.—Matters of excuse.
Subdivisions.—(*a*) Defective intelligence; (*b*) Mistake, consent, and accident; (*c*) Triviality; (*d*) Coverture.

Division 4.—Rights *in rem*.
Subdivisions.—(*a*) Nature of rights ; (*b*) Community of rights ; (*c*) Vicarious exercise of rights ; (*d*) Descent of rights.

Division 5.—Consensual obligations.

PART III.—ABSOLUTE PRIVATE DUTIES.

Division 1.—Self-regarding duties.

Division 2.—Household duties.

Subdivisions.—(*a*) Management; (*b*) Marriage; (*c*) Births; (*d*) Maintenance.

Division 3.—Duties concerning occupations.

Subdivisions.—(*a*) Observance of Sunday; (*b*) Licensed occupations; (*c*) Medical profession; (*d*) Printing and newspapers; (*e*) Factories and mines; (*f*) Pecuniary transactions.

Division 4.—Duties concerning importation and exportation.

Subdivisions.—(*a*) Influx of criminals; (*b*) Imports and exports.

Division 5.—Duties towards the Aborigines.

Division 6.—Duties towards and concerning lower animals.

Subdivisions. — (*a*) The treatment of animals; (*b*) The slaughtering of tame animals; (*c*) The diseases of tame animals; (*d*) The registration of dogs; (*e*) The preservation and capture of game; (*f*) The preservation and capture of fish.

PART IV.—ABSOLUTE PUBLIC DUTIES.

Division 1.—Duties of allegiance.

Division 2.—Duties concerning public servants.

Division 3.—Duties concerning elections.

Division 4.—Duties concerning the administration of justice.

Subdivisions.—(*a*) The conduct of justice; (*b*) The facilitating of justice; (*c*) Abuses of justice; (*d*) The officers of justice; (*e*) Arrest; (*f*) Jurors; (*g*) Witnesses; (*h*) Prisoners.

Division 5.—Duties concerning the public peace.

Subdivisions.—(*a*) Breaches of the peace; (*b*) Unlawful assemblies; (*c*) Riots; (*d*) Unlawful oaths.

Division 6.—Duties concerning public decency and good order.

Subdivisions.—(*a*) Public decency; (*b*) Disorderly houses and gaming; (*c*) Vagrancy; (*d*) Dangerous persons.

Division 7.—Duties concerning the public convenience and safety.

　　Subdivisions.—(*a*) Common nuisances; (*b*) Use of vehicles; (*c*) Use of fire; (*d*) Public health.

Division 8.—Duties concerning coins, weights, and measures.

　　Subdivisions.—(*a*) Coins; (*b*) Weights and measures.

Division 9.—Duties concerning the revenue and its protection.

　　Subdivisions.—(*u*) Customs; (*b*) Excise; (*c*) Post office; (*d*) Stamps.

Part V.—Relative General Duties.

Division 1.—Duties relating to the person of others.

　　Subdivisions.—(*a*) Duties relating to life; (*b*) Breaches of duties tending to loss of life; (*c*) Breaches of duties tending to bodily harm; (*d*) Duties relating to security; (*e*) Duties relating to chastity; (*f*) Duties relating to the disposition of the dead.

Division 2.—Duties relating to the feelings of others.

　　Subdivisions.—(*a*) Defamation; (*b*) Insults and threats; (*c*) Blasphemy.

Division 3.—Duties relating to the family of others.

　　Subdivisions.—(*a*) Members of the family; (*b*) Domestic and outdoor servants; (*c*) The Home.

Division 4.—Duties relating to the property of others.

　　Subdivisions.—(*a*) Duties towards property; (*b*) Criminal breaches of duty in taking property; (*c*) Criminal breaches of duty in damaging property; (*d*) Summary jurisdiction in offences against property; (*e*) Summary jurisdiction in offences against Crown property; (*f*) Restitution of stolen property.

Division 5.—Duties relating to the industry of others.

Division 6.—Duties relating to the privileges of others.

　　Subdivisions.—(*a*) Offices and franchises; (*b*) Copyright; (*c*) Patents; (*d*) Trade marks.

Division 7.—Duties relating to the obligations of others.

Division 8.—Duties of veracity towards others.

　　Subdivisions.—(*a*) Fraud; (*b*) Personation; (*c*) Forgery; (*d*) Preparations for forgery; (*e*) Criminal breach of trust.

Division 9.—Duties of diligence towards others.
Subdivisions.—(*a*) Use and management of property; (*b*)
Conduct and control of business; (*c*) Personal circum-
spection.

PART VI.—SANCTIONS.

Division 1.—Punishable offences.
Division 2.—Punishments.
Subdivisions.— (*a*) The kinds of punishments; (*b*) The
infliction of punishments; (*c*) The remission of punish-
ments.
Division 3.—Remedies for wrongs.

PART VII.—RIGHTS OF OWNERSHIP.

Division 1.—Collective rights of ownership.
Division 2.—Singular rights of ownership.
Subdivisions.—(*a*) Right to possess; (*b*) Right to use and
enjoy; (*c*) Right of abuser; (*d*) Right of disposition;
(*e*) Right of exclusion.
Division 3.—Qualified rights of ownership.
Subdivisions.—(*a*) Temporary ownership; (*b*) Conditional
ownership; (*c*) Expectant ownership.
Division 4.—Investitive facts of ownership.
Subdivisions.—(*a*) Occupancy and dereliction; (*b*) Pre-
scription; (*c*) Accession of land to land; (*d*) Accession
of movables to land; (*e*) Accession of movables to
movables; (*f*) Crown grants; (*g*) Private grants.
Division 5.—Divestitive facts of ownership.

PART VIII.—THE OWNERSHIP OF LAND.

Division 1.—Ownership of land in fee.
Subdivisions.—(*a*) Rights to surface; (*b*) Rights to water;
(*c*) Rights to minerals; (*d*) Rights to wild animals; (*e*)
Boundaries and fences.
Division 2.—Ownership of land for life.
Division 3.—Settled estates.

Division 4.—Non-possessory rights in the land of another.

Subdivisions.—(*a*) Profits à prendre; (*b*) Licences; (*c*) Highways by land; (*d*) Highways by water; (*e*) Annuities.

Division 5.—Duties and rights attached to the ownership of particular tenements.

Subdivisions.—(*a*) Easements; (*b*) Covenants that run with the land.

PART IX.—RIGHTS IN REM OTHER THAN THOSE OF OWNERSHIP.

Division 1.—Privileges.

Subdivisions.—(*a*) Copyright in designs; (*b*) Copyright in literature; (*c*) Copyright in art; (*d*) Patents; (*e*) Offices; (*f*) Trade marks; (*g*) Goodwill.

Division 2.—Fiduciary rights.

Subdivisions.—(*a*) Creation of trusts; (*b*) Beneficial interests; (*c*) Duties of trustees; (*d*) Powers of trustees; (*e*) Succession of trustees; (*f*) Vesting orders.

PART X.—OBLIGATIONS OR DUTIES AND RIGHTS IN PERSONAM.

Division 1.—The formation of contracts.

Subdivisions.—(*a*) Proposal and acceptance; (*b*) Form; (*c*) Consideration.

Division 2.—The avoidance of agreements.

Subdivisions.—(*a*) Mistake; (*b*) Illegality; (*c*) Method of avoidance.

Division 3.—The rescission of contracts.

Subdivisions. — (*a*) Incapacity; (*b*) Misrepresentation and fraud; (*c*) Duress and undue influence; (*d*) Method of rescission.

Division 4.—Contracts of imperfect obligation.

Division 5.—Contingent conditional and collateral contracts.

Division 6.—The enforcement of contracts.

Division 7.—The discharge of contracts.

Subdivisions.—(*a*) Discharge by agreement; (*b*) Discharge by performance; (*c*) Discharge by breach; (*d*) Discharge by impossibility of performance; (*e*) Discharge by operation of law.

Division 8.—Non-consensual obligations.

PART XI.—OBLIGATIONS ARISING FROM PARTICULAR CONTRACTS.

Division 1.—Contract of marriage.

Subdivisions. — (*a*) Parties to marriage; (*b*) Contract to marry; (*c*) Celebration of marriage; (*d*) Dissolution of marriage.

Division 2.—Contract of service.

Subdivisions.—(*a*) Work and labour; (*b*) Personal service.

Division 3.—Contract of agency.

Subdivisions.—(*a*) Appointment and revocation of agent; (*b*) Duties of agent to principal; (*c*) Duties of principal to agent; (*d*) Sub-agency; (*e*) Contracts by agents; (*f*) Powers of Attorney; (*g*) Auctioneers; (*h*) Brokers; (*i*) Factors and Commission agents; (*j*) Shipmasters.

Division 4.—Contract of partnership.

Subdivisions.—(*a*) The liability of partners; (*b*) The mutual relation of partners; (*c*) The dissolution of partnership; (*d*) The winding up of partnership affairs.

Division 5.—Contract of bailment.

Division 6.—Contract of hire.

Subdivisions.—(*a*) Hire of chattels; (*b*) Terms of years; (*c*) Tenancy at will; (*d*) Tenancy from year to year; (*e*) Obligations of landlord and tenant.

Division 7.—Contract of sale.

Subdivisions.—(*a*) Sale of chattels; (*b*) Sale of land.

Division 8.—Contract of security.

Subdivisions.—(*a*) Securities; (*b*) Land as a security; (*c*) The mortgage of chattels; (*d*) The pledge of chattels; (*e*) Charges upon chattels; (*f*) Priority in securities upon chattels; (*g*) The registration of bills of sale; (*h*) The registration of station securities.

Division 9.—Contract of carriage.

Subdivisions.—(*a*) Of goods by sea; (*b*) Of goods and of passengers by land.

Division 10.—Contract against loss.

Subdivisions.—(*a*) Indemnity; (*b*) Insurance; (*c*) Guarantee.

Division 11.—Negotiable instruments.

Subdivisions.—(*a*) Bills of exchange; (*b*) Cheques; (*c*) Promissory notes.

PART XII.—THE TRANSFER OF RIGHTS.

Division 1.—Alienation.

Division 2.—Transfer of land.

Division 3.—Transfer of chattels.

Subdivisions. — (*a*) Sufficient transfers; (*b*) Insufficient transfers ; (*c*) Defeasible transfers.

Division 4.—Transfer of other rights *in rem.*

Division 5.—Transfer of rights *in personam.*

Division 6.—Transfer of negotiable instruments.

Division 7.—Transfer of documents of title.

PART XIII.—THE SUCCESSION TO RIGHTS.

Division 1.—Intestacy.

Subdivisions.—(*a*) General provisions ; (*b*) Widows' share ; (*c*) Lineal descendents; (*d*) Ascending and collateral relatives.

Division 2.—Wills.

Subdivisions.—(*a*) The execution and the revocation of Wills ; (*b*) Wills of soldiers and of mariners.

Division 3.—Bequests.

Subdivisions.—(*a*) Void bequests ; (*b*) Vested onerous and contingent bequests ; (*c*) Conditional and directory bequests ; (*d*) Specific and demonstrative bequests ; (*e*) Bequests of certain things and to certain persons ; (*f*) Exoneration ; (*g*) Election ; (*h*) Gifts in contemplation of death.

Division 4.—Probate and Administration.

Subdivisions.—(*a*) Legal custody of vacant property ; (*b*) General grants ; (*c*) Grants limited in duration ; (*d*) Grants for another's use ; (*e*) Grants for special purposes ; (*f*) Grants of effects unadministered ; (*g*) Alteration and revocation for grants.

Division 5.—The distribution of assets.

Subdivisions.—(*a*) The powers and duties of executors and administrators ; (*b*) Payment of debts and legacies ; (*c*) Executor's assent to legacies ; (*d*) Payment of annuities ; . (*e*) Investment of bequeathed funds ; (*f*) Produce of and interest on legacies ; (*g*) The refunding of legacies.

PART XIV.—THE RECOGNITION OF FOREIGN RIGHTS.

Division 1.—Domicil.

Division 2.—Foreign rights *in rem.*

Division 3.—Foreign torts.

Division 4.—Foreign contracts.

Division 5.—Foreign judgments *in personam.*

Division 6.—Foreign bills.

Division 7.—Foreign marriages.

Division 8.—Foreign successions.

INDEX.

By Authority : JOHN FERRES, Government Printer, Melbourne.

2 c

www.ingramcontent.com/pod-product-compliance
Lightning Source LLC
Chambersburg PA
CBHW031350290326
41932CB00044B/867